MW01065178

How to:

R/S = Novell Application Launcher

NetWare® 5

24 seven™

John Hales
Nestor Reyes

NETWORK® PRESS
SYBEX

San Francisco Paris Düsseldorf Soest London

Associate Publisher: Guy Hart-Davis
Contracts and Licensing Manager: Kristine O'Callaghan
Acquisitions & Developmental Editor: Maureen Adams
Editors: Tracy Brown, Bronwyn Shone Erickson
Technical Editor: Brian Horakh
Technical Galley Reviewer: Paul Tronier
Book Designer: Bill Gibson
Graphic Illustrator: Tony Jonick
Electronic Publishing Specialist: Adrian Woolhouse
Project Team Leader: Shannon Murphy
Proofreaders: Elaine Lewinnek, Nancy Riddiough, Richard Ganis, Jennifer Campbell, Amey Garber, Molly Glover
Indexer: Ted Laux
Cover Designer: Ingalls + Associates
Cover Illustrator/Photographer: Ingalls + Associates

SYBEX, Network Press, and the Network Press logo are registered trademarks of SYBEX Inc.

24seven and the 24seven logo are trademarks of SYBEX Inc.

Screen reproductions produced with Collage Complete.

Collage Complete is a trademark of Inner Media Inc.

TRADEMARKS: SYBEX has attempted throughout this book to distinguish proprietary trademarks from descriptive terms by following the capitalization style used by the manufacturer.

The author and publisher have made their best efforts to prepare this book, and the content is based upon final release software whenever possible. Portions of the manuscript may be based upon pre-release versions supplied by software manufacturer(s). The author and the publisher make no representation or warranties of any kind with regard to the completeness or accuracy of the contents herein and accept no liability of any kind including but not limited to performance, merchantability, fitness for any particular purpose, or any losses or damages of any kind caused or alleged to be caused directly or indirectly from this book.

Library of Congress Card Number: 99-65210
ISBN: 0-7821-2593-X

Manufactured in the United States of America

10 9 8 7 6 5 4 3 2 1

I dedicate this book to my wife, Susan, for her constant love and support.

—NMR

I dedicate this book to my wife, Carin, and to my four children, Robert, Ashley, Brianna, and Andrew, for their love and support and for their sacrifices to let me complete this book.

—JRH

Preface

We have been in the industry now for over 25 years, and we can tell you one thing's for sure—it's not just death and taxes anymore. A new standard has appeared and that is "the next version of the software." New versions of operating systems are being developed at an increasing rate, and keeping up with it all is a constant challenge.

We can honestly say that things have gotten much better over the years for both users and administrators. These improvements have meant more features and ease of use to our users, and more administrative control to the administrators. With the advent of e-commerce, networks have gone from being just a tool to become a source of revenue. Extended networks are now literally retail outlets that generate income for the company.

This new structure stretches our capabilities to the max. As administrators of networks, our plates are full. From performance concerns to accessibility and security, we now have to deal with millions of potential users who also demand services.

Not to worry, the cavalry is here. Novell, with its new line-up of services and offerings and its committed support for the Internet and related applications, provides us with ample tools to support and manage our networks. From NetWare 5 to NDS v8 and all the software in between, we have a one-stop service provider who is on our side. The focus of this book is to help you access all these features and to use them on your network. We hope that we have gone beyond the standard "how-to book," by giving you a "this is how it is book."

—Nestor M. Reyes

—John Hales

Acknowledgments

How would you like to write a technical book about a product that has just been released and is constantly being revised as you are developing your content? Well that's exactly what happened to John and I, and we couldn't have done it without the support and participation of everyone involved in this book. This book is a result of this collective process, and we are very proud to have been part of it.

I am very grateful to my very patient wife, Susan, who believes in me and loves me. She has always been very supportive of any of my endeavors.

This book would have been next to impossible without the help of everyone involved at Sybex, the greatest people in the publishing industry. I want to thank Guy Hart-Davis, our Associate Publisher, who has published many wonderful books; Maureen Adams, our Acquisitions and Development Editor, who kept us on schedule and understood our challenges; and Bronwyn Shone Erickson, a great editor who gave us credibility as writers. Thanks also to Brian Horakh, the toughest and most demanding tech editor I have had the pleasure to work with. He tells it like it is and made sure that what we wrote was relevant to our readers. Thanks to Senoria Bilbo-Brown, Contracts and Licensing Assistant, who always made me feel like I was part of the family. Thanks also to Adrian Woolhouse, Electronic Publishing Specialist, Shannon Murphy, Production Team Leader, and Elaine Lewinnek, Nancy Riddiough, Richard Ganis, Amey Garber, Molly Glover, and Jennifer Campbell, Proofreaders.

During the development of this book, we talked to many Novell administrators who were going through the process of migrating to NetWare 5. I would like to give special thanks to Pete Gold, Mauricio Gonzalez, Paul Tronnier, Tracy Ingram, and Paul Haisman. Their support and participation provided invaluable information to the content of this book.

There are not enough words or deeds to describe and show my appreciation to John Hales, my co-author. He not only introduced me to my first book project, but invited me to help him with this one also. He is a true friend and a great professional.

I want to also give a special mention to my friend, Jane Gailey, who has had a lot of influence in my life. She was my mentor at a crucial point in my life. She saw hope and possibilities when I saw a dim light. She pushed when I dragged, and she stopped me when the cliff was near.

—NMR

I want to echo my gratitude to all of the same people at Sybex that Nestor mentioned. They are an excellent team who kept us focused on the subject at hand and tried hard to keep us on schedule.

I want to express my deep and heartfelt appreciation to my family for their encouragement to produce the best book possible. Their sacrifice of time with me has touched me deeply and inspired me to try harder to be a better father to my children. This is especially true of my wife: she handled many of the parenting tasks by herself to allow me uninterrupted time to work on the book.

—JRH

Contents at a Glance

Table of Contents

Appendix   451

Introduction

We can say that writing this book was quite a challenge because we started when the product was going from beta to a first release; you can imagine the updating we had to do. You may be standing in a bookstore right now trying to decide if this is the right book to purchase. You may be curious as to what's in this book and what approach we took to put it together. Well, we thank you for considering it and for the fact that you have read this far.

This Book and the Development Process

During the initial development of this book (and the entire 24seven series), an emphasis was placed on conveying what you, as an administrator, need to know to keep your NetWare 5 server healthy, happy, and operational 24 hours a day, 7 days a week. We queried many experienced NetWare administrators and asked them a few questions:

- What do you do to keep your NetWare network healthy and happy?
- What facts did you learn the hard way?
- What have you done wrong (and right)?
- What would you like to share with other NetWare administrators?

We assembled the book with the answers to these questions combined with our own experience as network administrators. We cover the whole spectrum of designing, installing and maintaining a NetWare 5 network with an emphasis on migration.

Throughout this book, you will find NetWare 5@Work, Sage Advice, and Case Study sidebars. The NetWare 5@Work sidebars contain specific situations and problems that we have encountered in the field while deploying NetWare 5. We felt it important to use some special mechanism to emphasize how other companies are approaching problems. The case studies at the end of each part of the book are often longer than the NetWare 5@Work sidebars and deal with more general problems and solutions that some companies have faced. (The actual names of the companies have been changed.) And the Sage Advice sidebars provide specific solutions or tips to various situations.

Who Should Buy This Book?

If you are standing in your neighborhood bookstore asking yourself this question, then ask no further. Maybe you are just starting a pilot deployment of NetWare 5. Or you are in the process of migrating to NetWare 5. Maybe you need to know how to upgrade your servers or add new servers to your site. Perhaps you are curious about some of the pitfalls and sticky situations that can happen with NetWare 5. If you are in any of these situations, this book is for you.

Are you wondering about the best management practices for a NetWare 5 Server? How often you should run backups? What you should do if disaster strikes? What you can do to prevent problems? Are you wondering what Novell recommends (versus what works in the real world)? If you answered yes to any of these questions, this book is for you.

Several of the NetWare server books on the market today seem to be applicable only if you are supporting 10,000 users or more. We have endeavored to keep the topics in this book useful for you whether you are supporting 10 users or 100,000. For those of you with larger sites, you are already aware that any guidance we can provide in a 500-page book will have to be generic enough for you to customize to your own environment.

This book is for the network administrator, new or experienced with NetWare. Its readers should have experience in network operating systems, communications media, and related technologies.

Assumptions

The book is centered on NetWare 5, but many of the things discussed here will work with all versions of NetWare. Some of the features described in this book require SP2 or later; we used SP3 for this book.

How This Book Is Organized

We have divided this book into four parts that consist of 18 chapters, plus one appendix. The topics and complexity of the book vary from chapter to chapter. Each chapter was intended to stand on its own; you can read the chapters in just about any order you wish.

Part 1—Implementing NetWare 5

The first part of this book, Chapters 1 through 5, covers important facts that you need to know when preparing your NetWare 5 environment, planning NetWare 5, and migrating to NetWare 5. We tried to emphasize things that have gone wrong with installations we've been exposed to, including common design mistakes with NetWare networks, and suggestions for how to plan, deploy, and migrate to NetWare 5. We have also included coexistence with previous versions of NetWare and mixed protocols. We concentrated in Chapter 5 on migrating from IPX/SPX to TCP/IP.

Part 2—NetWare Operations

Part 2 covers the NetWare 5 server operations. Chapter 6 deals with basic day-to-day server operations. Chapters 7 through 11 deal with more advanced issues.

Part 3—Desktop Management

Part 3 delves into things you can do as an administrator to make your job easier by providing centralized desktop management and software distribution. We concentrate on ZENworks in this part of the book.

Part 4—Maintenance and Troubleshooting

Part 4 focuses on monitoring and maintaining NetWare 5 networking to include system management and hardware maintenance such as cabling, file systems, and resource management. We end this part with some nifty troubleshooting tips.

Appendix

Appendix A goes deeper into the working of DHCP and DNS on NetWare servers, since this is a critical component to support TCP/IP.

Novell Announces Two New Directory Services Products: NDS eDirectory and NDS Corporate Edition

As of the writing of this book (actually right before we were going to print) Novell expanded its NDSv8 offering with two new products: NDS eDirectory and the NDS Corporate Edition. The new products follow Novell's strategic objective to ensure NDS as the Directory of choice for any network environment.

NDS eDirectory

For multicompany service providers such as Internet providers who run NT and Sun systems, you now can leverage the power of NDS on your systems with the use of NDS eDirectory. This version of NDSv8 runs natively without the need of Novell servers on Sun and NT servers. You can now take advantage of the most powerful Directory services in the market and manage all your users, regardless of the resources they use. For an ISP or ASP this is an invaluable service. Just think, you can centrally manage all your users with an incredible amount of customization capability. Soon Novell will release versions for Linux and Compaq Tru64.

NDS Corporate Edition

Expanding on the NDS eDirectory platform, Novell offers NDS Corporate Edition for networks behind the firewall. You can support multiple platforms with NDS and provide not only traditional services, but also those associated with encryption and VPN resources. From a single point of management, and natively, you can manage users who access SUN and NT resources. Soon you will be able to manage Windows 2000, Linux, and Compaq Tru64.

These two products are now available to you by Novell. Visit the Novell site for more info and case studies. We read several interesting cases by AltaVista and CNN.

More to Come

We could not fit everything we wanted to in this book. There is just too much information to share.

However, this book does have a Web site where we will periodically post additional information such as sample documentation sheets, a sample Service Level Agreement and anything else that may be relevant to the topics covered in this book. This Web page can be found on the 24seven series Web site at www.24sevenbooks.com. Information on other Sybex books is available at www.sybex.com.

We hope the material in this book answers some of those nagging questions you have had about NetWare 5 and that it helps you to prevent a few problems in the future. Most importantly, though, we hope it helps you get out of the office by 5:00 P.M.!

Part 1

Implementing
NetWare 5

Topics Covered:

- Designing a NetWare 5 network
- Designing a tree structure
- Selecting NetWare 5 protocols and topology
- Installing NetWare 5
- Planning for the hardware and software that NetWare 5 requires
- Avoiding installation gotchas
- Integrating NetWare with NT
- Using NT as an appplication server
- Execute a healthy migration to NetWare 5
- Licensing servers
- Migrating and coexisting with TCP/IP
- NetWare 5 WWW and FTP services
- Supporting intranet and Internet services

Designing a NetWare 5 Network

Choosing a network operating system for your organization is a process that involves many meetings. You will need to establish the company's goals and the current state of its IS infrastructure. You will base your decision on what services you will support and new technologies available. Taking all that into consideration, it's hard not to take a look, or even decide on, NetWare 5 as your solution. It brings support for many of the services you will want to implement.

NetWare 5 supports the newest technologies available in application, performance, and security support. Novell Directory Services (NDS) makes the management of the entire network a breeze and its new support for native TCP/IP makes it a logical solution for integration with the Internet.

This chapter discusses designing a NetWare 5 network. We will discuss the design of the Novell Directory Services (NDS), evaluate different network topologies and protocols, and then finally plan a strategy for integrating applications on a NetWare 5 network.

NDS Design

Making the initial sketches of the tree is the most time-intensive and difficult part of the design process. You will need to decide on the tree structure, naming conventions, resources users will need to access, and administration issues. Security is also a big topic, and as you will see with NetWare 5 there are many new features to consider.

On the physical side, you will need to analyze if the network infrastructure can support the new demands you will place on it. NetWare 5 and NDS come with added functionality, considerably increasing the network traffic. Existing systems will also affect your design process. Can the existing systems be integrated with NetWare 5? That depends on a lot of factors which we will try to discuss in this book.

> **NOTE**   Try to keep the design as simple as possible. Remember that your users are the ones needing access to their resources, and you need to manage resources for their easy access. Creating a complicated tree structure might look neat, but it's difficult to access and manage.

Designing a Tree Structure

Experience with previous versions of NetWare is certainly helpful in the design process. Prior versions of NetWare (4.*x*) are very similar to NetWare 5 in design and concept, and should put you a step ahead of the game. You are going to have to spruce up your knowledge of TCP/IP if you are considering migrating from IPX to IP networking. You should consider training your staff in TCP/IP for better results; IP networks are very different in configuration and demand a lot of planning.

> **WARNING**   Do not attempt to migrate your network to pure IP without expert knowledge of the TCP/IP protocol stack. If you do not have internal resources for this, use a consultant.

NetWare Directory Services

NetWare 5 has made some major improvements to NDS. The new NDS schema extensions and snap-ins make managing network resources a much easier task. Here are the latest improvements in NDS:

WAN Traffic Manager   This new tool, implemented as a snap-in for NetWare Administrator, is used to control the WAN bandwidth. These are the three components of WAN Traffic Manager:

- WTM.NLM

- WAN traffic policies
- NWADMN32 snap-ins - Windows mmc.msc

Implementing
NetWare 5

PART 1

Catalog Services   Installed by default on your NetWare 5 server, Catalog Services allows contextless logins for users. The service indexes NDS information, allowing quick lookups and enabling users to log in to the tree without knowing their current context. This also enables administrators to get a quick snapshot of a particular section of the tree, allowing them to search specific areas rather than the entire directory database.

LDAPv3   LDAPv3 (Lightweight Directory Access Protocol) is an ITU standard directory access protocol. It allows a client to query any X.500-based directory database regardless of the platform the database is on (ADSI or NDS, for example); this provides both intranet and Internet applications a standard protocol to access your Directory tree.

ADSI   ADSI (Active Directory Services Interface) provides an interface for accessing multiple directory services. NDS is compatible with ADSI implementation. It is important to note that ADSI will also be available with Windows 2000; this will allow for a seamless integration of directories.

DS Diagnostics   Also known as DSDIAG.NLM, DS Diagnostics is used to diagnose or find problems in NDS. This utility lets you know the current configuration and health of your NDS tree.

Transitive Synchronization   This feature allows replica synchronization between IP- and IPX-based networks.

NOTE   For more information on the new NetWare 5 features, see Novell's online documentation and the Novell Web site www.novell.com.

Designing Your Tree

When you design the proper tree structure it will be easy to manage and secure. Always think of the NDS tree as a file system containing network resources. By keeping this design simple you guarantee accessibility and ease of management.

TIP   You should consider getting up-to-date on your Novell Directory Services knowledge before starting on your design work. There are many self-study and instructor-led options available to you; visit education.novell.com.

What does it mean to keep the design simple? It should follow some basic rules of thumb. If your company has a distributed computing platform with servers at each site, you should:

- Design a tree structure that follows your company's geographical topology.
- Consider one Organization container for the company.
- Below the Organization use Organizational Unit containers that represent company sites.
- Once inside a company site, create Organizational Unit containers that represent logical workgroups or departments located in that site.
- Keep less than 1,000 objects in each container. Create only the necessary amount of containers. (Please note that there are different limits for NDS depending on the version; NDS 8 can support over 3,500 objects in a container.)
- If you have less than 100 users in a site, use only one container for the location.
- Keep no more than 12 child containers under each parent container object.

If your company follows a more centralized approach with servers located in a single location and not local to the sites, you can:

- Design a tree structure that follows the company's organizational chart or business groups.
- Create a single Organization container for the company, with Organizational Unit containers representing each company division.
- Add Organizational Unit containers for company sites only if they have their own servers.
- Add additional containers for the various groups at each division. This facilitates the distribution of login scripts and applications.

If you have a small- to medium-sized company with a single site, you should:

- Create a single Organization container for the company.
- Create only the necessary Organizational Unit containers to facilitate the distribution of login scripts and applications.

This should be the simplest design of all. You need advance notice of future growth plans so that you can adapt the tree to new needs.

WARNING   We are dealing with general principles; you'll need to make the necessary adaptations to suit your particular network environment.

> **NOTE** Most projects that we have worked on use the geographical approach to designing a tree structure. We prefer to use a mixed approach that concentrates on where the resources are located.

NDS for NT

If you are planning to integrate your Microsoft Windows NT 4 servers, or manage an Exchange server on your network, you will want to use NDS for NT. Here are some additional guidelines Novell recommends to use when you are designing the tree structure with NDS for NT in mind:

- Design upper levels of the tree to conform to your office locations. Each location should have its own container.

- Don't create containers for departments that have less than 10 users. Take care not to create unnecessary containers.

- Try not to create containers or groups (global groups) that include users in other offices connected by WAN links.

- As of this writing, a typical NDS object could be 2 to 4KB in size and growing. You may want to anticipate using a 4GB SYS volume to support growth for the next 2 years. (Novell says 3 years.)

- For large networks, install a series of servers dedicated as replica servers. A replica server is a NetWare server that stores NDS partition replicas. These servers are optimized for this purpose.

- Do not add more than 3,000 members to the NT Domain objects membership *MS=ACL* list; this refers only to NT users and groups.

- Place the NT Domain object in a container that is local to the users.

- Keep each NT domain in separate partitions.

- Run NDS for NT on every PDC (Primary Domain Controller) and BDC (Backup Domain Controller) for a domain.

> **TIP** You can stay updated on NDS for NT recommendations by visiting www.novell.com/products/nds/nds4nt.

WARNING   It's a good idea to verify any recommendation we make before you incorporate it into your design. Although we try to make sure our information is accurate, products are updated very frequently and strategies change. We do want to emphasize the need to be familiar with Web resources and how valuable they are.

ZENworks

If you are designing an NDS tree and you are planning to use ZENworks as the desktop management software, follow these basic guidelines:

- If you are adding a considerable number of objects to the tree, make sure the containers are not already at the recommended maximum.
- Have policies and profiles documented before installing ZENworks.
- Note that objects added by ZENworks only affect the lower layers of the tree.
- Keep ZENworks objects in containers local to the users.
- If you are planning to use ZENworks remote control policy, test your desktops to make sure they can handle it.   RAS?

NOTE   Check with Novell for updates to ZENworks at support.novell.com.

Deciding on a Naming Convention

You must consider several variables when deciding on a naming convention. You have to be very sensitive to the users. Access to applications and data can be affected as well as user and group accounts. Naming servers after a character or animal might look cute, but it doesn't help identify what the server is for. You need to be able to answer this simple question: "If I left, could my replacement understand what I did in a timely manner?" Naming conventions apply to the following:

- User and group accounts
- IPX network addresses
- Server names and internal IPX number
- Directories and files
- Container objects
- Application objects
- Profile login script objects

- Computer and User Policy objects
- NetBIOS naming standards
- E-mail user accounts
- Routers, hubs, switches, and gateways

As you can see, it is not a simple task to generate a naming convention. A good naming convention informs the users and the administrators what the object is, what it's for, where it's located, and who uses it. You can create forms to document this information (Excel spreadsheets are preferred). You can later dump the info into a SQL or Access database for tracking purposes.

NetWare 5@Work: Company A's Naming Convention

In the process of designing the NDS tree, Company A (name has been changed to protect the innocent) established a very comprehensive naming convention. The naming convention was discussed and decided on not only by the IS department, but by all interested parties including division heads, developers, user groups, and IS personnel. The final document included:

- Network resource names: type/function/location of a resource, brand/model/location of printers

- User accounts: initials/three digits for uniqueness

- Container objects: location or department initials

- Network addresses: IPX similar to IP subnets

- NetWare server internal IPX number: IP subnet/location

- Profile login scripts: department/location

- NetBIOS names: department\location\number

- E-mail addresses: first name and last initial *MAUREEN K.*

- All names had no more than ten characters, with containers three or two.

With these naming standards, the user could identify the resources they need and the administrator could allocate them according to their location.

Access to Resources

Accessing resources generally means using network applications and data. To accomplish this, design your tree structure with performance, reliability, and security in mind.

- Make sure resources are accessible only to the users who need them and not to others. This will ensure a secure network.

- Design the tree for local NDS accessibility, placing partitions in local servers.

- Distribute resources according to who is using them.

- Group your accounts and resources by container objects.

- Place user or group objects where they can get the best access to most of their resources.

- Ensure that non-mobile users are placed in departmental or site containers, where their resources reside.

- Assign Alias objects to your mobile users so they can log on locally. That way you can point them to local resources on the site and cut down on WAN traffic.

- Use Profile login script objects rather than Container login scripts. These allow you to adapt more quickly to moving users.

- Create a special Profile for remote users who need access through dial-up lines. They will require additional properties.

- Use Template objects as often as possible. These ensure that accounts with similar properties always get the same properties.

- To access general application servers that are used by a large group of people (i.e. mail and database servers), place them at a higher level in the tree structure. This makes it easier to assign access rights to groups and users from different containers.

NetWare 5@Work: How Company A Takes Care of Remote and Mobile Users

Company A has a very large corporate network spanning an entire state. Over 30,000 users are located throughout the company's many locations. A large number of these users roam from location to location, and were constantly having problems accessing their servers and applications.

To solve this problem the administrator opted to use Profile scripts that identified the location users were logging in from, instead of using Container login scripts. By indicating the location, the administrators mapped the users to local resources and gave them rights to access them.

NetWare 5@Work: How Company A Takes Care of Remote and Mobile Users *(continued)*

For more consistent roamers—users that went to the same sites—an Alias object was created for the user to login locally. A guest account for each site was also established for the less consistent roamers.

It is a good rule to always identify users by their jobs and locations they travel to. This way you can address any special needs that come up.

TIP   All the user sees is his or her desktop, they really don't know where anything is physically located. Document what users and groups need access to and make a chart cross-referencing the information. This way when a call comes in for support you are not blindsided.

Administration of the Tree

When you are designing the tree structure you also want to anticipate whether you are implementing a distributed or a centralized administrative approach. As we stated before, your tree structure will have an impact on the administration of the NDS tree.

Centralized administration is better implemented in small networks, whereas distributed administration is best suited for larger networks. In either approach it is recommended that you use Organizational Role objects to identify administration functions. You can create as many as you want, wherever you want.

The latest version of NDS allows for selected administrative tasks (and the inheritance of these tasks), greatly improving the flexibility of assigning specific capabilities to administrators.

NetWare 5@Work: Company A's Administration Approach

Company A has the following distributed administration approach:

- The Admin user account is reserved for network-wide administrative tasks such as partition and replica functions, general security emergencies, or overrides. The security group of the company controls its password.

NetWare 5@Work: Company A's Administration Approach *(continued)*

- There are multiple levels of Organizational Role (OR) objects that handle day-to-day tasks like user account management and application accessibility.

- An OR object is created in each container for the administration of that container.

- Department support and personnel user accounts are added to their respective OR objects.

- The network administrator and the designated NDS manager have their own OR object high in the tree structure for added accessibility to all the objects in the tree. They are responsible for moving and maintaining server objects and providing supervisor privileges to container OR objects.

- A separate applications OR object is responsible for all application management tasks. These include deploying and maintaining applications.

The whole purpose of distributed management is to give people access to their administrative domains and ensure proper security. But keep in mind that each person assigned with OR responsibilities should be properly trained in how to administer rights.

Security Options

When designing your secure tree structure you need to consider whether you are going to go beyond the login and file system security active on NetWare servers and NDS. You also need to consider physical security on the servers as well as all entry points to your network and physical site. You should start by identifying all the ways users can access your network, and through which components.

Analyzing your points of entry sounds like a logical process, but you will be surprised at how many avenues are available for security breaches. Let's list some of these:

- Dial-up lines
- Wiring closets
- Router terminal ports
- Hubs/switches
- Server consoles/floppy drives
- Desktops

- Laptops
- Company personnel
- The Internet
- The phone company

All of these are areas that you should be concerned about, and there are solutions for these. NetWare 5 comes with many of the solutions you need, and there are also third-party ones available. We will discuss these in more detail later in the book.

A good tree design will make it easier to identify security trouble spots on the directory and file system, but you will still need to plan for the other trouble spots listed.

NetWare 5@Work: A Security Plan

The following is a list of procedures that Company A is implementing for their security plan:

- All access to physical locations is card monitored; everyone has to have a badge with their picture on it to enter and exit the premises.

- Access cards are used at individual offices within each site. This is not for every location, just those that are restricted after hours.

- All contract personnel and guests are carded and assigned restrictions according to whom they visit or work for. These cards have unique colors to distinguish them.

- Contract personnel who need access to systems are issued temporary user accounts with the necessary permissions.

- Company employees are taught that they are an integral part of the security systems. An indifferent employee is as dangerous as an open door.

This security plan elaborates on how the company will implement its site security. Notice that it covers physical, systems, and personnel concerns. In this case you see that a good security plan involves more than a user account and password.

Network Topology

Your network topology has a big impact on the design of NDS. The network topology determines your available bandwidth, supported protocols, built-in redundancy for dependability, and available security. The area it covers will determine how large the tree can be and how many sites can be maintained by a single NDS tree, which is your ultimate goal.

There are several aspects that you will be interested in. The first is your site topology, which includes the network backbone and distribution layers if you have multiple LANs. You will also need to include the WAN connections you use to connect each site. This could be anything from a dial-up service to a high-speed ATM network using SONET. Finally, you'll want to know what protocols are available to disseminate directory information across your network.

This section covers how LAN/WAN issues, the use of SAP and SLP protocols, and dynamic routing options can affect your NDS design.

LAN/WAN Design

It will be obvious to you that the extent of your NDS design is limited by your network topology's capabilities. A single site network will not have the same requirements as a multi-site worldwide network. You have to gauge your network's current performance and its ability to support the added reliability, security, and performance required for a fully functional Directory Service.

If your intent is to manage all network resources from a single directory, you will need continuous connectivity to all sites. This involves ensuring that your LAN/WAN connections are always up, that you have adequate security, and that you have reasonable performance.

On the other hand, if you do not meet the criteria above, you will need to consider a multiple tree directory design. Then you will use LDAPv3 as a common interface between them (available through NetWare 5). Clients can then access network resources from multiple trees this way.

See the "NetWare 5@Work: Company A's Network Topology" and "NetWare 5@Work: Company B's Network Topology" sidebars to see examples of how two companies implemented their network topology.

NetWare 5@Work: Company A's Network Topology

Company A has a network that spans the entire state with over 100 locations. There are two corporate buildings, several major regional offices, and many smaller sites.

NetWare 5@Work: Company A's Network Topology *(continued)*

Company A needs to provide continuous communications for all its sites. It needs a single Directory tree that can administrate the entire network. To accomplish this, the following infrastructure was created:

- The two corporate buildings were designated as the WAN hubs for all routes.

- A T3 backbone was installed between the two corporate buildings, with future upgrade to ATM possible.

- From the main router hubs, redundant T1 links connect to the major regional centers.

- Regional centers were then connected to nearby smaller sites with T1, fractional T1s, or ISDN links, depending on the size of the site.

- All sites have redundant connections and dialup-on-demand backups.

- Main IS support offices were at the corporate centers, with a large help desk system in the main corporate office.

- A three-tier support staff was established and participated in the project from its inception.

- HP routers and switches were used for the backbone.

- At each location all LAN links were upgraded to 100baseT networks with SMC NIC cards and HP switches/hubs.

- HP Netserver servers were distributed throughout the locations.

- A core of Netservers were reserved for NDS services and software distribution only.

- Mainframe connectivity was migrated to the LAN/WAN infrastructure.

- All desktops were replaced or upgraded with HP systems supporting Pentium series processors, 32MB of RAM, 4GB HD, CDs, and 15" monitors.

This topology allows company A to support a continuous connection between all sites, with the desired bandwidths, server/desktops, and support staff. Company A is now prepared for the design and implementation of NDS.

NetWare 5@Work: Company B's Network Topology

Company B is a smaller company than Company A, but its reach is worldwide. It provides distance learning as its core business; therefore it needed to maintain both corporate and customer communications on a continuous basis.

The company has two objectives: 1) provide single-account access to all network resources and 2) provide a common directory interface from a mixed client/server base.

With two corporate offices in different states, the following is the network topology of company B:

- A T1 link connects the two offices. These are fractionalized to six voice, six video, and twelve data channels, using CISCO 2500 routers and CSUs for the segregation of voice and data lines.

- A full additional T1 is used for Internet connectivity. This provides access to six UNIX servers delivering Web and mail services to students.

- 100BaseT CISCO Catalyst switches with over a 100Mb-bandwidth capacity support internal networks.

- Gateway desktop and servers are used with NT 4 Workstation OS and a mixture of NetWare, NT, and UNIX servers.

- Main application platform is Notes.

Although Company B is in the beginning stages of a migration to NetWare 5, this topology will enable them to design an NDS directory service. This Directory service will enable them to manage the entire network, including users who access company resources over the Internet. These users will use LDAPv3-enabled applications to interface with NDS.

The two cases overviewed in the previous NetWare 5@Work box give you a pretty good picture of what you need to consider when designing an NDS tree. Certainly ensuring that you have enough available bandwidth is a critical issue, but a more important reason for this is access to network resources using a single logon account. We can't tell you how many times we have heard users complain about using various accounts and passwords to get to applications. Worst of all is the time they waste logging in to each system. NDS takes care of all this, assuming your applications can access NDS, or at least support LDAP.

TIP Applications which implement their own security mechanisms are not enhanced using NDS, and will still require a separate login and password. If you develop your own in-house applications, have your developers use the tools provided by Novell developer support which can be obtained at developer.novell.com.

SAP vs. SLP

Now let's consider how network resources are discovered by workstations and network applications. This is an important design consideration whether you are designing a new network or migrating from an existing one.

Using SAPs

In previous versions of NetWare, the clients discovered network resources with the use of SAPs (Service Advertisement Protocol). SAPs were broadcast on IPX/SPX-based networks by servers and routers to identify themselves to clients and list services available through them.

Information on the services was kept in the Bindery database of servers, and the routing tables of the routers. A workstation or application written to IPX and NetWare would make calls to Bindery objects to access a service. For an application or a workstation to find the right server or router it would look at the SAP packets which pointed to the resource location. In other words, SAPs allowed a server or router to build a map of all network resources available.

SAPs are transmitted in broadcasts throughout the whole network, and therein lies the problem. In current NetWare networks you need to provide adequate network bandwidth to support SAP traffic. By default, SAPs are broadcasted every 60 seconds, and the more network resources you have, the bigger the problem gets. To control this traffic you need to implement filtering throughout the network so you do not inadvertently advertise resources which are not relevant in other parts of the network. Don't get us wrong, all networks produce a certain level of broadcast traffic for information purposes.

There is a positive point to SAP broadcasts. Clients can identify resources very quickly and updates are relayed within minutes. This certainly helps in the maintenance of a large network across various locations. But functionality always comes at a price.

To alleviate and improve network traffic (among other reasons), Novell implemented NDS. With NDS, all network resources were integrated into a central database. All clients and applications look for resources on the NDS database. Only the changes in the database are shared with other servers, rather than the entire database every 60 seconds.

For backward compatibility, Bindery containers on NDS store information for Bindery-dependent applications and clients. SAPs are still the vehicle of choice to advertise service location. Having an NDS partition replica in the local network cuts down on traffic and time when an application or client needs to access a resource. All in all, this improves network performance and allows for the support of more network resources.

A well-planned NDS tree with partition replicas located strategically throughout the network ensures quick and reliable access to network resources. A single database is much easier to manage and is more secure.

If the database becomes too large, you can always partition it into more manageable sizes, strategically placing the partition replicas where they will be best utilized. In a real-world scenario the tree structure would reflect the distribution of resources by location or company organization.

NetWare 5@Work: Company A's Use of SAPs to Advertise Network Resources

Company A established a set of guidelines for the broadcast of SAP traffic and the placement of NDS replicas throughout the network:

- Designated servers at both corporate locations would hold all master replicas of NDS partitions for monitoring, redundancy, and maintenance purposes.

- Sites with their own servers and resources would carry a Read/Write replica of the partition that contained the resources available to it. This would provide access to local resources even if the WAN links to the corporate offices were down.

- The company organization chart and site distribution map were used to come up with an idea on how resources should be distributed while keeping in mind the natural business flow of the company.

- Time synchronization would also be ensured by this strategy.

This set of guidelines provided criteria for the tree design. The design had to reflect the location of network resources and take advantage of SAPs to advertise the services to clients.

Using SLPs

With the advent of NetWare 5 comes the support for native IP. This means that now you can connect all your network resources with TCP/IP as the underlying communications protocol. TCP/IP, as opposed to IPX/SPX, involves a different set of rules when advertising network resources.

To allow a more dynamic resolution of network services over TCP/IP, Novell introduced the use of SLP (Service Location Protocol). SLP provides service advertising of network services over IP, much like SAP does over IPX. The following is a list of SLP properties and services:

- SLP (RFC 2165) is comparable to SAP in that it allows clients and network applications the ability to discover network resources by inquiring to a single database. It differs from SAP in the way it distributes its packets.

- SAPs are distributed through broadcasts throughout the network, causing considerable traffic. SLPs, on the other hand, can use various means for distribution. It can use multicast and static entries to resolve the location of resources. This means that a client can access SLP information to locate a resource, or NDS data, by more manageable means. This has the net effect of reducing network traffic considerably.

- SLPs also provides backward compatibility to clients and applications that are Bindery- and SAP-based. It does this by translating SAP packets into SLP packets through the Compatibility Mode drivers. These are installed by default on all NetWare 5 servers running IP only.

- SLP's main function is to make IP infrastructure resources accessible to clients and applications. In a NetWare network these infrastructure resources are servers, routers, NDS, DNS, NDPS printing services, and gateways.

- SLP provides a Plug-and-Play environment to add services on the network which could be registered to NDS in a dynamic manner. This is an advantage of using NDPS; it takes advantage of SLP Plug-and-Play environment, and is able to add printers dynamically to the tree.

- SLP does not create NDS objects by itself, it just reports them to the clients, and, in the case of NDPS, allows services to be registered dynamically to NDS. However you look at it, SLP is a more efficient advertising protocol than SAP and allows for active directory registration.

Lets look at the components involved in SLP:

- SLP, in its default configuration, is composed of SLP user agents located at the clients and SLP service agents located at the servers. The user and service agents communicate via local segment broadcasts so you don't have to do any initial configuration.

- You can also configure the user and service agents to connect directly to a Directory Agent (DA), by static entry or by using DHCP services. The employment of DAs might become necessary when you have a large internetwork and you don't want to multicast between networks

Link-State vs. Distance-Vector Routing Protocols

For those of you who have multiple location networks, we are sure you have dealt with the dilemma of choosing between Distance Vector (such as RIP) or Link State (such as OSPF) based route discovery protocols in your quest to better manage your routing tables. Which is better? Which is more efficient? You know that in the world of networking there is nothing that's "better," just more compatible with your needs. That's the same situation with routing protocols. Neither is better, but one may be better suited to your needs than another. We will discuss the pros and cons of each, and how they affect your design.

If you have been installing routers and configuring them for a while, you may have been dismayed by the amount of information you had to enter so that your routers could forward packets. In the good old days of IPX this was fairly simple to configure. You only had to enter two addresses: the server's internal IPX and the network address. In the background RIP a distance vector protocol allowed routers to dynamically exchange routing information with each other by adding each other's known routes to their routing tables.

Unfortunately, this resulted in high amounts of broadcast traffic which could saturate a network. To overcome this you could use link-state protocols like NLSP for IPX and OSPF for IP networks. These allow for much more manageable traffic on your LAN and WAN internetwork.

Now that NetWare 5 is here and the push is to support pure IP networks, your knowledge of routing is more critical. Understanding your network topology will affect how you will design your NDS tree. The upper-layer containers of your tree will inevitably resemble the company's geographical makeup.

The implementation of DHCP and DNS for name and address resolution is imperative, and will cause additional routing concerns.

Here are some rules you should consider when designing your tree over a large multi-network environment:

- To place replicas in a local segment you need to analyze traffic from the physical to the network layer.

- You want to make sure you have enough available bandwidth, let's say no less then 60% utilization. Otherwise use DAs to advertise services.

- In internetworks with less than three routers, or with no redundant links, use static routing tables.

In medium-sized internetworks of three to ten routers, use a combination of local RIP and WAN static routes between sites (Leased, T carrier, Frame Relay, etc.).

Implementing
NetWare 5

PART 1

- With large internetworks you will need to use link-state protocols (NLSP for IPX or OSPF for IP) to connect large numbers of routers and limit IPX or IP RIP-based traffic to local segments.

- When planning to manage NDS traffic over WAN links, don't forget to use WAN Traffic Manager for NDS. WTM. NLM; WHN Traffic Policies; NWADMIN 32 Snapin

- Use a network-wide traffic analyzer such ManageWise from Novell or OpenView from HP.

- Also consider traffic generated by Microsoft NT and Windows systems on your network. Their browser services generate a lot of traffic. Plan for NDS for NT as a solution to this problem.

The following NetWare 5@Work has solutions implemented by companies A and B.

NetWare 5@Work: Company A's Routing Solution

This company is considered a large internetwork composed of multiple locations throughout the state and with hundreds of routers. The following is the company's routing architecture:

- This company is going through a migration and currently supports IPX- and IP-routed protocols.

- In the local segments within a location, RIP is used for route discovery. Since these are remote sites in most cases, sending network personnel to a site is limited; therefore dynamic processes are used to minimize the need to do this.

  vector

- The corporate backbone is controlled at the corporate offices, and the routing protocol used is NLSP for IPX and OSPF for IP. This ensures managed route discovery traffic.

  Link State

- To merge the RIP routing tables in the locations with the OSPF/NLSP tables, the company was divided into areas to group several locations. One area is designated a backbone network to which all areas connect to.

NetWare 5@Work: Company A's Routing Solution *(continued)*

- A router from each area is connected to the backbone. These are referred to as Area Border Routers, and they merge RIP with NLSP/OSPF data. In addition, they often provide route summarization to consolidate many smaller networks into a single larger one. This ensures that every area knows the topology of the backbone and the backbone knows of each area.

- Routing tables are shared within areas and only the backbone routers are aware of the entire network (where you have more bandwidth capabilities).

- This company has optimal performance with this design. They minimize routing table traffic over the WAN, and optimize route discovery in the local LANs. In this scenario they designed a multi-partition tree.

NetWare 5@Work: Company B's Routing Solution

Remember that Company B has a small internetwork. Its routing solution is much less demanding. They are also going through a migration to NetWare 5 infrastructure with Macs and NT Workstation desktops. They also have Lotus Notes servers and mainframe connectivity to support. Let's review their setup:

- There are two offices in different states connected with a full T1 multiplexed into data, voice, and video channels. Half of the T1 channels are dedicated to data.

- This company uses both IPX- and IP-routed protocols, with the intention to migrate to an IP-only network.

- Static routes are utilized between the two sites with SAP filtering enabled.

As you can see, this is a fairly simple setup, and the administrator designed a dual-container tree representing each site. No RIP traffic is affecting network performance over the WAN.

Bandwidth Issues

Overall, a well-planned network architecture will support your NDS design objectives. You want to provide a strong network infrastructure to ensure high performance and reliable connectivity. In some cases you will have to upgrade not only your WAN lines to accomplish this, but also the LAN.

Many readers still probably have 10Base2 and 10BaseT. This means you are barely getting 3 to 4 Mbs of usable bandwidth out of the advertised 10 Mbs, not enough in today's bandwidth-hungry applications. To improve this situation you should do the following:

- For those who have 10Base2, replace it with 100BaseTX full duplex and switches. Might as well go for the gold—at today's prices you can't lose. In the long run your initial capital outlay will be made up by the increase in performance and reliability (which could reach 200 Mbps per connection).

- If you have 10BaseT you can double your performance by just replacing your active hubs with 10/100 switches and creating a single 100Mbps network core. But you should still try to upgrade to 100BaseTX full duplex.

100BaseX is the most cost-effective LAN solution available and the easiest to manage and troubleshoot. There are a lot of people who like Token Ring, but it is difficult to troubleshoot and manage. Token Ring is also very slow and expensive to purchase and maintain.

For campus-wide connectivity, an FDDI or ATM backbone is an excellent solution. They have a high capacity and can handle heavy loads. But in particular, if you want to support voice, video, and data, the ATM solution is best. You might also want to consider Gigabit Ethernet as a backbone solution. Even though it's a fairly new technology, it has a large following.

The WAN can eat up quite a bit of your network budget. There are special deals through the different carriers, but cost versus bandwidth is always an issue. You need to concentrate on your capacity requirements more than up-front costs. The principle "Your network is only as good as your lowest bandwidth," is true. Analyze your traffic patterns and look for the bottlenecks. This way you can distribute the load on your WAN and only pay for what you need.

Supporting Applications

The final objective of all network administrators is timely, reliable, and secure delivery of applications and data to the users. That is the essence of our jobs. Just as we design our networks for delivering information, we should design them to access applications. NetWare 5, NDS, and ZENworks bring to the table superb features for supporting, managing, and deploying applications.

In the above segments of this chapter we overviewed design considerations for NDS and networks. These tie into the delivery of applications, but you need to know how NetWare 5 resources improve application support. We will also discuss the impact NDS and ZENworks have on the distribution and management of applications, and how to plan for them.

There are three basic types of application resources:

- Server-based applications
- Desktop-based applications
- Internet-accessible applications

You can distinguish them by where the processing occurs:

- Server-based applications are processed by a server, midrange, or mainframe system.
- Desktop applications are processed on the workstation.
- Internet applications are those that can be accessed by a browser and by definition are available to the world, or at least your intranet. The consideration for Internet-accessible applications is whether to process them on the server, at the client, or on both.

The data needed for these applications is kept on the server or the workstation, depending on the administrator's judgement. If you have Internet-accessible applications, you are extending your network beyond your walls. This incurs several logistical and security issues. Using Internet applications also implies that you are making services available to the public. Since this is a new arena, it is still in the developmental stage.

Let's discuss each type of application and how a design can affect an application's performance regardless of who processes it. We will also discuss Novell Replication Services (NRS) as an easy way to distribute applications and data to servers throughout the entire network.

Server-Based Applications

Server-based applications are divided into two categories: client/server, and stand-alone applications. These two types of apps are distinguished by the way in which they are accessed. A client/server application is accessed through a front-end application running on the workstation. The server portion of the application running on the server listens for requests from the clients. In essence you have two applications working in conjunction with each other over the network. The stand-alone application, on the other hand, runs only on the server and is typically accessed through a dumb terminal or terminal-emulation software. This is not the same as storing files on a server and running the application on the workstation, which refers to desktop applications.

We brought these up to highlight the different network and system needs associated with these two application platforms.

The following are some considerations associated with each type of server-based application:

- The stand-alone applications require less network traffic then the client/server ones, and are more secure.

- The client/server applications require more system resources at the workstation than a stand-alone. Consider this if you are upgrading applications.

- Consider upgrading your application servers to handle 32bit apps. Test the servers for load capacity.

- When designing the network or migrating an existing network you should take care of the types of applications you have and anticipate the impact of the changes.

- Set up a test environment where you can run your current applications on the new systems. Check for compatibility and performance.

- Develop a schedule on how much time it will take to deploy a complete system throughout your network. Take advantage of disk imaging software as part of your deployment strategy.

- Consider the use of thin-client technology. There are many advantages to this option, like the reduction in operating costs.

The NetWare 5@Work sidebar below shows how a company addressed server-based applications in their design.

NetWare 5@Work: Server-Based Applications, and Their Impact on the Network

Company A has both client/server and stand-alone business-critical applications. The following is a description of how the applications were deployed based on the network design:

- All server-based applications were placed on dedicated HP Netserver LC, HP9000, IBM\RS6000, and AS400 servers. The eventual goal is to migrate all the applications to UNIX and NT platforms.

- Application servers are placed in "server farms" located in the main corporate offices.

- NDS controls access to all applications through application objects and desktop properties (Profiles and Policies).

NetWare 5@Work: Server-Based Applications, and Their Impact on the Network *(continued)*

- NDS and File System Security control access to the terminal emulation and client portion software for the server-based apps.

- Terminal emulation and client portion software is stored on file servers throughout the network. This makes these applications easily accessible to clients and provides built-in redundancy since these servers have the same software files. No data is kept on these servers.

- Desktops only contain productivity software files and respective data, i.e. Office 97. All user data is stored in their home directories on a departmental NetWare server.

All server-based applications are kept on dedicated application servers. The files for the client portion of the applications are kept on NetWare 5 servers, which were distributed throughout the network.

Desktop-Based Applications

In addition to the server-based applications, you will also have to deal with the *productivity applications*. This is software for the individual user and the type that causes most of our headaches. In most cases your users need some type of word processor and spreadsheet application. But there is a whole new breed of productivity applications that have become *business critical*. Yes, e-mail is one of them. Recent versions like Exchange, Notes, and GroupWise are actually server-based applications. More importantly, their functionality includes groupware and scheduling capabilities. In most cases productivity software, such as e-mail, is stored and run on the workstation.

When designing your network, you should pay particular attention to how you are going to manage the applications users have access to. Desktop-based applications, depending on how you deploy them, can be very time consuming and demanding to support. Here are some basic tips on planning the deployment of desktop applications:

- Create a basic image of the desktop with all the standard applications already installed. Use disk imaging software or the software distribution capabilities of ZENworks to rapidly deploy the applications.

- Test the image within controlled environments that are not connected to the production network. Store the installation files on local servers for server-based installs.

- Create bootable disks with batch files so that IT personnel have the option to boot up a client, connect to a server, and download the image.

- Consider the use of terminal servers and thin clients if you are considering replacing your desktops. In some cases where the users use a limited number of applications, the need for a full-blown desktop is not necessary.

- In the planning stages, it's a good idea to explore as many options as you can. There are no specific guidelines for all networks, since no two networks are alike.

TIP Check out the Web site www.thinplanet.com; for thin-client solutions, the number of options there will surprise you. For a terminal server solution we also recommend www.mentasoftware.com.

NetWare 5@Work: Deploying Applications on Your Network

Company A developed a strategic plan to implement rapid deployment of desktop applications. This strategy also would be used when resolving future help calls to the desktop. The following is a description of how Company A designed their network for desktop applications:

- All application installation files were stored on local NetWare servers.

- A testing lab for R&D purposes was made available for the development of the desktop image.

- A bootable disk, with a network client and installation scripts, was developed.

- Images were created for various departments and used in the deployment of the workstations.

- A standard desktop architecture was used for all workstations that were compatible with the software package. These were HP Vectra series desktops.

- Remote-control agent-software was added to the software package so that IT personnel can do remote troubleshooting.

- Internet access was made available to all desktops requiring the installation of a browser. *Netscape IE,*

NetWare 5@Work: Deploying Applications on Your Network *(continued)*

Novell Replication Services (NRS) was used to update and maintain server-stored application files across multiple servers, which made it less time consuming to update application files (by doing the update on just one server), and let NRS synchronize all the servers with the same files.

Planning the desktop can reap many wonderful benefits down the road when it comes time to support a network. You know that 80% of your service calls are workstation and user related. The more standard your implementation is, the better it is for maintaining and monitoring the desktop.

TIP   For software packaging and distribution, check www.cai.com. Computer Associates has a product called ShipIT, which can bundle and automate the installation of applications to the desktop. They offer a free 30-day evaluation edition.

Internet-/Intranet-Accessible Applications

This is a fairly new field, but its development has been exponential. In the past five years we have seen the Internet grow from relative obscurity to its current stardom. More and more companies are considering the Internet as a valuable tool to access new customers, and customers see the Internet as a means to acquire goods and services.

The following are some guidelines you can use when planning for Internet-accessible applications:

- Plan NDS with LDAPv3 in mind, because LDAPv3 will allow those accessing your network via the Internet use of the Directory services. Then you can actively view and manage all users of network resources through LDAP.

- Take advantage of all the security features built in to NDS and link your Internet services to NDS through LDAPv3.

- You can force all your users to authenticate for secure access or use anonymous access. In any case you need to design your network with LDAPv3 in mind.

- Load balancing is a criterion when deploying Web sites with e-commerce in mind. This requires that your applications reside on more than one server, ensuring fault tolerance and performance.

- NetWare 5 provides support for Java applications, following Sun's pure Java specification. NetWare 5 also supports virtual memory, giving NetWare an added boost in its capabilities to support Internet-ready applications.

- Oracle 8 is integrated into NDS. You also get the necessary database capabilities to handle large data transactions over the Internet.

NetWare 5 brings many features to the table that allow you to integrate your network with the Internet and provide reliable, secure, and fast access to it. Both in-house users and customers can take advantage of a company's Internet applications, which allows the business to extend its reach to customers.

Novell Replication Services

If you have more than one server that provides application distribution services and are going to hold the same files, then use Novell Replication Services (NRS) to replicate the information. NRS (current version is v1.21) provides one-way distribution of applications and data of up to 241 servers. Being able to distribute files in an automated environment can free you up to take care of other management tasks. There are, however, planning issues associated with migrating to NetWare 5. Planning for NRS can be divided into two scenarios:

- Pre-existing NRS servers

- New NRS implementation

We will discuss both scenarios in this section.

NOTE   Check the Novell site: www.novell.com/nrs for the latest updates on NRS.

Pre-existing NRS Servers

Planning a migration to NetWare 5, as you have seen through this chapter, involves preparing and updating resources to support the new environment. NRS is no exception to this. Having existing NetWare 4.*x* servers running NRS is a consideration when planning a migration. In this scenario NRS is a mission-critical service involving several servers. These servers, in return, supply applications and data to a multitude of users. NRS basically keeps the files updated so you only have to physically update a single server.

Maintaining this service affects the network as a whole, from the network topology to the operating system. Here are some rules of thumb to follow when planning for the migration:

- Make sure all the servers have the latest service packs and NDS version.

- Make sure there are no synchronization problems. The tree has to be stable.

- Upgrade NRS to the current version and move the data to the target volume. Earlier versions of NRS stored data on the SYS: volume.

- Make sure you have ample space on the volumes where you will store NRS data. Link servers require more space than replica servers do.

- Locate the master replication server so it can provide the highest bandwidth to access link servers and replica servers.

- Plan to install the same server configurations, and software, on servers running NRS.

- Designate only one person to be responsible for maintaining the NRS services. The database can get corrupted when more than one person accesses the database, at the same time, from different workstations.

NetWare 5@Work: Company A's NRS Implementation

The following is a brief description of the NRS implementation for Company A:

- The current backbone of NetWare 4.11 servers used for NDS, and file distribution services populating the network, is updated with the use of NRS.

- There are two NRS master replication servers, one of each located at the corporate offices.

- Link servers are located at the corporate offices and major regional offices.

- A specific set of directories and files is replicated; these are files of applications ultimately downloaded to the desktops by ZENworks.

- All servers are updated regularly to keep up with the latest service packs and NDS versions.

- A test lab is available to review changes before they are carried out in the production environment.

- Care is given not to overload the replication servers with too many files.

- Login scripts are configured for redundant server access. If one server is down, users are connected to a backup server.

As you can see, Company A's whole infrastructure is geared to provide the highest level of bandwidth and server availability.

New NRS Implementation

You are designing a new network and you want to implement NRS for desktop application files being distributed to several servers in your new tree. Here are some tips you can use when designing a network with NRS in mind:

- Create a network topology with ample available bandwidth throughout the WAN infrastructure. (Depending on the amount and frequency you will be updating information, T1s may not provide enough bandwidth for medium to large organizations.)

- Use switching technology, with its full duplex network interface cards, to provide the highest bandwidth in each location.

- Use the main partition replica servers as the NRS servers also. Dedicate the servers for NDS, NRS, and IP services only. Do not use the servers for user access.

- Make sure that your routing paths favor master replication servers synchronizing with link servers first.

- Dedicate a volume on the replication servers and provide ample space for the volumes.

- Try to set up backup NRS servers. These servers will not be used for file distribution on a normal basis.

- Adjust your naming conventions to include replication servers.

There are many details to consider when you are designing a network. Add those features and services available to NetWare 5, like NRS, and you will spend some time planning the network. Our best recommendation is to focus on the needs of the company. You want to solve specific problems, not implement new technologies just for the sake of it.

2

Installing NetWare 5
the Right Way!

NetWare 5 is a modern, powerful Network Operating System (NOS), and along with power comes complexity. This complexity is not a bad thing. In fact, it is a good thing because it lets NetWare adapt to all environments—from the smallest, single-server office to the largest corporations in the world. In fact, Novell has demonstrated NDS trees that have over *one billion objects* in them. This far outstrips any other NOS on the market. On the other hand, managing and dealing with this complexity can be an overwhelming job. This means two things. First, you will need to plan, plan, plan. In fact, if you haven't already read, studied, and internalized the first chapter of this book, go back and do so now before you even think of installing NetWare 5. Second, after you have planned your network, you will need to consider several issues involved with installation.

Installation is a very broad topic; it includes installing new networks as well as interoperating with and upgrading existing ones. In this chapter, we will focus on installing new NetWare 5 servers. In Chapter 3 we will look at coexistence with Windows NT servers as many networks now have both, and in Chapter 4 we will look at the issues inherent in upgrading existing servers.

Within this chapter, we will break the installation process down into several components. We will begin with some of the planning you will need to do before you even take the NetWare CDs out of the package. We will follow that with a discussion of some issues that may arise during the installation of NetWare 5. From there we will list many of the "got-chas" that may happen and how to avoid, or at least deal with, them. Finally, we will conclude with a discussion of Support Pack 3, which was current when the book was written. We will look at the process of installing Support Pack and the need to do so as well. Are you ready? Let's begin.

Planning for the Hardware and Software That NetWare 5 Requires

For those of you who are familiar with previous versions of NetWare, you'll find that NetWare 5 has far greater minimum requirements than previous versions. In the following sections, we'll show you what Novell tells you you'll need and add some of our own recommendations as well.

Recommended Hardware

Let's begin with a tour of the hardware requirements necessary to install NetWare 5. Novell recommends the following hardware as the *minimum you would want to implement*:

- 100MHz Pentium.
- 64MB of RAM (128MB if using Java).
- 500MB SYS: volume.
- RAM plus 50MB DOS partition. The RAM component is for space for a core dump, which is a copy of memory that is saved to a file for analysis by technical support. Remember when planning the RAM component that you want to plan not only for the amount of RAM you have today, but also for the amount that you may eventually install in your server up to a maximum of 4GB. If you are upgrading an existing server and the DOS partition is too small, you may consider using PowerQuest Software's ServerMagic, version 2 or later. This product will allow you to resize your DOS and NetWare partitions, as well as to copy your data (DOS and NetWare partitions) from one hard drive to a new, larger hard drive. This product may prove to be a great asset to you.
- One or more Network Interface Cards (NICs) with Certified NetWare 5 LAN drivers.
- VGA card and monitor (SVGA recommended).
- CD-ROM that reads ISO-9660 formatted disks.

- PS/2 or serial mouse recommended, but not required (just like it's not required in Windows).

NOTE   More information on Server Magic is available on PowerQuest's Web site at www.powerquest.com/servermagic/index.html.

While this hardware will work, it will not work very well. Based on our experience using the product, we recommend the following hardware for adequate performance:

- 300MHz Pentium II or higher.

- 128-256MB RAM; more is always better. Remember that you can't have too much!

- 4GB SYS volume (to provide room for growth for new, and larger, NDS objects). As noted in the previous chapter, Novell says this size should be OK for the next 3 years.

- 3-4GB HD for the DOS partition (unless you plan on having more than 2 GB of RAM). This drive is rarely accessed, so a cheap IDE drive will be fine. This also allows you the space for diagnostic utilities, support packs, and other programs you may find useful in the troubleshooting and maintenance of the server.

- VESA 1.2 or higher compliant VGA card and monitor. You may want to reuse the monitor if you won't be using it much after installation, but installation is much simpler with a good video card and monitor.

- A PS/2 style mouse if at all possible. In some rare circumstances a serial mouse may cause problems with the installation or operation of the server.

NOTE   The list of certified NetWare 5 devices can be obtained at the following addresses: developer.novell.com.hpp.

Recommended Software

In addition to the hardware listed, we and Novell recommend the following software:

- DOS 3.3 or higher (Novell includes Caldera DR-DOS 7.02 on the license disk and the Operating System CD if needed). Novell does *not* recommend using the version of DOS that comes with Windows 9*x*.

- DOS CD-ROM drivers (unless installing from a bootable CD-ROM).

Additional Recommendations

In addition to the hardware and software recommendations for NetWare 5, here are some miscellaneous recommendations culled from our experiences with the product and Novell's recommendations:

- An IP address is required if you are installing IP, and more specifically a valid Internet IP address is needed if you are connecting to the Internet. (Contact your ISP if you have questions on this.)
- Document the IRQ, I/O Port, DMA channel, and so forth, used by all hardware devices—especially for any storage devices and NICs. If possible, Novell recommends that you not use interrupts 2, 7, 9, and 15; a few very rare problems have been traced to their usage. Related to this, you should disable any hardware devices not in use, such as parallel, serial, and USB ports.
- If you use the Novell Client for DOS and Windows 3.1*x* as your client software on a computer that will be installed as a server for a server-to-server install, you will need to add **FILE CACHE LEVEL = 0** in the NetWare DOS Requester section of the NET.CFG file so that enough RAM is free for the installation to be successful.
- **FILES=30** in CONFIG.SYS.
- Drive translation for drives larger than 1GB in the BIOS needs to be turned off because drive translation is incompatible with NetWare's method for accessing large drives.
- Unplug any mouse, keyboard, and video sharing switches in use by attaching the cables directly to the server for the installation. You may reconnect them after the installation without any problems.

Other Issues to Consider before Installation

The list thus far for getting your server installed properly is pretty extensive. However, there are still some other issues you will need to think about and plan for before you begin your installation.

First, if you are installing by booting directly from the CD-ROM, be sure the BIOS is set to boot from the CD before the hard drive and that your CD-ROM drive supports the El Torito (bootable CD-ROM) standard.

Second, the Adaptec AHA 1540 and 1542 Host Bus Adapters will only install if they are revision C or higher. Earlier versions will not work in NetWare 5 at all.

Third, your video card must support VESA 1.2 or 2 to work with the SVGA video setting. If your video card does not support one of those standards, use only the VGA setting. You will know that your card doesn't support VESA 1.2 or 2 if, when installing NetWare, the screen goes blank when the GUI is started. If this is the case, you will need to reboot, load the server manually with the –NA switch (to forego loading AUTOEXEC.NCF) and then run SYS:JAVA\NWGFX\DEF_RSP.NCF to switch back to standard VGA. You will then need to redo the installation from that point, using NWCONFIG. Your other choice is to reinstall the entire server, remembering to choose the VGA setting for the video. We recommend the latter approach. Common cards that fall into this category include ATI Rage 3D Pro Turbo Chipset based video cards, which are standard in many computers, including some made by Compaq, Gateway 2000, and Dell.

Fourth, if you are using an older 3C5x9 (3Com Etherlink III) card that is set to Legacy (in other words, non–Plug-and-Play) mode [PnP], the card will not be autodetected. If you manually select the driver, the system will attempt to load the driver and then hang to the point that you must manually reboot to continue. If the driver is manually loaded at a console prompt, it works fine, but installation will not continue. There are two possible solutions:

- Install the server with a different NIC, then replace it after the installation. You will then need to manually update the AUTOEXEC.NCF file to remove the NIC you used for installation and add the lines to manually load the 3C5x9 driver, which will work fine after installation.

- Set the card to use PnP. However, Novell recommends placing the card back in legacy ISA mode after the installation. Some communication problems may result while operating in PnP mode if the card is, in fact, a legacy ISA card.

Fifth, if you have an Adaptec AHA2940 PCI SCSI card and a Pentium II 200MHz (or faster) computer with four or more processors, the SCSI driver may hang during install. The cause is that the driver and NetWare can't switch together correctly at an extremely fast rate. The solution is to either not load the PSM (Platform Support Module), which will disable support for all but one processor, or try again, as the problem is intermittent.

Sixth, not all WAN drivers are automatically installed when NetWare 5 is installed. The most popular are installed by default, but the rest are available and may be obtained from the Operating System CD in the \PRODUCTS\WAN_SUPP directory. They are stored as self-extracting archive files that, when expanded, can be used to create the disks that will be needed for the installation. Before you begin the installation, make sure any needed WAN drivers are available.

Finally, don't set any adapter card to use the memory at 0A0000h because the GUI's splash screen uses this area as well. If this isn't possible, you will need to start NetWare with the –NA option.

TIP   If you are having trouble installing NetWare 5, be sure all shadowing is turned off in the BIOS because it can cause problems in rare cases. After installation, you will probably want to determine which type(s) of shadowing can be re-enabled for better performance.

Sage Advice

While you can use the minimum values listed, performance will be dismal in all but the smallest of networks. For example, while working on this book, we used as one of our servers a machine with 96MB of RAM and consistently found that there were only 1,000 cache buffers (approximately 4MB of RAM) or so available. 128MB is the minimum that should be considered, and even then only on small networks with light server usage. Choosing 256-512MB of RAM as a starting point works much better. Also, plan on getting lots of hard drive space and setting the 4GB aside for the SYS: volume—it sure fills up fast!

Performance and Maintenance Tips

While all of the previous tips and issues are important to a functioning server, they may not be enough. If your server will be called upon to be available 24/7 with little or no planned or unplanned downtime, or if the maximum possible performance is required, you may want to consider the technologies listed in this section.

PCI Hot Plug

Novell and Compaq created and then chaired the PCI Hot Plug SIG (Special Interest Group), which allows peripherals to be added, removed, and replaced while the server remains online. This is a great feature when maintenance must be done but 24/7 availability is required. This capability has been in place for years with hot swappable drives (typically in a RAID array), but this is relatively new technology for expansion cards.

PCI Hot Plug works by powering down individual PCI slots while leaving the remaining slots fully functional. For PCI Hot Plug to work, four conditions must be met.

1. The operating system must support PCI Hot Plug, which NetWare 5 does.
2. The hardware must be in place for the operating system to request that a slot be powered down.
3. The device drivers need to support PCI Hot Plug.

4. There needs to be simple and safe access to the slots so that an administrator can safely (electrically and mechanically) work inside the computer while the system is turned on. This is a design issue for PC manufacturers, not an issue for you, but you should know that the manufacturer had to think about the issue.

PCI Hot Plug allows the user to manually step through the process of replacing a component. This may be done to upgrade an existing component for performance or other reasons or due to the system detecting an abnormality with a particular component and shutting down the slot automatically. If the latter is the case, the computer will notify the operating system and the user of the failure of that component. One of the features included here is that almost all existing PCI cards can function in this environment, although device drivers will need to be Hot Plug aware to take advantage of the capability. NIC drivers that are ODI 3.31 compliant are already Hot Plug aware. The NetWare Peripheral Architecture (NWPA) supports Hot Plug as well, and any other driver can take advantage of Hot Plug functionality if it is programmed to interact with the Novell Event Bus.

NetWare is the first OS to support PCI Hot Plug technology. Many others, including Windows NT and various flavors of UNIX are expected to support Hot Plug shortly. Once again, Novell is leading the pack and pushing the performance envelope.

NOTE   More information on the Hot Plug specification can be found at www.pcisig.com. More information on Novell's implementation of the Hot Plug Specification can be found on Novell's Web site at www.novell.com/whitepapers/iw/hotplug.html.

Intelligent I/O

For maximum performance, Novell supports I_2O (Intelligent Input/Output, also known as Intelligent I/O). This is an open, cross-platform standard that will work with any operating system that supports it. Novell was one of the developers of this standard and NetWare is one of the first NOSs to support it. It offers several benefits in terms of performance, primarily by offloading most of the I/O from the computer's CPU to the I/O card in question. This frees the computer's CPU to perform many other tasks that only it can do. Novell supports I_2O for both network cards and for storage cards, such as RAID arrays. Because I_2O was a relatively new standard when NetWare 5 shipped, there were few I_2O products available. However, Novell is posting updates to drivers and additional driver support at developer.novell.com/npp/advanced.htm, and once there query for I2O in the Document Text field.

NOTE   More information on the I_2O specification can be found at their Web site at www.i2osig.org.

Installation Issues and Recommendations

Now that we have reviewed many of the pre-installation issues, let's move on to the issues and recommendations surrounding installation. This will be a rather short section because many of the issues will be addressed in the next section on "Gotchas" that may occur during the installation.

Novell states that the following sizes are the minimum SYS: volume sizes that you should use (you could use smaller sizes, but you will most likely run into problems using the server if you do):

- 350 OS only (minimum install)
- 450 OS and default components
- 500 OS and all optional components except the documentation
- 700 OS and all optional components including the documentation

Note that these sizes do not adequately allow enough additional space for NDS, Swap files (for virtual memory support), print queues, and especially space for new features, support packs, and so on. You should move the print queues and swap file(s) to other volumes to allow enough space for NDS data which must reside on SYS:. If this is not possible (for example, you only want a single volume), then additional space will be necessary, depending on your setup. Also, recall from our previous discussion that Novell recommends, and we also *strongly recommend*, a 4GB SYS volume to allow for future growth of both the operating system and larger and more numerous NDS objects.

Two important points should be brought up here, as they affect all installations.

- You can choose a volume's size when you define it, but you can't reduce it once it is created. You can add free space to a volume by clicking Modify when the GUI file system option screens are open. You can also create and delete volumes at these screens which would, in a roundabout way, allow you to reduce volume size.
- Locality objects don't display in the browser when you are setting your server and administrator contexts during installation, but they can be typed in if you need them.

Installation Gotchas

Now we come to the longest part of the chapter—the gotchas. This will be a relatively long list, and we'll explore many pitfalls. We culled many of these from Novell TIDs (which we will list hereafter) along with problems we have seen in the field. To help you better find the resolution to your problem, each problem will have its own heading. Updates for any of the files listed may be available. Check Novell's Web site at support .novell.com to find the file(s) in question. The minimum patches that you should have installed are available from support.novell.com/misc/patlst.htm#nw. Ready? Here we go!

Time Synchronization Issues

In an IPX environment, time synchronization works nearly flawlessly, but in a pure IP environment, the secondary servers occasionally won't find, and therefore use, a time provider (such as a primary or single reference server). This doesn't happen too often, but when it does, the solution is to list the IP address of the time provider as a configured time source and to enable configured time sources. Both of these changes are made with SET commands or in Monitor. You will want to use the latest version of TIMESYNC.NLM. Check with Novell for the latest patches and support packs on this issue; time is critical to the proper functioning of NDS. (For example, time synchronization is addressed in Support Pack 3, briefly described next).

If multiple IP servers are installed at the same time, they may configure themselves to point to each other, and not the necessary time provider, for time synchronization. In this case, there is a circular dependency between the servers so that they all point to each other, and none point to a time provider that already exists on you network. You should always verify the time synchronization parameters, therefore, to make sure that the configured sources list points to a valid time provider on your network.

Hardware Issues (Mouse and NIC)

The first hardware issue has to deal with mouse support. If you tell the installation program that a mouse is installed when, in fact, one is not, the server may hang during the installation. The solution is to tell the installation program that you don't have a mouse if one is not installed or to install a mouse. It sounds simple, but the question can easily be missed or you may have one installed, but it is either on the wrong port, is not the type you specified, or just doesn't work—all of which will cause the installation program to hang.

The second issue has to do with NICs. If your LAN Card isn't autodetected during install, the installation won't proceed until one is manually chosen and it loads. Either choose the card and its parameters manually, or install a different card for installation purposes, and then after the server is up, replace it with the original card and load the correct driver manually. Don't forget to update the AUTOEXEC.NCF file to reflect the new card.

CD-ROM Issues

There are a couple of issues related to CD-ROM support. The first has to do with a server-to-server installation. When the NetWare 5 Operating System CD is mounted as a volume in the source server, you must mount the volume with the CDINST.NLM module, not the normal CDROM.NLM. (The difference is that CDINST.NLM mounts the volume as a traditional file system volume, whereas CDROM.NLM mounts it as an NSS volume, and that format is not supported for server-to-server installations.)

The second issue relates to installing, or otherwise accessing a CD over the network when the source server is a NetWare 4.11 server. If you will need access to CDs that are mounted as volumes on a NetWare 4.11 server (such as for a server-to-server install), you will need to upgrade to the latest CD-ROM files (available in Support Pack 6.0a or higher) or the 4.11 server may abend (the technical term for crash; it stands for ABnormal END) when the CD is accessed.

Protocol Issues

There are a couple of problems that you may encounter if you are installing a NetWare 5 server with IP as the only protocol into a mixed IP/IPX or IPX-only tree. The first occurs when you are installing into an existing tree where the servers are running only IPX and you choose to install only IP on the new server. In this case, the server will not detect any existing trees, nor will it choose the correct IPX network numbers. To avoid this problem, load the LAN driver manually (if needed) and bind IPX to it using the correct IPX network number before you set the IP address during install. The other solution is to install both protocols and then remove IPX after the server is successfully installed.

The second issue also has to do with mixed IP/IPX environments and NDS replication. In this case if you are installing into a mixed protocol environment with some servers running only IPX and some only IP, you will need to make sure to place the migration agent—load SCMD with the /G switch—on the server(s) with the master replica(s) of the NDS partition(s) for NDS to replicate properly. See Chapter 5 for more on IP/IPX integration and migration issues, including the Migration Agent.

Installing a NetWare 5 Server into a NetWare 4.1x or 4.2 Tree

If you choose to install NetWare 5 into an existing NetWare 4.1x or 4.2 tree, the 4.1x or 4.2 servers will need DS.NLM and DSREPAIR.NLM (and all related files) to be at least the following (and preferably the latest version available):

- If the existing servers are running NetWare 4.10, you need *at least* DS.NLM v5.13 and DSREPAIR.NLM v4.58. As of the writing of this book, the latest versions of these files were in a file on Novell's Web site called DS410P.EXE, dated

March 9, 1999. The version of DS.NLM is v5.17 and the version of DSRE-PAIR.NLM is v4.63.

- If your existing servers are running NetWare 4.11 or 4.2, you need *at least* DS.NLM v5.99a and DSREPAIR.NLM v4.58. As of the writing of this book, the latest versions of these files were in the file NW4SP7.EXE (Support Pack 7 for NetWare 4), dated August 18, 1999, also available on Novell's Web site. The version of DS.NLM in that file is v6.04 and the version of DSREPAIR.NLM is v4.65.

In any case, if you choose to install any support packs on any server running any version of NetWare, see the notes accompanying it for more information on the minimum versions for interoperability with NetWare 5. The information on Support Pack 2 for NetWare 5 is provided next.

Licensing Issues

Licensing is one of the biggest areas (perhaps behind NDS issues only) that cause problems with the installation. There are several errors and different causes for each. We will put each one in its own section for easier reference.

Issue 1: Error 0xC0001003 and Policy Manager Error 5.00-89

One of the messages that may occur is Error 0xC0001003, which may appear during the GUI stage of the installation. You will also see at the console prompt a "Policy Manager Error 5.00-89, error number C0001002" after installation until the problem is resolved. This is a fairly complicated problem. Let's begin this section with the causes of the problem, and then we will discuss some solutions.

Error 0xC0001003 occurs primarily when *all* of the following conditions are met:

- You are installing into a partition below [Root].
- A valid license was installed.
- A server in the partition the server is being installed into that is running NLS (Novell Licensing Service) does not have a R/W (Read/Write) replica of that partition. The server running NLS can be either a NetWare 5 or a NetWare 4.11 server with Support Pack 6 or higher server.

This may also occur if you have previously installed the server and then did *any* of the following to this server:

- Moved it to another location in the tree
- Renamed the server
- Renamed the container the server was installed in
- Removed and then subsequently reinstalled NDS

If you get the error during installation, you will receive a message when installation is complete that a license must be installed later. Another byproduct of this error is that the license containers for the server (Novell NetWare 5 Conn SLC+500 and Novell NetWare 5 Server+500 [the 500 refers to version 5.00, not the number of connections purchased]) will not be created. If the Policy Manager error cited previously occurs for the second set of reasons listed, these containers may already exist from a previous installation, but even then the licenses will not be in those containers.

Another possible consequence of this error is that partitions may be placed (or omitted) on this server that you weren't planning on. The partitions that may be created on the server are as follows:

- A R/W replica of [Root]
- A Subordinate Reference replica to the partition that the server was installed in, if that partition is a child of [Root]

So, what is the solution to the error message? There are actually several steps that you must take to remedy the problem.

First, you will need to get the partitioning set up correctly. One approach is to place a replica of the desired partition on the NetWare 5 server with the error, and when the state of the replica changes to ON, install the license as described in the following section. If that is not possible or desirable, you may put a R/W replica of the partition you are installing into and/or NLS (so that *both* are on the same server) on a NetWare 4.11 server with SP6 or higher. Again you will need to wait until the replica state is ON before installing the license, as described next.

Another potential problem is that the network adapter driver may allow communication, but not some replication with other servers. The solution here is to apply the latest support pack from Novell and update the LAN Adapter if needed.

If the problem is occurring due to the second set of reasons (moving the server, renaming it, and so on), then in addition to making sure that the appropriate replicas and NLS are in place (as noted previously), you may also need to run SETUPNLS from the console prompt.

After the appropriate corrective action has been taken, you can then install the license. This can be done by any of the following methods:

- You can use NWCONFIG (at the server console, not via RCONSOLE—see the section entitled "License Installation and RCONSOLE" for more on this), choose Select License Options ➢ Install Licenses. After you install the license disk as prompted, the problem will be resolved. Also, the license will already be assigned to the server, as you did it at the server that had the error.

- Your second option is to use NWAdmin. Begin by selecting the container to install the license in, choose Tools ➤ Install License ➤ Install Envelope. Unless the license is an MLA (Master Licensing Agreement) license, you will need to assign it to the server, as described in the following steps. MLA licenses are described in a later section.

- Your third option is to use NLS Manager. Start by switching to Tree View (if necessary), then select the container that will hold the license containers, and choose Actions ➤ Install Envelope. You will need to select both the base and the connection licenses when prompted and assign the license to the server (again unless it is an MLA license) as described in the following list.

You can assign a license to a server by using NWAdmin. You will need to do the following for *each object in the license container:*

1. Expand the License container to view the serial numbers.

2. Select the serial number object and choose details.

3. Select the Assignments tab.

4. In the File Server Assignment box, type the server name or use the browse button to choose the server.

Licensing and replica issues are some of the more complicated problems that you can run into, but with proper planning and some foresight you can also easily avoid them.

Issue 2: License Ownership

When you are installing new licenses (either during installation or later), you should always use the same user name because the license certificates are owned by that user, and only that user can make some changes to that certificate. Note that ownership is independent of NDS trustee assignments. Specifically, only the owner (or someone who has security equivalent to the owner) can do the following:

- Transfer ownership of the license certificate to another user

- Assign other users, containers, and other NDS objects as valid users of the license

We want to point out, however, that once you have assigned one or more NDS objects as users of the license, that only those explicitly listed (and those who are security equivalent to those listed) may use the license. The default installation allows all users at or below the context of the certificate to use it.

Issue 3: License Installation and RCONSOLE

Licenses can't be installed in NetWare 5 with RCONSOLE. The option to press F4 to install a license in RCONSOLE is only in NWCONFIG.NLM v 3.03, which ships on the

English-only CD. The international version does not even have the option to press F4. You must either install the license directly at the server or through NWAdmin. Novell recommends the latter.

Issue 4: Installation Takes a Long Time or Appears to Hang When Installing Licensing

If the installation process seems to hang during the installation of licensing, it may be due to the need to walk the tree. Walking the tree refers to the process of moving through the tree, potentially across servers and WAN links. This is because the components used in licensing may be located anywhere above the server in the tree. Therefore, the larger the tree is, the longer the wait may be for this process to complete.

Information on Master Licensing Agreements

When NetWare is licensed, it can be done in several configurations. Very large organizations can purchase NetWare directly from Novell with an MLA (Master Licensing Agreement). The major difference is that in typical installations, there is a license for each server, and each server is allowed a certain number of simultaneous connections. If the same license is used on multiple servers, errors are sent throughout the network until the problem is resolved. With an MLA, however, licenses *can* be reused as often as desired, and each server will allow an *unlimited* number of connections. There are a few special issues surrounding this type of license that don't apply to other customers:

- An MLA license can only be installed a maximum of one time per container for any number of servers in that container.

- For performance reasons, you will typically want to install an MLA license at the root of each *partition* of the tree, although you may install the certificate (and the associated containers) at any point in the tree at or above where the servers are. You may even install them at the top level Organization and let all servers use the one set of objects. This may consume an undesirable amount of bandwidth so we recommend that you install one copy per partition root.

- If you choose to install the licensing objects once near the top of the tree, servers may not be able to access those objects if the NLS_LSP_*<servername>* object is configured to search only to the root of the partition. The default is to search to the [Root] of the tree. You can verify (and change if necessary) this setting by displaying the details for the NLS_LSP_*<servername>* object and ensuring that the Search to the Root of the Tree option is selected.

- Do *not* assign a server to the license certificate, or only the specified server will be able to use it. You will also not be able to install any more servers into the container because they can't use the certificate. Note that for all other license arrangements you must list a server here for it to function.

Reinstallation of NetWare 5

If you reinstall NetWare 5 on top of an existing version of NetWare 5 and choose to install a *new* server, a warning message will appear. The message will state that a previous version of NetWare 5 was found in C:\NWSERVER (or whatever directory), and that if you choose to install a new server, "all data on the existing server will be lost." The message does *not* refer to data on the *NetWare partition*, but rather to all the data in the C:\NWSERVER (or whatever) directory. Later in the installation process, you will receive a second message as follows: "Existing NetWare partitions and volumes have been detected. Removal of partitions and volumes will destroy any data on them." Along with that message, two options are given, including "Replace volume SYS and its NetWare partition." If you choose that option, *all data on the partition that contains the SYS: volume will be lost*, but not on any other volumes in other partitions.

These messages (and the potential loss of data associated with them) can be avoided by choosing to *upgrade* rather than install a new server. Even though the option is to upgrade from NetWare 3.*x* or 4.*x*, it will work fine if NetWare 5 is already installed. In that case, all existing data will be preserved.

Directory Services Installation Error

When you install NDS you may get the message "Error Installing DS, Error Code 1." This occurs when the *master* replica of the partition you are installing a NetWare 5 server into is located on a NetWare 4.1*x* server.

The solution is to place the master replica on a NetWare 5 server before installing a new server. Also, be sure that an Admin level user (with Supervisor rights to [Root]) exists in the partition you are installing into. In some circumstances, this may obviate the need for the master replica to be on a NetWare 5 server. If you create the Admin user *after* you get the error message and then attempt to continue the install, a dialog box will appear informing you that the server already exists. Simply ignore the error and choose to continue the installation and the installation will proceed normally.

Date and Time Issues

As you are well aware, NetWare, and particularly NDS, is very sensitive to time and date issues. This is because synchronization of NDS objects is based on time. Therefore, be very sure to set your internal clock properly before installing NetWare. Java won't work correctly (and therefore the install process won't complete) if the year is greater than 2039. This is a known bug in Java, not a Y2K issue.

General Information and Other Tips and Tricks

Before we conclude the Gotchas section, we want to review some other useful bits of information and help for you.

Country Codes

When you create a Country object, you need to name it according to the accepted two letter codes, as used on the Internet and defined by ISO standard 3166. A comprehensive list of those codes can be found by searching for "ISO 3166" on the Web. A few of the more popular country codes have been provided in Table 2.1 for quick reference.

Table 2.1 Codes for Creating Country Objects

Code	Name
ar	Argentina
at	Austria
au	Australia
be	Belgium
br	Brazil
ca	Canada
ch	Switzerland
cl	Chile
cn	China
co	Colombia
de	Germany
dk	Denmark
eg	Egypt
es	Spain
fr	France

Table 2.1   Codes for Creating Country Objects *(continued)*

Code	Name
gb	Great Britain
gr	Greece
hk	Hong Kong
ie	Ireland
il	Israel
in	India
it	Italy
jp	Japan
kp	North Korea
kr	South Korea
mx	Mexico
my	Malaysia
pa	Panama
pe	Peru
ph	Philippines
pl	Poland
pr	Puerto Rico
pt	Portugal
ru	Russian Federation
sa	Saudi Arabia
se	Sweden

Table 2.1 Codes for Creating Country Objects *(continued)*

Code	Name
sg	Singapore
tr	Turkey
tw	Taiwan
uk	United Kingdom
us	United States
ve	Venezuela
vg	Virgin Islands (British)
vi	Virgin Islands (USA)
za	South Africa

General Troubleshooting Techniques for Installation Problems

If you are having trouble with the installation, there are several switches for INSTALL.BAT that may prove useful. These include:

-frame *<frame>*   This will force the server to bind to the frame type specified.

-iipx /serv_id *<addr>*   This will set the internal IPX number to the one specified.

-lang <#>   This switch will allow you to set the language used for the installation. The list of numbers can be obtained by typing **Language List** at a console prompt. Since this may be the first server you are installing, and since you don't have a console prompt to go to look this up, Table 2.2 lists the supported languages and the associated numbers. Note that not all codes are valid with Netware 5; see the note at the end of the table for more information.

-n   Using this switch will let you do the installation without the required amount of RAM available. You would use this switch when DOS reports the wrong amount of available RAM. Using this switch is not recommended. If the requisite amount of RAM is not available, installation will not complete, even with this switch.

-conlog   This switch is on by default and enables logging during the installation. There are several other related switches listed as well. The default location for the log file is C:\NWINST.LOG. It will normally be 0 bytes, as the file is not written to the disk until CONLOG.NLM is unloaded, which doesn't happen during a normal install. To get a report of everything that happens at the console prompt during install, go to a console prompt during the install and type UNLOAD CONLOG *before rebooting* at the end of the installation.

-nolog   This switch is the opposite of the –conlog switch; it turns off console logging during installation.

-log *<path>*   This switch will allow you to set the location for the console log file. All system messages and errors will be logged to the specified path. This switch is often used when doing unattended or factory installations.

Table 2.2   Countries and Their Language Numbers

Language	Number
Chinese-Simplified	1
Chinese-Traditional	16
Czech	21
Danish	2
Dutch	3
English	4
Finnish	5
French-Canadian	0
French-France	6
German	7
Hungarian	20
Italian	8
Japanese	9

Table 2.2 Countries and Their Language Numbers *(continued)*

Language	Number
Korean	10
Norwegian	11
Polish	17
Portuguese-Brazil	12
Portuguese-Portugal	18
Russian	13
Spanish-Latin America	14
Spanish-Spain	19
Swedish	15

NOTE NetWare 5 does not support all of the languages listed in Table 2.2. Different products are available in different combinations of languages. As of this writing, only codes 1, 4, 6, 7, 8, 9, 12, 13, 14, and 16 are supported.

Another source of troubleshooting information is the files created in the C:\NWINST .TMP directory. Some of the errors that may occur during the installation may be saved there. You want to look in here for any log files that may exist; in particular, look for BOOT$LOG.ERR. Setuperr. Ms; for MS

Manually Installing NetWare 5

If all else fails and you're an advanced administrator, you can manually install NetWare without the INSTALL.BAT and the GUI by doing the following:

1. Copy the STARTUP directory from the CD-ROM to C:\NWSERVER (or whatever directory you wish).

2. Start the server by typing **SERVER**.

3. Install the operating system by loading NWCONFIG and choosing each menu item in order, from top to bottom, answering each question as appropriate.

Note that if you follow the preceding procedure, the GUI will not be fully installed, nor will any product that requires the GUI be able to be installed without it. We want to repeat our note of caution again: This is for advanced administrators only. We've provided this solution only for those who cannot get the GUI installation to work at all. Try this method only after trying all of the troubleshooting tips already mentioned.

When STARTUP.NCF Is Corrupted, What Next?

If you boot the server by using the syntax NWSERVER –NS to avoid running the STARTUP.NCF file, the server is not fully operational. You can load NWCONFIG to fix it and then reboot the server. But what if you want or need the server to be fully operational so you can test it out or set some parameters to determine their effect? When you load NetWare with the –NS, some functionality is missing. To fully boot the server you must execute the six load stages in order. This is accomplished by entering (at the console prompt, in the order listed): **LOADSTAGE 0, LOADSTAGE 1, LOADSTAGE 2, LOADSTAGE 3, LOADSTAGE 4,** and **LOADSTAGE 5**.

When you have finished, the server will be fully functional. However, remember that any commands in STARTUP.NCF and AUTOEXEC.NCF have not been executed, so you may need to go back and manually enter those as well.

How Do I Get Answers to Questions Not Addressed Here?

While we have tried to address many of the concerns and issues that you may run into during installation, it is impossible to address all of them or to address future products and upgrade, that you may install. The best source of support information is Novell's Web site at `support.novell.com`. From there you can search for any information of interest to you, including answers to questions, the latest patches and upgrades, and so on. One of the best places to search for this information is by clicking on the word Knowledgebase at the aforementioned Novell site. These articles have proven invaluable over the years that we've worked with NetWare when we've gone as far as we could with a problem. The answers to your problems are probably in there. In the rare case that a technical support call is required, the solution that they come up with will be added to the Knowledgebase to help everyone else in the future. Reports that Novell posts on its Web site are called TIDs (Technical Information Documents).

Table 2.3 lists some of the TIDs we found when searching for installation problems. You can find them by TID number or by searching Knowledgebase for Installation NW5.

Table 2.3   Some Common Installation TIDs

TID #	Description
2941991	NetWare 5 Release Notes—Server Installation
2944438	NetWare Server Setup Checklist
2946427	NW5 AHA154X will not install in NetWare 5
2943847	NW5 GUI in SVGA on ATI Rage Pro Video Cards
2947263	NW5 GUI Install Error 0xC0001003
2944739	Error installing DS, Error Code 1
2944209	NW5-Unable to open the license envelope file (RCONSOLE and installing licenses)
2943025	NW5 install: Does not autodetect LAN card
2946614	NDS Tree not seen when selected NW5 install
2938552	NDS guidelines for ZENworks and NDS for NT
2944009	NW5 Install fails with year 2039 or later
2942647	NW5 Install hangs with 3c5x9.lan
2944797	NW5 Installing MLA license certificates
2942539	NW5 OS installation issues
2941992	NW5 Release notes known software limitations
2942918	NW5: Warning a previous install will be lost
2942243	Server hang during NetWare 5 install
2951603	NetWare 5 Support Pack 3

Support Packs

From time to time as Novell develops patches for problems or adds features for existing products, they issue what Novell calls support packs (SP). These support packs are available free on Novell's Web site. The quickest way to get the latest SP for a product is to check the minimum patch list. As mentioned before, the quickest way to find out what patches are on the list is to go to support.novell.com/misc/patlst.htm#nw. You should always download and install the patches listed here before calling Novell for technical support. In fact, if you call and you haven't installed the patches yet, they will direct you to do so and call back if the problem persists. With this in mind, this section will review SP3, the latest SP available as of the writing of this book. Other ones will become available, but the basic ideas and concepts discussed here will apply to all support packs and we will get a chance to review them in this manner.

Now let's look at SP3's new features, installation procedures and prerequisites, and other notes.

Other SPs will have similar types of information. Refer to the documentation that comes with the SP for the latest information.

> **NOTE** Complete information on each support pack is available in the readme file that accompanies it. The information is also posted in a TID, allowing it to be easily searched.   *2951603*

New Features

Following are some highlighted new features added with this support pack:

- Improved Wan Traffic Manager policies
- Faster NSS with salvage capabilities
- Improved DNS/DHCP GUI
- IDE DVD-ROMs are now supported
- Updated Java Virtual Machine (VM) to 1.1.7b

Installation

To install a support pack, you must meet some prerequisites. For SP3 (they vary based on the updates in the support pack), they include the following.

- Unloading JAVA.NLM and any Java-based applications because the Java system will also be updated. You can do this manually or the installation routine will do it for you.

- Ensure that you have enough free space on the SYS: for the support pack. SP3 requires approximately 115MB free space plus an additional 140MB if you choose to back up the original files. The space requirements will vary depending on the options you have installed.

- If you have already installed NDS 8, be sure to back up SYS:SYSTEM\DSBACKER .NLM to another location.

- IPXSPX.NLM must be loaded on an IP-only server to install the support pack. It can be removed after that.

The installation of the support pack falls into two categories, namely preparing for the installation and the actual installation itself. The preparation for the installation is really quite simple. After you download the SP, you will need to copy the SP to a location where you can expand it. This can be on any volume with enough space or (if you are installing it via RCONSOLE) your local hard drive. Some of the paths to some files are very long, so you will need to put this file in a root-level directory (ex. SYS:SP3) to avoid any problems. One other note here: You can't install the support pack through the GUI, but must use NWCONFIG instead.

To actually install SP3, you will need to do the following:

1. At a console prompt, type **NWCONFIG** and then choose Product Options ➤ Install a Product Not Listed.

2. Depending on where you chose to put the support pack, do one of the following:

   - If the support pack is on a volume on the server you are installing it to, press F3 and enter the path (including the volume name), for example SYS:\SP2.

   - If the support pack is located on another server, press F3 and enter the path to it, including both the server and volume names, for example MY_ SERVER\SYS:\SP2.

   - If you are installing it via RCONSOLE and the files are on the client PC's hard drive, press F4 and enter the local path to it, for example C:\SP2.

3. If you want to be able to uninstall, be sure to choose to back up the original versions of the files. If you do choose to back up the files at the installation of the support pack, the original files will go in SYS:SYSTEM\BACKUPSP3\UNINSTALL. Novell also has warned against uninstalling the SP if you have added any options after the support pack was installed. This could corrupt some files. Complete instructions for uninstalling the SP are in the README.TXT file.

4. Press F10 to install.

5. If you are installing the support pack on a system with NDS 8 installed, you will get an error message that tells you that this is a second attempt at copying files and

asks if you want to copy all the files or only the remaining files. This is expected. Simply choose to copy all of the files again and installation will proceed normally.

6. When the process has completed, verify the .NCF files to be sure they are correct and that any changes made are okay.

7. If NDS 8 is already installed, restore DSBACKER.NLM to SYS:SYSTEM from the backup location you chose before installing the support pack.

8. To finish the installation and make the changes effective, you must reboot the server. This is accomplished by typing **RESET SERVER** at the console prompt.

> **TIP**   If you are installing the SP on many servers at once, you may want to purchase Config Central by NetPro, available on the Web at www.netpro.com/configcentral/default.asp.

> **TIP**   You may be allowed to install an individual support pack while you are installing a new server, instead of installing the server then the SP. Refer to the readme that comes with the SP for instructions on how to do this (if it is possible).

Miscellaneous Support Pack Issues

There are several miscellaneous issues and features associated with using SP3.

First, Novell has enhanced the SCMD (the compatibility mode driver for IPX) driver and removed many bugs. Refer to Chapter 5 for details.

Second, Novell has also improved time synchronization, as well as interoperability with other NTP time servers. For more information, refer to TID 2949483.

Third, ConsoleOne is no longer bundled with the support pack. To get the latest version, you will need to download and install it separately. It is available at www.novell.com/download#nds.

> **WARNING**   As with almost all SPs, all of the installed features are updated as necessary, but options that are installed after the support pack is applied will not be updated. To update those services, reinstall the support pack.

Once you have installed SP3, there are some updated requirements relating to installing NetWare 4.11 and NetWare 5 servers in the same tree. The following versions of DS.NLM are required (at a minimum): NetWare 4.11 servers must be running version 6 and NetWare 5 servers require 7.09.

3

Integrating NetWare and Windows NT

While NetWare is a great operating system, it is only an NOS; you still need an OS for the desktop. Some of the desktop OS choices include DOS, Windows 3.*x*, Windows 9*x*, Windows NT, OS/2, Macintosh, and Unix systems. By far the most popular OSs in use today are Windows-based systems. Windows NT is being pushed by Microsoft as the OS for business. NT offers many advantages, including scalability, the ability to run on multiple hardware platforms, and greater security and stability than any other version of Windows. In addition to having NT on many desktops, NT is often used as an application server. There are many popular applications designed to run on NT Server, including SQL Server (for database access), Exchange (for e-mail and groupware functions), and IIS (Internet Information Server, for Web and FTP capabilities). There are some manageability problems with NT, however, which we will discuss as we go on. We will also look at the solutions to those problems recommended by both Microsoft and Novell. Today, interoperability is a business necessity.

In this chapter we will review the options and products that Microsoft and Novell offer to provide interoperability between these two operating systems. We will begin by looking at Microsoft's offerings, including CSNW (Client Service for NetWare), GSNW (Gateway Service for NetWare), FPNW (File and Print Services for NetWare), and DSMN (Directory Services Manager for NetWare). We will look at Novell's offerings as well, including the Novell Client (which we will discuss in detail in Chapter 9) and NDS for NT. From there we will compare and contrast NT's current Domain structure with Windows 2000's Active Directory with NDS for NT. Finally, we will conclude with a discussion on how NT can be used effectively as an application server in a NetWare network, specifically as an Exchange server.

Microsoft's Interoperability Products

Microsoft offers several interoperability components that allow NetWare and NT to coexist. Before we discuss all of them, however, you must remember that while NT needs to be seen as coexisting with NetWare, it is in Microsoft's best interest to get you to move from NetWare to NT, so the products are not necessarily the best possible products. Novell, on the other hand, has every reason to give you the best possible products to keep you as a customer. With that said, let's begin with a review of Microsoft's offerings.

In this section, we will briefly discuss CSNW (Client Service for NetWare), GSNW (Gateway Service for NetWare), and the Microsoft Services for NetWare, which consists of FPNW (File and Print services for NetWare), and DSMN (Directory Services Manager for NetWare). Note that FPNW and DSMN were separate utilities that were packaged together and sold as Microsoft Services for NetWare beginning with the release of NT 4.

NOTE   There are known problems and issues with CSNW, GSNW, FPNW, and DSMN. For the latest information, query for the appropriate product at the following Web sites: www.microsoft.com/support and support.novell.com.

CSNW

CSNW (Client Service for NetWare) allows Windows NT Workstation computers to communicate with NetWare servers. It is the client software that Microsoft provides to access NetWare servers. While it does support NDS (in NT 4 and higher), it does not fully do so. For example, while you can enter a context and tree name as part of the configuration of CSNW and/or at login, you can't specify the username you would like to use for that server. It must be the same as the NT username. You also can't administer NDS through this client, although you can administer bindery-based servers. Another limitation of this (and all other Microsoft products that allow for interoperability with NetWare) is that it only supports the NWLink protocol. NWLink is what Microsoft calls IPX/SPX.

(3.X & below)

This product does allow you to log in and select a default server and allows some basic customization of the product. The customizations that you can choose are whether or not you want:

- Banner pages when you print
- Form feeds after each print job
- Notification after each print job has printed
- NetWare's login script to be executed when you log in

To configure CSNW, you can either specify your settings when you log in or you may modify them later by going to Control Panel ➤ CSNW. Note that you can't change the settings by going to Control Panel ➤ Network. The only thing you can configure under the latter choice is the Network Access Order. Here you can choose which type of resource will be accessed first when attempting to resolve a name as well as which will be chosen if there are duplicate names between your NT and NetWare servers. You can choose to set both the network and print priorities here.

There are several other issues with this client as well. First, it doesn't support synchronizing time with the NetWare servers, something that Novell's client always does. Second, you may have trouble accessing a user on a NetWare 5 server in any context unless Support Pack 4 (SP4) or higher is installed on the NT-based computer. Another pre-SP4 issue is that when you log off and then back on again, CSNW does not log you out of the NetWare server when you log out of NT. When you try to log on again, NetWare sees this as a "new" connection and if your maximum concurrent connections is set to one, you will get an error. Another problem with CSNW is that when you change your password in NT by pressing CTRL + ALT + DEL and choosing Change Password, the NT password will be changed, but not your password on a bindery-based NetWare server (3.x and below). This is not a problem with NDS-based servers.

Most networks that we have seen that use NetWare for the NOS and NT as the desktop OS use Novell's client software, the Novell Client (formerly Client32) instead of CSNW. As of the writing of this book, the latest version was 4.6.

GSNW

GSNW (Gateway Service for NetWare) allows NT server-based computers to communicate with NetWare servers. All of the configuration options and issues discussed previously in the CSNW section also apply to GSNW. The GSNW service also offers one feature that CSNW doesn't—the ability to act as a gateway. Until you enable the gateway, it acts essentially the same as CNSW, but after the gateway is enabled, you can share NetWare resources to Microsoft-based clients, with only the server running client software for NetWare networks.

To enable the gateway, three things must be done. You must:

1. Create a user account, with any name and password you wish, on the NetWare server.

2. Create a group called NTGATEWAY on the NetWare server.

3. Place the user you created in step 1 in the NTGATEWAY group.

At this point, however, the gateway is still useless. To make the gateway effective, you must choose to enable the gateway on the NT server by checking the box Enable Gateway and entering the username and password of the user created in step one. You still aren't finished, however. You must next choose to add shares (which is how resources are made available on Microsoft-based networks) to the resources that you want to make available. To do so, you will need to enter the share name and path, as well as a drive letter for each share. There are two points that need to be made here. First, a drive letter is required for each share and you only have 26 for all local and shared drives; this can be a limiting factor. Second, the path is entered using the Microsoft standard syntax, called Universal Naming Convention (UNC), rather than the Novell standard. The format of a UNC name is *server**volume**path*.

Now that you have done all the things listed in the previous paragraphs, the gateway is active. The next logical question, then, is what kind of security is effective on that share? The answer is the *most restrictive* of the NT share permissions and the NetWare user's rights. By default, all shares on an NT-based computer are configured with the group Everyone getting the Full Control permission. Be careful when it comes to security when using the gateway.

There is another issue here as well. As long as you are using the NT server as a gateway between the two networks, all of the traffic between the Microsoft-based clients and the NetWare server go through that NT server. While on the positive side this requires only one license on the NetWare server for all of the clients using the gateway, it also means that all network traffic must go through that NT server. This means more traffic on the wire. (All traffic must be sent first to the NT server and then sent on to the NetWare server, plus the reply traffic is sent to the NT server and then back to the client.) This can be a big bottleneck on the NT server.

Sage Advice

We highly recommend that you use Novell's client software. While Microsoft needs to have a "check box item" for the feature list that offers compatibility with NetWare, it is not in its best interest to be a great client. They really want you to use only Microsoft products. Novell, on the other hand, has a vested interest in providing the best possible performance and capabilities so that you keep your NetWare server. Refer to Chapter 9 for tips and ideas that can help the Novell Client perform even better.

FPNW

FPNW (File and Print services for NetWare) is designed to allow you to have an NT server on your network appear as a NetWare server. This is an add-on utility, meaning it does not ship with NT and must be purchased separately. The NT server will then appear to Microsoft-based clients as an NT server and to Novell-based clients (clients running only Novell client software) as a NetWare 3.12 server.

> ***WARNING*** NT servers without SP 3 or higher will cause Client32 and the Novell Client clients to be confused. This is because of upgraded NCP support in NetWare 3.11 and higher (which the NT server advertises itself as) while the NT server in actuality does not support the upgrades.

Once you install FPNW, it will create a SYSVOL directory, which corresponds to Net-Ware's SYS: volume. In it will be the standard NetWare 3.*x* subdirectories of Public, Login, Mail, and System. In the Login subdirectory you will find the Login command, and in Public will be Login, Logout, Attach, Map, Slist, Capture, Endcap, and Setpass. On the NT server in User Manager for Domains you will see two new items: a checkbox labeled Maintain NetWare Compatible Login and a button labeled NW Compatibility. With these two options you can control how the NetWare clients see the server.

As far as printing is concerned, users running Novell client software will see the printers installed on the NT machines just like they were print queues on a NetWare server. They can then print to them just like they were regular NetWare print queues. On the server side, the printer can be a local printer or a printer that is directly connected to the network, such as with a Jet Direct card. If it is the latter, and the card is in Print Server mode, it can directly service the printer (or queue depending on your point of view) on the NT server.

FPNW works in both a single and a multiple domain network. Users can log in to a single server in a domain or across a trust if multiple domains have been setup. If you are in a single domain environment, you may want multiple FPNW-based machines installed for fault tolerance, depending on the purpose of the machine(s). If you are in a multiple domain environment with two domains, for example DomainX and DomainY, you would establish a one-way trust between DomainY (the trusted domain) and DomainX (the trusting domain). Assuming that at least one domain controller in each domain is running FPNW, you would then create the user or users in DomainY. The Novell clients could then log in to the FPNW servers in either domain.

One note of caution here is also in order. According to TID 2947398, FPNW and NDS for NT 2 can't coexist on the same machine. These two products are at opposite ends of the scale. FPNW basically makes an NT server appear as if it were a NetWare server (at least to the Novell clients), whereas NDS for NT (as described below) allows NDS data to be stored on an NT server and replicated with NetWare servers. The two can't coexist at the same time. (It would cause a severe case of schizophrenia anyway!)

To conclude, let's review the positioning of this product, at least in Microsoft's view. FPNW is designed to fill two basic roles.

- The first is to act as an application server (for messaging, database access, and so on) in a NetWare network without requiring additional network clients.

- The second is as a migration tool. In this case, you are migrating away from Net-Ware servers, but don't have time or money to upgrade all of your servers and/or clients at the same time. This allows your existing NetWare clients to view the new NT servers as NetWare servers until, at some point in the future, you have upgraded everything to a pure NT (or at least Microsoft-based) network.

Sage Advice

We have known companies that have implemented this product instead of using Net-Ware servers. While they have a consistent platform and can be managed with standard NT tools, performance is below that of a native NetWare server. You really should only consider this as a transition tool to NT. If this is not your plan, consider using real NetWare servers for the increased performance and decreased hardware requirements that the NetWare server would provide.

DSMN

DSMN (Directory Services Manager for NetWare) is a Microsoft product that allows you to synchronize information between NetWare servers and NT servers. DSMN really only allows you to effectively synchronize bindery-based NetWare servers. It doesn't work very well with NDS-based servers because it only supports bindery emulation mode on NDS servers.

The positioning of this product allows you to centrally manage all of your server's users, whether NT-based or NetWare based. This is a very effective product for NetWare 2.*x* and 3.*x* servers. It works by copying the bindery from your NetWare server(s) to a Windows NT PDC (Primary Domain Controller), creating new users in NT for all of your existing NetWare users. Once that is done, any changes you make on the NT server, such as changing groups and passwords, creating new users, and so on, will be replicated back to the NetWare server(s). DSMN, as implied in the last sentence, will keep the username and password of each user synchronized across *all* servers that DSMN is configured to work with—both NT and NetWare.

There are only a few requirements and issues with using DSMN. The first is that you must have GSNW installed before you install DSMN. You must also be running Windows NT 4 Server as a PDC. One major issue that you must address is the initial password for all imported users. DSMN can *not* read your existing password when you create the new account on the PDC. You have several password options available to help you decide how you want to handle the initial password issue. You can choose for your passwords to all be the same one (which you define); to have no password; to be the same as the username; or you can manually create a file which maps NetWare usernames to the initial password created on the NT server.

You can backup the DSMN configuration, including the users and groups and the servers where these accounts are propagated. If the PDC goes down, you simply promote a BDC (Backup Domain Controller) to take the role of PDC, install DSMN, then restore the saved configuration to the new PDC.

There are, at least in Microsoft's view, a few reasons for using DSMN. The first is that if you are migrating from NetWare to NT, you can use this as a migration tool to help you keep all of your accounts synchronized. The second scenario is to add NT servers to your existing NetWare network, for SQL or Exchange for example, when you want to centrally manage your users. The third is strictly to keep synchronized all of your user accounts across all of your NetWare servers. In this case you are not using the NT server for any real purpose except account synchronization. We suggest you only use this product with NetWare 2.*x* and 3.*x* servers. DSNW

Sage Advice

We have three recommendations relating to DSMN.

First, you should do a trial run when you first run DSMN to see what will be migrated and any errors that may show up when you migrate the accounts. We have seen a few problems with this program before, so be aware of any errors and issues the trial run may produce and be sure to verify the migration after it is complete.

Second, we recommend that you either use the same password for all users (informing each user of the password with a mass e-mail where all users are BCC'd, so that they don't know the password is the same for everyone) or create a password mapping file. The other two options pose greater security risks and so aren't recommended except in possibly low-security situations.

> ### Sage Advice *(continued)*
>
> Finally, you should only use this product in low- to medium-security environments, as NT has far weaker encryption than NetWare does. The encryption mechanism used with passwords is different between the two systems. However, the reason that we recommend that you don't use this product when security is a great concern is that if the password were hacked on the NT side, the same password would also work on all of the NetWare servers as well.

Novell's Offerings

Novell has two main products that are designed to integrate NT into a NetWare network. These two products are the Novell Client and NDS for NT. We will briefly review the Novell Client for Windows NT in this chapter (all of the Novell Clients will be covered in more detail in Chapter 9) to compare it with CSNW. We will also review in greater detail NDS for NT 2.

The Novell Client

The Novell Client has the same purpose as all of the other Novell clients: excellent connectivity with Novell servers. The Novell Client offers the full range of connectivity options that any other Novell-provided network client offers, including the ability to manage NDS using NWADMN or ConsoleOne, to control profiles, and to choose your context, preferred server, and username at login. The Novell Client also fully supports both IPX and IP, unlike CSNW (which you may recall only supports IPX). With this client you can log on with one username to the NetWare network and a different one to the NT one, which is also impossible with CSNW.

All things considered, this is a great client, offering a broad range of options for connecting to your Novell (and NT) servers. This section has been kept very brief, as the client is covered in detail in Chapter 9. The main purpose here is to show how all of the limitations of CSNW are overcome when you use Novell's client software instead.

NDS for NT

NDS for NT is a major product from Novell's perspective. The current version even allows you to place replicas of NDS partitions on your NT servers, just as if they were NetWare 4 or 5 servers. We will focus in this section on the following topics: how NDS for NT works, the hardware and software needed on the NT server and the NetWare 4 or 5 servers, when and how to place partitions on the NT server, NDS for NT integration with Microsoft Exchange, and management of NDS for NT.

How NDS for NT Works

NDS for NT is a very simple product conceptually. As illustrated in Figure 3.1, client applications have no idea that NDS is involved at all; they still believe the NT domain is still in place. The basic process is that a client sends a request to a domain controller, just like normal. The domain controller doesn't even know that it is not a domain controller. NDS for NT replaces SAMSRV.DLL which normally queries the native SAM (Security Accounts Manager) database and replaces it with a new SAMSRV.DLL that queries NDS instead. That's really all that NDS for NT does (besides placing replicas on the NT server—if desired—as described later).

Figure 3.1   The conceptual framework of NDS for NT

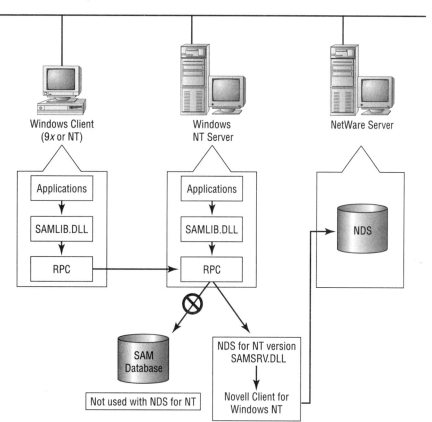

Implementing NetWare 5

PART 1

NOTE For more information on how NDS for NT functions, refer to the online documentation that comes with the product. There is also an excellent article on the subject on the NetWare Connection Web site at the following address: www.nwconnection.com/apr.99/nds49/index.html.

Hardware and Software Requirements on the NT Server and the NetWare Servers

To begin using NDS for NT, several requirements must be met. We will begin by listing the requirements on the NT server and follow that with a discussion of the requirements on the NetWare servers.

NDS for NT requires Windows NT Server 3.51 or 4 installed as a domain controller, among other things. The specific requirements are as follows:

- NT Server 4 with SP 3 or higher or NT Server 3.51 with SP 5 or higher
- 32MB RAM minimum (64 recommended) if you plan to place a replica on the server
- An NTFS Partition
- 90MB free disk space on the NTFS partition
- An additional 150MB free disk space per 1,000 objects in the partition on the NTFS partition
- Administrator rights to the NT server

There are a few other things to consider when you get ready to install NDS for NT. To begin with, you should install it first on the PDC, and then, ideally, on all of the BDCs. Second, you can't rename the domain (or the Domain object) while NDS for NT is installed, so you should carefully choose the name and modify it if needed before you install NDS for NT.

On the NetWare server side, the requirements are quite modest. All that is required is either a NetWare 5 server or a NetWare 4.11 server with SP 6 or later and DS 5.99a or higher. As mentioned in the previous chapter, installing the latest SP is always recommended. As far as rights are concerned, you will need Supervisor rights to the [Root] for the first NDS for NT server installed to extend the schema of the tree, and Supervisor rights to all parts of the NDS tree that will be "Domain Enabled." Domain Enabled simply means that that part of the tree will appear in an NT domain.

Implementing NetWare 5

Placing Partitions on the NT Server

Novell recommends that you place a partition on an NT server if that server will be located across a WAN link from a NetWare server with the partition that contains the Domain object and the users that will be using that NT server. Otherwise, if both the NT server and a NetWare server are on the same LAN, Novell recommends not placing a replica on the NT server. The reason is that NetWare is faster than NT when it comes to accessing and using partition data.

There are a couple of issues that should be considered when placing a partition on an NT server. First, when you place a replica on an NT server it becomes an NDS Server object in the tree and it gets a R/W (Read/Write) replica of that partition. Second, to be able to repair the replica should anything go wrong, you will need at least one replica of the partition on a NetWare server. This is because only NetWare servers can run DSREPAIR. This limitation will be overcome in a new version of NDS for NT slated to be available around the end of 1999.

The ability to place partitions on an NT server is due to a service, called NDS Server (you will see it listed in Control Panel ➤ Services as NDS Server.*DOMAINOBJECTNAME.CONTEXT* and in other places simply as NDS Server), that runs on your NT machines. This service is only installed when a partition is placed on the NT server. The first partition needs to be installed on the server using the Domain Object Wizard (available at installation of NDS for NT or from the Start menu). Once the service is installed and functioning, you can add additional partitions using NDS Manager. To determine which partitions, and therefore which container, user, and group objects are in a single domain, view the Details of the Domain object and select the Replica Advisor page. In viewing this information, remember to place a replica on the NT server if there is no local NetWare server with a replica of the data. Otherwise, use the NetWare server—it's faster.

WARNING   To place a replica on a server, you must have purchased a server license. Information on licensing can be found at the following address: www.novell.com/catalog/pl/pl14315.html.

Integration with Microsoft Exchange

NDS for NT allows you to integrate with Exchange to automatically create and manage Exchange mailboxes. You can use this capability to create a user, add him or her to a domain, and create an Exchange mailbox in one step and in one program, NWAdmin. You can also use NWAdmin to change mailbox information for users, as well as manage Distribution List information. To reiterate, you can only take advantage of this capability when you have NDS for NT installed. This capability is called the Mailbox Manager for Exchange. To install it, you can choose Mailbox Manager from the menu that appears when you insert the CD or run SETUP.EXE from the I386\MM4X directory. Mailbox Manager for Exchange will be described and discussed in the section entitled Exchange Interoperability Issues.

Management of NDS for NT

To manage your NDS for NT servers, you will usually use the familiar tool NWAdmin. If you, or some of your employees, are more comfortable with the NT tools, such as User Manager, then they may be used as well. You will, however, lose access to many of the advanced capabilities and settings that are not available in User Manager. You can create users and then place them in one or more domains at the same time. You can also manage the shares on your NT server and the permissions (NetWare calls them rights) on those shares from NWAdmin.

The ability to create users and have them in one or more domains, as necessary, is a great feature and one that saves time and bandwidth in maintaining trust relationships between your NT domains.

Let's begin with a brief discussion of the Domain Object Wizard (the primary tool to setup NDS for NT), and then we will look at the day-to-day management duties using NDS for NT.

The Domain Object Wizard   Once you have installed NDS for NT, the Domain Object Wizard (SAMMIG.DLL) will run. This Wizard can do the following:

- Extend the NDS schema to support the NT-related objects (this happens only once per tree).
- Move objects (users, groups, and NT computer accounts) from an existing NT domain to NDS.
- Install the first NDS partition on an NT server (as mentioned earlier, the rest are installed with NDS Manager). This installs the NDS Server service.
- Remove the last NDS replica from an NT server. This removes the NDS Server Service.
- Remove NDS for NT, allowing the NT server to act as a native NT server using its native SAM (Security Accounts Manager) database.

One very important note must be mentioned here with regard to passwords. As discussed in the DSMN section, NDS and NT store and manage passwords differently, so to make the two systems completely compatible, once NDS for NT is installed *two* passwords are stored for each user. One password is stored in the NDS format and the other in the NT format. If you want those two passwords to be the same, and to be kept synchronized (and normally you would want them to be the same), then you will want to check the

Force password sync checkbox. Once checked, the user will need to enter a new password when they next log in, and that password will be stored for both NT and NDS use. These two passwords will remain synchronized as long as the user changes his or her password with a Windows-based utility (such as when prompted at login or when the user presses CTRL + ALT + DEL on an NT-based computer and chooses Change Password). They will also remain synchronized if you change them with NWAdmin. They will *not* remain synchronized if the user changes his or her password with a DOS-based utility, such as SetPass.

> **TIP** You may want to rename SETPASS.EXE to another name and create a batch file named SETPASS.BAT with instructions to your users to change their passwords with a Windows-based utility instead.

As part of the initial migration process, you have the ability to match up NT user accounts to existing NDS users in any context. This allows you to eliminate duplicate users at the time of the migration. This is particularly useful if you are migrating multiple NT domains into a single NDS tree. You can also specify (if you are matching NT users to NDS users), what to do with users that don't exist in the NDS tree, such as the built-in NT-user Guest. You can either create a new NDS user or choose not to migrate it at all. You should be aware, however, that any accounts that you don't move at this point will *not* be able to access the domain after NDS for NT is installed (because they won't exist in the NDS tree). We recommend that you migrate everything and then disable those accounts you don't need after the migration. You would be surprised how many times a user that everyone thought was unused *is* used after all, such as by an NT service. Deletion should *only* be done after you are *sure* that the account is not needed. After you have made your selections, a summary screen will be displayed where you can make any modifications before the changes are committed to NDS.

If you place a replica on this server (as previously described), an NDS Server object will be created (also previously described) and you will be given a chance to specify the directory on the NT server in which you want to place the replica. Remember that this directory must be on an NTFS volume.

Day-to-Day Management   Once you have installed NDS for NT, the ongoing task of daily maintenance begins. To manage your new and improved tree, you will need to install the administration utilities, which also come with the NDS for NT CD. Most are already installed by default on the machines that you installed NDS for NT on at the time of installation, but NWAdmin and NDS Manager are not. For remote administration of the server or to install the two management tools just listed, simply choose to install them from the menu that appears when you insert the CD or run ADMSETUP.EXE from the I386 directory. When you do so, the following tools will be installed:

- Domain Object Wizard
- NWAdmin
- NDS Manager
- Novell Login
- Novell Send Messages

These are either the standard Novell utilities, designed for NT, or have already been discussed previously. These utilities can either be installed locally or on a NetWare server.

When you create new users, you follow one of two approaches: domain-centered or user-centered. The domain-centered approach is useful when you want to add many users to a domain at the same time. The user-centered approach is useful when you create a new user and want him or her to belong to one or more domains. Once NDS for NT is properly set up, the latter one is the approach you will probably use most often.

To use the domain-centered method, simply display the details of the Domain object, select the Members tab and add the users that you want to be a part of that domain. You can use the same technique to remove members of the domain by selecting Delete instead of Add. Note that this will remove the member from the Domain object, but not from NDS. If you delete the user (by selecting it in NWAdmin and choosing Delete), the user is removed everywhere, including NDS and any domains, groups, or other objects where it was referenced.

To use the user-centered approach, display the details for the user and select the Domain Access tab. From this tab you can view all of the domains that the user belongs to, as well as what groups (both global and local) in the domain the user is a member of. You can add the user to the domain, and—once added to the domain—to groups in the domain, by selecting Add and then choosing the domain or group object(s) that you want the user added to. You can remove a user from a domain or group by selecting it and choosing Delete. Note that when a user is removed from a domain, the user is automatically removed from all the groups it belonged to in the domain.

NDS for NT also greatly simplifies the process of moving users from one domain to another. Doing so with standard NT 4 domains is a complicated process because you can't move a user between domains with any of the standard Microsoft tools (although third-party tools that can do so exist). Instead, you must document what the user had (in terms of rights, permissions, and so on) in the original domain, delete the user from that domain, and re-create the user in the new domain. You must then add the user to all of the appropriate groups in the new domain, and then reassign the new user all of the rights and permissions that were documented earlier. This is not a trivial task and can take many hours (which is why the third-party tools exist). After the change has been made, the user must know the new domain he or she needs to log in to, as well as the initial password for the new user account. With NDS for NT, you simply change the domains and groups listed on the Domain Access tab. If you move the user in the NDS tree, however, you will need to tell the user the new context, unless you enable contextless logins (described in Chapter 9).

Another great time saving feature of NDS for NT is the NT Tools tab that is added to the Domain object's Details dialog box. Several standard NT tools, namely Server Manager, User Manager for Domains, and the Event Viewer are automatically added, and you can add any other tool that you find useful.

Finally, there is a wizard called the File and Folder Sharing Wizard added to the NT Tools tab that allows you to manage local or remote shares and to assign access permissions to the shares as well as manage NTFS permissions for folders and files. If you select a folder, you can assign NTFS permissions (if it is on an NTFS partition) and you are then asked if you want to share it as well. If you choose to share it, you can specify a share name and what types of users you want to have access to it (Windows, NetWare, and/or Macintosh). One major weakness of this tool is that you only have three combinations of NTFS or share permissions that you can assign (although you can choose to leave the permissions as they are). The combinations are:

- Administrators: Full Control
- Administrators: Full Control and Everyone: Read
- Everyone: Full Control

Sage Advice

While Novell says the File and Folder Sharing Wizard is a great tool and you can manage everything from one place, we disagree. Based on our experience with the tool and the limited permissions you can assign, we recommend that you continue to manage your NTFS and share permissions with the native NT utilities and consider this tool a work in progress.

Conclusion

While NDS for NT is not a perfect product, it does go a long way towards making management of an integrated NetWare and NT network simpler. If this product is something that interests you, check with Novell for more information and pricing. Novell has been offering a 60-day trial of the product as well. Novell plans to offer the ability to use NDS for NT without any NetWare servers on the network around the end of 1999.

TIP   The latest information on NDS for NT can be found on Novell's Web site. In fact, the product has its own home page that collects all of the relevant information in one place. The trial version is available from this site, as are comparisons with Microsoft's offerings. The address is: `www.novell.com/products/nds/nds4nt/index.html`. You may also want to check out the cool solutions site under the NDS heading for more information on the product. The address is: `www.novell.com/coolsolutions/nds`. An excellent source of troubleshooting information can be found in TID 2934901, entitled "NDS4NT Troubleshooting Summary."

Domains vs. AD vs. NDS

In this section we will compare and contrast the two ways that NT can (or will) manage the network with Novell's NDS for NT. The method used in all versions of NT below Windows 2000 is the domain. One of the major advances of Windows 2000 is the invention of Active Directory (AD). This Directory is not X.500 compatible, but it does support LDAP, allowing it to synchronize with NDS. The simplest way to compare and contrast the three methods is with a table. This information was compiled with information from our own experiences, as well as both Microsoft's and Novell's Web sites.

Table 3.1   Domain vs. AD vs. NDS

Feature	NDS	Domain	Active Directory	Purpose/Comments
Trusts Required	No	Yes, manual creation	Yes, automatic creation	Multi-domain environments only.
Trusts Transitive	N/A	No	Yes	A trust is transitive if X trusts Y and Y trusts Z, then X trusts Z.

Table 3.1   Domain vs. AD vs. NDS *(continued)*

Feature	NDS	Domain	Active Directory	Purpose/Comments
Frequency of required reboots for upgrades and new features	Very rarely required	High	Low	Domains in this case means NT 4 and below and Active Directory means Windows 2000 and above.
Hierarchical name space	Yes	No	Yes	
Uses OUs to create hierarchical structure	Yes	N/A	Yes	
Standards name space based on	X.500, LDAP	Proprietary	Proprietary, LDAP	
User can be assigned rights to resources on multiple platforms	Yes	No	No	NDS allows rights assignments on Net-Ware, NT, and Unix servers.
Administra- tive authority can be dele- gated by type of object	Yes	Yes	Yes	In Domains, account operators have access to all users and groups, except those users and groups that have administrative capabilities.

Table 3.1 Domain vs. AD vs. NDS *(continued)*

Feature	NDS	Domain	Active Directory	Purpose/Comments
Administrative authority can be granted for a portion of the tree or domain	Yes	No	Yes	In NT 4, a user can't be granted control over a group of users, for example, only all users or no users as just described.
Administrative authority can be delegated to individual objects	Yes	No	No	
Administrative authority can be delegated to individual properties or attributes of objects	Yes	No	Yes	NDS uses the term properties, whereas AD uses attributes, but they are essentially equivalent.
Rights and permissions assigned to OUs flow to the members of the OU	Yes	N/A	No	AD allows permissions to be assigned to *Security principles* (users, groups, and computers) only. Permissions can't be assigned to OUs, so many groups must be created, often with the same membership as the OU itself.

Table 3.1 Domain vs. AD vs. NDS *(continued)*

Feature	NDS	Domain	Active Directory	Purpose/Comments
Rights can be assigned to OUs for folders and files	Yes	N/A	No	See previous line's notes.
Uses Multi-Master replication model	Yes	No	Yes	In the domain structure, all information flows from the PDC to each BDC individually. Changes can *only* be made at the PDC. When using AD, multimaster replication takes place between all AD-enabled domain controllers (those running Windows 2000 and higher only); uses the domain model for replicating with NT 4 and lower domain controllers.
Multiple replicas can be stored on a single server	Yes	No	No	A domain controller can only be a domain controller for a single domain.

Implementing
NetWare 5

PART 1

Table 3.1   Domain vs. AD vs. NDS *(continued)*

Feature	NDS	Domain	Active Directory	Purpose/Comments
Inheritance model for Access Control Lists (ACLs)	Dynamic	Static	Static	With dynamic inheritance, changes are reflected immediately and the objects (file, user, and so on) below the parent are no larger in size. With static inheritance, when a change is made to an ACL, you are given the opportunity to copy that change to all of the objects below that object. This modifies the ACL of each subordinate object with the change; therefore the object also grows in size.
Central Administration ability	Complete (entire tree)—automatic	Within domain — automatic; between domains— manual	Within domain— automatic; between domains— manual	With either AD or Domains, cross-domain administrative capabilities can be accomplished by using various groups.
Primary GUI Administrative tool(s)	NWAdmin, NDS Manager, ConsoleOne	User Manager, Server Manager, Disk Administrator, Explorer	Microsoft Management Console (MMC), Explorer	

Table 3.1   Domain vs. AD vs. NDS *(continued)*

Feature	NDS	Domain	Active Directory	Purpose/Comments
Where an object can be moved	Anywhere in tree	Anywhere in domain	Anywhere in tree	Any other move requires the object to be deleted and then recreated in the new location. Rights and permissions will need to be reassigned for the new object.
Support for roaming user profiles and system policies	Yes	Yes	Yes	

TIP   For a good overview of AD and NDS, you can visit Microsoft's and Novell's Web sites. The comparison that Novell makes between AD and NDS can be found at www.novell.com/advantage/nds4nt. There is a lot of good information there, as well as links to more information. Microsoft's AD vs. NDS information (which is very pro-Microsoft) can be viewed at www.microsoft.com/windows/server/eval/comparisons/ADandNDScomp.asp.

NT as an Application Server

NT can make an excellent application server, particularly when combined with the manageability that NetWare 5 offers. There aren't any real interoperability issues with NetWare and NT servers for most Microsoft BackOffice applications. The big exception to the rule is Microsoft Exchange (the BackOffice product, not the wimpy program that comes with Windows 95). There are quite a few issues with Exchange, which we will cover in this section.

Exchange Interoperability Issues

When you run Exchange on an NT server (the only platform you can run it on), it requires you to create an NT user for each user who will use Exchange. The user must exist in a domain for Exchange to function. The simplest way to meet these requirements of Exchange and still have a single point of administration for your networks is to use NDS for NT, as described previously. As we mentioned before, if you want to extend the concept of a single administration point to your Exchange servers and the users on them, you will need a component of NDS for NT called the Mailbox Manager for Exchange.

There are several components of the Mailbox Manager for Exchange. The first is the snap-in for NWAdmin, which will allow you to manage Exchange information in NWAdmin. Second is the NDS schema extensions that allow you to add and manage the Exchange objects. The new Exchange-related objects are:

- Site
- Recipient container
- Distribution List (DL)
- Exchange Server

NOTE   Although these objects have the same names in Exchange, they do not have most of the properties and tabs that are accessible with Microsoft's administrative tool for Exchange—Exchange Administrator.

- The third component is the import utility (IMPORT.EXE), which is used to bring the Exchange information into NDS.
- The final component is BACKEND.DLL, which keeps NDS and your Exchange servers synchronized.

To use Mailbox Manager for Exchange, you need to meet the following prerequisites:
- Exchange 5 SP 1 or higher or Exchange 5.5
- NetWare 4.11 SP 4 or higher
- NDS for NT installed on all domains with Exchange servers
- Administrative rights to the NT domain
- Administrative rights to the Exchange directory if you want to use the import utility

The computer that will run Mailbox Manager needs to meet these requirements:

- Exchange Administrator installed.
- Operating System: Windows NT.
- The computer must belong to the same domain that the Exchange server belongs to.

Once you have installed the Mailbox Manager, you can administer your Exchange information from NWAdmin. One of the options presented to you at the end of the installation is to run the Import Utility (IMPORT.EXE; located in SYS:PUBLIC\WIN32 and SYS:PUBLIC\WINNT). This utility will gather the information from Exchange and place it in NDS. It will build the Exchange hierarchy, match mailboxes to the associated NDS users, and import the mailbox attributes from the Exchange server into NDS. Be sure that Exchange Administrator is set up on the computer that you will be using Mailbox Manager on and it is working properly before installing Mailbox Manager.

Sage Advice

After using Mailbox Manager, we personally don't care for the interface. For example, when creating a user, you first have to create the user, then add the user to the domain (so that there is an account for Exchange to associate with). That is normal; we expect that. However, when you add the user to Exchange, you will be told that you need to add the user to the domain first. You need to click OK in the Details dialog box, then go back and redisplay the details to add the user in Exchange. Once you have done that, the information will be grayed out and you will then need to click Cancel to get out of the dialog box, even though the information is saved. We personally don't like the fact that some of the tabs displaying various properties of the mailbox are not accessible in NWAdmin (the Limits, Email Addresses, and Protocols tabs).

The are a few other issues with using the Mailbox Manager for Exchange. The first is that once it is installed, any changes you make with the Exchange Administrator will *not* be replicated back to NDS. Another way of saying this is that all changes to mailbox information must be done from NWAdmin (if you want to display the information in NWAdmin), which will then replicate that information to the Exchange servers. The way around this, if you choose to use the standard Exchange Administrator tool, is to run the Import utility to update NDS whenever you want NDS updated. Second, the current version of Mailbox Manager (1.01) doesn't support custom recipients, including in DLs. This means that DLs that contain them, when imported with the import utility, will be empty; not even the normal recipients will be in the DL.

Because of these issues, we can't recommend this solution at this time. If you want to be able to view Exchange information in NDS, do all of your administration in the standard Microsoft tool, Exchange Administrator, and then run the import utility as needed to update NDS. Hopefully Novell will increase the value of this tool to provide real integration between the two products.

4

Migrating to NetWare 5

Whether you have an existing NetWare network or you are migrating from a mainframe-based system to a distributed network, you need to be aware of hardware, system, and software requirements to migrate or upgrade to NetWare 5. Based on these requirements, you will have to choose between doing a same-server upgrade or a server-to-server migration. Finally, you will need to determine the appropriate utility to perform the upgrade.

Novell has made considerable efforts to make the upgrade to NetWare 5 as painless as possible. You will see that there have been considerable improvements from previous versions of upgrade and install utilities. But, as always, there is the real world of "gotchas" and "not compatibles" to contend with.

There is no way that you could ever anticipate all the problems you might encounter during a migration or upgrade. All you can do is have many resources and backups to help you overcome any potential disasters. Planning is essential to avoid running into problems, but you need to be prepared and informed as much as possible.

This chapter will try to help you through some known issues, but our main objective is to show you all the resources that we used and found useful so that you can benefit from them as well.

Sage Advice: Tip for a Successful Migration

The most important tip for a successful migration to NetWare 5 is to make a backup first. To be completely safe, make two backups, and restore a few files to test the backup. This may sound paranoid, but there are many steps involved in the upgrade process, and many things can go wrong. Ninety-five percent of the time, everything works fine—but it isn't easy to explain to the CEO of the company that you're in "the other five percent." Play it safe.

Hardware Tips

You can upgrade some existing NetWare 3.*x* and 4.*x* servers to NetWare 5 without purchasing additional hardware. However, NetWare 5 is a more sophisticated operating system and requires more resources to run efficiently. You may need to upgrade the processor, install additional RAM, or add more disk storage space (in other words, a new system) in order to achieve optimum performance.

Existing Hardware

Table 4.1 summarizes the hardware requirements for NetWare 3.*x*, 4.*x*, and NetWare 5. Minimum requirements are given, along with suggested hardware for optimal performance in a simple network. Use the information in the following sections to determine if your server supports, or is capable of being upgraded to, the minimum system requirements.

Table 4.1   Hardware Requirements for NetWare 3.*x*, 4.*x*, and NetWare 5

Operating System	RAM (Minimum/ Optimal)	Disk Storage (Minimum/ Optimal)	Processor (Minimum/ Optimal)
NetWare 3.*x*	4MB/8MB	50MB/ 500MB	386/486
NetWare 4.*x*	20MB/32MB	90MB/ 500MB–1GB	386/486, Pentium, or Pentium Pro
NetWare 5	64MB/ 128MB	230MB/ 5GB	Pentium 200MHz/Pentium Pro 200MHz or higher

> **TIP** If you do have to buy a new server, don't write off the old server completely. If it's not too old, it will probably make a fine workstation. Be sure the upgrade is a success before you reformat that hard drive, though.

Memory

NetWare 5 definitely requires more memory than any previous version. Your NetWare 3.*x* server may have run just fine with 8MB, but you'll need at least 64MB for an efficient NetWare 5 server. If you are planning to use Java applications, including running ConsoleOne on the server, you will need a minimum of 128MB.

Be sure that you also have plenty of room for additional memory. If you add a disk drive, additional software, or additional users to the network, you'll need more memory.

Disk Storage

Disk storage requirements have changed considerably between previous versions of NetWare and NetWare 5. You'll need a minimum of 50MB for the DOS partition, but Novell recommends you use 1GB. The SYS: volume requires a minimum of 200MB, but Novell also recommends that you use 4GBs. The large difference between the partition minimum and recommended sizes is due to future expansion of NetWare's capabilities and services. Altogether, you'll need 5GBs of disk storage so that you can handle future growth on the operating system and additional space for applications and data.

If your existing server doesn't meet the DOS and SYS: partition requirements, but does meet all the other hardware requirements, resize the partitions on your drive. There are many partition-resizing tools on the market that support DOS and NetWare partitions. Server Magic and Partition Magic are excellent tools.

> **NOTE** You can obtain additional information on Server Magic and Partition Magic by visiting their site at www.powerquest.com.

CPU

You will need the power of a good processor to run NetWare 5. NetWare 5 puts a higher load on the processor (CPU) than previous versions. A 486 might suffice for NetWare 3.*x* networks of up to 30 or 40 users, but for NetWare 5 you will want a Pentium 200MHz or higher for that number of users. Since they're fairly low-priced, you might even consider starting with a Pentium III with a speed of 450 MHz or higher. The older motherboards do not support the newer Pentium II and IIIs, so you might have to upgrade your motherboard also.

Implementing NetWare 5

PART 1

You should think seriously about purchasing an entirely new machine. There are very few machines that can be upgraded to a higher processor without great expense and inconvenience. In addition, a new machine comes with parts that were intended to work together, and are new and unlikely to fail—or if they do fail, at least they'll be under warranty.

As a final benefit, a new machine will allow you to perform a server-to-server upgrade or across-the-wire migration to upgrade the server. A *server-to-server* upgrade transmits data across the network to create a copy of the old server's setup on the new server. This method doesn't make any changes to your existing server, and if something goes wrong, you can quickly bring the old server back online.

New Hardware

In all upgrade and migration scenarios you have to tackle the problem of selecting the right hardware combination. This is not a simple task due to the different systems needing support. Here is our recommended hardware combination:

- A high-speed bus motherboard—EISA or the more recent PCI. VESA local bus is another alternative, but is not well supported by network card manufacturers.

- Network cards that support the bus you've chosen and support NetWare 5 specifically.

- A PS2 mouse and VGA color monitor (so that you can enjoy the new graphic features of NetWare 5).

- Disk controllers that support the high-speed bus and fast disk drives. RAID 5 subsystems are the way to go in our book. You should always consider your drive system your most precious resource. NetWare 5 does not support the older .DSK format.

- Hot swappable components. NetWare supports this architecture.

- A CD-ROM drive. Unless you have another server with a CD-ROM drive on the same network, you'll need this for installing the server and for occasional maintenance.

- A brand name server built for the capacity you estimate the server needs to support.

Sage Advice: Novell Partners

When it comes to picking new hardware, be sure to check out the Novell partners. In conjunction with Novell, they develop the best hardware platforms for the scenario they are designed for. Compaq, Dell, and HP, are but a few of these partners, and they offer a wide variety of server platforms that include hot swappable components and redundant storage units. These partners assemble servers with performance and reliability in mind.

> **Sage Advice: Novell Partners** *(continued)*
>
> The Novell Tested and Approved symbol is an indication that the component was tested in Novell labs and meets Novell's standards.
>
> The Novell Web site has a current list of its OEM partners. Check it out.

Pre-Migration Issues

Upgrading your network to NetWare 5 is definitely not something that you should do spontaneously. In order to upgrade successfully, you must plan the process carefully. This includes choosing the best method for your upgrade and preparing hardware, software, and users for the transition.

There are multitudes of scenarios that exist, one of which might fit your migration, but every network is different and requires special attention.

This is the stage of your NetWare migration where you want to ask yourself the following questions:

Have you identified which existing severs will run NetWare 5?   You need to know exactly how many servers you will use in the migration. You will also need to determine their configuration and the best migration strategy applicable to them.

Have you selected the system requirements you will incorporate into the new NetWare 5 servers?   Setting a standard configuration for new servers will start you on the path of going home on the weekends. No more endless hours of work trying to figure out what you have in order to troubleshoot the problem.

Do you have your network documented and the topology drawn out?   Do not expect a smooth migration without this documentation. You will find yourself in a sea of surprises if you haven't done a proper inventory of hardware and applications.

Is your network stable or do you have outstanding problems to resolve?
Please note that if your current network is not stable your migration will fail. We have found that previous versions of NetWare are a lot more tolerant of an unstable network than NetWare 5 is. Test your cabling thoroughly; make sure you can certify that all links are CAT 5. Redesign your network to support layer 2 and layer 3 switching at the core, with high-speed routers linking to the WAN.

Have you designed your network for the applications you are planning to use?   Upgrading to a new operating system is not going to fix old problems, and you can certainly create new ones if your applications aren't compatible with your new environment.

Do you have a test lab for applications?   Set up a test lab to simulate a typical office. This way you can test applications on your new network before it goes into production. A test lab should consist of a standard workstation and servers connected with the topology you are going to use.

Can your servers and networks handle the load?   Use load testers for applications in your test lab; there are many available and they are relatively cheap. You can test if your servers can really handle the anticipated load on the servers and on the network.

The following sections deal with more specific topics addressing steps you should take before doing the actual migration.

Make Sure Your Tree Is Healthy

When you are migrating an existing NetWare 4.x network, you must follow some basic recommendations issued by Novell regarding the tree:

- Check for incomplete replication processes. The replica ring of a partition must be synchronized for all the partitions. The tree must be stable.

- Make sure there are no unknown objects in the tree, which could indicate an incomplete replica synchronization. Also look for unreachable replicas and objects not visible to the tree.

- Make sure all servers have synchronized their time.

- Make sure that all servers use the same and latest DS.NLM and dependent NLM versions.

- Keep the number of replicas of a partition between three and four. Locate the Master replicas at the main IS offices and leave a Read/Write replica at their respective office.

- Backup NDS and all server apps/data files.

- Migrate by partition, starting with the Master replica servers.

- Ensure that transitive replica synchronization in a mixed IPX and IP network environment is possible. You will need to make sure that at least one NetWare 5 server is configured with both protocols. This will make it possible to install the Migration Agent on that server and allow transitive replica synchronization between servers using IP and IPX.

- Use DSTRACE to monitor the tree for its health, and DSREPAIR.NLM to check Directory status.

- Use NDS Manager and DSREPAIR.NLM to repair tree errors and database corruption.

- To perform replica synchronization with DSREPAIR.NLM a server must have a replica for this operation to display replica synchronization status. In DSREPAIR go to the Available Options menu and select Report Synchronization Status.

- To check external references in DSREPAIR go to the Available Options ➤ Advanced Options Menu ➤ Check External References. This option will display external references and obituaries (deleted objects). It will also show you the status of all servers in the back link list for the obituaries. A healthy tree will have no outstanding obituaries waiting to disappear.

- Check the replica state. In DSREPAIR go to the Available Options menu and select Advanced Options Menu ➤ Replica and Partition Operations. Verify that the replica state is On.

- Check remote server IDs in DSREPAIR from the Available Options ➤ Advanced Options Menu ➤ View Remote Server ID List ➤ Remote Server ID Options ➤ Verify All Remote Server IDs. This option executes authentication from server to server using the remote server's ID. This option verifies this server's ID on the other servers. This is a good way to find out if replica servers are up and running.

- Check replica ring. Run DSREPAIR on the server holding the Master replica of each partition and also on one of the servers holding a Read/Write replica to check for replica ring mismatches. From the Available Options ➤ Advanced Options Menu ➤ Replica and Partition Operations ➤ View Replica Ring, verify that the servers holding replicas of that partition are correct.

- Check NDS schema health. Go to the server console and create a server batch file containing the following:

    SET DSTRACE=ON   Activates the trace screen for Directory Services transactions

    SET TTF=ON   Dumps related screen information into the DSTRACE.DBG file for later viewing

    SET DSTRACE=*R   Resets DSTRACE.DBG file

    SET DSTRACE=+SCHEMA   Displays schema information

    SET DSTRACE=*SS   Initiates schema synchronization

- To view the DSTRACE.DBG file run the following:

    SET TTF=OFF   Stops DSTRACE from dumping information to the file. View the file with a text editor, and check for the message "SCHEMA: All Processed = YES." This will indicate a healthy schema.

- Make necessary repairs to the local database. Use DSREPAIR to perform this function. Repairing the local DS database will lock the Directory Services database. Authentication cannot occur to this server with Directory Services locked; in other words, users will not be able to log in to this server during this operation. For this reason, this operation should be performed after business hours.

- DSTRACE, if left operating, in some cases will increase utilization. After completion of all DSTRACE checks, enter the following DSTRACE commands:

  Set DSTRACE=nodebug

  Set DSTRACE=+min

  Set DSTRACE=off

This will minimize filters and turn DSTRACE off.

NetWare 5@Work: Directory Services Health Check

To maintain a healthy NDS, Company A performs the following operations:

- The DS.NLM is the same version on every NetWare 4.1x file server in the tree.

- Time synchronization is continuously checked.

- To monitor server-to-server synchronization with DSTRACE, a server batch file is run with the following commands:

SET DSTRACE=ON Activates the trace screen for Directory Services transactions.

SET DSTRACE=*H Initiates synchronization between file servers.

SET TTF=ON Sends screen data to a file: SYS: SYSTEM\DSTRACE.DBG.

SET DSTRACE=*R Starts the file at 0 bytes. This batch file dumps screen data into DSTRACE.DBG, which can be viewed from a text editor.

Then, when they are ready to view the file, they run SET TTF=OFF (once NDS has completed synchronizing all partitions) to turn off sending data to the file. They can then map a drive to their server's SYS: SYSTEM directory and bring the DSTRACE.DBG file up in a text editor. The file is reviewed for -6__s (this will show any NDS errors during synchronization, such as -625), or YES (this will show successful synchronization for a partition).

NetWare 5@Work: Directory Services Health Check *(continued)*

When we were consulting at Company A, it was very convenient to use this batch file when we suspected NDS problems. This batch file produced a log file with the pertinent information we needed on obituaries, back links, and synchronization errors. We used this information to ascertain which server was not synchronizing with the replica ring.

Preparing for the Migration

Before performing an upgrade, you must prepare for it. Aside from choosing which method to apply, there are other considerations. If you are upgrading from an existing server, you will need to do the following:

- Upgrade DS.NLM on all the 4.*x* servers when installing into an existing tree.

- Install the latest service pack for your current version of NetWare. When installing NetWare 5 into an existing tree, the 4.11 servers need to be upgraded to ROLLCALL.NLM version 4.10 or later. (This version is available in NetWare's Support Pack 5 or later.)

- Novell Licensing Services is required to run NetWare 5 servers. If you are installing into an existing tree with NetWare 4.11 servers, you need to setup NLS on the 4.11 servers prior to installing NetWare 5 (NetWare 5 installs NLS by default at installation). To do this you will need to run SETUPNLS.NLM on the NetWare 4.11 server to install NLS, and extend the schema. NLS also requires that at least one server in each partition have a Read/Write replica with NLS installed.

- Schedule a time for the upgrade. Estimate how many hours of downtime you'll need, then double that number. Be sure that all users are informed of the upgrade time and that they are logged out when you begin.

- Schedule your upgrade at a time of day when you can reach Novell technical support, your Novell reseller, or a qualified consultant (unless you're *really* confident).

- Make a backup. Then hide it and make another one. Nobody has ever regretted making too many backups.

- Delete all unnecessary files from the server.

- If you are upgrading from NetWare 3.1*x*, run the BINDFIX utility twice on the NetWare 3.1*x* server. The first run will repair any problems with the bindery; the second will ensure that you have a backup copy of the bindery files.

- If you are upgrading from a 2.*x* or earlier version of NetWare, you will first need to upgrade the server to a 3.12 version, then prepare for the migration.

- Copy the CD-ROM drivers to the DOS partitions prior to installing NetWare.

- If you need to expand your existing DOS partition, there are some utilities that can help you modify it. You can use Server Magic from Power Quest, or Partition Magic.

NOTE   You will need to check for the latest version of DS.NLM online at support .novell.com.

Reality Check: Notes from the Front

You are going to find yourself up against a roadblock if you are migrating an existing 4.11 network. Planning is crucial here. You want to determine what your current system configuration is, and what capacity your network has. It doesn't take much to saturate a 10BaseT network. And the server requirements for NetWare 5 are so great that you will more than likely have to replace all your systems.

Company A is going through just that. It planned for an eventual upgrade from 4.11 to NetWare 5, but underestimated the system requirements. All their plans have had to be re-evaluated.

The company is pushing back the migration to a single protocol suite (TCP/IP), until they can stabilize the current infrastructure.

Upgrading to an existing tree is the most complicated scenario. You will need to make sure all existing servers are upgraded to the latest NetWare support pack for the operating system you are running. Document the hardware settings on your system and plan for any customization ahead of time. Finally, perform at least two backups of any server being upgraded.

> ***TIP*** When upgrading an existing tree to NetWare 5, always start with the servers that hold the Master replica of the [Root] partition! We must emphasize though that Novell does not recommend this; this advice is based on our personal experience.

Internal Hardware Considerations

You will need to evaluate the internal hardware in the existing server you are planning to use for the upgrade. You might have met the basic system parameters on your server, but not for your SCSI drives, or any other component for that matter.

Compatibility problems in the world of IT are half science and half guessing; the results can slow or even stop a migration project.

NetWare 5@Work: Pre-Migration Considerations

Anything you can do to minimize the impact a migration will have on your network will save you time and money in the long run. The following are some suggestions that can help you avoid some problems during the migration:

- Inventory all components on your existing NetWare servers. Sort them by manufacturer, category, and age if possible.

- Check with the manufacturer for any compatibility problems with NetWare 5. Don't forget to check for any Y2K problems.

- Get the latest drivers on devices like NIC, video, and CD-ROMs.

- Set up a test bed with a comparable server.

- Look for the latest TIDs on installing and migrating to NetWare 5 for the latest information on the subject. Lots of great tips and solutions to problems are posted there.

- We always check with the Novell Web site for approved hardware components and software compatibility issues.

Choosing a Protocol

In a move to support standard protocols, be a more open network operating system, and be easily integrated with Intranet and Internet resources, NetWare 5 defaults to a pure IP installation. Current NetWare installations are on an IPX-based network; you will have to select IPX on your new server for compatibility with your old system. Whether your plans are to migrate to an IP network or just to access resources in an Intranet or Internet environment, you have the option to select various protocol combinations. By selecting both IP and IPX during the upgrade, you'll make it easier for your network to work with both protocols. We will cover this topic in greater detail in Chapter 5.

> **NOTE** For more information on IP/IPX compatibility and migration, consult the IPXTOIP.HTM file on your NetWare 5 CD.

Migration Methods

The first consideration when migrating is deciding which method of migration you will use. First you need to determine whether you are going to use the existing server or migrate to a new server platform. You may also want to initially use a lab to determine the best course of action.

You can migrate using one of the following tools:

Install Wizard   Use this tool to quickly upgrade NetWare 3.1*x* or 4.*x* servers to NetWare 5 using current hardware. This is also known as an *in-place upgrade*.

Upgrade Wizard   Use this tool to move data and users from a NetWare 3.*x* or 4.*x* server to a new server running NetWare 5. This method is also called a *server-to-server* upgrade or an *across-the-wire* migration.

DSMAINT.NLM   Use this tool if you are moving your NetWare 4.*x* server to new hardware before upgrading to NetWare 5. There are some specific scenarios you want to watch out for which we will discuss later in the chapter. Primarily, this tool is used when you want to upgrade the hardware of the original server, before upgrading to NetWare 5.

In practice, you'll usually use the Install Wizard program for upgrades on the same server; the Upgrade Wizard if you are upgrading an existing 3.*x* or 4.*x* server to a new NetWare 5 server; and DSMAINT.NLM if you are keeping the existing server but you want to upgrade the hardware.

> **NOTE** The Install Wizard is used for new installs as well as upgrades. There is no "custom" or "simple" install option in NetWare 5. The customization is done at the end of the installation process, when you will be able to set a custom server ID, select sub-components, and so on.

Migrating from NetWare 2.*x* and 3.*x*

Now you're ready to begin the actual upgrade process. Before you start, carefully read all of the following instructions, as well as those given in the NetWare manuals. Make sure you have a good backup of all the data and bindery information on the server, and that you have chosen the best upgrade method for your particular needs.

If you are planning to migrate from NetWare 2.*x* to 5 you are more likely to migrate to a new server. In the case of NetWare 2.*x* you will have to upgrade the old server to NetWare 3.*x*, then migrate to NetWare 5.

Upgrading with the Install Wizard

Using the Install Wizard is the easiest method of upgrading. All you have to do is run the install program from the NetWare 5 installation CD-ROM. This method works only for systems that already have NetWare 3.*x* and 4.*x*. All of the previous version's files and settings—users, trustee rights, and all other information—are converted to NetWare 5 format.

Because no data is copied over the network, this is the fastest method of upgrading. In fact, if all goes smoothly, you could be done within a couple of hours. However, there are some disadvantages to consider:

- Once you've started the upgrade, there's no turning back. If something goes wrong, you'll need to either resolve the problem or reinstall the old NetWare version and restore a backup. If you are upgrading from a version of NetWare 3.*x* supplied on floppy disks, you might be busy for quite a while.

- The server must be brought completely down before you can begin the upgrade, causing user downtime.

- This method won't work if you're replacing the NetWare 3.1*x* server with a new machine, or if you need to change the partition sizes on the hard disk. Be sure your existing machine can handle NetWare 5 before you begin.

Most importantly, keep a backup of the old server, and be sure you know where the disks or CD-ROM for the old NetWare version are in case you have to revert to the old system.

After the upgrade, test the server. Be sure all of the old applications work. You will also want to install the new client software on all workstations to take advantage of NDS.

Upgrading with the Upgrade Wizard

If you're replacing your old NetWare 3.*x* server with a new NetWare 5 server, using the Upgrade Wizard is the only way to go. With the Upgrade Wizard method, you install a new NetWare 5 server on a new machine, then add it to the network. While running the Upgrade Wizard from a workstation, you copy all data, users, and trustee assignments from the old server to the new server. Once you're sure the new server is operational, you can bring the old server down and start using the new one.

The Upgrade Wizard method is much safer than the Install Wizard method. Here are some additional advantages:

- Since you're keeping the old server intact, you can put it back online at a moment's notice.
- There are always two copies of the data, so there is less risk of data loss (but make a backup anyway).
- You can actually migrate data from multiple volumes on the old server to a single volume on the new NetWare 5 server. In addition, you can migrate multiple NetWare 3.*x* servers to the same NetWare 5 server. This allows you to easily reconfigure the network for efficiency if the new server can handle the load.

The Upgrade Wizard has one principal disadvantage: It's *slow*. The process can take anywhere from half an hour to four or five hours. The actual time will depend on the speed of the servers (both the new one *and* the old one) and the speed of communication over the network. Be prepared to spend the better part of a day completing this process—or a night, if the company doesn't want users to spend a day without network access. You'll also need to keep users off the old server during the Upgrade Wizard process.

Once you have upgraded and migrated the NetWare 3.*x* server to NetWare 5, you need to modify any configuration files that were in place in the old server to comply with NetWare 5 settings and commands.

NOTE Refer to the online documentation for the Upgrade Wizard for more post-upgrade issues.

Migrating from NetWare 4.*x*

NetWare 4.*x* versions can be migrated to NetWare 5 using the following three tools:

- Install Wizard
- Upgrade Wizard 3
- DSMAINT

NOTE   Upgrade Wizard 3 will allow you to upgrade your NetWare 3.*x* and 4.*x*
servers to NetWare 4.11 or 5.*x*. Previous versions of Upgrade Wizard will only
upgrade 3.*x* to 4.11 or higher, and cannot be used to upgrade to 4.10. Any version
of Upgrade Wizard can be used to upgrade NetWare 3.12 to NetWare 5 without
upgrading to NetWare 4.11 first, but it is recommended that you use Upgrade
Wizard version 3.

Upgrading with the Install Wizard

Using the Install Wizard is the easiest method of upgrading. All you have to do is run the
install program from the NetWare 5 installation CD-ROM. This method works only for
systems that already have NetWare 3.*x* and 4.*x*. All of the previous version's files and settings—users, trustee rights, and all other information—are converted to NetWare 5
format.

Since no data is copied over the network, this is the fastest method of upgrading. In fact,
if all goes smoothly, you could be done within a couple of hours. However, there are some
disadvantages to consider:

- Once you've started the upgrade, there's no turning back. If something goes
  wrong, you'll need to either resolve the problem or reinstall the old NetWare version and restore a backup.

- The server must be brought completely down before you can begin the upgrade,
  causing user downtime.

- This method won't work if you're replacing the NetWare 3.1*x* server with a new
  machine, or if you need to change the partition sizes on the hard disk.

Here are a few rules you should follow before using this method:

- Be sure your existing machine can handle NetWare 5 before you begin.

- Load the latest patches before running the Install Wizard.

- Make sure that you have the latest drivers for your server components handy.

- Before upgrading your servers, move all Master replicas for your partitions to specific servers, and start the upgrades with those servers.

- Start the upgrade with the server that contains the Master replica of the [Root]
  partition. Work your way down the tree, upgrading parent replicas before child
  replicas.

- Make sure that you select IPX and IP during the upgrade, especially if you are
  planning to migrate to IP in the near future.

Most importantly, keep a backup of the old server, and be sure you know where the disks or CD-ROM for the old NetWare version are, in case you have to revert to the old system.

After the upgrade, test the server. Be sure all of the old applications work. You will also want to install the new client software on all workstations to take advantage of NDS.

Upgrading with the Upgrade Wizard

If you're replacing your old NetWare 4.*x* server with a new NetWare 5 server, using the Upgrade Wizard is the way to go. With the Upgrade Wizard method, you install a new NetWare 5 server on a new machine, then add it to the network. While running the Upgrade Wizard from a workstation, you copy all data, users, and trustee assignments from the old server to the new server. Once you're sure the new server is operational, you can bring the old server down and start using the new one.

The Upgrade Wizard method is much safer than the Install Wizard method. Here are some additional advantages:

- Since you're keeping the old server intact, you can put it back online at a moment's notice.
- There are always two copies of the data, so there is less risk of data loss (but make a backup anyway).
- You can actually migrate data from multiple volumes on the old server to a single volume on the new NetWare 5 server.
- In addition, you can migrate multiple NetWare 3.*x* servers to the same NetWare 5 server. This allows you to easily reconfigure the network for efficiency if the new server can handle the load.

The following are some rules you should follow before using this method:

- Since you are probably migrating an existing tree, all existing servers need to have the latest patches and DS.NLM version installed.
- The tree should be stable before starting the process. See the sidebar "NetWare 5@Work: Directory Services Health Checks."
- Migrate the servers that hold the Master replicas first. Start with the parent partitions, and work your way down.
- Have replacement login scripts ready to update existing scripts.
- A quick way to copy and paste the login scripts is using the CTRL + INSERT keys to copy, and SHIFT + INSERT to paste.
- Once you have upgraded and migrated the NetWare 3.*x* server to NetWare 5, you need to modify any configuration files that were in place in the old server to comply with NetWare 5 settings and commands.

___

NOTE Refer to the online documentation for the Upgrade Wizard for more post-upgrade issues.

Using DSMAINT

There are two ways in which a NetWare 4.*x* server can be migrated to a NetWare 5 server using DSMAINT. You can upgrade to:

The same server   In this scenario the server will be upgraded (not migrated) from an older version of 4.*x* to NetWare 5. Hardware will not be changed, just the OS on the existing server.

A different server   In this scenario you want to upgrade the hardware in a existing NetWare 4.*x* server before you upgrade it to NetWare 5. All of the data and Directory Services database information needs to be migrated to the new machine.

___

WARNING You cannot go back to the original configuration once you have used DSMAINT. You cannot use DSMAINT in a test environment.

This procedure uses an NLM called DSMAINT or the DSMAINT functionality that is built into INSTALL.NLM. DSMAINT allows for a complete backup of Directory Services into a single file. It keeps DS IDs intact (therefore, no printing or trustee relinking problems), and it keeps all partitions from the server complete and intact.

You will run DSMAINT on the source server, and make a backup to a floppy drive. Then you will run DSMAINT on the target server and place the tree backup file you created earlier on the new server. This lays the exact same DS database down on the new server, and it picks up communication with the other server(s) as if nothing happened (except that it was down for 20 minutes or so). After DS is restored on the new server, a restore operation will place the file system and trustees on the NetWare volumes, thus completing the upgrade.

If you would rather have the existing server left untouched, then you could:

1. Install the exact same version of NetWare on the new box that the old box has.
2. Run DSMAINT on the old server and the new server and follow this with an in-place upgrade on the new server.

For example, if you want to move NetWare 4.10 to NetWare 5 using new hardware, you would keep the existing 4.10 server and install NetWare 4.10 on the new hardware. Use DSMAINT to bring the DS information across the network to the new hardware and then do an in-place upgrade to NetWare 5 on the new hardware.

Notes from the Field: Using a Test Lab

We would say that many of the tools and techniques recommended by Novell have only been tested in a lab environment, which means they haven't seen the real world yet. An example is the almost immediate release of Support Pack 2. We recommend that you set up a test lab with a typical desktop and server system. This will allow you to test any solutions in a controlled environment before releasing it to your network.

A sample lab environment should include the following:

- Two servers: one setup for file and print services, the other setup for applications and a database.

- Two workstations set up with the typical office application suite. You want one with monitoring applications.

- Two networks separated by routers with a serial (null modem) connection between them to simulate a WAN topology.

With this setup you should be able to test systems before going to production.

The reason you need to run DSMAINT and then do an in-place upgrade is because you can't run a DSMAINT from a NetWare 4 to NetWare 5 server. This is due to the great differences in the NDS schemas between the two servers. If a DSMAINT procedure were to be done directly from NetWare 4.10 to NetWare 5, the licensing information and schema extensions would be lost on the new server.

Another problem is that the names and number of the files containing the DS database will change between 4.*x* and 5.*x* servers; this creates restoration problems. Essentially, DSMAINT would have to be removed from the NetWare 5 server and then re-installed to restore the correct database format if DSMAINT were used directly to perform a migration.

Licensing Servers

NetWare implements licensing in a very different way with NetWare 5. You keep track of licensed products through Novell Licensing Service (NLS), and store this information in NDS. This makes it a lot easier to manage and provides you with a central point of administration.

Novell Licensing Service Components

To understand how the Licensing Services work, you need to know the three basic components that make up NLS. They are:

NLS Clients   The NLS client is an NLS-enabled, or a ZENworks-configured, software package that will request a license before it executes. If the software does not get an available license it will not run. This ensures that the user can not use software beyond its licensing limitations, protecting the company from any liabilities.

License Service Provider   A License Service Provider is a NetWare server running the NLSLSP.NLM, and its function is to respond to NLS client requests. When an NLS client requests an available license, the LSP scans the NDS tree for a License container object that represents the software for an available license (the License container object is discussed in the next section). This process of scanning the tree for License container objects is done until a license is found or the LSP has contacted all License container objects. You need at least one LSP per tree.

Licensing Objects   There are two Licensing objects that are configured for NLS. These are the License container object and the License Certificate objects. The following sections discuss the two objects.

License Container Objects

License container objects are special purpose container objects. Like any other container object, they hold leaf objects. Unlike most other containers they can only contain License Certificate objects. Each product gets its own container, but there may be multiple certificates in any container.

By default, NetWare creates two of these containers to keep track of licenses for the operating system itself, which describe the type of license and license connections. They are Novell+NetWare 5 Conn SCL+500 and Novell+NetWare 5 Server+500. The name of the container is derived by taking the following three components and concatenating them with plus (+) signs:

- Publisher
- Product
- Version

Hence, you can see that the information for the two default objects is as follows:

- Publisher: Novell
- Product: NetWare 5 Conn SCL (user connection licenses) and NetWare 5 Server (licenses for the operating system itself)

- Version: 5.00 (it is simpler to leave off the period, as NDS attaches special meaning to the period. If you choose to use it in objects you create, it will appear like this: 5\.00.)

License Certificate Objects

The reason that License container objects exist is to hold License Certificate objects. By default, a server-based connection certificate is installed in the Novell+NetWare 5 Server+500 container. The certificate typically supports one server. User licenses are stored in the Novell+NetWare 5 Conn SCL+500 container. There is one License Certificate installed, but if you display the details for the certificate, you can see how many user licenses that certificate supports.

You can't modify the properties of License Certificates that relate to the license itself. You can, however, create what Novell calls a Metered Certificate for any product that doesn't support NLS, and for those products you can specify all of the details. Information on Metered Certificates, the objects involved, and where to place them in the tree can be found in the online documentation.

There are several concepts you need to know to manage License Certificate objects, namely assigning ownership of the object and assigning users who can use the license.

Assigning Ownership

The owner of the license has several special abilities which will be covered shortly. First, however, we need to discuss who the owner is by default, and how one gets to be the owner. The owner of a license certificate is, by default, the user who created the certificate. Usually the person who creates them is, therefore, Admin or another administrator.

The owner of a certificate is the only person who can assign another owner. The owner is also the user who assigns other users who may use the certificate. The information on ownership can be found on the Owner tab in the details of the certificate.

Assigning Users

By default, no objects are assigned to the certificate. This means that anyone can use the certificate. Once you assign an object or objects here, however, only those objects can use the certificate. Although the name implies assigning specific users to the certificate, we (and Novell) don't recommend doing so. Instead, you will want to assign groups or containers and allow all of those users in the group or container to use the certificate.

This allows you to control who can use what license. This might be useful if, for example, different departments purchased their own licenses to keep one department from poaching licenses from another. Assigning users is done on the Assignments tab of the certificate.

Licensing Services Administration Tools

There are two tools you can use for the administration of licenses; one is a stand-alone tool called NLSMAN32.EXE and the other is a snap-in (NLSADMN32) for NetWare Administrator that incorporates the functionality of NLSMAN32.EXE. These tools for Windows 95/98 and Windows NT-based computers allow you to view the licenses that are installed anywhere in the tree.

You can view what was installed, usage over time, and so on. This is a great analysis tool. To use the stand-alone tool, run SYS:PUBLIC\WIN32\NLSMAN32.EXE, and to use it from NetWare Administrator select from the menu bar Tools ≻ NLS. You can do everything from both tools except generate reports.

You should be aware of how much impact the NLS service has on your NetWare 5 servers and network in general. The following is information that can be helpful to you as you migrate to NetWare 5:

- NetWare 5 will allow two grace login connections without any license installed. If there is no license installed, error messages will be displayed at the server console.

- Each License Envelope contains a server license and a user license.

- NetWare 5 has two built-in debug tools which may help troubleshoot licensing issues. During the installation a file called SYS: \SYSTEM\NLSI.DBG will be created to trace NetWare 5 licensing. You will also want to use the SET parameter **SET NLSTRACE=2** to create a file called SYS: \SYSTEM \NLSTRACE.DBG.

- Following is a list of options you can use with the SET parameter NLSTRACE:

    NLSTRACE = 0 Write file

    NLSTRACE = 1 Output to screen

    NLSTRACE = 2 Create file

- There are two SET parameters which deal with licensing:

    SET Dirty Certificate Cache Delay Time = 1 minute

    Limits: 1 minute to 1 hour.

    This SET parameter can be set in the STARTUP.NCF file description: Minimum time the licensing services wait before writing a dirty certificate cache to DS.

    Set NLS Search Type = 0

    Limits: 0 to 1

    Description: 0 = Stop upward search for license certificate at tree root.

    1 = Stop upward search at partition root

- The following are licensing messages reported by the policy manager:

  0 Success

  C0001001 Bad Handle

  C0001002 No license has been installed at or above the server's context.

  C0001003 The NLSLSP.NLM is not running, DS is not running, or you must "Setup licensing service" using NWCONFIG.

  C0001004 License Terminated

  C0001005 License is assigned to a different file server. If user assignments have been made, then the user is not assigned to the license.

  C0001006 License has been installed but all units are in use.

  C0001007 Resources Unavailable

  C0001008 Network problem. This is usually some sort of NDS issue.

  80001009 Text Unavailable

  C000100A Unknown Status

  C000100B Bad Index

  8000100C License is expired.

  C000100D Buffer Too Small

  C000100E Bad argument

  C0004001 Mismatched versions of NLSLSP.NLM on servers

  C0004002 License is already installed.

- Troubleshooting licensing issues:
  - DS needs to be healthy for NLS to function properly.
  - Download and apply NLSLSPx.EXE. This has all known NLS issues resolved. You can download this from Novell's Web site: support.novel.com.
  - The container that holds the licensing objects must be a trustee of [Root].

- Licenses can be installed during the NetWare 5 installation with the graphical user interface NWCONFIG and NWADMIN.

- Licenses with a nine-digit serial number cannot be installed while upgrading an existing server to NetWare 5. If the serial number printed on your license diskette label has nine digits, you must check the Install Without Licenses box on the License Installation screen during the server install.

- The GUI install will give the user the ability to enter an Activation key, which has been processed by the Activation Web page. This will only work on EPFIGS NetWare 5 CDs. The activation Web site can be found at www.novell.com/products/activation.

Implementing
NetWare 5

PART 1

- NWCONFIG will allow the user the ability to enter an Activation key obtained from the Web page even if the serial number is 9-digits long. NUMLOCK is not needed or provided with NetWare 5.

- During license installation, the License objects will be created in the same container as the server object.

- In order to obtain a licensed connection, the License container must be in the same container as the server object or in a container above the one which contains the server object.

- The Policy Manager will walk up the tree to find the License container and not down the tree.

- The NLS_LSP object will govern how far to walk the tree.

- Changing the name of the file server will affect licensing.

- A base license must be installed with a number of connection licenses. If no base license is installed, the server will generate a message similar to:

  "Policy Manager 5.00-89: Server < ServerName> was unable to obtain a valid server base license. Connection to this server will not be allowed."

- NetWare 5 requires a NetWare 5 license. No license from a previous version of NetWare will function, i.e. NetWare v.4.11, NetWare v.4.10, and NetWare v.3.12.

- Install the latest support on the NetWare 4.11. This will update NLS and other modules.

- The Property Rights box should have All Properties selected and the Read right. If the rights are not granted to the object, check for Inherited Rights Filters (IRF).

As you can see, Novell Licensing has become very complicated and so has the rest of the operating system. Proper planning and documentation will be critical for the successful migration to NetWare 5.

5

Migrating from IPX to TCP/IP

The NetWare 5 operating system and Novell Directory Services (NDS) now feature full native support for TCP/IP. This means that the core operating system and clients can communicate with each other using TCP/IP as the communication protocol stack. This provides many advantages for the NetWare 5 user.

If you're familiar with TCP/IP, you will have less of a problem understanding specific issues related to this protocol. If you're new to TCP/IP, this is a good time to start learning about it. In the sections that follow, you'll find in-depth information on migrating to TCP/IP and coexisting with IPX/SPX. These sections will help you plan for, and implement, a migration strategy that best fits your company's goals. We will also review implementing WWW, FTP, firewalls, and SAS on the network.

Migration to—or Coexistence with—TCP/IP

In an increasingly Internet-aware market, supporting TCP/IP natively allows NetWare to fully integrate with the Internet and company intranets. With these new TCP/IP services and features you no longer need to support multiple protocols (IPX/SPX and TCP/IP), as previous versions of NetWare required.

All the network services available on IPX/SPX in previous versions of NetWare are available over TCP/IP. The new services added to support TCP/IP are tightly integrated with NDS for ease of management and use common management interfaces. Services like Domain Name Services (DNS) and Dynamic Host Resolution Protocol (DHCP) were integrated into NDS. The following sections discuss the components, features, and implementation strategies that enable native support for TCP/IP.

When you install NetWare 5, it defaults to a TCP/IP-only configuration; you can then select the protocol you need (IPX or IP). Therefore, you need to plan ahead to decide which protocol is best suited for your network.

The most striking benefit of NetWare 5 is that it gives network administrators the ability to implement a single protocol over their networks with NetWare 5 servers. If you have an existing IPX-based network, you can implement a coexistence, or migration, strategy with TCP/IP.

NetWare 5 also includes support for TCP/IP-based applications, which are included with the server package. Novell and third-party applications are supported over a pure IP (TCP/IP-only) network. Novell allows third-party application support through the Transport Layer Interface (TLI) or BSD 4.3 Sockets Interface. Netscape FastTrack Server for NetWare, developed by Novonyx (a joint venture between NetWare and Netscape recently absorbed by Novell), provides WWW Services for an intranet or the Internet. This service is managed by NDS. NetWare servers can also be configured to provide FTP Services.

Supporting a Mixed Environment of IPX and IP

NetWare 5 maintains compatibility with the existing IPX network used by previous versions of NetWare. While NetWare defaults to a pure IP protocol, you have the option of using IPX also. Every network should be designed in the manner that best supports the company's goals. This includes selecting the transport protocol best suited to your particular situation.

In today's networks, you will find two predominant protocol stacks: IPX/SPX and TCP/IP. Each has advantages and disadvantages. With the increased interest in the Internet throughout the business world, TCP/IP has become a more sought-after protocol. This means that you may be faced with having to migrate your network (if you had an IPX-based network) to TCP/IP.

You may have to maintain compatibility with IPX if you have existing applications that require it. In that case, you'll use the Compatibility Mode (discussed later in this section). You may also decide that you want to migrate your network in stages. If so, you will need to support both protocols for some time. In very few instances would you decide to implement TCP/IP from the get-go, but you would still have to provide backward compatibility. The great news is that NetWare 5 supports all of these options.

The following sections will discuss supporting coexistence with IPX and migration from IPX to pure IP networks.

Choosing a Protocol Configuration

As mentioned, NetWare 5 lets you choose the protocol(s) that best suits your network needs. There are three possible server and client configurations:

- IP-only (including Compatibility Mode)
- IPX-only
- The IP and IPX option

Server or Client with IP Only   This configuration will only allow the NetWare 5 server to communicate with clients and services that use the TCP/IP stack. The IPX stack is loaded as well, but it is not bound to the network card. IP-only servers and clients can execute IPX-based applications using Compatibility Mode (loaded by default), but you will need to install the Migration Agent (Gateway) to connect to IPX-based servers and clients. (The Migration Agent will be discussed later in this chapter.)

Server or Client with IPX Only   IPX-only servers and clients can communicate with previous versions of servers and clients without any special configurations. Although both IPX and TCP/IP stacks may be loaded, only the IPX stack is bound to the network card. If you were using NetWare/IP on the existing NetWare servers, both the IP and IPX stacks should be loaded on the new NetWare 5 servers. The servers establish connections to clients and other servers using only the IPX stack. To communicate with IP-based NetWare 5 servers, the IPX-only servers and clients will need to use a Migration Agent (Gateway).

Server or Client with Both IP and IPX   Servers and clients installed with both protocols have the ability to communicate with either protocol. The NCP packets can be transported over TCP/IP or IPX. This allows the servers and clients to execute IPX-based applications and to communicate with pre-existing IPX-based or IP-based clients. These IPX-based servers and clients can communicate with IP-based servers through a Migration Agent. A client configured with both IP and IPX is not guaranteed to establish a connection with an IP-only server unless you use a Migration Agent. The same thing is true of applications that use bindery information.

Compatibility Mode

In all the protocol configuration options we've discussed, you can always execute IPX-based applications, or connect to IPX-based servers and clients, between IPX- and IP-based networks. A feature called Compatibility Mode provides this capability. All the Compatibility Mode server components are integrated into the SCMD.NLM module. There are three main components that make up Compatibility Mode (SLP, which provides SAP encapsulation for Compatibility Mode, is discussed later):

- Compatibility Mode Driver
- Migration Agent
- Bindery Agent

Compatibility Mode Driver   The Compatibility Mode Driver (CMD) is loaded by default when the IP-only protocol option is installed. This enables the server or client to execute applications that require IPX. The server views the Compatibility Mode Driver as a network adapter card and, if bound to both IP and IPX, it acts as an internal router for the server. This allows the server to route IPX packets to itself, a capability that is used when the server is executing IPX-based applications. Also, if the CMD is loaded with the Gateway option (/G), it provides communication between the IP and IPX worlds. In this scenario, you need to bind IP and IPX to the network adapters before loading SCMD with the Gateway option.

NetWare only uses these services when needed. If they are not needed, the CMDs are idle. For the CMDs to communicate with IPX-based applications or IP-based systems, SLP must be implemented across the network. This means that the CMDs are dependent on the services provided by SLP. At least one Migration Agent must be used to connect an IP-only segment with an IPX-only segment.

> **NOTE**   See Novell's online documentation for information on CMD configuration options.

Migration Agent   You need to install the Migration Agent, also called the Migration Gateway, to enable communication between an IP-based network and a IPX-based one. You will need at least one server configured with both IP and IPX, and the CMD loaded with the Gateway option on the server console:

```
SCMD /G
```

This server would have to be connected to both networks, and would be responsible for routing requests between each network. For example, an IPX-based client would connect to an IP-based server by establishing a connection with the server that has the Migration

Agent installed. The IP-based server would respond to IPX-based calls using the CMD it has, and connect to the client using a server with the Migration Agent.

Bindery Agent   The final component of Compatibility Mode is the Bindery Agent, which provides compatibility with Bindery Services. This allows a client to access services on an existing 2.*x* or 3.*x* server or application that requires Bindery Services. To enable the Bindery Agent, you will need to create an Organizational Unit (named *Bindery*, for example), under the Organization object. On the server where you are enabling the Bindery Agent, make sure there is a Read/Write replica of the partition that contains the Bindery container object. Then set the bindery context with a command such as this: **SET BINDERY CONTEXT=.Bindery.***Organization object name.*

Once the bindery context is set, load BINDGATE.NLM on the console. Clients attached to this server can now make bindery requests to NetWare 2.*x* and 3.*x* servers.

Sage Advice: Before Migrating to TCP/IP

Migrating from one protocol to another is a nightmare in itself, but when you are unfamiliar with the target protocol, in this case TCP/IP, you can really create traps for yourself.

One of the first things we did before we migrated to TCP/IP was to establish a well laid-out plan where we assigned IP subnets and established IP address scopes for various hosts. For instance, we assigned all workstations a range of addresses from x.y.w.50 through x.y.w.200. The servers were assigned from x.y.w.10 through x.y.w.49. Routers are assigned x.y.w.1through x.y.w.9. This way you can easily identify hosts by the address range they belong to and also avoid conflicts.

If you didn't understand what we just described above, then we strongly suggest you take a TCP/IP class. Knowledge of this protocol is paramount to planning and implementing it.

The reason we bring this topic up is because most NetWare administrators have had limited exposure to TCP/IP. In most cases, we were not exposed to the initial implementation phase, much less the planning stages.

IPX-to-IP Migration

You may want to consider your options before migrating your network to IP only. For smaller networks, or even medium-sized ones, IPX is still a viable solution. The administration costs for an IP network are considerably higher than those for an IPX network, which requires much less configuration and administration. You can configure an IPX/IP gateway to access the Internet if you want to provide IP services without configuring IP on the clients.

In some cases, though, it makes sense to migrate to an all-IP network. If you are supporting both protocols already, migrating to an IP-only network means you can reduce the costs associated with running both. NetWare 5 enables you to manage both protocols and related services from a central Directory service. This allows you to manage diverse clients. It will also support you through a phased migration from one protocol platform to another.

These new features provide the components for this transition:

- Migration Agent (discussed in earlier sections)
- Protocol-independent client and server software (discussed in earlier sections)
- Protocol-independent NDS
- Service Location Protocol (SLP)
- Network Time Protocol (NTP)
- Transitive Synchronization
- DNS
- DHCP

All of these components provide the vehicle for the migration. These components are critical to the support of NetWare services when migrating to an IP-only environment.

SLP

SLP is a standard Internet protocol (RFC 2165) used for the discovery and registration of services over an IP network. SLP is not a name resolution protocol like DNS, but a service locator for clients, much like the SAP protocol was for IPX clients in previous versions of NetWare. The main purpose for SLP is to discover infrastructure services like NDS, DHCP, DNS, and NDPS. A second objective is to import SAP packets when running Compatibility Mode with IPX-based services.

One of SLP's advantages over SAP is that it registers its information with NDS and therefore does not need to broadcast across networks as SAP does. The client only needs to query NDS for services rather than using the entire network.

SLP Components   Basic components include the SLP user agent (on the client), SLP Directory Agents, and the SLP service agents (on the servers). SLP uses broadcasts to connect an SLP user agent with several SLP service agents. For non-local service agents (on a separate network), you can use DHCP to help user agents access those service agents.

An optional method to multicast, and one that is more appropriate for a large network, is to have multiple SLP Directory Agents (DAs) scattered across your network. The SLP DAs will then replicate information between each other. Both options have costs and benefits associated with them.

SLP Configurations   SLP is critical to a NetWare 5 implementation or migration to IP because it provides the services that SAP did in previous versions of NetWare. In small networks the default configuration works well. But as your network becomes more complicated, broadcasts are not recommended, and DAs are used to advertise network services. Information collected by a DA is stored in its own NDS container which can be replicated and made available to other DAs on the network.

You can also specify concentration in services, or scopes, with DAs. This new service advertising architecture, together with the implementation of native IP, brings new considerations to NDS designs.

Sage Advice: Migrating to TCP/IP and NDS—SAP vs. SLP

You are probably thinking to yourself: "How does migrating to IP affect my NDS design?" Well, to start with, implementation of native IP brings new considerations to NDS designs. Here are some guidelines you should follow:

- Keep the design simple. If you have a small network, you should create a single container and anticipate the use of a default SLP configuration.

- In the case of a multi-network design with geographic considerations, you want to keep as many resources local to users as possible.

- Locating these resources in a central location across WAN links will require additional containers, partitions, and replicas. You will also need to configure DAs.

- If you anticipate using DAs, plan for the deployment of at least two DHCP and DNS servers.

- Placing partition replicas on local servers can be minimized with the use of DAs.

- You will be dependent on DHCP and DNS servers to distribute DA location information to clients. Make sure you have redundant servers.

- Plan for servers to use DAs; this will require additional processing power and memory.

Sage Advice: Migrating to TCP/IP and NDS—SAP vs. SLP *(continued)*

- You should create servers dedicated to DHCP and DNS services, with DAs configured on them. These servers would only have NDS information and be strategically located for maximum effect. No user access should be allowed to these servers.

One DA per organizational group should be enough to cover service scopes within a company. This limits the growth of DA NDS containers.

There are a series of SLP parameters to configure if you decide to use DAs. These can be found on the NetWare 5 online documentation and on the Novell Web site at support.novell.com.

WARNING You should always consult the Novell Web site (support.novell.com) for updated information before you employ any of these guidelines. It has been our experience that Novell constantly makes adjustments and improvements to services.

Server SLP parameters are configured with SET console commands and stored in the STARTUP.NCF file and the Client SLP parameters are configured in the client configuration property page under advanced settings.

NTP Services

This service is used to coordinate time in an IP or mixed IP/IPX environment. The IPX-based servers can only be secondary time servers in a mixed IP and IP/IPX environment. IP-based servers can be one of two modes: They can be server mode (analogous to Reference Time server) or peer mode (analogous to a primary time server).

You should be using TIMESYNC.NLM v5.09 or later on the Single Reference or Reference servers to support NTP services. NTP relies on multiple redundant sources of time; therefore you should coordinate what external time sources you should use. The protocol recommends that you use at least three external reference sources.

You need to identify the primary NTP time sources on the NTP network; these are the time sources that obtain time from a source external to NTP and then distribute it to the rest of the NTP network.

If you configured time to flow from Timesync to NTP, then any atomic clock or an authentic Internet source of time should be applied only to the Timesync network and not to the NTP network. You will find that NTP is a very sensitive protocol; if it detects large differences of time between reference time sources, it will likely reject one or more of them. When configuring NTP, you only need to worry about the primary or reference servers because these are the ones synchronizing with NTP time sources.

Keep in mind the fact that NTP uses UDP port 123 which means that your routers and firewalls need to be able to have this port enabled. You will need to enable this port to allow traffic so that time can be synchronized.

We strongly recommend that you check the Novell support site for the latest TID on the subject. They constantly update this information.

Transitive Synchronization

Transitive synchronization allows for synchronization of replicas to occur in a mixed protocol environment. With mixed protocols, it's not always possible for all servers to communicate with each other. However, if a NetWare 5 server in your tree is set up to run multiple protocols, transitive synchronization is enabled by default. This allows a server configured as a Migration Agent to act as a transit between servers with IPX and IP and to synchronize their replicas with each other.

Actually, the IPX-based servers synchronize their replicas with the server configured as a Migration Agent, and this server synchronizes with servers on the IP network. Thus the replica ring can be maintained on different protocol networks.

DNS

With traditional DNS services, you had to do some planning to configure servers properly. Based on your network's load, number of domains, and number of users, you determined how many master and secondary name servers you wanted to configure. By placing the right number of DNS servers, you ensured proper load balancing for quicker name and address resolution.

NetWare 5 DNS services store all DNS records in NDS, and they are replicated throughout the tree. That means you can select NetWare 5 servers that are strategically located to be DNS servers for better response time. NetWare servers designated as DNS servers then retrieve DNS information from the NDS. This ensures that DNS data is replicated efficiently through NDS.

DNS Zones   DNS information is stored in zones. Zone information is stored in NDS as Zone objects. A zone contains DNS information pertaining to a domain name and is managed and replicated throughout the Directory Services.

There are three Zone objects you can create: a standard DNS zone, an IN-ADDR.ARPA zone, and an IP6.INT zone. All DNS zones must be configured as primary or secondary DNS zones.

If you select a NetWare server to support a primary DNS Zone object, it can do the following:

- Resolve host names to IP addresses by querying the NDS tree
- Add or delete DNS records
- Update the SOA (Start of Authority) serial number

If you select a NetWare server to support a secondary DNS Zone object, it can do the following:

- Receive DNS information from a primary DNS zone not stored in the NDS tree
- Place DNS information in the NDS tree, which NDS distributes throughout the tree

DNS Objects   DNS objects are NDS objects formed when the NDS schema is extended, and are used to administer and control DNS services. There are four objects you need to configure before you can run DNS services:

- DNS Server objects
- DNS Zone objects
- Resource Records objects
- Resource Records Set objects

We will walk through the configuration procedure for each object in the following sections. In addition, you will need to start the DNS services from the server console after the objects are configured and configure your clients to use DNS.

Configuring DNS Server Objects

The DNS Server object is responsible for resolving DNS requests. It contains information on zones such as resource records, DNS server IP addresses (for the purpose of forwarding requests not resolved locally), and related information.

Configuring DNS Zone Objects

A DNS Zone object is a container object in the NDS tree. It stores the data for a single DNS zone, which can be a primary or secondary zone. DNS Zone objects contain the resource records needed to resolve DNS requests from clients.

Configuring DNS Resource Records Objects

A Resource Record object maps a host name to an IP address. DNS servers need this information to resolve DNS clients' requests. Resource records are entered in the respective zones. When a Resource Record object is created, a Resource Record Set object, which holds the DNS Resource Record objects, is created by default.

Resource records cannot be modified. If you want to make changes, you will have to delete the record and create it again. Here are the most important types of resource records and their functions:

Address (A) records: Maps standard host names to IP addresses.

Canonical Name (CNAME) records: Maps aliases to standard host names.

Start of Authority (SOA) records: Shows server's zone of authority.

Name Server (NS) records: Delegates authority of subdomains to other DNS servers.

Pointer (PTR) records: Maps IP addresses to host names (known as reverse lookup or IN-ADDR.ARPA).

Mail Exchange (MX) records: Maps SMTP addresses to domain names.

DHCP

To facilitate the administration of IP configuration on clients you can use DHCP services. NetWare 5 DHCP is fully compliant with TCP/IP protocol standards. All DHCP data is stored on NDS; this makes it available to the entire network.

The following sections will walk you through the process of creating and configuring each of the DHCP objects.

DHCP Server Objects You'll need to create DHCP Server objects to make DHCP available to your network. Deciding how many is the trick. You don't need more than one server, but you may want to watch its performance to make sure it can handle its load. Adding an additional DHCP server can provide redundancy and load balancing.

Subnet Objects A subnet object represents an IP subnet assigned to a physical network segment. You can configure the IP address and range of the subnet. The subnet object can be created in a container object to reflect that container's location in the physical network.

Once you have created the subnet object, you can configure the following settings in the subnet object details window:

- DNS zone for dynamic updates
- Domain name

- Subnet pool reference
- Default DHCP server

DHCP Subnet Address Range Object and IP Address Object   You can configure DHCP for dynamic addressing with the Subnet Address Range object or for manual addressing with the IP Address object.

Subnet Pool Object   Many TCP/IP protocol stacks allow you to configure more than one subnet in a single network segment. The subnet pool object can assign IP addresses to multiple subnets in a single physical segment. You can also configure this object using the DNS/DHCP Management Console.

Additional DHCP Options   You can configure additional DHCP options—either for a global or specific subnet—to further facilitate the administration of your IP network. These options include DNS servers, default gateways, the preferred server, and the NDS context. For more information on how to get to this table, and to configure it, see the Novell online documentation.

See Appendix A for more on DNS/DHCP services.

NetWare 5 WWW and FTP Services

As part of your migration to TCP/IP you might want to also consider intranet and Internet services available to you through NetWare 5. NetWare 5 includes the Netscape FastTrack Server for NetWare as its Web server offering, providing TCP/IP standards-compliant WWW Services for intranets and the Internet. We'll look at the Netscape FastTrack Server in detail in this chapter.

Although it doesn't get as much publicity as the Web does, FTP (File Transfer Protocol) is one of the most commonly used Internet protocols. FTP is used with a Web server to allow visitors to your Web site to download files or browse directories on your network. Novell FTP Services, included with NetWare 5, adds support for this protocol on a NetWare server. You can use this protocol for general-purpose file transfers over the Internet or an intranet, or even across multiple platforms.

WWW Services

The Web has evolved from publishing simple text documents to presenting complex graphical and business-capable applications. These provide users with many services and functions. You can make Web services available to your users through the Internet or your company's intranet by using a TCP/IP network and HTTP (HyperText Transfer Protocol). TCP/IP provides the transport mechanism to move data between computers, and HTTP provides the request/response mechanism between the Web server and a client browser. HTTP version 1.1, or later, bring considerably enhanced performance and security.

Netscape FastTrack Server

The Netscape FastTrack Server is Novell's solution to providing WWW services on NetWare 5 servers. It is a complicated piece of software and may require a slight upgrade to your server.

Check System Requirements   You should have no trouble installing the Netscape FastTrack Server on most servers that can run NetWare 4.11 or higher, but make sure your server meets all of the following system requirements:

> **Memory**   The Netscape FastTrack Server requires 64MB of RAM and, as always, the more the better.

> **Hard Disk Storage**   The Netscape FastTrack Server software requires 100MB of free hard disk space on the SYS: volume. In addition, be sure you have sufficient space for the HTML documents and graphics that you'll make available on the Web server.

> **TCP/IP**   The server needs to be configured to use the TCP/IP protocol.

> **Long Name Space**   You'll need to ensure long name space support for the volume that will hold your Web content. (NetWare 5 supports long name space by default.)

> **Unique IP Address**   A unique IP address must be assigned to the NetWare server.

Manage Files and Directories   During installation, Netscape FastTrack Server creates a directory to store Web documents and related files: SYS:NOVONYX\SUITESPOT\DOCS. Subdirectories can also be created under this directory to organize Web content and make it available to clients.

> **NOTE**   For more information on using the Netscape FastTrack Server for NetWare, go to these files on your intranet (using the server name and host name for your system): For the readme file go to `server_hostname/readme/readme.htm`. For scripting information go to `server_hostname/Netscape_scripting.htm`.

Configure the Web Server

After you have installed the FastTrack Server, you will need to configure the WWW Services. You will need to spend some time planning in order to develop the Web environment that best suits your client's needs. You can configure and manage your FastTrack

Server using the Administration Server and Server Manager. All run on the NetWare 5 server designated as the Web server.

The Administration Server is a group of NLMs that run on the Web server, providing a single interface to help you manage the FastTrack server. The Administration Server is accessed through its own home page. The Server Manager is a series of forms used by the Administration Server to configure and manage the FastTrack Server. Both tools will be described in the following sections.

Administration Server   The Administration Server is accessed from a browser, but you must first run ADMSERV.NLM from the server console to enable the administration Web pages. (The Administration Server is automatically started when the NSWEB.NCF is used also.) If you add the FastTrack startup file (NSWEB.NCF) to AUTOEXEC.NCF, this NLM loads automatically when the server is started.

When you run ADMSERV, the port number for the home page of the Administration Server will be displayed. Make sure you document this number. To access the Administration Server home page from a browser, type the Web site's URL, using the Web server's host name and port number: `server_hostname:admin_port_number/`.

Server Manager   The Server Manager allows you to configure the entire FastTrack Server or specific resources like a directory or a file.

After making changes on the FastTrack Server or a particular resource, you must save and apply the changes. Then return to the Administration Server home page.

Manage Web Server Security

After you install the FastTrack Server, default rights are assigned to the directories. All users receive read and file scan rights to the directories, including documents, and users are given full rights to logs and sample directories.

If you are making your Web site accessible to the Internet or you don't want anyone modifying the site, leave the default rights. This is especially true if you allow anonymous users to access the Web site. An anonymous user is anyone who accesses your Web site without a specific user account.

You can also change the server port number from the default port 80 to improve security. It's a good idea to change the default port number, because port 80 is a standard number for the HTTP protocol. Changing the port number forces hackers to guess which number you used, making it more difficult for them to break into your Web site.

Once you have changed the server's port number, you will need to use the new number when accessing the Web site. Use your machine's host name and port address in the following format: *HOST_NAME:NEW_PORT_NUMBER*.

Tune Your Web Server

The Netscape FastTrack Server will most likely meet your needs without modification. However, if it is heavily used, you may need to change its configuration to optimize performance. To do this, you will need to use the Administration Server and Server Manager.

These are some of the configuration options you can change:

- Directories in the document tree
- Document preferences
- Access to the Web site

We will discuss ways to modify these parameters in the following sections.

Modify Directories in the Document Tree   By default, Web documents are stored in this directory: SYS:\NOVONYX\SUITESPOT\DOCS.

This is the root directory of the home page. You can also use Server Manager to create additional directories to store Web documents.

Configure Document Preferences   With the FastTrack Server, you can predetermine how the Web server responds to document requests made from browsers by using:

Index Filenames   When a browser requests access to your Web site by entering your domain name, but not specifying a filename, you can specify which file will be displayed as the home page. The default files that will be displayed are INDEX.HTML and HOME.HTML. If you specify more than one filename to be the default home page, the server will look in the primary document directory of the Web site for the files in the order in which the filenames appear until it finds one. These files are what a user sees as your Web site's home page.

Directory Indexing   The Netscape FastTrack Server automatically creates an index of the files and subdirectories your document directory holds. Typically when a user accesses your Web site, a predetermined index file is displayed, but if one is not present the server will display the index file it created when the server indexed the document directory. This index file displays the contents of the DOCS directory.

Server Home Page   By default the server uses the INDEX.HTML file as your Web site's home page. You can select a different file to be the home page through the Server Manager if you prefer. From the Server Manager, click the Content Management button and then click the Document Preferences link in the left window.

Restrict Access   By default, anyone can access the Netscape FastTrack Server Web site you create on your server. If your Web site is meant to be public, then this default setting is fine. On the other hand, if your Web site is for internal use only, you need to restrict access to it which you can do by binding the FastTrack Server to NDS. Using NDS, you can create users and groups to set access restrictions to the Web site.

Beware, once you enable NDS authentication, everybody will be prompted to enter a password whether the document is secure or not. If you want to be able to differentiate which documents require authentication and which documents do not, you must use LDAP authentication.

The next step to restrict access to your Web site is to make trustee assignments to the Web contents, directories, and files. When a user tries to access the Web site, they will be prompted to enter a login name and password. The login name has to be an NDS user account with access rights to the Web site or the login request will be denied.

Web Server Troubleshooting

The Netscape FastTrack Server will work well in its default configuration under most circumstances. If the server is getting heavy traffic and performance is disappointing, there are a few settings you can change to improve speed:

- Tune server performance with FastTrack Server Manager. Use this tool to manage and adjust the settings for concurrent requests, simultaneous connections, and other settings that affect the server's performance.

- Modify the Maximum Packet Receive Buffers setting, which controls the amount of memory set aside for incoming network packets.

- Modify the Maximum Physical Receive Packet Size setting, which controls the maximum size for incoming network packets.

- Regulate Web server content. Sometimes problems with server performance are not caused by the server but by the number of large files and complex programs—images, multimedia, Java, image maps, and CGI programs—that users must download when they access your Web pages. You might need to regulate and tune this area as well.

These adjustments are explained in detail in the following sections.

Tune Server Performance with the Server Manager   The Server Manager can manage the following settings, which can affect the Netscape FastTrack Server performance:

Maximum Number of Simultaneous Requests   This parameter controls how many concurrent requests the server can respond to. The default is 48. Since every situation is different, we recommend that you closely monitor your Web servers for performance and adjust the parameter as needed. Always keep in mind that an increase in this parameter adds load to the server.

Domain Name System Lookups   This parameter is off by default. If you suspect slow response from the server, you may want to check whether this feature's setting has been turned on. If it has, then turning the setting back off can improve performance.

Listen-Queue Size   This is a socket-level parameter that indicates how many simultaneous connections the socket can accept. The default is 100 connections. You should be careful when changing this parameter. Again we recommend that you monitor the performance of the server and adjust as needed. The main reason for this setting is to avoid overloading the server with too many connections.

HTTP Persistent Connection Timeout   Persistent Connections is a feature of HTTP 1.1. A lot of overhead was created in earlier versions of HTTP because a browser had to establish a connection with each Web page in a downloaded Web site. With HTTP 1.1, a client connects to the FastTrack Server and establishes a connection that can be maintained for a pre-established period of time. All the pages of a Web site can be download on the same connection. This reduces overhead and improves performance.

Supporting persistent connections on the Web server ensures that you will only need one connection to the Web site for all your requests. Setting the timeout properly ensures a persistent connection for the right amount of time without overloading the server. We can't really recommend a setting because every installation is unique, but with good monitoring and analysis you can determine the right setting to use.

Modify Maximum Packet Receive Buffers   The Maximum Packet Receive Buffers setting controls the amount of memory set aside as a buffer for packets. This value can range from 50 to about 4 billion, and defaults to 100. Larger numbers use more memory.

You may wish to change this setting to a higher number if you have a large amount of Web traffic and have memory to spare. To change the setting, add a command like the following to your STARTUP.NCF file: **SET MAXIMUM PACKET RECEIVE BUFFERS = 2000**.

NOTE   This parameter and the Maximum Physical Receive Packet Size parameter (explained in the following sections) can only be changed in the STARTUP.NCF file, since memory for buffers is allocated when the server starts.

Modify Maximum Physical Receive Packet Size   The final parameter you may need to change is Maximum Physical Receive Packet Size. This parameter controls the amount of memory set aside as a buffer for each packet. Since different network topologies use different packet sizes, this parameter should be set to accommodate the largest packet size used by your network.

The following list shows the default maximum packet sizes for common network topologies (unless you are using a different topology, you shouldn't need to change this parameter):

Topology	Maximum Packet Size
Ethernet	1514
Token Ring	4202
ARCnet	512

If you do need to change this parameter, you must do so in the STARTUP.NCF file. Add a line like the following: **SET MAXIMUM PHYSICAL RECEIVE PACKET SIZE = 4202**.

Regulate Web Server Content   If users are complaining about slow performance when accessing your Web site, changing the parameters may help. However, it's possible that the problem lies in the content of your Web pages.

Since most Web content is created on a local network, it's easy to forget that the majority of Web users are accessing your site with modems with typical speeds of 33.6K baud. Be especially wary of the following items when creating pages for a public-access Web site:

Images   Full-color image files can be quite large. In addition, a page with a large number of images will require several threads to load, slowing down the server. You can speed up the server by reducing the number of images where possible. Also, when saving images, set the quality to 256 colors or less, rather than full color, to reduce their size. Also offer users text-only versions of the Web pages.

Multimedia   Audio and video clips are usually many times larger than image files. Keep these to a minimum, or at least warn users that downloading them may take some time. Audio files can be reduced in size by converting them to a lower-quality format (such as 8-bit rather than 16-bit).

Java   Complex Java applets tend to require a large amount of download time, and may take several minutes to start over a modem connection. You may want to weigh the benefits a Java applet may bring to your Web page against the cost in performance. Monitor the performance of the browsers downloading the applets to ensure acceptability by the users.

CGI programs   Although CGI programs aren't transmitted to clients, the user has to wait while the program executes. Complex programs can delay this response and put a heavy load on the server's processor. You must ensure that the use of CGIs or ISAPI filters does not overload your server; you should monitor server performance and adjust accordingly.

Image maps   Clickable images also require a bit of processing at the server. You can use client-side rather than server-side maps to improve the server's performance.

FTP Services

FTP Services is a powerful tool used to transfer files among dissimilar operating systems. For example, a Unix client can communicate and transfer a file to a NetWare server. NetWare uses two NLMs to provide FTP Services and the NFS (Network File System) name space to support Unix naming conventions and security. The two modules are:

FTPSERV.NLM   This module provides FTP Services on a NetWare server.

INETD.NLM   This module activates FTPSERV.NLM when an FTP client makes a request. This saves resources on the server when FTP Services is not being used because this module is much easier on the server.

Before you can install FTP Services, make sure you have the required hardware (including a CD-ROM) and software loaded. The FTP server requires TCP/IP to run. You also need to load NFS name space support on the volume where FTP documents are going to be stored.

Manage FTP Services

The main utility for configuring FTP Services is UNICON. You can use this utility to manage all aspects of FTP Services, as well as the other services supported.

To launch the UNICON utility, enter UNICON at the server console. You will be prompted to enter the username and password for the Admin account. After you do, you will be presented with a menu of options. In the following sections, we'll discuss these options and how to configure them.

UNICON Options   After you launch the UNICON utility, you will see the main menu.

Use these menu options to configure FTP Services:

Change Current Server   Allows you to manage FTP and other services for a different server on the network.

View Server Profile   Displays a list of information about the server and the services running on it.

Manage Global Objects   Allows you to manage users and groups for FTP access.

Manage Services   Displays a list of services currently running. You can select each service to access a menu of options specific to that service.

Start/Stop Services   Allows you to start and stop various services from FTP Services.

Configure Error Reporting   Allows you to choose a log file that will store error messages relating to the various services.

Perform File Operations   Allows you to perform simple file maintenance operations.

Start or Stop Services   The Start/Stop Services option displays a list of services that are currently running. By default, only DNS or NIS are running. If the FTP Services were running you would see it displayed here. The available services include the following:

DNS Server (Domain Name Service)   Provides identification for domain names.

NIS Server (Network Information Service)   An alternate protocol for domain management, which can be used instead of DNS.

FTP Server (File Transfer Protocol)   Allows users to transfer files via FTP.

NetWare-to-Unix Print Gateway   Allows clients on the NetWare network to print to Unix machines.

Unix-to-NetWare Print Server   Allows clients on a Unix network to print to NetWare printers.

NOTE   The last two services are collectively called Novell Unix Services.

To start a service that is not currently running, press Insert and choose the service from the list on the screen. To stop a currently running service, highlight its entry and press Delete.

Manage the FTP Server   To manage the FTP server, go to the UNICON Main Menu ➤ Manage Services ➤ FTP Server. Select from the following options:

View Current FTP Sessions   Displays a list of users who are currently connected to the FTP server, along with the files they are accessing.

Set Parameters   Allows you to set various parameters for the FTP server. These options are described in detail in the next section.

View FTP Log File   Displays the FTP log file, which logs all FTP accesses.

View Intruder Log File   Displays a separate log of failed logins to the FTP server such as an intruder attempting to hack your server, or simply a valid user entering the wrong password.

Restrict FTP Access   Allows you to edit a file that can restrict access to certain users or domains.

Clear Log Files   Resets both of the log files.

Set FTP Parameters   The Set Parameters option in the FTP Administration menu (covered in the previous section) allows you to configure settings for the FTP server.

Use the FTP Server Parameters screen to adjust the following settings:

Maximum Number of Sessions   Controls the maximum number of users that can be simultaneously connected to FTP. Depending on the speed of your server and the number of users, you may need to adjust this parameter to limit connections. The default is 16.

Maximum Session Length   Sets the maximum length of a single FTP session. Modifying this setting can be useful, ensuring that users log out and make a session available to another user within a reasonable length of time.

Idle Time Before FTP Server Unloads   Sets the amount of time a connection can be open with no FTP access before the server automatically unloads.

Anonymous User Access   Lets you choose whether anonymous (guest) access is allowed. The setting you select depends on the security level you want and the purpose of the FTP site.

Default User's Home Directory   Sets the default directory that users will use when they first connect to the FTP server.

Anonymous User's Home Directory   Is made accessible to anonymous users.

Default Name Space   Sets whether the FTP server accepts DOS filenames or long filenames. You must have the long name space module loaded in order to use non-DOS filenames.

Intruder Detection   Enables intruder detection when set to Yes. This disables the FTP server temporarily after a certain number of unsuccessful login attempts are made.

Number of Unsuccessful Attempts   Sets the number of unsuccessful login attempts that will be permitted before the user account is locked out.

Detection Reset Interval   Controls the amount of time after an intruder is detected before other users regain access to the FTP server.

Log Level   Controls how much detail is included in log entries.

Configure the FTP Server

After you've installed the FTP server, there are a few tasks you'll need to perform to configure the server for your needs. By default, no one has access to the FTP site when you install the FTP server. You need to decide who can access the server and what they can do, which depends on the purpose of the site and the type of files users can download.

Anonymous FTP is the most common type of FTP access. It allows you to make files publicly available over the Internet or to all users on your network. This is not a good option if you are providing sensitive files for download.

In addition to allowing access to anonymous users, you can configure your FTP server to allow wider access to users with passwords. This procedure allows you to improve security on your FTP server by restricting access based on individual user needs, rather than one general account such as the anonymous user. A combined approach is generally used so that guests can use Anonymous FTP and your users can use their accounts. This allows for a more secure environment.

Troubleshoot FTP Services

Like most other parts of the network, FTP does not always run smoothly. In the following sections we'll look at some of the common problems you may encounter while using FTP and how to solve them.

Users Can't Connect to FTP Server   If users are unable to connect to your FTP server, check the following:

- There may be a network problem. Verify that the server is up and that there are no problems with the network wiring.
- The FTP server may not be running. Use the Start/Stop Services option on the UNICON main menu to verify that the FTP service is started.
- The client software may not be correctly configured. If your users cannot reach *any* FTP sites, verify that FTP is configured on their workstations and that the FTP software is installed correctly.

Connection Refused by FTP Server   If users are able to connect to the FTP server but receive an error message, check for the following:

- The FTP server may be overloaded. Check the Maximum Number of Sessions parameter and increase it if necessary.
- Access to the FTP server may be restricted. Go to the Restrict Access page from the FTP Administration menu to check whether restrictions have been set appropriately.

Users Cannot Download a File   If users can connect to your FTP server but can't download a particular file, check for the following:

- Check that the file exists in the proper directory.

Implementing
NetWare 5

- Check that its rights have been set to readable—both in the NetWare file system and in UNICON.
- If a user needs to upload a file, be sure that the directory is set to allow write.

If a download stops during a file transfer or is extremely slow, the server may be overloaded. To alleviate this problem, upgrade the server or limit the number of concurrent users by adjusting the Maximum Number of Sessions parameter.

Securing Your Intranet and the Internet

If you want to monitor and control network traffic between your intranet and the Internet, you will need a firewall. If you want to secure communications between your browser users and your Web sites then you will need to support SSL (Secure Socket Layer) services. These are complex solutions, which require considerable planning before implementing them. Novell's firewall solution is BorderManager and Secure Socket Layer solution is Secure Authentication Services (SAS).

Firewalls

A firewall is a brick wall placed between buildings or houses to block a fire from spreading. In networking, the term firewall is used to indicate a control mechanism for inbound and outbound communication between networks. Firewalls provide added security to prevent unauthorized users from accessing the Internet (outbound access) or unauthorized people accessing your private network from the Internet (inbound access). You can also apply firewalls to prevent interdivisional communications; for example, you may not want a user in the Sales department to have access to a resource in the Accounting department.

A firewall can be composed of a packet-filtering router, circuit gateway, or an application gateway. Most firewalls are made up of a combination of these components, providing security at all layers of the OSI. Firewalls offer control mechanisms to various layers of the OSI model.

The following firewall types affect all layers of the OSI model:

Packet-Filtering Routers   Also called screening routers, *packet-filtering routers* restrict incoming packets from the Internet to your network (intranet). These routers can use source IP addresses, port numbers, and node addresses to restrict access to your internal network from the Internet. By denying access to a specific port number, IP address, or node address, a packet-filtering router can affect the datalink, network, and transport layers of the OSI model.

Circuit Gateways   These are also called *circuit-level proxies*, and they control outbound connections from your intranet to the Internet. This component acts on behalf of the client making the request. When a user wants to access the Internet, the request is forwarded to a port on the circuit gateway. The circuit gateway then replaces the user IP address with its own, accessing the Internet for the client. This firewall component affects the session layer of the OSI model. Circuit gateways allow you to implement RFC 1918 (Address Allocation for Private Intranet); the terms Network Address Translation (NAT), Port Address Translation (PAT), and IP Masquerading may all be grouped into this category. For more information on these terms please refer to the Novell online documentation.

Application Gateways   These application-level proxies control access to the presentation and application layer of the OSI model. Firewalls that include application gateways are considered the most secure type, because the data must actually be handled by the firewall, processed, and then sent back to the client. Sometimes other features such as caching are integrated into Application gateways; these are also called *caching proxies*.

Novell's Firewall

To address the need for firewalls on NetWare networks, Novell offers BorderManager. BorderManager for NetWare offers a comprehensive suite of services that include routing, remote access, IP gateway, proxy cache, and Virtual Private Network (VPN) encryption software. The following components provide these services:

NIAS 4.1   This software provides routing gateway services and remote access to your network for dial-up clients. These services include Multi-Protocol routing, WAN support, packet filtering, Network Address Translators which translate private IP addresses to registered ones, an IPX mapping gateway which translates private IPX addresses to registered IPX addresses, and inbound/outbound remote access. NIAS 4.1 also provides Virtual Private Network encryption software through its tunneling and encryption services over the Internet, eliminating the need for private lines.

HTTP Accelerator   This is used to accelerate access from the Internet to your company Web sites. In this situation, BorderManager is used as a front end to your public Web sites, reducing access to your internal network from the outside and improving response time to client requests from the Internet. You configure your DNS to point the host WWW to your BorderManager server(s). Then, when a client requests a document, the BorderManager server requests it from your real Web server. After receiving the document, it keeps a copy in its cache for future reference. All subsequent requests for the same document result in faster access times. All updates can be done in a secure network to the Web server, then the contents are cached to the disk on the BorderManager server.

Hierarchical Proxy Cache   This is used to place multiple caches on Border-Manager and to hold information from sources frequently accessed by users on both sides of your network. The objective is to make users request the Border-Manager server, which will accelerate response time and improve your Web security and performance, rather than having requests processed by your Web servers.

WARNING Be sure not to use BorderManager FastCache with pages that have dynamic content or need to be updated frequently.

TIP For more information on BorderManager, visit Novell's Web site www.novell.com/bordermanager.

As you can see, BorderManager is a comprehensive solution for various network services and should be considered whenever you do any network planning.

SAS

SAS is designed to provide support for new and evolving industry authentication mechanisms. The SAS design also includes a framework for distinguishing between authentication mechanisms of various qualities as well as support for the introduction of third-party authentication services. SAS also provides server-based user applications with controlled access to files and NDS objects based on the user's SAS authentication. NetWare 5's SAS will support SSL and use the SAS API set to establish encrypted SSL connections.

To support SSL communications you can use Novell's Public Key Infrastructure Services (PKIS) to provide the digital certificates and certificates of authority. The digital certificates contain the respective public and private keys needed for the signing and sealing of packets during communications.

Comparing Company A and B's New Server Installation Procedures

In all our years as systems engineers, we have yet to see a common setup for networks and systems between companies. In fact there is no right way to design, plan, and implement a network. We don't mean that there aren't rules to follow, just that there is more than one way to do it. Here you will see how two companies approached their server installs; you will see the differences and some common rules each followed.

Company A's Installation Process

Company A wanted to standardize their approach to new server installs. They had more than 400 servers to deploy, which would support a tree that spanned the entire network. This network supports over 30,000 users. The following is a synopsis of their process:

- Standard HP Netserver configuration is dependent on the use of the server. For example, the NDS backbone servers are LC series servers, with SMC 10/100BaseT cards.

- Standard drive partitioning depends on use. DOS partitions are set at 1GB for future expansion. The SYS: volume is set at 1GB with the rest of the drive reserved for data and application volumes.

- All servers have a standard AUTOEXEC .NCF and STARTUP.NCF configuration, with the latest support pack installed.

- Servers are installed at the main IS staging office where they are connected to a

NetWare server with the distribution files stored on it. From this server, a network install is performed.

- Naming convention reflects purpose and location of the server.

- A bootable disk with a batch file to automate the install process is used.

- Necessary files are copied to the server to complete the install.

- Server's configurations are adjusted before they are sent to their destination for Plug-and-Play setups.

Company B's Installation Process

Company B is going through a two-stage upgrade process. This is a very small network compared to company A, but it includes a WAN and has about 300 users. Never underestimate potential problems, no matter what the size of the company. All clients are being upgraded to Microsoft NT 4 Workstations with Gateway desktop clients. The servers are being replaced with Gateway servers and NetWare 5 as the backbone network operating system to take advantage of NDS and ZENworks. The focus is to manage the users and desktops through NDS and ZENworks.

Installing NetWare 5 on the Gateways is in the test stage to identify any potential problems before the actual rollout. There are existing NetWare 4.11 and 3.12 servers that need to be upgraded. These will be migrated to new hardware and then upgraded also.

The biggest issue confronting company B is the compatibility of the hardware and that's why they are upgrading to Gateway systems and testing them.

Both companies are using DSMAINT.NLM as the primary tool to migrate NetWare servers from older to new hardware, and then they will upgrade the servers to NetWare 5.

Conclusion

We were involved in both projects and have to say that both companies' approaches make sense because their installs took a cookie-cutter approach to deploying servers on their network. This, in return, enabled them to minimize errors and installation problems. While there are many ways to install a server, one standard should be chosen for your network. In both cases the companies tested their strategies and corrected any potential problems before the actual implementation.

24seven **CASE STUDY**

Part 2

NetWare Operations

Topics Covered:

- Using console commands

- Managing your server with ConsoleOne

- Managing your server with NWCONFIG and INETCFG

- Optimize performance with SET parameters

- Gather performance data with Monitor

- Remotely manage servers

- Optimizing remote access performance

- Selecting a connection service

- Implementing security

- Optimizing network traffic

- Selecting the right Novell and Macintosh installation opitions

- Administering NDS objects

- Managing users and groups

- Using contextless login and Catalog Services

- Maintaining NDS

- Managing partitions and replicas

- Troubleshooting NDS with DSREPAIR

6

Basic Server Operations

Now that you have installed your servers, planned your network, and determined what protocols you want to use and how to implement them, it's time to turn to the day-to-day operation of your server. In this chapter, we will cover the use of the server console and GUI that are new with NetWare 5. We will cover many useful tools and utilities to help you manage your server. We will also briefly discuss ConsoleOne at the server, workstation, and even via the Web, and how you can perform basic management tasks with it. Finally, we will conclude with a brief review of NWCONFIG and INETCFG.

Server Console

With the advent of a GUI on the server, many have thought that the command-line interface of the server console would be a thing of the past. Nothing could be further from the truth. Just as with the various versions of Windows where certain tasks can more efficiently (or in some cases only) be performed at the console prompt, the same is true with NetWare 5. The Console prompt is still alive and will be an important location where commands are issued, environments are configured, and so on.

Because most people reading this book have been with NetWare for a long time, and because the interface hasn't changed much, we will only focus on new features and capabilities in this section. The first (and probably most long sought-after feature) is the ability to load NLMs without having to specify LOAD first. DOS has the ability to load programs without using LOAD or a similar command, and has since version 1, and now any NLM can be loaded in NetWare 5 by just typing its name as well. UNLOAD, however, is still needed to unload an NLM, as most don't have an interface from which the option to exit could be chosen.

The second new feature is the expanded list of commands, and provided with it is a new and improved help system. Table 6.1 lists some common, new, and changed commands.

Table 6.1 Important, New, and Changed Console Commands

Command	Purpose and Notes
ADD NAME SPACE	Used to store variously named files on a volume. NSS volumes automatically have all name spaces listed below installed on them. Traditional volumes have the DOS and LONG (formally OS/2) name spaces added. The available name spaces are DOS, Long, Mac (for Macintosh files), and NFS (for Unix formatted files).
ALIAS	Allows you to substitute a short name for a longer command; similar to an ability of DOSKEY in DOS. For example, to view the loaded NLMs, you could type **M** instead of **MODULES** if you had first set up the alias by typing **ALIAS M MODULES**.
APPLET or **APPLETVIEWER**	Allows you to run Java-based applets at the server.
BINDERY	Allows you to set or remove bindery contexts for the server; formerly done with SET BINDERY CONTEXT =.
BROADCAST or **SEND**	Send a message to all users (or selected users) connected to a server, to inform them of maintenance, for example.
CPUCHECK	Used to view CPU information, such as speed, amount of L1 and L2 cache, and so on; often used with Display Processors (see "Display Processors.")

Table 6.1   Important, New, and Changed Console Commands *(continued)*

Command	Purpose and Notes
CSET	Displays a list of Set categories or the SET parameters and their current values for each category if a category name (not number, as with SET) is entered. Similar to typing **SET** and pressing ENTER in earlier versions. The difference is that you are prompted to change or not to change each value in the category. This allows you to change a parameter's value without having to type its name.
DISPLAY IPX NETWORKS	Shows the known IPX networks, along with their external IPX network number, and the number of hops and ticks (1/18th of a second) away. Same as **DISPLAY NETWORKS** (which still works, although not listed in Help) in previous versions.
DISPLAY IPX SERVERS	Displays the servers that the server is aware of via SAP (Service Advertising Protocol), hence only IPX-based servers will be listed. Also lists the number of hops away. Same as **DISPLAY SERVERS** (which still works, although not listed in Help) in previous versions.
DISPLAY INTERRUPTS	Displays the total number of interrupts for each processor since the server was brought up.
DISPLAY PROCESSORS	View the status of each processor in your system (online or offline). Additional information on each processor can be displayed with CPUCheck, Display Interrupts, Start Processors, Stop Processors, and through Monitor. Multi-processor behavior can be adjusted through SET parameters.
DISPLAY ENVIRONMENT	Displays the current values of most Set parameters; similar to doing a SET for each category of information.

NetWare
Operations

PART 2

Table 6.1 Important, New, and Changed Console Commands *(continued)*

Command	Purpose and Notes
DISPLAY MODIFIED ENVIRONMENT	A variant of **DISPLAY ENVIRONMENT** that shows only those Set parameters that have been changed from their default values; displays both current and default values.
DOWN	Accomplishes what was formerly achieved by both **DOWN** and **EXIT** with one command.
ECHO ON or **ECHO OFF**	Same functionality as Echo On or Echo Off in a DOS batch file for NCF files.
ENVSET	Displays, adds, and removes environmental variables; similar to SET in DOS.
JAR, JAVA, JAVA-RMI.CGI, JAVAC, JAVADOC, JAVAH, JAVAKEY, JAVAP, JRE, RMIC, and **RMIREGISTRY**	Java related commands and utilities. For more information on Java, refer to the online documentation or Novell's Web site. Note that these commands are only available while JAVA.NLM is loaded, but as with many things requiring Java, it is normally loaded.
LIST STORAGE ADAPTERS	Shows all registered storage adapter (IDE, SCSI, and so on) HAMs and the devices (CD-ROMs, hard drives, and so on) associated with each; part of NPA. See also "List Devices."
LIST DEVICES	Lists all registered storage devices, without displaying the associated adapter; part of NPA. See also "List Storage Adapters."
LOAD	Now an optional keyword; useful with optional switches to specify where a program or driver will load, if it is restartable, and so on.

Table 6.1   Important, New, and Changed Console Commands *(continued)*

Command	Purpose and Notes
MAGAZINE INSERTED, MAGAZINE NOT INSERTED, MAGAZINE NOT REMOVED, MAGAZINE REMOVED, MEDIA INSERTED, MEDIA NOT INSERTED, MEDIA NOT REMOVED, and **MEDIA REMOVED**	Used with devices that support multiple pieces of media simultaneously (such as a CD-ROM jukebox) to inform the system of the status of a given magazine (collection of media) or individual piece of media (such as a CD).
PROTECTION	Displays the protected memory address spaces and the things (such as NLMs) in them.
PROTOCOL and **PROTOCOL REGISTER**	Displays (or, with Protocol Register, adds) protocols and associated frame types registered with the system; it is better to manipulate with INETCFG (described in the INETCFG section).
REGISTER MEMORY	Registers additional memory with the NOS. Rarely needed as NetWare automatically detects the installed quantity of memory. See the warning following the table for important information about this command. Values must be specified in hexadecimal.
RESET ENVIRONMENT	Allows you to reset some or all SET parameters back to the default values. You should execute a **DISPLAY MODIFIED ENVIRONMENT** first to be sure you understand what will be changed.
RESET SERVER	Will **DOWN** and warm boot the server; See also "Restart Server."
RESTART SERVER	Will Down and immediately restart the server (all components *except for SERVER.EXE* will be reloaded). The machine is not warm booted. See also "Reset Server."

NetWare
Operations

PART 2

Table 6.1   Important, New, and Changed Console Commands *(continued)*

Command	Purpose and Notes
START PROCESSORS and **STOP PROCESSORS**	Allows you to selectively start or stop (respectively) any or all secondary processors. (Processor 0, the primary processor, can't be stopped.)
SWAP	Allows you to view or modify virtual memory settings. See the following note for more information on this command.
VMDISMOUNT, VMMOUNT, and **VMVOLUMES**	Can be used instead of Dismount, Mount, and Volume (or Volumes) respectively.

Swap by itself displays current settings. Use it with the Add or Del parameters to add or delete a swap file on a volume; and change settings of an existing swap file with the Parameter = parameter. You can set minimum and maximum sizes for the file as well as the minimum free space to leave on the volume. You can add a swap file to a volume that isn't currently mounted; if you do so, it will automatically be created when it is next mounted. When you dismount a volume, any swap file on that drive will automatically be removed. By default, the only swap file created is on the SYS: volume. Generally it is recommended that you move the swap file off of SYS: to prevent it from filling up and, because it is used frequently, it may also improve performance. Place the appropriate commands in AUTOEXEC.NCF to automate this.

Sage Advice

Register Memory is normally not necessary anymore. Using this command can cause memory fragmentation and other problems. Before using this command try the following:

- Look in AUTOEXEC.BAT and CONFIG.SYS for any program or driver that may prevent NetWare from seeing all of the installed RAM. Typically that limits the amount that NetWare can see to 64MB.

- If you have an old ISA or MCA NIC, upgrade to a newer card.

- Search Novell's Web site at support.novell.com for any known issues with devices and memory registration problems by querying for Register Memory.

Sage Advice *(continued)*

- Upgrade the motherboard to a model that allows NetWare to see all of the installed memory.

- NetWare will automatically detect up to 16MB of RAM if the system has only an ISA bus (you should *strongly* consider upgrading if this is the case); all available memory should be detected on EISA, MCA, and PCI based computers.

If you find that you need to use this command, keep in mind the following:

- You should place this command in the STARTUP.NCF file before the command(s) to load the disk driver(s) so that the memory will be available when mounting the SYS: volume. Otherwise you may get memory related errors.

- Be very careful to avoid memory conflicts with adapter cards that are not 32 bit.

As you can see from the preceding table, a lot has changed in this version of NetWare. More complete information is available by consulting the online documentation. There are many other NLMs and a few new Java-based applications as well. Before leaving this section, let's also review some useful server-based tools and scripts that can make your life a little (or in some cases, a lot) easier.

Tools and Useful Scripts

There are many useful tools that can help you manage your NetWare server. Many are available from Novell's own Web site (`support.novell.com`), as well as from Novell Consulting (`www.novell.com/coolsolutions/nds/subject_index.html`). The consulting Web site, in particular, has a goldmine of information. There is technical documentation, as well as applications to help you manage NDS, ZENworks, and other products. There are links to Novell's Web site and their products and even links to third-party tools. Speaking of third-party tools, there are many great applications that can help you in your quest to maximize the productivity and manageability of your network. One of the best places we have found for any Novell related utility is `www.novellshareware.com`. Let's look at some of the tools that we have found useful.

CRON: The Command Scheduler for the Console Prompt

CRON allows you to schedule events at the server. You can schedule any event to run whenever you want. An event is the execution of any command, NCF, NLM, and so on that can be entered at the console prompt. To install it, simply download and expand the program, copy CRON.NLM to the SYS:SYSTEM directory and the associated message file (CRON.MSG) to the appropriate NLS subdirectory (for example, in English this would be SYS:SYSTEM\NLS\4). To execute the utility, simply type CRON at the console prompt, and optionally add the maximum size for the log file it will create (the default is 5MB). Every event is logged, along with the time and date it occurred in SYS:ETC\ CRONLOG.

To schedule the events, simply edit the CRONTAB file. A few sample entries will help you understand the structure of the file; shown in Table 6.2.

Table 6.2   The Structure of CRONTAB

Minute	Hour	Day of Month	Month	Day of Week	Command
*	*	*	*	*	Memory
30	*	*	*	*	Volumes
0	7	*	*	1–5	Mount Accounting
0	18	*	*	1–5	Dismount Accounting
0	0	1	1	*	Broadcast Happy New Year!

Before we look at the entries in Table 6.2 , we will briefly define the parameters. Minute is a value from 0–59, Hour from 0–23, Day of Month from 0–31, and Month is from 1–12. The only one that is slightly tricky is Day of Week, where the values range from 0–6, and where 0 = Sunday. An asterisk (*) matches any value, and comments are denoted with the pound sign (#). Note from the table that ranges can be specified by using a dash (–) to separate the start and end values. If the range is not contiguous, separate the values with commas instead. With this information in mind, let's look at the examples in Table 6.2 to determine what each does.

The first entry runs the Memory command every minute, all day, every day. It is not very useful to do this, but it shows the effect of setting all of the time entries to asterisks. The second entry displays the mounted volumes and their attributes at half past every hour. The third and fourth entries mount and dismount the accounting volume at 7 A.M. and 6 P.M. (18:00), respectively, Monday to Friday. The final entry will send a message to all users who are attached or logged in to the server at midnight, January 1ˢᵗ, stating, "Happy New Year!"

As you can see from the examples, this is a very versatile and powerful tool. Let your imagination run wild with ways to automate routine processes for you.

> **Sage Advice**
>
> There are some processes you should do periodically to properly maintain your server. Here are some that we like to automate and the frequency that we prefer to do them:
>
> **DSREPAIR**   General maintenance of the NDS database; use with the –U switch to automate the program so no user intervention is required. We like to do this weekly in general. This should be done when server and NDS usage is minimal, such as on the weekend.
>
> **MIRROR STATUS**   Displays a list of all mirrored partitions and the mirroring status of each. We like to do this daily as a review of mirroring status and an early warning system when trouble starts to occur. This is really only useful when used with CONLOG and when the log is checked frequently.
>
> **MOUNT and DISMOUNT**   If you have volumes that are only used occasionally, you can schedule them to be MOUNTed and DISMOUNTed as needed.
>
> **REMOTE and UNLOAD REMOTE**   If you want to restrict remote access to your servers to certain times (such as when you're at work), you can schedule REMOTE.NLM to be loaded and unloaded as needed. This approach could be applied to RCONAG6 .NLM as well.

NetWare Operations

PART 2

NOTE   CRON is available at `support.novell.com/cgi-bin/search/patlstfind.cgi?2939440`.

Config and Config Reader: A Simple Method of Viewing and Documenting Server Configuration

Config and the associated tool, Config Reader, are very powerful yet simple-to-use tools to view the configuration and parameters associated with your server. To install the server portion, simply copy CONFIG.NLM to SYS:SYSTEM. When you load CONFIG (and you will need to use LOAD CONFIG or the console command of the same name will run) it will create a file called CONFIG.TXT in the SYS:SYSTEM directory that will be used by Config Reader. You will know that is has finished when you see the message on the console "Config Done." There are a couple of switches you can specify when you load it, including /D to also list the files in SYS:SYSTEM, and /S to add to the output the SET parameters. By default, if CONFIG.TXT exists, it will be overwritten. This behavior can be changed so that the contents are appended by using the /A switch. That's all there is to the server side.

On the client side, simply run SETUP.EXE. It runs on any Win32 platform (Windows 9x and NT). When installed, an icon will be added to your Start menu to run the program. When you run it, begin by opening the CONFIG.TXT file, created by CONFIG.NLM as described in the preceding paragraph. Through the product, you can view basic server information, such as the name of the server, the version of NetWare it is running, the amount of memory registered, the number of licenses installed, and so on. You can also view relevant configuration files, including CONFIG.SYS, AUTOEXEC.BAT, STARTUP.NCF, and AUTOEXEC.NCF. In addition, you can view information on your volumes, including size, free space, and purgable space and you can compare two servers to see how their configuration differs. Finally, and this is our favorite part, it can make recommendations on how to improve your configuration. Figure 6.1 shows that output on our server.

Figure 6.1   Config Reader's suggestions

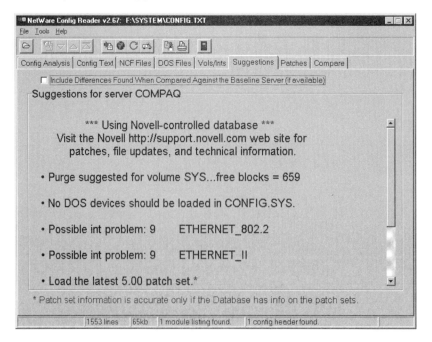

> **NOTE** The Config utility is available at support.novell.com/cgi-bin/search/
> patlstfind.cgi?2954578 and Config Reader is at support.novell.com/cgi-bin/
> search/patlstfind.cgi?2943247.

DSRIGHTs: A Utility to See What Rights One Object Has to Another Object and/or Effective Rights and Where They Come From

The DSRIGHTS utility allows you to view the rights that one object has to another, similar to NWAdmin's capabilities. The power of this utility, however, lies in its ability to show where the effective rights to an object come from. The output to this program will be similar to this (when the following command is entered at the console prompt: DSRIGHTS John Corp):

```
How John got rights to Corp.

                                             All
                                  Object Property

[Root]


Inherited Rights Filter          [SBCDR][SCRWA]


Inherits from above              [   ][    ]


Equivalent to [Public]           [ B  ]


Effective Rights                 [ B  ][   ]


EMA...


Inherited Rights Filter          [SBCDR][SCRWA]


Inherits from above              [ B  ][    ]
```

NetWare Operations
PART 2

```
Effective Rights                          [ B   ][    ]
```

```
NYC..

Inherited Rights Filter                   [SBCDR][SCRWA]

Inherits from above                       [ B   ][    ]

John                                      [ BCD ][ CR ]
```

```
Effective Rights                          [ BCD ][ CR ]
```

```
Corp.

Inherited Rights Filter                   [SBCDR][SCRWA]

Inherits from above                       [ BCD ][ CR ]

                                          _____
Effective Rights                          [ BCD ][ CR ]
```

```
Selected Property Rights

Login Script
    Equivalent to Corp.                        [ cR ]
                                               _____
    Effective Rights                           [ cR ]
```

```
Print Job Configuration
    Equivalent to Corp.                              [ cR  ]
                                           _____

    Effective Rights                                 [ cR  ]


WM:Registered Workstation
    Equivalent to Corp.                              [ CRWa]
                                           _____

    Effective Rights                                 [ CRWa]
```

As you can see from the preceding sample output, this is a very handy tool to view *where* rights come from. It is easy to find one object's effective rights to another, but finding out where those rights come from so they can be modified appropriately has been a challenge. We hope you find this as useful as we do.

> **NOTE**   DSRIGHTS is available at support.novell.com/cgi-bin/search/ patlstfind.cgi?2924751.

CPUTrace: A Graphical View of CPU Utilization Over Time

If you use Windows NT, you are probably familiar with Task Manager. With this program, you can view a few simple, but important statistics relating to memory and processor usage. While there isn't currently a product that does the same for your NetWare server at the server console, CPUTrace does offer some of the same functionality. It allows you to view CPU Utilization over time in a graphical format. We recommend that you use this tool as a screen saver, allowing you to view CPU utilization as you walk past the computer or see a brief history when you RCONSOLE into it. This is not to say that you shouldn't also use a password-protected screensaver, such as SCRSAVR.NLM. While it does provide a graphical view of CPU utilization, it does this with simple graphics that can be displayed on any monitor (in your choice of colors even!) and is visible as a normal text screen.

To install this product, simply download it and place CPUTRACE.NLM in the SYS: SYSTEM directory. As you can see in Figure 6.2, you can see the minimum, maximum, and average values for CPU utilization, as well as the current value.

Figure 6.2 The CPUTrace screen

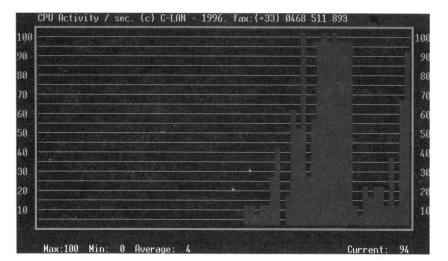

> **NOTE** CPUTrace is available at www.novellshareware.com in the NLMs area.

Enhanced Toolbox: A Broad Collection of Useful Tools

The Enhanced Toolbox program lets you do many of the management tasks that you normally do at the console prompt, as well as automating some tasks normally accomplished at the server. This utility comes with a strong recommendation on the Novell Consulting Web site, as well as from many administrators.

To install the utility, simply download and expand the downloaded file, then copy TOOLBOX.NLM to SYS:SYSTEM. When you load the NLM, it will inform you how to get help; simply type TOOLBOX for the main help screen or TOOLS for a list of available commands. The commands are listed in Table 6.3.

Asterisked (*) commands denote those commands that can be placed in the startup file.

> **NOTE** This Enhanced Toolbox is available at support.novell.com/cgi-bin/ search/patlstfind.cgi?2954421.

Table 6.3   Commands Available When TOOLBOX.NLM Is Loaded and the Tools Command Is Executed

Command	Purpose
AUTH*	This command allows you to display your connections (for toolbox utility purposes) to other servers (in Bindery mode) or trees (in NDS mode), much like the old WHOAMI command did. You can also log in or log out with this command. This information can also be saved and loaded for automation in NCF files.
BEEP*	Causes the computer to beep once (no /? Help available).
CHDIR (CD)*	Allows you to view or change the current directory and set the default path that will be prepended to all commands entered at a console prompt.
COPY (CP)	This utility lets you copy or move files between volumes and servers and between a DOS partition and the volumes on that server. It also allows you to copy/move subdirectories as well, meaning it acts more like XCOPY than COPY.
DEL (RM)	Allows you to delete files on any volume of any server, as well as files on the DOS partition of the local computer. It can optionally remove directories when all the files in a directory have been removed (when the /S switch is used), similar to DELTREE.
DELAY*	Gives you the ability to pause execution of commands at the console prompt while a utility initializes, for example. The delay is specified in milliseconds (default is 1,000) and once started, it can't be stopped. Very useful in NCF files.
DIR (LS)	Displays a directory for a given path (or the default path). Includes the file size (incorrect if it is greater than 2GB), date and time, and name in a format similar to the one used in Windows 9x or DOS (with the –N switch). Can be displayed in a wide format (like /W for DOS) with –W and totals only can be displayed with –T. Also works with the local server's DOS partition, although free space will not be reported.
ECHO*	Use this command to display a message to a user in a NCF file to tell the user what is happening, for example, "There will be a 10 second delay", "I am deleting all temporary files", and so on (no /? Help available).

NetWare
Operations

PART 2

Table 6.3 Commands Available When TOOLBOX.NLM Is Loaded and the Tools Command Is Executed *(continued)*

Command	Purpose
FLAG	Allows you to set file attributes on any file on any volume on any server, but not on DOS partitions. Similar to the Flag command on the workstation.
MAP	Create a named alias (such as system:, public:, server7data:, and so on) to refer to a specific file or directory on a volume on any server. The mappings can be saved and used later.
MKDIR (MD)	Utility to create a directory (or multiple directories if a path is specified and any of the directories listed don't already exist) on a volume on any server.
MOVE (MV)	Allows you to move files. Actually, it is an alias for COPY /MS.
PURGE	Allows you to purge (permanently remove) deleted files. All directories below the specified directory can be purged as well (when using the /A switch). Similar to the PURGE command on the workstation. Note: filenames must be specified using the DOS-name-space-name (in other words, the 8.3 name).
RMDIR (RD)	Will remove a directory, but only if it is empty (like the DOS command RD). To remove all directories below it, either remove them one at a time or use DEL with the /S switch as described above.
SHUTDOWN	This command allows you to shut down (and restart if desired) the server. With the /F switch, shutdown will be completed even if there are open files, otherwise an error message will be returned. You can avoid the confirmation prompt by using the /Q switch. If you are issuing the command on the server you want rebooted, you can also restart the server (with /R, the default in NetWare 5), and in the case of NetWare 5 only, reset (or reboot) the server (with /S) as well. Fortunately, you must be authenticated for this command to succeed. You need to have at least the Write right to the server's Object Trustees (ACL) property or you will get an error message.
STARTFILE	Allows you to edit the Startup file for TOOLBOX.NLM. This file, SYS:SYSTEM\TBOX.CFG, is full of comments on its proper usage.

Table 6.3   Commands Available When TOOLBOX.NLM Is Loaded and the Tools Command Is Executed   *(continued)*

Command	Purpose
CDV4 (only in startup file)	Allow the CD alias (described above) in NetWare 4.*x*, if CDROM.NLM is not loaded.
NONS (only in startup file)	Disable long name space support on a NetWare 5 server for those commands described above that will accept long filenames.
NSV4 (only in startup file)	Enable long name space on a NetWare 4.*x* server with Support Pack 6 for the commands listed here that support them; otherwise only DOS (8.3) names may be used.
TAPPLET	Allows you to start a Java-based applet; it is only available on the local server, and JAVA.NLM must already be loaded. Similar to the APPLET command.
TEXP	Allows you to quickly export (copy) the TOOLBOX.NLM and all associated configuration files to a specified location, usually another server. Note that while you can choose any directory to copy the files to, they must be placed in SYS:SYSTEM to work properly.
TJAVA	Allows you to start a Java-based application. Only available on the local server and JAVA.NLM must already be loaded. Similar to the JAVA command.
TLOAD	Allows you to load a NetWare module located on a specified server from the specified path.
TMODULES	Allows you to view the loaded NetWare modules on any server; a module name or wildcard (such as an *) can also be used to view only specified modules.
TRUN	Allows you to run an NCF file on any server.
TUNLOAD	Allows you to unload a NetWare module from a local or remote server.
TOOLBOX	Toolbox main help listing the two help commands available, toolbox (this command) and TOOLS.

NetWare Operations

PART 2

Table 6.3 Commands Available When TOOLBOX.NLM Is Loaded and the Tools Command Is Executed *(continued)*

Command	Purpose
TOOLS	Lists all of the Toolbox Commands.
TYPE (CAT)	Allows you to view one or more files on the screen; similar to the DOS command TYPE.
XTD,XTB,DTX	A simple hex, decimal and binary calculator that allows you to convert hex to decimal, hex to binary, and decimal to hex. Simply enter the appropriate command and the value you want converted, and when you hit ENTER, the answer is displayed.

MakeSU and Recover: Powerful Backdoors and a Hacker's Delight

MakeSU and Recover both do the same thing—create a user with Supervisor rights to your tree. If you have ever forgotten your Admin user's password, have had a former administrator leave without disclosing the password, had a disgruntled employee cause problems, and so on, you may find these utilities very helpful. On the other hand, if a hacker has either of these tools, he or she could cause lots of trouble as well.

WARNING Both MakeSU and Recover are *very* powerful and should be kept in a safe place, *never on any volume on any server.*

Both of these utilities sound like a security nightmare, correct? Both utilities do offer some level of security, which, when combined with your standard security measures, allows you to rest a little easier. The primary security measure that both offer is linking the registered product to a specific tree name. MakeSU also allows the registered product to only be run from a floppy disk. The standard security measures that should be in place for any server include securing physical access to the server and limiting or disallowing remote access to the server (for example, by RCONSOLE).

Although there are many similarities between them, let's look at each utility individually.

MakeSU This utility is easy to use. Simply download MAKESU-D.ZIP, expand it, and sample the demo version. The demo version creates a user called Demo2 in the Organization DreamLAN2. You must have already created the Organization DreamLAN2. This user will be given full rights to [Root], just like the full product, and a password will be assigned (although you will not be told what the password is). With the full version you will be able to create a user with any name you desire. As for passwords, a password is required for the utility to run and you will be given the password to the user you create. The full version also affords you the ability to assign supervisory rights at any point in the tree, not just at the [Root]. You can register this product by going to DreamLAN's Web site at www.dreamlan.com/order1a.htm and completing the order form. The cost is $99. The output of the demo version (MAKESU-D.NLM) is shown in Figure 6.3.

Figure 6.3   The output of MAKESU-D.NLM

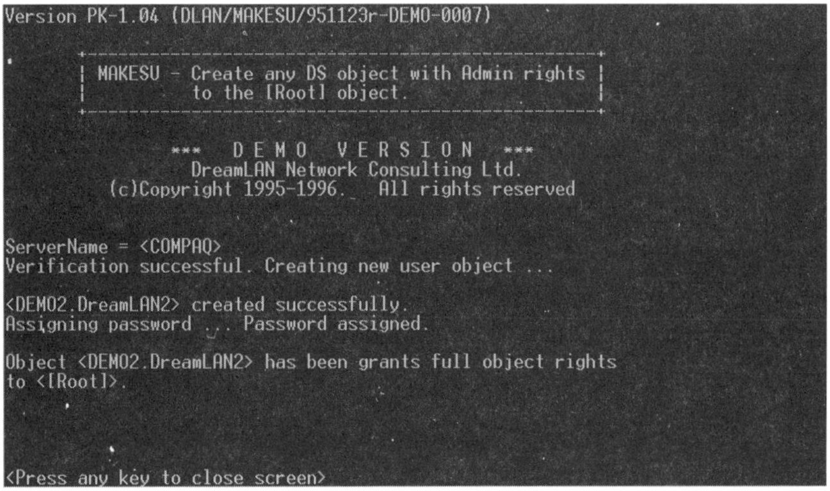

```
Version PK-1.04 (DLAN/MAKESU/951123r-DEMO-0007)

+------------------------------------------------------+
| MAKESU - Create any DS object with Admin rights |
|             to the [Root] object.                    |
+------------------------------------------------------+

           ***  D E M O   V E R S I O N  ***
              DreamLAN Network Consulting Ltd.
        (c)Copyright 1995-1996.   All rights reserved


ServerName = <COMPAQ>
Verification successful. Creating new user object ...

<DEMO2.DreamLAN2> created successfully.
Assigning password ... Password assigned.

Object <DEMO2.DreamLAN2> has been grants full object rights
to <[Root]>.


<Press any key to close screen>
```

NOTE   This product is by DreamLAN Network Consulting, which offers many great NDS-related products that you may find useful. Another DreamLAN-product, NDSDir, is also discussed in a later section of this chapter. Both products are part of their NDS utility suite called NDS ToolKit ($750). The latest information on their products may be obtained from www.dreamlan.com.

Recover   The second utility, Recover, is easy to use as well. Simply download RECOVER1.ZIP, expand it, and try out the demo version. The demo version allows you to create a user, but that user will be restricted to browse rights only. To get supervisor rights, you will need to either register online or by mail, e-mail, fax, or phone as described in the FORM.TXT file that comes as part of the RECOVER1.ZIP download. The registration fee is currently $75. With the registered version, you will be able to create a user with supervisory rights to any object you desire. Loading the demo version of RECOVER.NLM produces the output shown in Figure 6.4.

Figure 6.4   The output of RECOVER.NLM

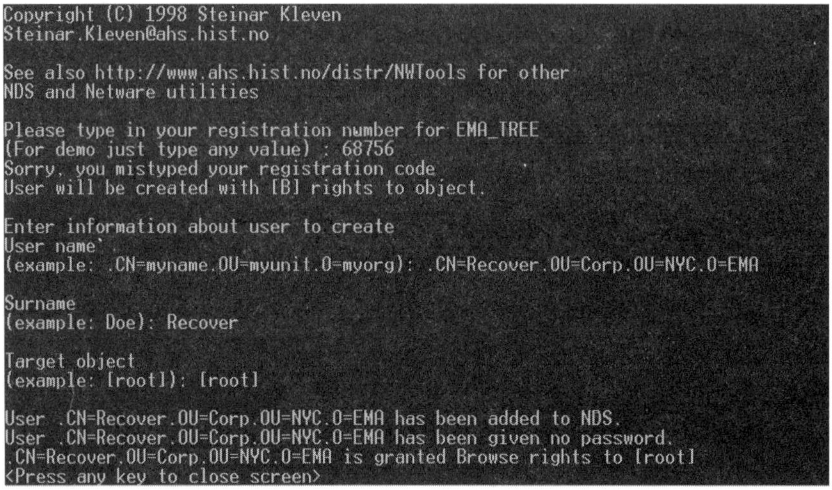

NOTE   These two utilities are both available at www.novellshareware.com (in the NLMs area).

NDSDir: A Tool to View the Hidden Components of NDS and Keep Track of Their Sizes

NDSDir allows you to view the files that make up the NDS database and see the size of each. These files are stored in a normally inaccessible directory named SYS:_NETWARE. One quirk of this tool is that it can't be run from a volume on the server, only from a floppy disk. You can also copy these files to a standard directory that can be accessed normally, and you could easily backup the NDS database without software that specifically knows how to back it up. If you choose to back up NDS with this method, be sure to read the warning at the end of this section.

To use this product, simply copy NDSDIR.NLM and NDSDIR.LIC to a floppy, and then at a console prompt execute NDSDIR.NLM (remember to include the proper path to the floppy). Note that without the NDSDIR.LIC file, the program will only run in demo mode. In demo mode, you are unable to sort the output and you can't use any of the command line options described in Table 6.4, but the –list switch, the default, is always used. To license this product, go to DreamLAN's Web site at www.dreamlan.com/order1a.htm and complete the form. The cost of this product is currently $99.

The output of the program will be similar to that seen in Figure 6.5, although only the first (of possibly many) screens is shown. In addition, the total number of files is listed on the last screen.

Figure 6.5 The first screen of the output of NDSDIR.NLM

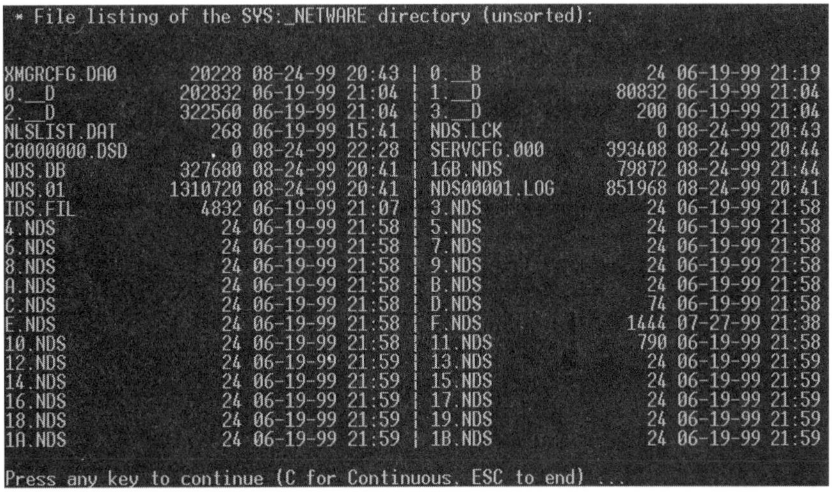

```
* File listing of the SYS:_NETWARE directory (unsorted):

XMGRCFG.DA0     20228 08-24-99 20:43 | 0._B             24 06-19-99 21:19
0._D           202832 06-19-99 21:04 | 1._D          80832 06-19-99 21:04
2._D           322560 06-19-99 21:04 | 3._D            200 06-19-99 21:04
NLSLIST.DAT       268 06-19-99 15:41 | NDS.LCK           0 08-24-99 20:43
C0000000.DSD        0 08-24-99 22:28 | SERVCFG.000  393408 08-24-99 20:44
NDS.DB         327680 08-24-99 20:41 | 16B.NDS       79872 08-24-99 21:44
NDS.01        1310720 08-24-99 20:41 | NDS00001.LOG 851968 08-24-99 20:41
IDS.FIL          4832 06-19-99 21:07 | 3.NDS            24 06-19-99 21:58
4.NDS              24 06-19-99 21:58 | 5.NDS            24 06-19-99 21:58
6.NDS              24 06-19-99 21:58 | 7.NDS            24 06-19-99 21:58
8.NDS              24 06-19-99 21:58 | 9.NDS            24 06-19-99 21:58
A.NDS              24 06-19-99 21:58 | B.NDS            24 06-19-99 21:58
C.NDS              24 06-19-99 21:58 | D.NDS            74 06-19-99 21:58
E.NDS              24 06-19-99 21:58 | F.NDS          1444 07-27-99 21:38
10.NDS             24 06-19-99 21:58 | 11.NDS          790 06-19-99 21:58
12.NDS             24 06-19-99 21:59 | 13.NDS           24 06-19-99 21:59
14.NDS             24 06-19-99 21:59 | 15.NDS           24 06-19-99 21:59
16.NDS             24 06-19-99 21:59 | 17.NDS           24 06-19-99 21:59
18.NDS             24 06-19-99 21:59 | 19.NDS           24 06-19-99 21:59
1A.NDS             24 06-19-99 21:59 | 1B.NDS           24 06-19-99 21:59

Press any key to continue (C for Continuous, ESC to end) ...
```

The available switches and their functions are listed in Table 6.4.

Table 6.4 Switches Available with NDSDIR.NLM

Switch	Purpose
LIST	The default switch, if none is specified. Displays the name, size, and date and time of each file to the screen in a two-column format. The output is sorted alphabetically by filename unless the -NOSORT switch (see "NoSort switch" in this table) is used. Note that the sorted list is limited to 1,000 files.
REPORT	This switch causes the list of files to be sent to a file instead of to the screen. The information that will be listed includes the following: name, size, date and time, and file attributes. Unlike the output generated by the list switch, the output is in a single column format. By default, this report will be stored in a file called NDSDIR.LST and will be stored in the root of SYS:. The file name and location can be changed with the -V and -F switches (described later in this list). If the file already exists, the output of this command will be appended to the existing contents.

NetWare
Operations

PART 2

Table 6.4 Switches Available with NDSDIR.NLM *(continued)*

Switch	Purpose
NOSORT	Displays the report or list output in the order they actually exist in the directory. There is no limit to the number of files that can be displayed with this switch.
V	Allows you to enter the volume that you want the report output written to; SYS: is the default.
F	File name for use with other switches (see REPORT, GET, PUT, and ZAP). The path may also be specified here; if not specified the root directory is assumed. If the file already exists, the new data will be appended.
GET	This switch will copy the contents of the SYS:_NETWARE directory to SYS:DREAMLAN. By default, all files in the directory will be copied, but when the -F switch is used, individual files (or groups of files when wildcards are used) may be specified. Note that files related to auditing (NET$AUDT.*) will *not* be copied.
PUT	This switch is the opposite of the Get switch. It will copy files *from* SYS:DREAMLAN *to* SYS:_NETWARE. By default all files will be copied, but individual files (or groups of files when wildcards are used) can be specified by using the -F switch. *WARNING: This will overwrite all of your NDS information*. Be very careful when using this switch. To provide a measure of security with this switch, you will need to enter the authentication code that will be sent to you when you purchase the product.
ZAP	This is a feature not documented in help, but listed with the documentation that comes with the product. *WARNING: This switch will delete any files specified with the -F switch (except the *.NDS files)*. You should always back up NDS (with GET) before using this switch! The -F switch is mandatory. Files associated with auditing (NET$AUDT.*) can not be deleted. As with the PUT switch, you will need to enter your authentication code for this command to work.

NOTE   Whenever you use the Get, Put, or Zap switch, the NDSDIR.LOG file is updated. This file is always located in the root of SYS:, and the new information will always be appended to the file.

Now that you have an idea as to what NDSDir can do, we want to go into more detail on the use of Get, Put, and Zap. Before we can do so, however, you need a brief explanation of the types of files that are stored in this directory. Table 6.5 lists that information for you and Figures 6.6 and 6.7 graphically show the relationships between the files.

Table 6.5   NDS-Related Files and the Purpose of Each

NetWare Version	File name or Type	Purpose
NetWare 4	PARTIO.NDS	Contains information on NDS partitions (one record per partition), including when to next replicate changes with the other replicas in the replica ring. High priority changes (those related to security, such as password changes, deleting a user or a user from a group) occur immediately. Medium priority (such as adding a user or adding a user to a group) occur two minutes from the change (unless the regularly scheduled replication is less than two minutes away), and the default is every 30 minutes.
	ENTRY.NDS	Contains information on each object stored locally (one record per object), including the partition it belongs to, the first child object (if a container object), first NDS attribute (the rest are stored in VALUE.NDS), the object class (such as user or group) the object is based on, and the number of subordinate objects (leaf objects always have this set to 0; for container objects it is the number of objects in the container).

Table 6.5 NDS-Related Files and the Purpose of Each *(continued)*

NetWare Version	File name or Type	Purpose
	VALUE.NDS	Contains information on each attribute of each object in the ENTRY.NDS database (except the first). Note that records are only created for attributes if a value is set, so that values that may not be set (such as mailing address or location) do not take up space in the database. However, all mandatory attributes always have a value set (though the system may use default or system-generated values for some attributes). Information included here is the attribute ID, value of the attribute, a link to the next value (for multi-valued properties such as group membership), a link to the next attribute (for the same object—to make finding all of an object's values quicker), and a timestamp (for replication. If a medium or high priority change is made as described above, it will also modify the partition replication schedule as described. If an attribute's value is too large to fit in one record, the overflow data is stored in BLOCK.NDS.
	BLOCK.NDS	As all records are fixed-length records in all NDS databases, some attributes may have values too large to fit in one record in the VALUE.NDS database (such as a long description). In such a case, the overflow data is stored here in one or more records, as needed.
	*.000	These files, known as Stream files, store information for attributes that are typically very long, such as login scripts and print job configurations. It is inefficient to use many records in the BLOCK.NDS database, therefore separate files are used that simply link to the associated object and are as long as necessary.
	MLS.*	Licensing information files; one per license installed. There is no equivalent in NetWare 5 because licenses are stored in NDS just like any other object.

Table 6.5   NDS-Related Files and the Purpose of Each *(continued)*

NetWare Version	File name or Type	Purpose
NetWare 5	0.NDS	Corresponds to PARTIO.NDS.
	1.NDS	Corresponds to ENTRY.NDS.
	2.NDS	Corresponds to VALUE.NDS.
	3.NDS	Corresponds to BLOCK.NDS.
	4.NDS	Stores NetWare 5–specific information, such as licensing objects, SLP-related objects, and so on.
	*.000	Correspond to the *.000 files mentioned above.
NetWare 5 with NDS 8	NDS.DB	This file contains the overall control information for the NDS database, as well as the roll-back log, which is used to undo changes that don't get properly completed (due to problems such as power or hardware failures).
	NDS*.LOG	This file keeps track of transactions that have not yet been completed and written to the NDS.0? files (described next). Data is first written to this file and then to the appropriate NDS database, so this type of log file is known as a "roll-forward" file, where changes can be applied after a failure with no data loss.
	NDS.01, NDS.02, and so on	Contains all of the information formerly stored in PARTIO.NDS, ENTRY.NDS, VALUE.NDS, and BLOCK.NDS, as well as indexes on all of the data. Each file has a maximum size of 2GB, so when one fills, a new file with the next number is created (for example NDS.01 is followed by NDS.02). NDS.01 has some special responsibilities as well in maintaining some indexes that NDS needs to maximize performance.
	*.NDS	Corresponds to the preceding *.000 files.

NetWare Operations

PART 2

Figure 6.6 Relationship of NDS files in NetWare 4 and 5 (pre-NDS 8), using the NetWare 4 file names

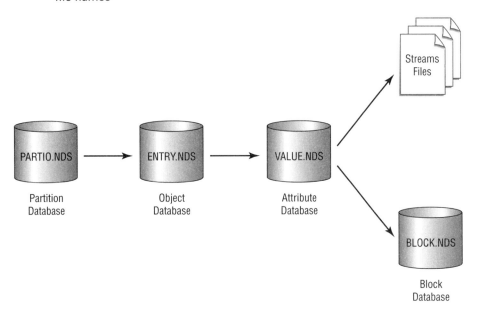

Figure 6.7 Relationship of NDS files in NDS 8

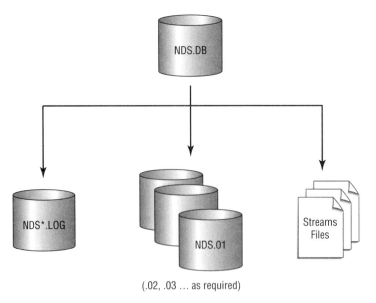

More information about the files that make up the NDS database and the purpose of each is beyond the scope of this chapter, but can be obtained from Novell. Specifically, Novell provides Advanced Training Videos, BrainShare and TechShare conferences, and the best source for advanced NDS information, LogicSource for NDS. More information on NDS can also be found in Chapters 11 and 15 of this book.

We know that the above information was quite a detour, but it is necessary to understand the output of NDSDir. Let's turn our attention now back to NDSDir. NDSDir's Get and Put switches are not intended as a substitute for a good backup program. They are designed to allow you to make simple backups in a test environment where things are tried, and then you can quickly reset to a known configuration. These commands can also be of use in a training environment.

The Get switch is not designed to backup a multi-server NDS tree. You can back up individual servers this way, but restoring one (with the Put switch) is likely to cause corruption of the NDS database. Use the standard NDS tools and a good backup program instead.

> **WARNING** The primary purpose of this product is to view the files used by NDS and the backup files created by DSREPAIR. You should not, unless you are highly trained and absolutely sure of what you are doing, use the Put switch or *irrevocable damage* could result to your NDS tree.

> **NOTE** NDSDir is available at www.novellshareware.com (in the NLMs area).

StuffKey: A Simple Method to Automate Those Pesky Interactive Programs

StuffKey allows you to automate programs that require manual intervention at the server. For example, you may want to automate running DSREPAIR.NLM to repair the local database and then exit when it finishes using any option but Unattended full repair (which, while you can still use it, can also be accomplished with the –U switch). Another useful application of this program is to capture data that a screen creates to a file—the output of NDSDir to document changes over time, for example. To install the program, simply copy STUFFKEY.NLM to SYS:SYSTEM (if you have versions of NetWare other than version 5, refer to the documentation that comes with the NLM for required updates). In this section, we will give two examples of how you can use this utility. In the first, we will look at how to use StuffKey to automate the DSREPAIR process and in the second how to capture the output of NDSDir.

To load StuffKey, simply type **STUFFKEY**, optionally followed by a command file or /?, at the server console. Running STUFFKEY.NLM by itself or with the /? Switch will display help on its use. The command file listed here will automate the DSREPAIR process (lines that begin with a # are comments and this documentation should be typed with the file as a reference for future modifications):

```
#This example will load DSREPAIR and do an automated repair of
#the local database. Console commands and Stuff Key tags are
#listed in UPPER CASE, Stuff Key commands in Proper Case, and
#other key strokes are in lower case.
#Written by Bryan Amundson (Author of StuffKey). This file
#is included with the help file.
#Modified 6/21/99 by John Hales to support the DSREPAIR
#interface that comes with NDS 8, (DS 8.11, DSREPAIR 6.28),
#and assumes that it will be used with NetWare 5
#-----------------------------------------------------------
#The only known screen is the console screen, so we will start
#there and then load DSREPAIR. If it is already loaded, an
#error would be generated, so we will begin by unloading it.
<Screen=System Console>
UNLOAD DSREPAIR<CR>
DSREPAIR<CR>
#Depending on the activity on the server, it may take a few
#seconds to load, so we will wait until DSREPAIR is loaded,
#and then make it the active screen.
<WaitFor Screen=Dsrepair Status Screen>
#From the "Available Options" menu choose "Advanced options
#menu" and press Enter (by specifying the <CR> tag)
adv<CR>
#Choose "Repair local DS database" and press Enter
rep<CR>
#Choose the "Exit automatically upon completion" choice and
#set it to Yes, then press Enter. Making that choice is done
```

```
#by pressing the down arrow a number of times that varies
#depending on the version of DSREPAIR you are using. To repeat
#a keystroke, type the number of times before the tag. The tag
#for pressing the down arrow is DN, and for pressing the
#function key F10 is <F10>
<11DN>
y<CR>
<F10>
#When the process has completed, dsrepair will automatically
#exit and you will be left at the console prompt.
```

Note that when typing these commands that you must be very careful to place spaces where they are required and leave them out where they shouldn't be. Type carefully! You should also plan on spending some time debugging your scripts. We have found that, unless they are short, you should write them a little at a time, debugging as you go. To use this command file, create a text file with any name you like and save it on the server (SYS:SYSTEM is preferable because they are console commands and we don't want them generally available). If you named it REPAIR.TXT and saved it in SYS:SYSTEM, you would execute it by going to a console prompt and typing STUFFKEY SYS:SYSTEM\ REPAIR.TXT. Note that the path to the command file is required.

For the second example, we will look at how NDSDir data can be saved to a file for later analysis. We will assume that you have already installed the demo version of NDSDIR.NLM (the full version lets you write the output to a file anyway) and know how it works. The command file is listed here:

```
#This example will load NDSDir and display the NDS database
#files, which will also be copied to the file
#SYS:SYSTEM\NDSDIR.TXT. If the file already exists, the new
#data will be appended, making for a simple method of
#archiving changes. Console commands and Stuff Key tags are
#listed in UPPER CASE, Stuff Key commands iin Proper Case, and
#other key strokes are in lower case.
#Written by John Hales 6/22/99
#This file is designed to be used with NetWare 5
#----------------------------------------------------------
```

```
#The only known screen is the console screen, so we will start
#there.
<Screen=System Console>
#Now we will initialize the log file, SYS:SYSTEM\NDSDIR.TXT.
<Log Append=SYS:SYSTEM\NDSDIR.TXT>
#Now we need to load NDSDir, which must be loaded from a
#floppy drive. We will assume that the A: drive is being used.
#If it is already loaded, an error will be generated, but that
#is not likely as this is a special purpose utility. After it
#is loaded, we will need to make that screen the active
#screen.
LOAD A:NDSDIR<CR>
<Screen=NDS Toolkit - NDSDir>
#The opening screen is an informational screen, listing the
#server name, NDS tree name, and copyright information. Since
#we are storing the output on the local server, there is no
#need to keep this screen, so well will press any key to give
#us the first real screen of output. Any key can be pressed,
#but I chose to use Enter because it shows up better in this
#file.
<CR>
#Now that the first real screen is displayed, we will dump it
#to a text file, press any key (again, I have chose Enter for
#ease of display in this file), dump the new screen again, and
#so on, until the process is completed. Depending on how mnany
#objects you have in your directory, there may be multiple
#screens, you may need to modify the number of Dump commands
#followed by Enters until the process is complete. If you have
#too many, you will be getting captures of the System Console,
#which you can edit out of the resulting text file.
<Dump>
```

```
<CR>

<Dump>

<CR>

<Dump>

<CR>

<Dump>

<CR>

<Dump>

#At this point all screens have been captured, so well will

#press any key one more time to end the utility.

<CR>
```

Just as with the first example, all you need to do to use this command file is to create a text file with any name you like and save it on the server (we prefer to save it in SYS:SYSTEM as described previously). If you named it NDSINFO.TXT and saved it in SYS:SYSTEM, you would execute it by going to a console prompt and typing **STUFFKEY SYS:SYSTEM\ NDSINFO.TXT**. Note that the path to the command file is required. As NDSDir was designed to write information to the screen and StuffKey is imperfect, we sometimes lost a couple of files (though not always—it depended on how full the last screen was). We found that the output was not displayed very well with Notepad, but looked very good with WordPad. The output of this command is shown next (We left out several of the screens in the middle to reduce the output):

```
[John"]''--Screen: "NDS TOOLKIT - NDSDIR" dumped 06/22/1999 11:42:26

---------------------------------------------------------------------------
------

NDS Tree name = <EMA_TREE>

<Press any key to continue>
 * File listing of the SYS:_NETWARE directory (unsorted):

XMGRCFG.DA0     20228 06-22-99 10:31 | 0.__B           24 06-19-99 21:19

0.__D          202832 06-19-99 21:04 | 1.__D        80832 06-19-99 21:04

2.__D          322560 06-19-99 21:04 | 3.__D          200 06-19-99 21:04

NLSLIST.DAT       268 06-19-99 15:41 | SERVHAND.DAT     4 06-22-99 10:46

CONNHAND.DAT    24000 06-22-99 10:46 | SERVCFG.000 393408 06-22-99 10:33
```

```
NDS.DB          327680 06-21-99 08:34 | NDS.LCK             0 06-22-99 10:31

NDS.01          983040 06-21-99 08:34 | NDS00001.LOG   851968 06-21-99 08:34

IDS.FIL           4832 06-19-99 21:07 | 3.NDS              24 06-19-99 21:58

4.NDS               24 06-19-99 21:58 | 5.NDS              24 06-19-99 21:58

6.NDS               24 06-19-99 21:58 | 7.NDS              24 06-19-99 21:58

8.NDS               24 06-19-99 21:58 | 9.NDS              24 06-19-99 21:58

A.NDS               24 06-19-99 21:58 | B.NDS              24 06-19-99 21:58

C.NDS               24 06-19-99 21:58 | D.NDS              74 06-19-99 21:58

E.NDS               24 06-19-99 21:58 | F.NDS               0 06-19-99 21:58

10.NDS              24 06-19-99 21:58 | 11.NDS            790 06-19-99 21:58

12.NDS              24 06-19-99 21:59 | 13.NDS             24 06-19-99 21:59


-------------------------------------------------------------------


Screen: "NDS TOOLKIT - NDSDIR" dumped 06/22/1999 11:42:26
-------------------------------------------------------------------

4.NDS               24 06-19-99 21:58 | 5.NDS              24 06-19-99 21:58

6.NDS               24 06-19-99 21:58 | 7.NDS              24 06-19-99 21:58


-------------------------------------------------------------------


Screen: "NDS TOOLKIT - NDSDIR" dumped 06/22/1999 11:42:27
-------------------------------------------------------------------

A2.NDS              83 06-19-99 21:59 | A3.NDS             24 06-19-99 21:59

A4.NDS               0 06-19-99 21:59 | A5.NDS             24 06-19-99 21:59


A6.NDS             766 06-19-99 21:59 | A7.NDS           2664 06-19-99 21:59

A8.NDS              24 06-19-99 21:59 | A9.NDS            129 06-19-99 21:59

AA.NDS              24 06-19-99 21:59 | AB.NDS             24 06-19-99 21:59

AC.NDS              24 06-19-99 21:59 | AD.NDS             24 06-19-99 21:59
```

AE.NDS	24 06-19-99 21:59	AF.NDS	1696 06-19-99 21:59
B0.NDS	24 06-19-99 21:59	B1.NDS	137 06-19-99 21:59
B2.NDS	24 06-19-99 21:59	B3.ND	0 06-19-99 21:59
B4.NDS	44 06-19-99 21:59	B5.NDS	766 06-19-99 21:59
B6.NDS	24 06-19-99 21:59	B7.NDS	24 06-19-99 21:59
B8.NDS	344 06-19-99 21:59	B9.NDS	24 06-19-99 21:59
BA.NDS	24 06-19-99 21:59	BB.NDS	24 06-19-99 21:59
BC.NDS	24 06-19-99 21:59	BD.NDS	24 06-19-99 21:59
BE.NDS	752 06-19-99 21:59	BF.NDS	24 06-19-99 21:59
C0.NDS	137 06-19-99 21:59	C1.NDS	24 06-19-99 21:59
C2.NDS	0 06-19-99 21:59	C3.NDS	24 06-19-99 21:59
C4.NDS	5702 06-19-99 21:59	C5.NDS	527 06-19-99 21:59
C6.NDS	24 06-19-99 21:59	C7.NDS	540 06-19-99 21:59
C8.NDS	24 06-19-99 21:59	C9.NDS	24 06-19-99 21:59
CA.NDS	24 06-19-99 21:59	CB.NDS	24 06-19-99 21:59
CC.NDS	24 06-19-99 21:59	CD.NDS	1367 06-19-99 21:59
CE.NDS	24 06-19-99 21:59	CF.NDS	137 06-19-99 21:59

We have found this to be a very handy utility for automating many things on the server. We think you will find it useful as well. Best of all, it's free!

> **NOTE** StuffKey is available at support.novell.com/cgi-bin/search/patlstfind.cgi?2948742

ConsoleOne

Many readers may not be familiar with ConsoleOne. ConsoleOne is Novell's replacement for NWAdmin and many of their other administration tools, even across product lines. For those of you familiar with Microsoft's MMC (Microsoft Management Console) for Windows 2000, the concept is similar: single point administration for all network services across all servers using a single tool. All future development of administrative tools will be in ConsoleOne, so it is a good time to become acquainted with it. While NWAdmin is currently supported and can do most administrative tasks, those tasks are being migrated to ConsoleOne as well.

Currently, there are two "versions" of the tool, one for use at the server (with SP 3 or later installed) and the client, and the latest offering—one for use within a Web browser. We will look at each in turn, although we will not focus on them in detail. Chapter 10 deals with administrative tasks, which is where this tool will be covered more completely. We will discuss ConsoleOne version 1.2B in this section.

NOTE ConsoleOne is no longer automatically updated with the NetWare 5 Support Packs or with other Novell products because it is the common administrative tool for many products. Instead you download it as an individual product. It can be downloaded from www.novell.com/download#nds.

ConsoleOne on the Server

At the server, there can be two versions of ConsoleOne. The first is the one that comes with NetWare 5 and must be used if SP3 or later hasn't been installed. This is the original version of the tool and the most limited. If you do use this version of the tool, however, you can accomplish many tasks that were difficult or impossible to do at the server. These tasks include: viewing the files and directories on the server and displaying the contents of text files; using RCONSOLEJ to remotely view and administer other servers; and viewing and modifying NDS objects. You will be required to log in to the server to access some functions, such as viewing and managing the NDS tree.

You don't have the ability to manage all objects, nor even all of the properties of the objects, but even with these limitations there is more manageability than we have ever had at the server. (You can always, however, manage the NDS trustees with this tool.) The main objects that you can create and manage include Users, Groups, Organizations, and Organizational Units. There are also a few Java demo applets, and some shortcuts to folders that are available to you, but as we mentioned, it is not a very powerful, nor widely used tool. In fact, this tool on the server is seen more as a "proof of concept" that administration can be done at the server than as a serious tool for actually doing it.

The second version can be downloaded from Novell's Web site and can be used once SP3 or higher is installed. This tool offers the same capabilities available at the workstation (see the following section, "ConsoleOne at the Workstation"). You will need to log in before you can do anything; this is a great security-related improvement in version 1.2B over the original version. This is reason enough to upgrade.

TIP   Either version of ConsoleOne at the server is really only useful if you are physically at the server, (as graphical screens can't be viewed remotely) which is rarely done. In our experience, very few people do any administration at the server. It is, however, a "checkbox" item when comparing NetWare with NT. Now administration can be done on either system at the server for that system itself.

ConsoleOne at the Workstation

ConsoleOne at the Workstation is the most powerful of the ConsoleOne family of tools. This tool is designed to be run on a Windows 9*x* or NT computer (or the server, as described in the previous section) and should eventually replace NWAdmin. The latest version of this tool is 1.2B. This tool will be discussed in detail in Chapter 10, but a brief overview of new features and requirements will be presented here.

NOTE   The primary source of documentation for this tool is Novell's Web site. Documentation for most of Novell's current products is available at www.novell .com/documentation.

You can do many new tasks with this version of the tool, including the following:

- Browse very large containers more efficiently (it only downloads the objects you will see on the current screen instead of all objects in the container), making screen refreshes faster, saving RAM, and providing access to very large containers (those with millions of objects or more).

- Create, modify, and delete any kind of NDS object, as well as work with multiple objects.

- Use template objects to control the creation of new users.

- Control NDS rights and IRFs (Inherited Rights Filters). Note that Object rights are accessed under the Property rights, and are called Entry Rights.

- Control File system information, including rights and attributes.

The minimum system requirements for using this tool are as follows:

- At the server:
  - NetWare 5
  - NDS 8
  - Support Pack 2 or higher (3 or higher for use of the tool at the server)

- At the workstation:
  - Windows 9*x* or NT
  - 64MB RAM—more will increase performance (128MB if you want to use it at the server)
  - Swapfile at least the amount of RAM in size
  - 200MHz or faster processor
  - Java 1.1.7 (included with the product for use at the workstation and SP3 for use at the server)
  - The Novell Client (at the workstation only)

As you can see, the requirements are somewhat high, but certainly not exotic for most environments.

> **NOTE** ConsoleOne 1.2 comes as part of NDS 8, as well as individually. You will want to download ConsoleOne 1.2B for the greatest functionality. They are available at `www.novell.com/download/#NDS` (for NDS 8) and `www.novell.com/download/#Management` (for ConsoleOne 1.2B only).

ConsoleOne over the Web

The latest addition to the ConsoleOne family is ConsoleOne Web Edition. This tool lets you manage your NDS tree with any Web browser, even over the Internet. However, you will want to have SSL enabled if you choose to do so. Like the original version of the server product, this is not a full-featured product but rather a starter product—one that will let you accomplish the basic tasks necessary to manage your tree. Specifically, this tool is user focused, allowing you to only manage users; other objects must be managed with other tools.

With this tool, you can:

- Create and delete users
- Manage the properties located on the identification tab for users (Yeah, we know, big deal, except you can get the person's phone number, e-mail address, and so on if you need to contact them.)
- Disable the account
- Reset an account that has been locked out by intruder detection
- Modify the groups a user belongs to
- Change a user's password

At this point, those are all of the tasks that can be done. It is a simple tool, but one that allows you to reset the backup operators password at 2 A.M. from home. You may also find this to be a useful tool to give to frontline help-desk personnel so that they can do basic tasks with users without having to learn the complexity of NWAdmin or the workstation version of ConsoleOne.

The minimum requirements for using this tool are as follows:

- At the server:
  - NetWare 5
  - NDS 8
  - Support Pack 2 or higher
  - Netscape Fastrack (included on the Operating System CD) or Enterprise (a free download from Novell's Web site) Web server installed (We recommend you upgrade to the Enterprise edition, as all future work and development will be on it.)
- At the workstation:
  - Netscape Navigator 4 or higher OR
  - Internet Explorer 4 or higher

There will be a little more information on this tool in Chapter 10.

NOTE ConsoleOne Web Edition can be obtained from Novell's Web site at www.novell.com/download/#Management.

NWCONFIG

As you may or may not be aware, NWCONFIG replaces INSTALL used in earlier versions of NetWare. The underlying program, however, has changed only a little from earlier versions. You can still do some basic tasks with this tool, and in some cases you will need to use it, but some tasks can also be performed through the GUI interface. The main menu is shown in Figure 6.8.

Figure 6.8   The main menu for NWCONFIG.NLM

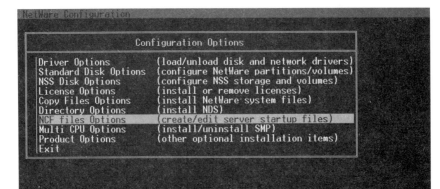

For those of you familiar with previous versions of NetWare, this looks pretty familiar. With this tool you can do many of the basic configuration items that must be completed for NetWare to work properly. We will break the menu choices into several categories for this section and discuss the choices available in each.

First, there are the hardware-related options. From here you can choose Driver Options to load and unload disk and network drivers, including automatically detecting new hardware in these two categories. This is useful when you change hardware to automatically determine which drivers are needed. You can also control how your system will use (or not use) multiple CPUs (if they are installed). This is done by choosing Multi CPU Options. You will be given the chance to select a Platform Support Module (PSM) which tells NetWare how to utilize multiple CPUs for your specific hardware, and install SMP (Symmetric Multi Processing) automatically as well. You can also uninstall PSMs here as well.

Second, there are the volume and disk options (not disk *driver* options; they are in the Driver Options menu just described). There are two menu choices here, Standard Disk Options for standard (also called traditional) NetWare volumes, and NSS Disk Options for managing NSS volumes. The options for standard volumes include scanning for new devices (such as when a new hard drive is added to the system), mirroring options, and configuring some properties of traditional volumes, such as enabling compression or suballocation or changing the size of the volume. For NSS volumes, you can configure NSS storage options and volume options, create and delete existing volumes, and modify parameters associated with an NSS volume (such as increasing its size or renaming it).

Third, you can do basic setup tasks like modify licensing, copy NetWare files, and install, remove, and maintain NDS. The first choice in this category, License Options, allows you to install and remove licenses, as well as to set up NLS (this should be done automatically as part of the normal setup procedure; it is here for those who had trouble with the standard installation routine). For an in-depth discussion of licensing installation issues, see Chapter 2. The second choice in this category, Copy Files Options, allows you to copy files to the server. Again, this is basically for redundancy if you had trouble with the standard installation procedure. Under normal circumstances, you will not need to use this option. The third choice in this group, Directory Options, is rarely used. It allows you to remove NDS if it is hopelessly corrupt, reinstall NDS back on the server after it has been removed, upgrade NetWare 3 bindery information into NDS, and add mounted volumes into NDS (in other words, create Volume objects). New in NetWare 5 is the ability to back up NDS and then restore it after a hardware failure or upgrade. Be very careful with this set of options, especially if you only have one server, as you will destroy *all NDS data* if you remove NDS. You will be warned several times of the implications of doing so before the change is finally made.

Fourth are the configuration options. There are two options in this category: NCF Files Options and Product Options. NCF Files Options let you create and edit the two most important configuration files for NetWare, STARTUP.NCF and AUTOEXEC.NCF. Product Options allow you to view, configure, and remove installed products, as well as install some other products. Some products can only be installed by choosing Install from the Novell menu in the GUI, others can only be installed through Product Options; check your product's documentation for which method to use. If you choose to install a product, you will need to know the path to the product's installation information (contained in a *.IPS file or in PINSTALL.NLM), whether on a CD, floppy, volume, or another system altogether. Choosing to View/Configure/Remove Installed Products will produce a screen similar to that shown in Figure 6.9. Note that many, if not most, products are not really configurable through this interface.

NetWare
Operations

PART 2

Figure 6.9 The View/Configure/Remove installed products screen

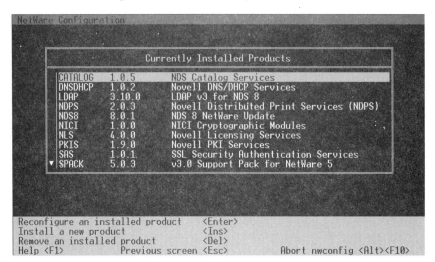

Please note that many upgrades are listed in Figure 6.9, including NDS 8, LDAP for NDS 8, and version 3 of the support pack. Other options are standard installation choices that were (or can be) chosen during installation.

To summarize, this tool offers many of the same basic options as previous versions of NetWare, and while you probably won't rely on this tool as heavily as you did in previous versions, it is still useful and you should be at least familiar with the interface. Many changes, such as the driver and volume-related ones already mentioned, can only be changed here after installation.

INETCFG

INETCFG.NLM is used for configuring your network cards and protocols which you may want to do as soon as your server is installed. You can do it at any point, however. When you choose to configure your network cards and protocols you will be prompted, as shown in Figure 6.10, to have INETCFG manage your network drivers and protocols which removes any associated commands from the AUTOEXEC.NCF file. You should answer Yes to this question to gain the full functionality offered by this tool.

Figure 6.10   The INETCFG prompt lets you manage your network cards and protocols.

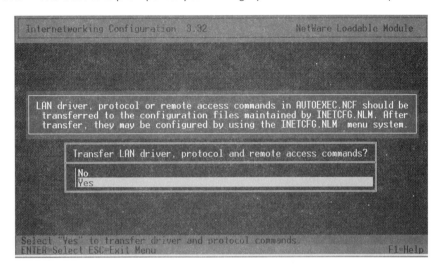

After you do so, you will be prompted to reboot the server for the changes to take effect. After you agree and the server is rebooted, you can go back and make any desired changes. Note the changes to AUTOEXEC.NCF as shown in the following code:

```
; Network driver LOADs and BINDs are initiated via
; INITSYS.NCF. The actual LOAD and BIND commands
; are contained in INITSYS.NCF and NETINFO.CFG.
; These files are in SYS:ETC.
sys:etc\initsys.ncf
#LOAD IPXRTR
#LOAD CPQNF3.LAN SLOT=10002 FRAME=ETHERNET_802.2  NAME=CPQNF3_1_E82
#BIND IPX CPQNF3_1_E82 NET=EC76152A
#LOAD IPXRTRNM
#LOAD TCPIP
#LOAD CPQNF3.LAN SLOT=10002 FRAME=ETHERNET_II  NAME=CPQNF3_1_EII
#BIND IP CPQNF3_1_EII ADDR=131.107.2.200 MASK=255.255.255.0
```

As you can see, all of the commands that loaded protocols (such as TCP/IP) and network card drivers (in this case CPQNF3.LAN) and the associated BIND commands have been commented out by placing a "#" in front of each line. There is also a note that INITSYS.NCF handles those functions now. If you load that file, the following warning is at the beginning of that file:

```
#! --- WARNING -- WARNING -- WARNING -- WARNING -- WARNING -- WARNING
#! This file was created by the Internetworking Configuration Console.
#! It is intended to be modified ONLY by the configurator (INETCFG.NLM).
#! Tampering with this file may cause severe malfunctioning of the system.
#! The configurator will check for tampering and abort if it is detected.
#! ----------------------------------------------------------------
```

As the warning states, all network configuration should now be done with INETCFG. When you first start the program after rebooting, the message shown in Figure 6.11 will appear.

If you are configuring only TCP/IP or IPX in a LAN environment or have permanent, synchronous WAN connections in addition to your LAN environment, you can use the fast setup. If you don't meet those requirements, you will need the standard setup. We recommend the fast setup in either case, and then if you have more advanced configuration to do, you can still go back and do it. The output you will get will be similar to that shown in Figure 6.12.

Figure 6.11   Fast or Standard setup prompt

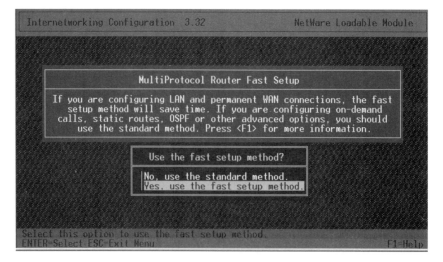

Figure 6.12   The results of the Fast Configuration choice, with the Configuration Options menu visible

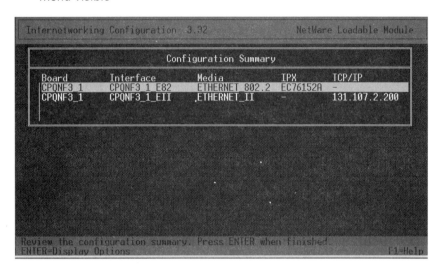

If you choose the fast setup method, you will be presented with the same prompt and information shown in Figures 6.11 and 6.12 every time that you load INETCFG. To get to all of the options that INETCFG offers, simply choose Go To INETCFG Main Menu. Once you have done this, you will always be brought directly to this point when you load INETCFG and bypass those two screens. The main menu is shown in Figure 6.13.

Figure 6.13   INETCFG's main menu

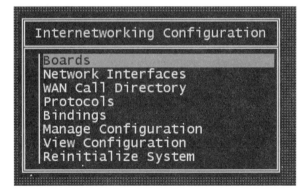

Fortunately, you will probably only use a few of the menu options shown in Figure 6.13. They are Boards, Protocols, Bindings, and Manage Configuration. Even with these options, you will probably never have to use all of the choices available in each.

The Boards menu item allows you to view your loaded LAN drivers, and optionally install and configure a new board, similar to the choices presented in NWCONFIG, although without the auto-detection offered by that utility. Pressing ENTER on any board will allow you to configure it, specifying things such as I/O port, Memory Address, IRQ, and slot (depending on the card). You can also view any other options the board offers, such as UTP vs. BNC connections, speed (10Mbps, 100Mbps, and so on), and duplex (half vs. full), depending on the card.

The Protocols option allows you to configure any installed protocol, including IPX, TCP/IP, and AppleTalk. Let's briefly focus on the two primary protocols, IPX and TCP/IP.

Some of the more popular IPX configuration options include:

IPX Status   Enabled or disabled (useful when you want to stop using IPX)

Packet Forwarding   Enabled or disabled (the server will act as a router when it is enabled)

Routing Protocol   RIP/SAP only or NLSP with RIP/SAP compatibility (NLSP offers many advantages over RIP and SAP, but requires more expertise and configuration. Refer to the online documentation for more details.)

TCP/IP configuration is similar in many respects. The TCP/IP status and IP Packet Forwarding options are the same as the IPX options. The RIP and OSPF options are analogous to RIP/SAP vs. NLSP already mentioned. OSPF is more complicated and beyond the scope of this chapter to discuss; see the online documentation for more details. There are a few specific options that you may need that should be discussed here as well. They include:

LAN Static Routing   Disabled or Enabled (Enable this to set a default gateway. You must then choose LAN Static Routing Table, press ENTER, press INSERT to add a new route, change the Route Type to Default Route, and specify the IP address of your default gateway in the Next Hop Router on Route field. Intuitive, isn't it? See Figure 6.14 to see what your screen will look like when you are finished. Press ESC twice and choose to update the database to save your changes.

SNMP Manager Table   Specify the IP addresses of those nodes that should receive SNMP traps generated by the server.

DNS Resolver Configuration   Allows you to specify your domain name for DNS and up to three DNS servers for name resolution.

Figure 6.14   Configuring a default gateway

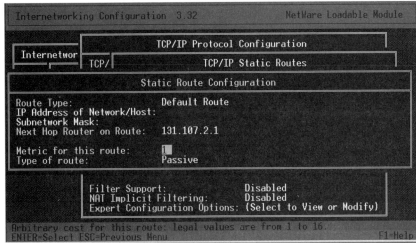

The bindings menu choice allows you to view the protocol(s) bound to each network card and the address associated with it (typically an external IPX address or an IP address). For IPX, you can also view the frame type being used. You may also modify the address choices here, and in the case of TCP/IP, you can also specify a subnet mask.

The primary reason you are likely to use the Manage Configuration option is to configure remote access to the server with the Configure Remote Console Access choice. You may also use this menu to configure SNMP. When configuring remote access you can configure the following parameters:

Remote Console Access   Enable or disable any remote access to the server

Password   The password that will be needed to gain access to this server remotely

RCONSOLE Connection   Enabled or disabled (allowing or disallowing remote access over the network; if enabled, it will load RSPX.NLM)

ACONSOLE Connection   Enabled or disabled (allowing or disallowing remote access over a modem; if enabled, it will load RS232.NLM. You will need to configure baud rate and COM port, as well, in addition to loading AIO.NLM and AIOCOMX.NLM to control access to the COM port. You can, if enabled, modem into your server and manage it by running ACONSOLE.EXE, or with newer versions of RCONSOLE, by choosing Asynchronous as the connection type.)

TELNET Connection   Enabled or disabled (allowing remote administration of the server through TELNET or an equivalent X Windows interface; if enabled XCONSOLE.NLM will be loaded)

As you can see from this brief description, this is a very powerful product. More information on using this product is available in the online documentation.

7

Performance Optimization

Now that you have seen some of the tools available to manage and monitor your network, it's time to turn to the other part of your job, optimizing the network. In this chapter we will look at the primary method for maximizing performance (besides buying more RAM, which always helps), SET parameters. Once we have covered what they are, we will cover when to modify them, and some of the more useful and important ones (there are literally hundreds of them). Then we will turn our attention to the primary tool for monitoring your network that comes with NetWare 5, MONITOR.NLM.

This does not mean that the tools discussed in the previous chapter aren't valuable; quite the contrary. However, there is some information that can best be seen using Monitor, and this is the tool that ships with NetWare 5, so it's free.

Finally, we will spend the remainder of the chapter covering miscellaneous performance optimization tips and guidelines. One more quick note before we begin: most of the hardware optimization tips are covered in Chapter 2 (on installation of NetWare 5); only a few hardware-related suggestions will be reviewed here. Instead, we will focus on software optimizations in this chapter.

SET Parameters

As you are probably aware, SET parameters help you modify how NetWare behaves. The good news is that NetWare is basically self-tuning. In fact, *all of the default values for the SET parameters have been set only after extensive testing by Novell for optimal performance*. However, you can manually override default settings to improve performance even more in some cases.

Sage Advice

One quick note before we begin, the common SET parameters are available by either typing **SET** at a console prompt or by going to Monitor and choosing Server Parameters. To gain access to the advanced SET parameters, you can load Monitor with the !H switch.

As an illustration of the difference between the standard and advanced SET parameters, there are 22 SET parameters in the communications category when you view them with Monitor, and 78 SET parameters when you view with Monitor using the !H switch. Most of the advanced SET parameters are not documented in the online documentation (or anywhere else) and will need to be modified only in the *rarest* of circumstances; probably at the behest of Novell Product Support Services. Be very careful when making any SET parameter changes, especially the advanced parameters, or you may actually *decrease* performance, or even worse, make the system unstable or unbootable.

The focus in this section of the chapter will be on the more important and useful parameters and how and when to modify them to maximize performance. Not all parameters will be discussed. They will be reviewed in the same categories that Novell uses, and the section headings will be the names of the categories as displayed in Monitor. Some of the acceptable and default values are different in the following tables from that which is described in the documentation. The documentation has incorrect information relative to the base product (no Support Packs installed), and changes have been made in various Support Packs. The values listed are the values when SP3 is installed.

NOTE   Information on most of the SET parameters is available in the online documentation, or, for the latest information, check out Novell's online documentation on its Web site at www.novell.com/documentation/lg/nw5/usreflib/utlrfenu/data/hgdzhwr7.html.

Communications

The parameters related to communications and how and when to optimize them are listed in Table 7.1.

Table 7.1   Communications Parameters

Parameter Name	Acceptable Values	Default Value	Notes/Recommendations
Maximum Packet Receive Buffers	50–6,949,785	500	Refer to the Packet Receive Buffers (PRB) statistic on Monitor's General Information screen to see how many are in use. You should increase this in increments of 10 if it is at or near the maximum. If the "No ECB Available count" is large, it means that packets are being dropped because there are no available PRBs. This statistic is related to service processes, which take packets from the PRBs and process them. The analogy we like to use to describe the relationship between PRBs and service processes is that of a bank. To accommodate customers, the size of the lobby can increase (PRBs), you can have more tellers (service processes), or some combination of both. The Maximum Packet Receive Buffers should be at least as large as the Minimum Packet Receive Buffers. If not, NetWare will set the maximum equal to the minimum. Novell recommends setting this value to 4,000 or higher, assuming that you have enough memory to do so.

Table 7.1 Communications Parameters *(continued)*

Parameter Name	Acceptable Values	Default Value	Notes/Recommendations
Minimum Packet Receive Buffers	10–65,536	128	This is the number of PRBs that are automatically allocated when the server is booted. If the number is substantially above the default after the server has been running for a while (as viewed in Monitor), you may want to use that number as the minimum so that the server won't have to spend time allocating more buffers, one at a time, to get to this level. Novell recommends starting by setting this to three times the number of licenses for the server.
New Packet Receive Buffer Wait Time	.1 second–20 seconds	.1 second	Specifies how long the operating system waits after receiving a packet with no free PRBs for the packet before creating a new buffer. Increasing this value will cause the occasional spike in demand for PRBs to not allocate many new buffers that will be unused most of the time, but packets may be dropped. Consider increasing this parameter only if you are low on memory.

Memory

The parameters relating to memory that you may find useful in optimizing your system are listed in Table 7.2.

File Caching

File caching is what makes NetWare so fast compared with other operating systems. File caching is the key to fast file access, and to rapid NDS access as well. The reason is that portions of the NDS database are cached just like data from any other application, using the memory that is used to cache any file, NDS related or not. Memory needs for file caching must be balanced against all other memory needs and against directory caching in particular.

Table 7.2   Memory-Related Parameters

Parameter Name	Acceptable Values	Default Value	Notes/Recommendations
Average Page In Alert Threshold	1–4,294,967,295	2,000	When the average (over the last five seconds) page ins per second from the Virtual Memory (VM) system reaches this level, an alert is sent to the console. We have found this value too high to be of use. For Windows NT, Microsoft recommends that 20 is a useful value in determining if too much paging is going on. We prefer this value to be in the range of 20–50. We have found in working with systems that have 64–128MB of RAM, that values between 25 and 50 are typical. We have also noticed that performance suffers and that there are large lags as the hard drive thrashes to provide the needed data. When we see this level of activity, it is an indication that more RAM is needed. By the time you get to 2,000 per second, performance is usually dismal at best.
Reserved Buffers Below 16 Meg	8–2,000	300	This parameter is for reserving memory for those drivers that can't access memory above 16MB (mainly older ISA drivers). If you still have many older drivers, you may need to increase this value.

Another large consumer of memory is that required to cache the FAT when mounting traditional volumes. Large volumes have a large FAT, requiring large amounts of memory to mount. Consider using NSS volumes instead of traditional volumes to free up the RAM that would be used for caching the FAT. Refer to Chapter 2 or the online documentation for a discussion of NSS. Remember that the SYS: volume must be a traditional volume.

Table 7.3 lists the most useful parameters relating to file caching.

Table 7.3 File-Caching Parameters

Parameter Name	Acceptable Values	Default Value	Notes/Recommendations
Minimum File Cache Buffers	20–2,000	20	This is the smallest number of Cache Buffers that NetWare will reserve for file caching. All RAM not allocated for other purposes is for file caching, but when the remaining File Cache Buffers get to this point, other things that need RAM (NLMs, Packet Receive Buffers, and so on) will be denied. Because all File Cache Buffers are 4K in size, there is only 80K of unallocated RAM when the default value is used. The server will not be stable with so little RAM, so there is really no reason to have this value set so low. Even with 2,000, it is only 8MB of RAM for caching. We recommend that you set this value to at least 1,000. See also Minimum File Cache Report Threshold.
Minimum File Cache Report Threshold	0–2,000	20	When you reach this number of buffers above the Minimum File Cache Buffers, a warning will be issued that you are almost out of RAM. Again, this number is ridiculously low. Using default values, when you have 20 buffers over the 20 Minimum File Cache Buffers, or 160K of RAM left, you will be warned. Most things that use memory use far more than 80K, so often you will get a warning that you are almost out of RAM followed by an error that you have reached the minimum setting. Consider setting this value to 500 (2MB above the minimum) or more.

Table 7.3   File-Caching Parameters *(continued)*

Parameter Name	Acceptable Values	Default Value	Notes/Recommendations
Maximum Concurrent Disk Cache Writes	10–4,000	750	This value is the maximum number of write requests that can be in the queue awaiting processing before data is written to the disk. Smaller values are more efficient at reading, but less at writing, but larger values make writing more efficient at the expense of read performance. Generally it is recommended that if 70% (some sources say 50%) or more of your Total Cache Buffers are Dirty Cache Buffers (as reported by Monitor), you should increase this parameter. We usually increase this parameter when the ratio reaches 50%. Of course, the best course of action would be to increase the performance of the disk subsystem or getting a faster processor (if the CPU is the bottleneck), but these solutions require money.
Dirty Disk Cache Delay Time	.1 second–10 seconds	3.3 seconds	This is the minimum amount of time that NetWare will wait before writing a partially full Dirty Cache Buffer to the disk. Increasing this time can make writing more efficient if many small write requests are made (such as often occurs when using a database). Decreasing this value, on the other hand, can radically reduce performance (as the system makes many small writes) with little difference in the possibility of losing data in the event of an equipment or power failure. This is especially true if you are using a UPS, as you should be, on all servers. If your Dirty Cache Buffers are greater than 50% of your Total Cache Buffers, however, decreasing this value (to as low as 0.5) will make writes happen more frequently, freeing more RAM for file caching. The better solution, however, is to buy more RAM.

NetWare Operations

PART 2

Directory Caching

As mentioned in the preceding section on file caching, directory caching and file caching go together hand-in-hand. Directory caching allows the server to find data quickly on the volumes, whereas file caching keeps the data available for faster access. Many of the parameters referred to here are similar to those used in file caching, so reference will be made to the impact of changing that parameter to the file caching table. Table 7.4 lists the directory caching related parameters. Note that many of these parameters apply only to traditional volumes, not the newer NSS format.

Table 7.4 Directory-Caching Related Parameters

Parameter Name	Acceptable Values	Default Value	Notes/Recommendations
Maximum Concurrent Directory Cache Writes	5–500	75	This value is the maximum number of directory write requests that can be in the queue awaiting processing before data is written to the disk. Smaller values are more efficient at reading, but less at writing, whereas larger values make writing more efficient at the expense of read performance. Novell recommends setting this value to 100 if there is a lot of activity that generates writes to the directory (creating and deleting files, and so on).

Table 7.4   Directory-Caching Related Parameters *(continued)*

Parameter Name	Acceptable Values	Default Value	Notes/Recommendations
Dirty Directory Cache Delay Time	0 seconds–10 seconds	.5 second	This is the minimum amount of time that NetWare will wait before writing a partially full Dirty Directory Cache Buffer to the disk. Increasing this time can make writing more efficient, but increases the chances of directory corruption, which can lead to data loss. Decreasing this value a little, on the other hand, can reduce performance a little but can reduce the possibility of losing data in the event of an equipment or power failure. This is especially true if you are using a UPS, as you should on all servers. Setting this value to 0, however, will drastically reduce performance.
Directory Cache Buffer Non-Referenced Delay	1 second–1 hour	5.5 seconds	This is the length of time after which a Directory Cache Buffer that hasn't been used (referenced) can be reused for caching other directory entries. Increasing this parameter increases the length of time an entry is cached, thus increasing the chances that it will be in cache when it is next referenced. This implies, of course, that additional Directory Cache Buffers will be needed, reducing the memory for file caching. Decreasing this value will reduce performance, but will also require fewer Cache Buffers. If you have a lot of RAM and a lot of data in many files, consider increasing this parameter to increase performance.

NetWare Operations

PART 2

Table 7.4 Directory-Caching Related Parameters *(continued)*

Parameter Name	Acceptable Values	Default Value	Notes/Recommendations
Directory Cache Allocation Wait Time	.1 second–2 minutes	2.2 seconds	This is the length of time that the system will wait after allocating a directory cache buffer before allocating an additional one. Note that there is no delay in allocating buffers until the number of buffers specified by the Minimum Directory Cache Buffers parameter has been allocated. This helps flatten out the spikes in demand for directory caching, as new requests for Directory Cache Buffers during this interval are ignored. Setting this value too low will cause many more Directory Cache Buffers to be allocated than are normally needed, while setting this value too high will cause the system to perform poorly as directory data will often not be cached due to the lack of available buffers. The general recommendation is that if searching directories is slow, even after the server has been up for a while (at a minimum 15 minutes), then decrease this value. Specifically, if you have plenty of RAM, Novell recommends that you decrease this value to .5 second. See also the Minimum Directory Cache Buffers parameter.

Table 7.4 Directory-Caching Related Parameters *(continued)*

Parameter Name	Acceptable Values	Default Value	Notes/Recommendations
Minimum Directory Cache Buffers	10–100,000	150	The server will automatically allocate Directory Cache Buffers (DCB) as needed with no delay up to this value. Novell recommends setting this to 3 times the number of licenses for the server as a starting point.
Maximum Directory Cache Buffers	20–200,000	500	This is the maximum number of DCBs the server will allocate. This number needs to be carefully balanced against the number of File Cache Buffers for optimal performance. Novell recommends setting this to 4,000 if you have sufficient RAM.

NetWare Operations

PART 2

File System

The parameters that are in this section control how NetWare deals with issues such as compression, salvaging of files, warnings about volumes being almost full, and a few other miscellaneous settings. Most of the parameters in this section are self-explanatory, and so will not be discussed here, but you should review them and set them to the appropriate values for your environment.

You should take special note of the compression settings; although compression will reduce performance, it will provide additional disk space that may be needed in a pinch. The compression algorithm is designed to be CPU-intensive to compress the files (typically when no one is using the system), but to be very quick to decompress them (when the user is waiting). Because disk space has become cheaper, many administrators have decided against using compression, preferring to buy more disk space instead, and thereby saving CPU time for other tasks.

We recommend that you consider compression when you are almost out of space—when an alert has been generated due to low disk space, for example—and you need some temporary space until more disk space can be purchased and installed. Once the new space is installed, you can decompress all of your files and disable compression until it is once again needed.

By default, compression is enabled on traditional volumes (it is not supported on NSS volumes), and once a volume is created with it enabled, it cannot be disabled without deleting and recreating the volume. Compression can be disabled on all volumes, however, as described in Table 7.5.

Table 7.5 lists the values that relate to warnings when a volume is at or near capacity and a couple of the most important compression-related parameters. Refer to the documentation for a list of all of the compression-related parameters.

Table 7.5   File-System Parameters

Parameter Name	Acceptable Values	Default Value	Notes/Recommendations
Volume Low Warn All Users	On or Off	On	If this parameter is set to On, all logged-in users will receive a warning when the volume is almost full (as defined by the Volume Low Warning Threshold parameter). If you change this to Off, the warning will only be reported on the console and you may not be aware how full the volume is. Check the available free space daily, at a minimum, and preferably more often as your volumes fill up, especially if you turn this parameter Off. You should be doing this anyway as a preventative measure. It is especially imperative that SYS: does *not* fill up, as the NDS files are on that volume. If it does, the system will experience severe problems, and may hang or abend.

Table 7.5   File-System Parameters *(continued)*

Parameter Name	Acceptable Values	Default Value	Notes/Recommendations
Volume Low Warning Threshold	0–1,000,000 blocks	256 blocks	The actual amount of free space depends on the volume's block size. For example, with 4K blocks, it would warn you when there is 1MB free; with a 64K block size, the warning would come when there is 16MB free. We believe the value is too low in any case. Today, 1MB or even 16MB of free disk space is nothing. You should consider setting this to at least 1,000 (64MB with a 64K block size), or even larger values if the block size is smaller. Novell recommends 2,048 blocks as a good value for the "average volume." As most volumes today are multi-gigabyte in size, we would be concerned if the free space were below 100 MB, maybe even more depending on what the volume is used for.
Volume Low Warning Reset Threshold	0–100,000 blocks	256 blocks	Once a low volume warning has been issued, another will not be issued until the free space rises above the space dictated by the following formula: (Volume Low Warning Threshold blocks + Volume Low Warning Reset Threshold blocks) * block size. Using the default values and a 64K block size, a warning would be issued when there is less than 16MB free space remaining and another would not be issued until the free space went above 32MB and then dipped back below 16MB. This prevents frequent warnings from being issued, but requires you to act on low disk space warnings quickly. Novell recommends that you consider 2,048 for this parameter as well; we recommend that you set this value to the same value you used for Volume Low Warning Threshold.

NetWare
Operations

PART 2

Table 7.5 File-System Parameters *(continued)*

Parameter Name	Acceptable Values	Default Value	Notes/Recommendations
Enabled File Compression	On or Off	On	Turning this parameter off will disable compression (though of course not decompression) on *all compression-enabled volumes* on the server. Anything that is flagged IC (Immediate Compress) will be queued until compression is enabled again. The normal process that looks for files that haven't been used lately (as specified by the Days Untouched Before Compression parameter) will not take place either until it is enabled again. Then it will resume as if it had never been disabled. This is a great compromise parameter, because compression can be disabled until you become low on disk space, at which time it can be enabled until more space is purchased and installed. This can be especially important for SYS:, which as mentioned earlier, must never be allowed to run out of space.
Days Untouched Before Compression	0–100,000 (about 274 years)	14	Many compression parameters refer to this parameter to determine when a file should be compressed or when an uncompressed file should replace the compressed version. Increasing this value means that fewer files will be compressed, while decreasing it means more will be. Novell generally recommends increasing this to 30 unless disk space is at a premium.

Disk

This group of parameters relates to how NetWare interacts with physical disk drives. Most of them are related to mirroring, which is a fault tolerance measure that can have a slight performance impact, but that impact is usually outweighed by the increased reliability and up time it affords. There are two parameters that deal with every write, however, and they are discussed in Table 7.6.

Table 7.6   Disk Parameters

Parameter Name	Acceptable Values	Default Value	Notes
Enable Hardware Write Back	On or Off	Off	This parameter will enable writing to cache on the hardware device (typically a caching controller), which will later be committed to the physical disk. NetWare will report the file as successfully written when it is written to cache. Writes done by the TTS (Transaction Tracking System) are never written to cache. Obviously, this parameter has no effect on those devices that don't have cache on them. If you have devices that have cache on them *and* a UPS on your system, you should enable this parameter to increase write performance.
Enable Disk Read After Write Verify	On or Off	Off	When enabled, this parameter will read back data that has just been written to the disk to make sure that they are identical. In previous versions of NetWare, the default was On, but with the increased reliability of today's media, the default is now Off. Enabling this parameter will provide greater fault tolerance, but will reduce write performance.

NCP

This group of parameters affects the behavior of NCP (NetWare Core Protocol). Those listed in Table 7.7 are the main ones that affect performance.

Miscellaneous

This group of parameters is truly eclectic, hence the name for the category. That does not mean that these parameters are not useful; quite the contrary. Table 7.8 lists some of the more useful and interesting ones.

NetWare Operations

PART 2

Table 7.7 NCP Parameters

Parameter Name	Acceptable Values	Default Value	Notes/Recommendations
NCP Packet Signature Option	0–3	1	Packet signature prevents forgery (modification of packets or impersonation of a user on another workstation) by placing a digital signature on each packet. If the signatures don't match, the packet is discarded. In addition, an alert is sent to the affected workstation, the console, and the server's error log. The signature changes with each packet, further reducing the chances that a forgery could be produced. The values for this parameter are cryptic. The values and the definition of each are as follows: **0** Disable packet signature. **1** Server will sign packets only if the client asks for it (client setting is 2 or higher). **2** Server will sign packets if the client is able to as well (client setting is 1 or higher). **3** Server always signs packets. The latest version of the client calls this parameter Signature Level. Servers and clients that are set to 0 and 3 (or 3 and 0) respectively, will cause the client to be unable to log in to that server. Packet signature is set to 1 by both sides by default, meaning that both are capable, but neither will request it. This means that packets will not be signed by default. Another interesting requirement of this parameter is that once set, it can never be lowered without rebooting the server. It can, however, be raised any time. Packet signature increases the load on both the server and the client, and so is usually disabled unless security is very important. Enabling this parameter will decrease performance.

Table 7.7   NCP Parameters *(continued)*

Parameter Name	Acceptable Values	Default Value	Notes/Recommendations
Allow LIP	On or Off	On	LIP stands for Large Internet Packets. With this parameter set to Off, all packets that are sent over routers are limited to 576 bytes. When set to On, the client and server negotiate the largest size packet that both can support and are also supported by all intermediary routers. Large packets are more efficient than small packets, as there is a greater percentage of the packet that has data in it, compared to control information and headers.

Table 7.8   Miscellaneous Parameters

Parameter Name	Acceptable Values	Default Value	Notes/Recommendations
Allow Unencrypted Passwords	On or Off	Off	This setting exists to provide compatibility with versions of NetWare before 3.1x and servers and services designed to operate with those versions. Allowing passwords to traverse the network unencrypted is a big security risk and should be avoided unless connectivity with the aforementioned devices is absolutely required. In fact, Novell recommends you upgrade any servers, services, and clients to versions that do support using encrypted passwords.

NetWare
Operations

PART 2

Table 7.8   Miscellaneous Parameters *(continued)*

Parameter Name	Acceptable Values	Default Value	Notes/Recommendations
Enable SECURE.NCF	On or Off	Off	SECURE.NCF is designed to set the options necessary to put NetWare in the trusted configuration for the government's C2 security rating. This does not mean that your system is C2 certified when you run this file, but it is more secure and the parameters required to be C2 certified are set. There are also additional parameters in this file designed to further enhance your network's security. If you set this parameter to On, it will execute after the AUTOEXEC.NCF file has finished.
Sound Bell For Alerts	On or Off	On	Causes the server to beep whenever a warning or error is sent to the console screen. You may want to disable this if others need to work near the server and "it keeps beeping." This can happen, for example, if the server's clock gets set back, causing synthetic time to be issued and the computer to beep frequently.
Display Lost Interrupt Alerts	On or Off	Off	You may want to set this parameter to On to notify you (at the server console) when lost interrupts occur. A lost interrupt happens when a card or driver requests the services of the CPU (through an interrupt), but drops the request before the CPU can respond. This message is generally indicative of either a problem with your hardware or a bad driver. Lost interrupts lower performance because CPU time is wasted as it is interrupted, finds nobody needs it, and then resumes what it was doing. See also the Display Lost Interrupt Alerts Threshold parameter for the number that must occur per second to trigger the alert (the default is 10).

Table 7.8 Miscellaneous Parameters *(continued)*

Parameter Name	Acceptable Values	Default Value	Notes/Recommendations
Display Spurious Interrupt Alerts	On or Off	On	You may want to set this parameter to On to be notified (at the server console) when spurious interrupts occur. A spurious interrupt happens when a card requests the services of the CPU (through an interrupt), but that interrupt is being used by another device. This message is generally indicative of an IRQ conflict or a hardware problem. Spurious interrupts lower performance because CPU time is wasted as it is interrupted, finds that the incorrect device made the call, and then resumes what it was doing. See also the Display Spurious Interrupt Alerts Threshold parameter for the number that must occur per second to trigger the alert (the default is 200).

Error Handling

Most of the parameters in this category have to do with log file sizes and what to do when the log file in question reaches its maximum. These parameters affect free disk space, but not performance specifically. If hard drive space is an issue (especially with SYS:), review and set these parameters carefully. The only other parameters deal with how the server will react to an abend (abnormal end). Table 7.9 discusses those two parameters.

Directory Services

Most of the parameters in this category are for debugging purposes and background processes that NDS undertakes to maintain proper synchronization and the validity of the data. There are no specific parameters that we want to mention in this context; we simply wanted to make you aware that these parameters can be modified if needed to control what NDS does in the background. Like the rest of the SET parameters, there generally is no need to modify any of these values.

NetWare Operations

PART 2

Table 7.9 Error-Handling Parameters

Parameter Name	Acceptable Values	Default Value	Notes/Recommendations
Auto Restart After Abend	0–3	1	This parameter tells NetWare what to do when an abend happens. The four possible values are cryptic; the meaning of each is as follows: **0** Do not attempt to recover from the abend. The server crashes and sits there until someone manually reboots it. **1** Attempt to recover from the abend, follow with a downing and restarting of the system (after the configured amount of time) for the more serious errors. For errors of a less serious nature, suspend the process that caused the fault and leave the server up. **2** Attempt to recover from the abend, follow with a downing and restarting of the system (after the configured amount of time) for *all* errors. **3** Same as number 2, but reboot immediately, instead of waiting for the configured amount of time to elapse. This option is disabled if the Developer Option parameter is enabled.
Auto Restart After Abend Delay Time	2–60 minutes	2 minutes	The amount of time to wait before restarting the server to allow users to finish saving any open documents and shut down gracefully. Users will be notified every 2 minutes, regardless of this setting. Remember that this parameter is meaningful only when the value of Auto Restart After Abend is 1 or 2.

Managing the Configuration Environment

There are a few commands that can help you manage your environment and the SET parameters that you have in use. Let's briefly cover them here before we turn our attention to Monitor.

The first two commands that you have at your disposal are closely related. Both are new to NetWare 5. The first is DISPLAY ENVIRONMENT, which displays the current value of your SET parameters. The second is DISPLAY MODIFIED ENVIRONMENT, which shows only those parameters that have been changed from the default. We really like the second one, because we often want to see what has changed, not all the default stuff. You may want to use this command in conjunction with Stuff Key (discussed in Chapter 6) to put this information in a file for documentation purposes. You could do the same to document all SET parameters, but there is a simpler method. Simply start Monitor, choose Server Parameters, then press F3 to write these parameters to a file (by default SYS: SYSTEM\SETCMDS.CP). You should then print this out as part of your documentation. Note that neither of the console commands will display the advanced parameters. The documentation method that uses Monitor will save all of the parameters that you can view, which by default include only the standard parameters. If you want to see and therefore be able to document all of the parameters, you can use the "!h" switch when loading Monitor.

Second, if you really make a mess of SET parameters and want to return some or all of them to the default values, you can type **RESET ENVIRONMENT** at a console prompt. This command will also allow you to selectively reset only desired parameters to the default by prompting you for each modified parameter to leave it alone, change it to the default, change all parameters to the default, or quit the command.

Monitor

Now that we have covered how to use SET parameters to maximize performance, let us turn our attention to the primary tool that will allow us to monitor the server to see how well it is performing. That tool is Monitor. This tool has been around for many years, and much of the interface should seem familiar to users who have used NetWare before. In this section, we will focus on a few of the screens that are very important in performance monitoring and optimization and we will review some of the parameters and the acceptable value ranges for them. Remember that these are general guidelines; you will need to test them in your specific environment to determine the optimal values for your configuration.

When Monitor is first started, you are shown the General Information screen, as shown in Figure 7.1. This screen is probably the most important screen in Monitor. To give you a quick overall view of performance, we will discuss each parameter. Table 7.10 details each parameter, what it is for, and the desired value (according to Novell) for each. Note that some vendors have specific guidelines that can be very different from those presented here. You should always take into consideration the hardware manufacturer's guidelines in your testing to determine what is optimal for your environment. Most of the menu options are hidden below this screen, but the General Information portion of the screen can be shrunk to allow access to the menu choices by pressing either ESC or TAB. Likewise, the information can be restored to its original size by pressing TAB again.

Figure 7.1   The General Information screen of Monitor

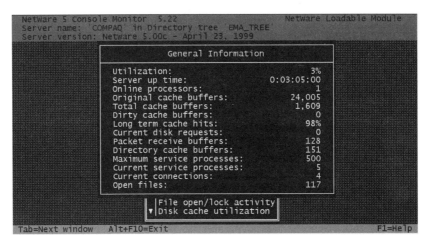

Table 7.10   Monitor's General-Information-Screen Parameters

Parameter Name	Desired Value	Notes/Meaning
Utilization	Average < 80%	The percentage of CPU time spent doing something productive. Short spikes to 100% are OK.
Server up time	As long as possible	Use this statistic to keep track of how long the server has been up since the last reboot. If it is shorter than you expect, check your UPS, the abend log, and for intruders who may have downed the server.

Table 7.10   Monitor's General-Information-Screen Parameters *(continued)*

Parameter Name	Desired Value	Notes/Meaning
Online processors	As many as you have in your system	This parameter reports how many of the CPUs installed in your system are being used by NetWare. Platform Support Modules (PSMs) are required to utilize all CPUs beyond the first.
Original Cache Buffers	This number times 4K should be approximately the amount of RAM installed in your system.	This number by itself is not very useful, but it is important when viewed relative to Total Cache Buffers (described next)
Total Cache Buffers	Ideal: 70% of Original Cache Buffers; Acceptable: 40% of original	The more file cache buffers available, the better the performance you will get out of the server. This statistic is usually used in conjunction with Original Cache Buffers, Dirty Cache Buffers, and Long Term Cache hits. Everything that needs RAM on the server gets it from these buffers. If the ratio is less than 40% Total Cache Buffers: Original Cache Buffers you need to buy more RAM.
Dirty Cache Buffers	Ideal: < 50% of Total Cache Buffers; Acceptable: < 70% of Total	This represents buffers that have been modified in RAM and are waiting to be written to disk. If the number is above 50% (some sources say 70%), consider either increasing the Maximum Concurrent Disk Cache Writes parameter, buying a faster disk subsystem, or buying more RAM. A short-term solution that might help is to set Dirty Disk Cache Delay Time = 0.5 so that many small requests don't clog the system.
Long Term Cache hits	> 90%	Whenever the system can respond to requests for data out of RAM instead of the hard drive, performance will improve dramatically. If this value drops below 90%, buy more RAM.
Current disk requests	Low	If this number is usually high, the disk subsystem may be a bottleneck, and you may want to consider upgrading it.

Table 7.10 Monitor's General-Information-Screen Parameters *(continued)*

Parameter Name	Desired Value	Notes/Meaning
Packet Receive Buffers	< Maximum Packet Receive Buffers (PRBs)	If this value is substantially above the minimum PRBs, consider adjusting the minimum to this value. As this value approaches the maximum, either increase the maximum and/or allocate more service processes. The size of each PRB depends on the underlying network architecture, for example Net-Ware uses approximately 1.5K for Ethernet and 4K for FDDI.
Directory Cache Buffers	< Maximum Directory Cache Buffers	If this value is substantially above the minimum Directory Cache Buffers, consider adjusting the minimum to this value. As this value approaches the maximum, you may want to increase the maximum value, remembering you need to balance file and directory caching.
Maximum service processes	> Current service processes	This value represents the number of threads (task handlers) available to process packets in the PRBs. When the number of Current service processes approaches this value, consider increasing it, unless you are low on memory. Novell recommends allocating at least 2–3 per connection, and preferably setting this value to the maximum (1,000), as they will not be allocated unless they are needed.
Current service processes	< Maximum service processes	Yes, we know that this is circular logic, but the values don't matter so much as long as this value is less than the maximum.
Current connections	N/A	Represents the number of current connections to the server. Some of them may be internal server resources that don't consume a connection license.
Open files	N/A	Number of open files on the server.

While the General Information screen is the single most important source of information on the functioning of your server, there are many other useful pieces of information available to you.

First, there is the functioning of the disk drives. All of the disk and most of the volume related information is available in Monitor by choosing Storage Devices from the Available Options menu. A drive must be activated, functional, and registered to be able to be used and therefore monitored. As you can see from Figure 7.2, you want to make sure that the values for these three parameters are all Yes. This is particularly important with infrequently accessed and mirrored drives where a failure would not be as immediately noticeable.

Figure 7.2   Some information on a properly functioning drive

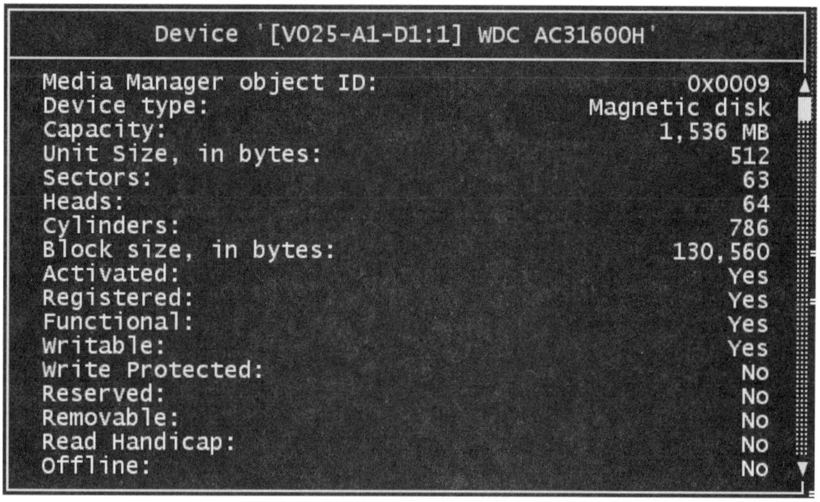

```
          Device '[V025-A1-D1:1] WDC AC31600H'
    Media Manager object ID:                 0x0009  ▲
    Device type:                      Magnetic disk
    Capacity:                             1,536 MB
    Unit Size, in bytes:                       512
    Sectors:                                    63
    Heads:                                      64
    Cylinders:                                 786
    Block size, in bytes:                  130,560
    Activated:                                 Yes
    Registered:                                Yes
    Functional:                                Yes
    Writable:                                  Yes
    Write Protected:                            No
    Reserved:                                   No
    Removable:                                  No
    Read Handicap:                              No
    Offline:                                    No  ▼
```

Another thing that you want to track for your NetWare partitions is the Hot Fix information, found under the Hotfixed Partition entry under your NetWare Partition(s). Figure 7.3 shows a healthy drive, with no Hot Fix blocks in use. Novell says that when half of Total Hot Fix blocks available are used, the hard drive is in danger of crashing. Be sure you have proper backups of all data and order a replacement drive so that you are ready when it goes. Even better, mirror that drive now so that access to the data on that drive will be uninterrupted.

> **NOTE**   When you use a RAID array, most faults are not reported to the operating system, though most vendors have a tool to allow you to view the health of your disk subsystem. In these cases, there is no reason to reserve Hot Fix space, as the system will be dead long before any errors will be reported to NetWare and these reserved blocks will never be used.

Figure 7.3   Hot Fix information

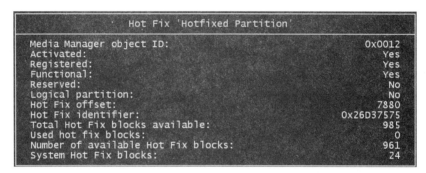

A third thing that you need to monitor is free space on each of your volumes. One of the simplest ways to do this is to choose Volumes from the Available Options menu in Monitor. When you do so, you will see the name of each volume, along with its total space and the percentage used, as shown in Figure 7.4. More detailed information on any volume can be displayed by selecting it and pressing TAB. In general, you want to keep the free space on each volume at 15–20% of the volume's total space. This is especially true for SYS:, which should always have 20% or more of its space free because all of your NDS data and many of the system's logs, among other things, are stored on that volume. You should become very concerned when any volume drops below 10% free, and should consider deleting files, adding more space, and/or enabling compression to make more space available.

Figure 7.4   Volume usage information

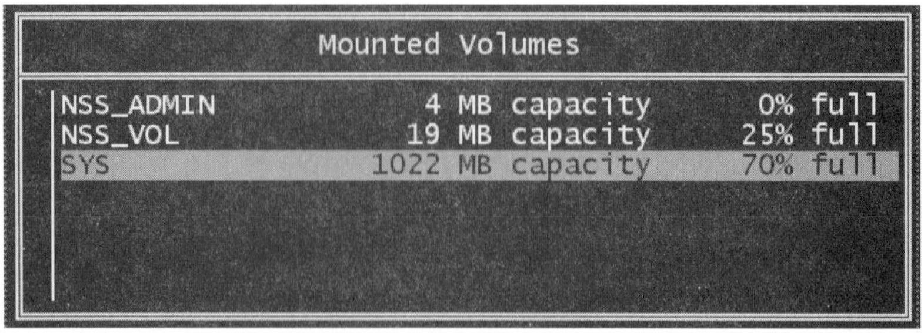

The final area that we want to discuss in connection with Monitor is the information on cache utilization. This information can be gathered by choosing Disk Cache Utilization from the Available Options menu in Monitor. This is shown in Figure 7.5. Table 7.11 reviews some of the most important values necessary in optimizing cache usage.

Figure 7.5   Cache statistics

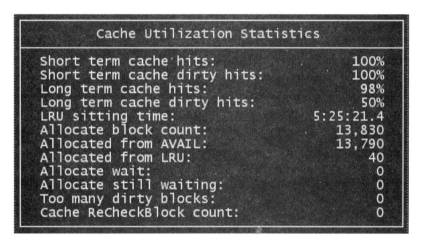

Table 7.11   Important Cache-Utilization Parameters

Parameter Name	Desired Value	Notes/Meaning
Short Term Cache Hits	> 98%	The percentage of requests for data in the last second that were filled out of cache instead of having to go to the disk drive. If this value is less than 98%, consider purchasing more RAM.
Long Term Cache Hits	> 90%	This figure represents the overall percentage of times that requests for disk-based resources were filled from cache instead. If it is less than 90%, consider buying more RAM.
Long Term Dirty Cache Hits	Low	The lower this value the better. Dirty Cache Buffers can't be used until the existing contents are written to disk, so the lower the value the better. If it is high and/ or increasing steadily, you should buy more RAM.

Table 7.11   Important Cache-Utilization Parameters *(continued)*

Parameter Name	Desired Value	Notes/Meaning
LRU Sitting Time	A long time	This represents how long the Least Recently Used (LRU, or oldest) buffer has been in RAM. The longer this value, the better, as it means there is sufficient RAM for caching. If it is a small value (especially one less than 15 minutes), you may need more RAM.
Allocated From AVAIL	High relative to Allocated from LRU	Ideally, this value is high relative to Allocated from LRU, because it means that memory needed for caching was not taken from memory that was being used to cache something else, but instead from free memory. In this case, you have enough RAM for caching.
Allocate Still Waiting	< 7	This represents the number of times in the last 10 minutes that the OS itself had to wait for an LRU buffer to become available to process a request. If it is above 7, you will need to buy more RAM.

Miscellaneous Performance Guidelines

This chapter will conclude with some other helpful tips and things to watch for to help you optimize you system.

First, as is preached in almost every document, class, and discussion on servers in general, or NetWare specifically, you should have a UPS on every server. That is not enough, however. You need to test it occasionally to be sure that it works as expected. We can't tell you how many times we've heard or seen a server protected by a UPS go down right after a power failure because no one had ever (or at least recently) tested the battery and made sure it was still good. Novell recommends the following test procedure:

1. During a scheduled maintenance period or other time when the server is not in use, Down the server and exit to DOS, but don't shut down the server.

2. Pull the plug and see what happens. If the system shuts down within a few seconds or even a minute or two, it is time to upgrade, repair, or replace the UPS.

3. Plug the system back in and reboot the server.

> **TIP** The battery will probably last half as long (or even a little less) than the amount of time you experience with this test. This is because the server will be actively using its hard drives, NICs, and so on, which consumes a lot more power.

Second, Novell always recommends that you apply the latest support packs to be sure that the latest patches, fixes, and enhancements are installed. Some of them improve performance. The latest support pack is SP3.

> **NOTE** The latest support pack, as well as any other recommended patches, updates, and so on, are available at support.novell.com/misc/patlst.htm.

Third, be sure you are using the latest version of NDS and DS.NLM. At the time this book was written, the latest version of NDS was version 8 and the DS.NLM version was 8.17. NDS 8 is a free download from Novell's Web site as well. It is also very important to design your NDS tree and the partitioning and replication strategy well, or performance can suffer greatly. Chapters 1 and 11 contain information on these subjects.

> **NOTE** NDS 8 is available from Novell's Web site at the following address: www.novell.com/download/.

Fourth, there are four hardware-related tips to help with performance.

1. Place slow devices (such as CD-ROMs and Tape Backup devices) on different Host Bus Adapters (HBAs) from fast devices, such as disk drives.

2. Set your interrupts according to the priority you wish a device to have. IRQ priorities are as follows (from highest to lowest): 0, 1, 8, (2/9), 10, 11, 12, 13, 14, 15, 3, 4, 5, 6, and 7. Recall that IRQ 0 is reserved for the system timer and IRQ 1 is reserved for the keyboard.

3. *Always* use hardware-based versions of mirroring, duplexing, and RAID as opposed to software-based solutions whenever possible. The software-based solutions will add an additional load to the host computer's CPU and are slower.

4. If you are using traditional volumes, use a 64K block size. NetWare has been optimized for this size, and when combined with suballocation, the amount of wasted space is minimal. When using suballocation, however, try to always keep at least 1,000 free blocks and 10% free space on the volume. When the system detects fewer than 1,000 free blocks or less than 10% of the total volume space remaining, the suballocation system goes into "aggressive mode" looking to free space,

causing CPU utilization to increase and disk performance to decrease until the process has completed. It could even max out Packet Receive Buffers and service processes, potentially causing connections to be dropped. If there are fewer than 1,000 free blocks available, consider going to the root of the volume and issuing a **PURGE /ALL** to remove all of the deleted files, making all of those blocks free blocks.

NOTE There are several TIDs that relate to performance monitoring. They include 2944438, 2943356, 2943472, and 2944533. The latest information from Novell can be found at support.novell.com and searching for **Performance Optimization NW5** and **Performance Monitoring NW5**.

8

Advanced Server Operations

It is often said that installing software and operating systems is the easiest part of our jobs, but we all know that planning and maintenance take up most of our time. In the previous chapter, you were exposed to more day-to-day aspects of getting NetWare 5 servers running properly and tools you could use to optimize performance. In this chapter you will be exposed to tools that offer advanced features. The following is a list of advanced management tasks and the tools you will need to accomplish them:

- Remote Server Management
- Additional Security Enhancements
- Remote Network Access
- RAS and VPN Solutions
- Selecting a Connection Service
- Server Application Support
- LDAPv3 (Lightweight Directory Access Protocol) Services
- Optimizing Network Traffic

These sections will help you to not only understand these services, but also to determine when it's best to utilize them in your environment. You should always follow the "KISS" principle, so only use what you need and stay away from the rest.

Remote Server Management Tools

NetWare 5 installs with remote management capabilities and you need to consider them in your planning. Planning should include the server and workstation platforms, the types of communications you will have available to access the servers, and the functionality you want.

You will need these tools to get access to the servers and manage them properly. The following is a list of some of the advanced services you will be able to manage using the remote management tools:

- Access to the server console
- Configuring and managing LDAP services
- Viewing and managing large containers
- Managing Directory Services
- Managing Catalog Services
- Managing database services
- Time synchronization
- Advanced security features

From previous chapters and hands-on experience, you should be familiar with remote-management server-based tools such as ConsoleOne, RCONSOLE, and RCONSOLEJ. You have probably also used client-based tools such as NetWare Administrator, RCONSOLEJ, RCONSOLE, NDS Manager, and ConsoleOne (new version is 1.2b) to manage your servers. With NetWare 5, a series of snap-ins are added for additional administrative capabilities to NetWare Administrator and ConsoleOne.

As far as communications go, you will be able to access servers over LAN, WAN, or DIALUP services. By allowing the servers and clients to use IP natively, you can also access the servers over the Internet, and enhance your communications options. With these tools, you will be able to use your workstation to access the servers from your home or office. Therefore you should consider what system and type of hardware you want to use on your workstation. We would use Microsoft NT Workstation 4 as the OS and install really good hardware for the system. This ensures that you will have enough horsepower to run the utilities and manage the network servers.

The following sections go over details of the functionality associated with these tools, and updates since the release of NetWare 5 and the advent of NDSv8.

Accessing the Server Console

You can use RCONSOLEJ (written in Java) or the traditional RCONSOLE to access the server console from a workstation. To use RCONSOLEJ on the workstation, it is preferable to have TCP/IP as your default protocol in the server and workstation. You can also run RCONSOLEJ from NetWare Administrator using the menu bar (Tools ≻ Pure IP Remote Console). You will then have text access to the target server's console.

To use RCONSOLE, you will have to determine if you are going to access the server via a network connection over IPX or through a modem. You will lose some functionality when using modem access. When running RCONSOLE or RCONSOLEJ from your workstation, you can use the following shortcuts and keys to navigate the screens and activate the RCONSOLE menu screen:

- Press ALT + F1 to activate the Options menu.
- Press ALT + F2 to display an Exit Menu Option screen.
- Press ALT + F3 or F4 to change console screens.
- Press ALT + F5 to make the workstation's network and MAC address appear.
- You can invoke the Options menu by pressing ALT + F1 only from RCONSOLE. This gives you the option to go back to the workstation's operating system, exiting temporarily from the remote session. You can also transfer files and upgrade servers from this menu.
- RCONSOLEJ has a menu bar that allows navigating from screen to screen and will allow you to control the server from another server.

The ability to access the server console remotely brings risks; unauthorized intruders could shut down the server, for example. The following sections discuss ways that you can restrict access to the console.

Securing the Server Console

Securing the network from unauthorized access is a key task for the network administrator. One aspect of network security that is often overlooked is the physical security of the server itself. A server that is accessible to the public is very vulnerable to attack.

Consider locking up the server in a cabinet specially designed for servers and then locking the cabinet in a room with restricted access. Locking up the server keeps unauthorized individuals from accessing the server console. You can further protect the server console by entering **SECURE CONSOLE** on the console screen. This command disables NLM loading from any directory other than SYS: SYSTEM and it prevents intruders from changing the server time and date.

NetWare 5 further restricts access to the console screen with the use of a screen saver. You can run SCRSAVER.NLM from the server console and a screen saver appears. To return to the console screen, just press any key on the keyboard to display a prompt for a user-name and password. Only authorized users can access the server console.

Password Encryption

The console agents RCONAG6.NLM and REMOTE.NLM require that a password be assigned when you load them. You can generate encrypted passwords using RCONAG6 .NLM or REMOTE.NLM, which further restricts access to the server console via a workstation.

> **NOTE** Physical security is, by far, the most important factor in network security. If someone can walk up and access your file server without being watched, he or she can do damage no matter how secure your network is.

ConsoleOne

ConsoleOne is a graphical utility written in Java that allows you to manage the server and NDS. It implements Novell's Open Architecture, which encourages developers to add customized applications, objects and services to the operating system and management tools. Specifically, you can use ConsoleOne to manage the server, and third-party developers can use it as a front end for their applications.

When ConsoleOne loads, it will display a toolbar, menu bar, and two windows. The left window of ConsoleOne allows you to navigate from object to object, and the right window displays the properties and values of the objects. To access properties and values, use the menu bar or toolbar at the top of the display. Your menu and toolbar options will vary depending on the object that is highlighted.

Access Remote or Local Server Consoles

You can access the local server or a remote server console screen through ConsoleOne using one of two utilities—Console Manager or RCONSOLEJ. In order for you to gain access to local or remote servers using these tools, your target server must have the agent RCONCAG6.NLM loaded. The RCONSOLEJ RCONCAG6 agent can be accessed through a TCP or SPX port configured during the loading of the agent. The auto loading of this agent is marked in the AUTOEXEC.NCF by default at installation. The Console Manager's main screen can be accessed through ConsoleOne.

Access NDS Objects

ConsoleOne gives you access to NDS trees, allowing you to manage objects, delete objects, and create new objects in very much the same way NWAdmin does. You can also manage object properties and values, which is new with ConsoleOne.

Access Files and Folders

Administrators can add shortcuts to resources on the ConsoleOne interface which allows you to access files, folders, and applets more quickly. A shortcut is a text file that specifies a file, folder, or applet to be added to the ConsoleOne interface.

By default ConsoleOne includes several shortcuts. You can access frequently used configuration files by going to My Server ➢ Configuration files object. You will then be able to select the files you want to view.

ConsoleOne v1.2b

When you install NDSv8, a new version of ConsoleOne is installed (v1.2b). It includes new features for managing additional NDS object types, customizing the NDS schema, configuring NDS for LDAP-based access, and managing properties of files and folders on NetWare volumes.

With the new features added to ConsoleOne, you can:

Browse huge NDS containers   You can browse NDS containers containing thousands of objects. ConsoleOne gets and displays the contents one page at a time.

Search or customize views   In an NDS tree, you can search or filter the contents of the right window based on object name and type. You can also search based on specific property values.

Configure LDAP services   You can configure LDAPv3 services on individual NetWare servers and control how LDAP-based access to NDS works for different groups of users.

Administer all NDS objects   You can create, move, rename, delete, and modify any type of NDS object defined in the schema of your NDS tree. Custom property pages are available on most object types, and a generic Other page lists any leftover properties. You can modify multiple objects of the same type simultaneously.

Extend the NDS schema   You can extend the NDS schema to allow the addition of new types of objects and properties to your NDS tree. This includes the ability to create auxiliary classes.

NetWare
Operations

PART 2

Set up user accounts by template You can create templates for setting up new user accounts. A template supplies initial values for most properties of the User object, including a home directory in the NetWare file system.

Control NDS rights inheritance You can control whether NDS rights assignments are inheritable to lower levels in the tree, even for specific properties such as login passwords.

Manage NetWare file services You can manage the file system on individual NetWare volumes. You can create, move, copy, and delete individual files and folders. You can modify file and folder attributes, including rights assignments and owners. You can view and change volume statistics and control disk space allocations by user or by folder.

NOTE ConsoleOne v1.2b will only run on a 32-bit Windows workstation. You will also need to have Java 1.1.7. Check the Novell Web site for the latest info on system requirements.

When you install NDSv8 on a NetWare 5 server, the installation procedure copies the new ConsoleOne v1.2b files to the server and deletes a few of the old ConsoleOne files. You can still run the old ConsoleOne on the server, but on the client you will always get the new ConsoleOne.

The new ConsoleOne files that get copied to the server include a SETUP.EXE program that you can run on a 32-bit Windows client which will configure that client to run the new ConsoleOne.

WARNING NetWare Administrator is a better tool to manage small- and medium-sized NDS trees and is required for configuring Secure Socket Layers (SSL) for LDAP.

Additional Security Enhancements

NetWare 5 takes security to the next level by providing the next generation of authentication services named Secure Authentication Services (SAS). SAS provides server-based user applications with controlled access to files and NDS objects based on the user's SAS authentication. NetWare 5's SAS supports Secure Socket Layer (SSL) and use the SAS API set to establish encrypted SSL connections.

NetWare 5 implements the Public Key Infrastructure Services (PKIS): a set of services that enables the use of public key cryptography and digital certificates in a NetWare system.

PKIS for NetWare 5 allows you to establish a Certificate Authority (CA) management domain within NDS. Then you can use the CA and key management activity to enable certificate-based security services such as Secure Socket Layer (SSL) security for Web and LDAP servers.

The advent and increased popularity of e-commerce also requires the use of PKIS to secure Web sites containing customer sensitive information. This information includes purchase transactions as well as personal information.

PKIS also works with most commercial certificate authorities such as VeriSign, and with certificate authority software packages such as Netscape CA Server, and Microsoft CA Server. PKIS optionally generates PKCS #10 formatted Certificate Signing Requests (CSRs) that can be used by commercial or external certificate authorities.

Novell PKIS consists of a PKI.NLM and a snap-in module to NetWare Administrator. A network administrator uses NetWare Administrator as the administration point for PKIS.

> **NOTE**   Browsers will issue a warning saying that they don't trust you as a certificate authority unless the browser has been configured properly.

The following is a brief overview on installing and configuring SAS and PKIS:

- When installing a NetWare 5 server, you can install SAS, PKIS, and the NICI Cryptographic Modules through the Other Installation Items/Products menu. If you did not install these when you installed NetWare, you can still do so by using ConsoleOne's Install option at the NetWare 5 server and then installing these components through the customization menu.

- You must create the Certificate Authority object before you can perform any other administrative tasks using PKIS. The NDS tree CA object is created through NetWare Administrator. Once created, the NDS tree CA object resides in the Security Container in the NDS tree.

- You then create a Key Material object in the container where the NetWare 5 Server object resides. It is recommended that you create a separate Key Material object for each security application (for example LDAP services for NDS) on the server. Key Material objects are created through NetWare Administrator.

- To configure a security application to use a Key Material object you must look at that application's documentation. Each application has its own particular way of setting this up.

> **NOTE**   We strongly recommend that you review Novell's latest information on SAS and PKIS before implementing it on your network.

> *NOTE* The server to which a Key Material object is associated must be able to communicate with at least one other server holding a writable copy of the Key Material object. You must ensure that the servers are running the same protocol (IP and/or IPX). In addition, both servers must have all of the components listed installed and running on it.

NIAS Remote Access and Mobile Users

Today we live in a time of constant movement. Companies have employees traveling via plane, train, and car to remote locations to do business. These employees have to be able to stay in contact with the company and access the resources they need. Remote access has become the buzzword for mobile users. Or you may be involved in providing and maintaining a VPN network over the Internet so that the company doesn't have to pay for long distance charges.

You don't have to be a rocket scientist to provide these services. There are many solutions out there, including Novell NIAS Remote Access Server.

What Is NIAS Remote Access?

NIAS (Novell Internet Access Server) Remote Access Server runs on a NetWare 5 server, and provides the ability to support multiple modems and give users access to network resources. NIAS is part of the NetWare BorderManager server, which bundles many services for secure remote access and Internet access. These services include Firewall, Proxy, Cache Accelerator for Web sites, Remote Access Server, and many more features. NIAS also allows flexibility in the type of connections you want to use. You can provide a low-cost solution like an analog modem or high performance frame-relay connections.

There is a variety of equipment needed for NIAS to work. These include:

- One or more modems connected to the NIAS Remote Access Server
- A modem connected to the remote workstation or laptop
- An extra 5MB of RAM in the NIAS Remote Access Server
- A login and password for the user to access the remote network
- Remote workstation or laptop configured for remote access services
- Remote workstation or laptop and NIAS Remote Access Server set up with some type of data communication connection between them

In the case of supporting a VPN connection you will need a BorderManager server with a dedicated connection to your ISP, and the ISP has to support Virtual Private Networks (VPN) services. The clients also need to be configured, in addition to Dialup, as a VPN client. You can use RADIUS or PPTP as your VPN protocols (RADIUS is an authentication and accounting database, PPTP [Point to Point Tunneling Protocol] is a proprietary Microsoft protocol.).

In many companies, hardware solutions from CISCO and Bay Networks (Nortel) are commonly used. Microsoft NT also has a viable solution that we have used in the past.

Figure 8.1 illustrates the different RAS implementations you might consider:

Figure 8.1   A local area network and remote access via a laptop computer using RAS and VPN solutions

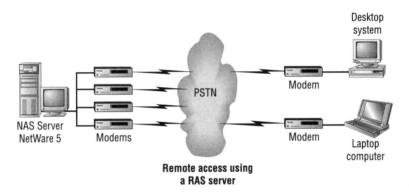

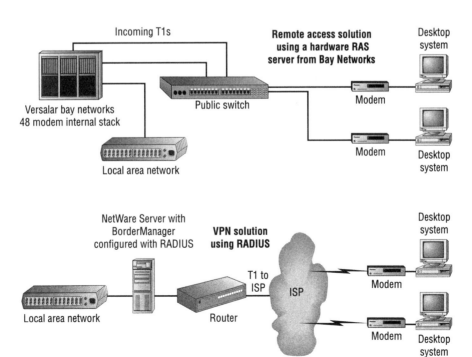

Sage Advice: Planning for RAS

There are several factors you need to consider when planning for remote access:

- Which users need remote access?

- Where are these users located? How many are at each location?

- Do you have enough phone lines/WAN links to handle additional network traffic and routing?

- How many NIAS Remote Access Servers will you need?

- Where are the best locations to place the NIAS Remote Access Server? (Think about how many remote users you'll have in that area.)

- What type of services or resources will the mobile users need while attached to the network remotely?

- How many simultaneous remote access connections will you need per NIAS Remote Access Server?

There is no standard set of rules when you plan for remote access services. You will have different needs from company to company so you will benefit from asking a lot of questions.

The following sections explore each of the elements that you will need to establish remote access.

Who Needs Access?

The first question or two you might consider during the remote access design phase is who needs remote access and why do they need it? This privilege should not be given lightly to every user who asks for it. You must determine whether they truly have a need for resources while at home or some other location. Are they a regular mobile user, or is this the only time they will need remote access? Security is always at risk when you give remote access, even though NIAS includes security measures. We will discuss remote access security later in this chapter.

Remote access allows mobile users to perform the following tasks:

- Send reports to the company via e-mail or even print to a printer on the network at a different location

- Access the resources in their files and directories on the NetWare 5 network

- Teleconference with the boss or attend a company business meeting without leaving home
- Print a document remotely by attaching and printing to a company printer
- Administrate the network remotely, if they have rights as the Admin user

NIAS versus LAN Connections

While in the planning stage of remote access, there are a few concerns you need to take into account. Not only do you need to decide who needs access, and where to place NIAS Remote Access Servers, but what kind of connection you'll provide and how fast you will connect them. Here are the key steps:

1. Select a data transmission media. Even if users connect with a 56KB modem, their access speed will be much slower than it is when they are attached locally to the LAN. The xDSL connections, described later in this section, can provide much faster speeds than POTS or ISDN, but a LAN, with the Ethernet transferring data at 10 to 100 megabits per second, will always be much faster.

2. Design an effective security plan. In most companies, this is the number-one concern. It's less secure to access the network via a voice telephone connection than by a local connection on the LAN. NIAS remote access includes some measures to increase security which we will cover later in this section.

3. Select locations for your NIAS Remote Servers. Place your NIAS servers in locations where you have large numbers of mobile users. By doing this, you cut down on the phone bills incurred when remote users access the NIAS via modem.

These steps illustrate the importance of having a well thought-out plan of action before you start deploying the NIAS Remote Access Servers. Your goal as administrator is to provide efficient and secure network access to remote users just as you do for other users.

Designing an Effective Security Plan

Network security is probably one of the most important issues you will face when designing a remote access plan for your users. Your main objective is to protect your network data against unauthorized access. It has become a pastime for hackers to see how many network systems they can break into. This is a serious problem, but the risk of break-ins can be reduced with some advanced planning for remote access.

The network administrator assigns rights in NDS which allow only authorized users to access particular files and directories. This is where designing a good Directory tree is very important. Assigning too many, or inappropriate, rights to users can really hurt the security of your company.

There are three main ways to ensure remote access security. You can:

- Create security policies for remote access
- Establish demilitarized zones for Remote Access Servers
- Ensure effective security configurations

Security Policies for Remote Access

First you need to decide on some guidelines for remote access. Establish policies such as these: Each user will be given a unique user ID and a password and users will be given rights only to the resources that they need while accessing the network remotely and so on. To design a remote access security policy appropriate for your company, use these questions as a starting point:

- Who are the remote users? Make a list of jobs, NDS groups, resources needed, and locations they need to access.
- Who will be in charge of security in your network?
- If you discover that an intruder has been on your network, what measures will be taken?
- Will the remote passwords be encrypted? Will users use the same password as their LAN password or a different one when connected remotely?
- Are there some data files or applications that you won't grant remote access to at all?
- Will remote connections be encrypted?
- Do you want the remote server to do callbacks to remote users?

Demilitarized Zones (DMZ) for Remote Access

You will want to set up an area of access for both your users and the public, yet still have some firewall security. Such an area is called a demilitarized zone or DMZ. This is done with a firewall that has at least three interfaces, one of which is assigned a DMZ. Web and FTP servers can be placed within a DMZ. This is a good use of the DMZ; you can filter public access, and allow unfiltered access for administrators.

Although creating a demilitarized zone goes beyond the scope of this book, it is important that you understand the concept. A screening router is the main component in the demilitarized zone and a basic component of most firewalls. Screening routers do just as their name implies: they screen packets, therefore allowing you to filter them.

NetWare 5 servers, hardware RAS solutions from Bay or CISCO, commercial routers, or a host-based router with packet-filtering capabilities can screen and connect remote access users to the network. A very popular firewall in the market today is Checkpoint.

This product provides excellent firewall services including a demilitarized zone capability and VPN services.

TIP DMZ's are very tricky to set up properly and they can be implemented in several different ways. Consult a network security analyst before attempting to implement a DMZ yourself.

Effective Security Configurations

By default, the NIAS Remote Access Server offers remote users unrestricted access. That's why it is very important to develop an effective security configuration for your network, before a problem happens. You'll need to:

- Set company restrictions to your NIAS Remote Access Server.

- Design a demilitarized zone to secure sensitive information. Firewalls are a big part of network security.

- Make the security administrator in your company a part of the remote access design team.

- Always be proactive, not reactive; this will save you a lot of headaches down the line.

Location of NIAS Remote Servers

You'll need to take into account several cost considerations when deciding on the location of the NIAS remote servers. Here are some questions to help you find the best choice for your company:

- **Will you need new servers, or do you have servers available at each site where you plan to place a NIAS remote server?** A low-cost option would be to install NIAS Remote Access Servers on existing servers provided that they can handle the added workload.

- **How many remote users are there at each location?** Locate the areas where you have the most remote users and place NIAS Remote Access Servers in those areas. Then you can minimize the expense of long-distance connections.

- **Will you need to buy more hardware for the LAN because of the increased traffic remote users will bring to the network?** Design your remote access plan to anticipate who needs remote access and who doesn't. Every user that is connected, whether remotely or directly on the LAN, causes increased traffic on your network. So plan your user access carefully. Make sure your network routers and WAN links can handle the extra traffic. If they can't, fix the problem before it hurts your network performance.

Optimal Remote Access Performance

Users accustomed to the speed of a fast local connection may perceive even optimal remote access performance as slow. You should consider, as part of your implementation plan, educating users on what performance to expect when dialing in to their network resources. At the same time, you should anticipate where bottlenecks might occur as users connect remotely to their network. There are three areas you need to monitor and optimize for the best possible performance discussed in the following sections: the server, the client user, and the remote access service.

Optimal Performance on the Server

NIAS Remote Access Servers should have the recommended amount of hardware to optimize remote access. The bandwidth for connections to the NIAS Remote Access Server should be adequate for all locations on the network.

This is where planning the appropriate data communication media is important. Your goal is to have a high-performance, low-maintenance NIAS remote access service.

Optimal Performance for Users

Servers can't complain, but remote users can—and that's exactly what they will do if remote access to your network is slow. It is normal for remote access to be slower than LAN connections, but it is still important to optimize the performance as much as possible for your users to ensure that their work is productive.

Here are some ways to optimize performance for the remote user:

- Load the programs or resources that remote users use frequently on the remote workstation or laptop.

- Install the newest modem version in the remote workstation or laptop. (Believe us, we find there are still many laptops with 28KB modems out there.)

- Tell the remote user to expect slower connections so they won't be disappointed when it happens. (This is very important; most of your support calls are due to user expectations not being met.)

- Limit the login scripts for the remote user. (Reducing the number of connections speeds up the login process.)

- Evaluate different data communication connections, keeping in mind the type of resources and needs the remote user will have when connected remotely. This should help you determine which type of connection is best suited for them.

Optimal Performance for Remote Access Service Administration

You can manage remote users and groups through NetWare Administrator or the Remote Access Server console. The Remote Access Server uses the Remote Access Management Agent (RAMA), which is compatible with SNMP (Simple Network Management Protocol), in order to be managed by ManageWise or any SNMP-based management tool.

NIAS Remote Access Server can also provide DHCP services to clients, thus eliminating the need to manually configure and administrate IP addresses for them. DHCP, discussed in more detail in Appendix A, provides the following services for remote users:

- An IP address while they are remotely connected
- A DNS server address and domain
- A default gateway router

RAS and VPN Solutions

There are many solutions out there that support remote access to corporate as well as ISP networks. You need to be aware of them so you can make decisions that best fit your company.

As a Novell network administrator, you have increased responsibilities for remote users accessing your enterprise LAN and internetwork. Remote access includes not only dial-in users, but also access from the Internet through your firewall or virtual private network.

The challenge is to provide a centralized form of authentication, authorization, and accounting for your entire network, no matter which type of remote access you may have. And you'll want to use the existing authentication framework you have in place such as Novell NetWare Directory Services.

To meet this challenge, a new standard—RADIUS (Remote Authentication Dial In User Service) has emerged which is supported by the leading remote access and firewall vendors.

Some of the products that support the RADIUS standard are Ascend MAX, Bay Networks' Annex, Shiva LAN Rover, Telebit NetBlazer, and the US Robotics' Total Control. Firewall products include Raptor's Eagle, CISCO Pix, and Cheyenne's Checkpoint. Most RAS devices can handle multiple dial-in users at once, and the corporate network might include a single RAS or multiple RASs working in tandem.

A typical installation will include a single RADIUS server like NetWare BorderManager, for example, to handle all the Remote Access Servers. Companies with Remote Access Servers at multiple sites could elect to have a separate RADIUS server at each site. If the various sites were linked over a WAN of reasonable speed or over the Internet, a single RADIUS server could be made to handle multiple Remote Access Servers at multiple sites.

RADIUS Protocol

RADIUS consists of a RADIUS server that retrieves all user information from a central database (like NDS) and a RADIUS accounting server that logs information on remote dial-in users. These two components run on your network. To accept VPN connections through your ISP you need to use a proxy RADIUS that runs at the ISP. Novell's implementation of RADIUS provides the following services:

- Centralized administration
- Client/Server environment
- Security over an Internet connection (VPN)
- Support for multiple platforms
- Customization options
- User authentication for dial-in services

In the following sections you will see how RADIUS accomplishes authentication and how it supports these features.

Authentication Types

During an authentication transaction, password information is transmitted between the RAS and the RADIUS server. The password information is encrypted using a secret key that you enter both at the RAS and at the RADIUS server.

The password information originally comes from the user, usually as part of PPP negotiations. The RAS is really just an intermediary, and it is best to think of authentication as being a transaction between the user and the RADIUS server.

Authentication Between Users and RAS

There are two types of authentication transactions used between a remote access user and RAS. Each represents a method of authentication used in PPP:

PAP (Password Authentication Protocol) is very simple. The user sends his or her password to the RADIUS server, and the RADIUS server validates it, either against its own database or against the NetWare Bindery or NDS. Of the two legs of the journey the password takes between user and RADIUS server, the first leg is usually unencrypted, and the RAS gets the password from the user in clear text. For the second leg, the RAS encrypts the password and the RADIUS server decrypts it using a shared secret key. Ultimately, the RADIUS server has the password in clear text form and is able to make use of it directly for authentication.

CHAP   (Challenge Handshake Authentication Protocol) avoids sending passwords in clear text over any communication link. With CHAP, the RAS generates a random number (the challenge) and sends it to the user. The user's PPP client creates a *digest*—a one-way encryption—of the password concatenated with the challenge, and sends this digest to the RAS. Because the digest is a one-way encryption, the RADIUS server cannot recover the password from the digest. What it can do is perform the identical digest operation using its own copy of the user's password stored in its database; if the two digests match, the user is authenticated.

RADIUS Attribute Exchange

The authentication transaction serves an additional purpose beyond simply authenticating the user. Along with the authentication information that the RAS includes as part of a RADIUS request, the RAS also passes information about the type of connection the user is trying to establish. The RADIUS server can use this information to further qualify the user, possibly issuing a reject based on this information.

Similarly, the RADIUS server includes additional information as part of the accept response it issues to the RAS. The RAS uses this information to control various aspects of the user's connection. This aspect of the authentication transaction is called *attribute exchange*.

Attribute exchange is controlled by the user's profile. Each profile lists attributes of two types:

- Checklist attributes define a set of requirements for the connection. During the authentication transaction, the RAS must send attributes to the RADIUS server that match the checklist; if they don't, the RADIUS server will issue a reject even if the user can be authenticated. For example, by including appropriate attributes in the checklist, a variety of rules could be enforced. Only certain users might be permitted to use ISDN connections or dial into a particular RAS. Or, caller ID could be used to validate a user against a list of legal originating phone numbers.

- Return-list attributes are the attributes that the RADIUS server sends back to the RAS once authentication is successful. The return list defines additional parameters that the RAS should assign to the connection, typically as part of PPP negotiations. For example, specific users could be assigned particular IP addresses or IPX network numbers, IP header compression could be turned on or off, or a time limit could be assigned to the connection.

NetWare
Operations

PART 2

Dictionary Files

The RADIUS server uses Dictionary files to establish checklist and return-list attribute values. The Dictionary file contains the RAS-specific proprietary items, which may be set for a user. Steel-Belted RADIUS provides pre-configured Dictionary files for popular RAS products.

RADIUS Accounting and Reporting

RADIUS Accounting is an additional feature of the RADIUS standard that permits a RADIUS server to track when users start and stop their dial-in connections and to acquire statistics about each session.

Using RADIUS Accounting, the RADIUS server can maintain:

- A history of all user dial-in sessions, indicating start time, stop time, and various statistics for the session
- A current User list indicating which users are currently connected to which Remote Access Servers

BorderManager fully supports RADIUS Accounting. All Accounting transactions are logged to a comma-delimited file that can be imported into standard word processors, spreadsheets, and database programs for report generation and billing.

One of the most useful capabilities provided by BorderManager is a real-time list of active RADIUS users displayed from the Administrator program in the Current Users dialog. For every active dial-in session, a line is displayed containing the following fields:

Distinguished Name   Shows the full username, which was used for the authentication

RAS-Client   Shows the Remote Access Server identification, which will either be the RAS's name or IP address

RAS Port   Shows the Remote Access Server port number, which represents a unique port number on the RAS

Time   Contains the date and time which the connection was started, according to the accounting transactions

While remote access offers tremendous opportunities for organizations, it brings with it a set of management issues. Most environments today are already using some type of authentication to manage access such as that provided by Novell. It makes sense to use the existing infrastructure to manage all types of remote access for authentication, authorization, and accounting. Plus, this yields increased security, since all access is managed centrally and can be audited with full assurance that all entries into the LAN can be accounted for.

RADIUS Proxy

For VPN services you will need a RADIUS proxy (which allows an organization to outsource its modem bank or dial-up hardware resources) to an ISP. The RADIUS proxy is located with the ISP. Clients connecting through the Internet then access the RADIUS proxy at the ISP, which forwards the connection request to the RADIUS server in your network. Once the client is authenticated, the user is given access to your network through the BorderManager server. This process requires a dedicated connection to the Internet from the BorderManager server to the ISP.

NetWare 5@Work: An Administrator's Nightmare

What would you do if you just purchased and installed a Remote Access Server costing several thousand dollars only to realize that it couldn't authenticate your users?

Such was the case for a medical training facility at a health science campus. Administrator's wanted to give employees at the center dial-in access to the university's 90-server Novell network (for e-mail, clinical data research, and Internet access). The MIS manager purchased a Bay Networks Remote Annex 4000 Remote Access Server. But once he installed the unit, he discovered a serious problem: Yes, it could provide dial-in access to the LAN, but it could not authenticate dial-in users against the information in NDS. He would have to manually recreate the appropriate entries in the RAS authentication database (a very big and tedious job).

Steel-Belted RADIUS for NetWare to the Rescue

For a few months, we settled for providing remote access to a few key and trusted users while we sought a solution. Then, at NetWorld + Interop, we visited the Bay Networks booth which referred us to a company called Funk Software. They had what we were looking for: a program that sits on the Novell server, waits for authentication requests from any dial-in server on the network, and handles the authentication via NDS.

A custom implementation of the RADIUS authentication standard, Steel-Belted Radius lets you authenticate all dial-in users against the existing information in your NetWare Bindery or NetWare Directory Services (no matter how many remote access servers are connected to your network).

We called Funk Software to purchase a copy. It was just a 50-page manual and a single diskette! And even more surprising was that from the moment we installed it, it worked! We've never done anything so easily before.

NetWare 5@Work: An Administrator's Nightmare *(continued)*

Steel-Belted Radius provides single-server implementation and thorough reporting on any RAS server on the network. Steel-Belted Radius logs all dial-in activity and lets you display a list of currently connected users. Plus, any changes you make to NetWare authentication apply to Steel-Belted Radius as well, so your dial-in users are always authenticated against the latest security information.

The fact that Steel-Belted Radius administration program runs in Windows scored heavily with us. This made the learning curve manageable, and deployment was done quickly.

Selecting a Connection Service

Selecting the connection services of both the remote user and your NIAS Remote Access Server is one of the key steps in designing a remote access system.

A connection service is the physical connection by which information travels. Your connection determines the speed of your service. In a LAN, the connection is usually cable, fiber optic, and so on. But data for data transmission between the NIAS Remote Access Server and remote users is provided through telecoms *(telephone company connections)*. You need to choose the best connection service for your NIAS Remote Access Server and your remote users. The telecom options are explained in the following sections.

ISDN

ISDN (Integrated Services Digital Network) is an evolving set of standards for a digital network that carries both voice and data communications. It requires the support of a TA (Terminal Adapter) and NT1 (Network Termination 1 device) on the client and server. The NT1 connects the server to the telecom.

ISDN connections are more costly than traditional analog connections. They are typically billed on a per-channel basis. If you are designing a plan of action, you need to decide if the need for speed outweighs the cost of providing it. The following questions will help you decide whether ISDN service is the best solution for your company:

- Will remote users be sending or receiving voice or video transmissions?
- Will remote users need high digital speeds for data transmissions?
- What type of resources will remote users need to access through the NIAS Remote Access Server?

Answering "Yes" to any of these questions is an indication that you need ISDN services.

ISDN offers two services for the customer: Basic Rate Interface and Primary Rate Interface.

Basic Rate Interface (BRI)

BRI is ISDN's basic service, which is made up of two 64KB B (bearer) channels and one 16KB D (delta) channel.

- Bearer or B-channels are circuit-switched connections that carry voice and data. Each B channel is capable of sending data at 64KB. Two B channels combined together through a process called bonding can deliver an aggregate throughput of 128KB. This is possible through your hardware and NIAS software, which supports MPPP (Multilink Point to Point Protocol).

- Delta or D channels use packet-switched connections and are used to control signals. For example, the D-channel can be used to hold or activate conference calling, call forwarding, and caller identification.

Primary Rate Interface (PRI)

PRI is ISDN's high-speed service. It is equivalent to a T1 (in North America and Japan), or E1 (in Europe) circuit, with ISDN software installed on it. PRIs can be used to consolidate multiple BRI circuits into a single larger circuit which is easier to manage and sometimes more cost effective. A T1 is a network communications line that has 24 64KB channels. With ISDN software installed you get 23 B channels, and one 64KB D channel. An E1 is a network communications line that has the same configuration but offers thirty B channels and one D channel (remember a T1 is 1.544Mb and an E1 is 2.048Mb).

POTS

POTS (Plain Old Telephone System) can be used for data communication between the remote user and the NIAS Remote Access Server. The equipment needed by both the remote user and the NIAS Remote Access Server is a modem and access to POTS. For basic communication between the remote user and their office, this service could provide a low-cost solution.

If your users need remote access to attend videoconferences or to upload or download large files and graphics, this service probably won't be suitable for your company. Once again, you need to weigh the pros and cons.

In today's POTS environment you typically find 33.6KB and 56KB modems. The biggest difference between the two is that 33.6KB modems provide the same speed on download as well as upload. By contrast, 56KB modems can only provide a maximum of 53.3KB per FCC regulations. There is no such thing as being able to transfer at 56KB in both directions using an analog connection.

PART 2

NetWare
Operations

xDSL

xDSL (Digital Subscriber Line) increases the speed of traditional analog telephone lines. This enables the remote user to have high-speed remote access to the NIAS Remote Access Server over POTS. This family of DSLs is called xDSL, and here are several examples:

HDSL (High Speed DSL)   Downloads at a rate of 1.544Mb and uploads at the same speed. Requires two cable pairs and provides symmetric transmission.

ADSL (Asynchronous DSL)   Downloads at a rate of up to 8.192Mb, but upload rates are slower. Requires a splitter at the remote user's site as well as some extra installation costs. Typically this speed is determined based on your proximity to the nearest DSLAM (Access Multiplexer), and the type of equipment your provider is using.

"Splitterless" DSL   Downloads at a rate of less than 1Mb, and upload rates are about the same. This doesn't require a splitter, which will reduce installation costs but also slow performance.

DSL uses packet-switching technology. It can be either asymmetric or symmetric. Asymmetric DSL allows for video on demand and Internet access at faster downstream speeds. Symmetric DSL allows for the same bi-directional speed.

NOTE   xDSL is not available in all areas. Before you spend hours designing a remote access plan around xDSL, check with your local telephone service or Internet provider to make sure that option is available to you.

Server Application Support

NetWare 5 brings enhanced application support with its improved memory management architecture. Virtual memory features provide better application support also. When an application requires more memory than is physically available, the operating system creates temporary memory that extends actual RAM in the system.

A new Java-based GUI and several Java-based applications are also included with NetWare 5. ConsoleOne and DNS/DHCP Management Console are examples of these. By being Java compatible, Novell makes it possible for developers to implement their own application with NetWare 5 servers.

These features, coupled with multiprocessor support, combine to enhance performance in all situations and have made NetWare 5 a capable application server.

Virtual Memory

Virtual memory (VM) has been incorporated into NetWare 5's memory management process to use physical RAM for maximum efficiency. Virtual memory allows an application to address memory space larger than the amount the server has in physical RAM. This is accomplished through the use of swap files.

A swap file is a file on the hard drive that simulates RAM, expanding as needed. A swap file is created on the SYS: volume by default, with a minimum size of 2MB; since the file can grow, you need to be careful that you do not run out of space in the SYS: volume. You can also create swap files in other volumes; doing so allows you to remove the swap file from the SYS: volume, preserving more space there.

You must be careful when adding a swap file to another volume, however. You need to add the file commands to the AUTOEXEC.NCF file to delete the swap file from the SYS: volume, and then create the swap file in the desired volume. If you do not add the necessary commands to the AUTOEXEC.NCF, the changes are not permanent.

NetWare
Operations

PART 2

WARNING   When you reboot the server, it will automatically put the swap file back in the SYS: volume unless you enter commands in the AUTOEXEC.NCF.

As part of the virtual memory system, NetWare monitors application codes, which will be explained in more detail. Codes that are inactive for a period of time are moved to the swap file on SYS: or another volume where you've created a swap file. When the code is needed, it is moved from the swap file to the server's physical RAM.

The default setting for a swap file is as follows (values are in MB):

MIN = 2

MAX = Free volume space

MIN FREE = 5

Note that the minimum free space of 5MB is what would be left on the volume when the swap file grows to full capacity. To change Virtual Memory parameters, use MONITOR !H on the server console. The !H option gives you access to hidden SET parameters, including Virtual Memory parameters.

WARNING   The MONITOR !H command displays hidden SET parameters. These should only be displayed and viewed by an administrator.

You will use the SWAP console command to add swap files to volumes, or to delete them. Enter **HELP SWAP** at the server console to list all the swap commands available to you.

Applications and Threads

NetWare 5 allocates CPU time to all applications that are running on the server. An administrator can allocate more CPU time to business-critical applications, allowing them to finish before other applications use the resources. This is a welcome addition with NetWare 5.

Applications are composed of many threads, which are each a path of code, like an IF statement routine. An IF statement is built into a program to define how to proceed once the individual using the program enters data. These codes have a beginning and an end, but the end can include numerous different paths or endings, each with its own thread.

NetWare 5 uses application groups to gather a number of threads and ensure that they have appropriate time on the processor. An administrator can create an application group and assign this group more threads so it can have additional processor time. The more threads that are assigned to an application, the more processor time the application gets. A NetWare 5 server's CPU can suspend threads from one application that is not in use at the time and allow threads from another application waiting in line to run. The system can then allow the threads that were suspended to start back up where they left off.

Share value of an application can be adjusted once the application is loaded. Share value is the amount of CPU time an application has, as opposed to the amount that other applications have. You can adjust this by using the Monitor utility and going into the Kernel option. Once in the Kernel options, select the Application option. You'll be able to see the applications that are running. The share values will be listed and you'll be able to adjust them at this point. The default share value is 100. To change this value, press F3 and enter your new value.

The NetWare Application group is the only application that is created by default when you install a NetWare 5 server. Some applications are created when programs load their NLMs. Other programs don't create applications, and these are assigned to the NetWare Application group by default.

Protected Memory

In NetWare 5, protected memory (an area of memory that is shielded from the operating system to protect it from injury or damage) can be used to protect the server from crashing because of corrupt NLMs. The NetWare operating system can't run in this area, it runs in an area called OS address space or the kernel address space. You can load one or more NLMs into protected address spaces that you create by using the commands in Table 8.1.

Table 8.1 Commands for Protected Address Spaces

Commands entered at server console	Results of the command function
MODULES	Lists the NLMs that are loaded along with the name of its address space.
PROTECTION	Lists all the address spaces on the system and the NLMs that reside in them.
LOAD PROTECTED *Module_Name*	Loads a specified NLM into a new protected space.
RESTART *Module_Name*	Loads a specified NLM into a new protected space with restart enabled. This means that if the NLM abends, the system will shut down and restart the space and reload the NLM into that space.
LOAD ADDRESS SPACE=*Address_Space_Name Module_Name* (Write complete command on one line.)	Loads the specified NLM into the protected space, plus this command allows you to load more than one NLM into the same protected space.
PROTECT *NCF_File_Name*	This is an address space where you will load all the NLMs listed in NCF files. This is a new protected space with the same name as the NCF file name.
UNLOAD ADDRESS SPACE=*Address_Space_Name Module_Name* (Write complete command on one line.)	This command allows you to unload a specified NLM from the address space but the address space remains.
UNLOAD ADDRESS SPACE=*Address_Space_Name* (Write complete command on one line.)	Allows you to unload all the NLMs in that particular address space while removing the address space at the same time.
UNLOAD KILL ADDRESS SPACE=*Address_Space_Name* (Write complete command on one line.)	Allows you to remove the address space without first removing the NLMs. The NLMs are then returned to the system.

NetWare
Operations

PART 2

SYSCALLS (the common name for the NetWare Operating System Call and Marshalling Library) is an NLM that intercepts corrupted calls and blocks them from passing calls to the core operating system, thus protecting the operating system. Together SYSCALLS and memory protection act as the interface between the server and the protected address spaces. To load SYSCALLS, use the server console command **SYSCALLS**. When SYSCALLS is loaded, the screen displays a list of NLMs for which calls to the system are filtered.

LDAPv3 Services

The Lightweight Directory Access Protocol (LDAP) is an Internet communications protocol that allows client applications to access directory information. It is based on the X.500 Directory Access Protocol (DAP) but is less complex than a traditional client and can be used with any other directory service that follows the X.500 standard.

The most popular current use of LDAP is to allow clients to access directory services that store and publish telephone numbers and e-mail addresses. But newer implementations of LDAP include stand-alone LDAP Directory servers.

Novell LDAP Services for NDS

Novell LDAP Services for NDS is a server application that allows you to set up and configure an LDAP service for your network. Using ConsoleOne or NetWare Administrator, you can set up and manage your Novell LDAP server and control the access you want to give to LDAP clients accessing your NDS directory.

Two new objects will be added to your Directory tree:

LDAP Server Object   Use this object to set up and manage the Novell LDAP Server properties.

LDAP Group Object   Use this object to set up and manage the way LDAP clients will access and use the information on the Novell LDAP server.

LDAP Services for NDS is also integrated with NDS Catalog Services to help improve the performance of search results requested by LDAP clients.

This product is LDAPv3 compliant.

NOTE   For more information about LDAP, refer to the University of Michigan at www.umich.edu/~dirsvcs/ldap/ldap.html and Critical Angle Inc. at www.critical-angle.com/ldapworld/index.html.

SSL for LDAP

LDAP Services for NDS supports the Secure Sockets Layer (SSL) protocol to ensure that the connection over which data is transmitted is secure and private.

To ensure message privacy, SSL provides for the creation and use of encrypted communications channels. To prevent message forgery, SSL allows the server and, optionally, the client to authenticate each other during the establishment of the secure connection. This release of LDAP does not ask the LDAP client to authenticate itself.

Key Material Object

To implement the authentication and encryption processes, SSL uses a cryptographic mechanism called public keys. To establish a secure connection, the server and the client exchange their public keys to establish a session key. The session key will be used to encrypt the data for the life of the connection. A subsequent LDAP connection over SSL will result in the generation of a new session key that is different from the previous one.

Digital certificates, digital IDs, digital passports, or public key certificates are critical for verifying the identity of the contacted server. They are similar to an employee badge that identifies the wearer as an employee of a company.

Each LDAP server requires a digital certificate to implement SSL. A certification authority (CA) issues digital certificates. Certificates are stored in a new NDS object, the Key Material object. Use Novell PKIS, a snap-in of the NetWare Administrator utility, to request, manage, and store certificates in NDS.

In order for the LDAP server to use a specific certificate for LDAP SSL connectivity (once it is stored in NDS), you must indicate the Key Material object containing the certificate on the LDAP Server General page in NetWare Administrator.

> **WARNING** The Key Material object must be in the same container as the NetWare Server object that will use it.

SSL Configuration

Although SSL can be configured on both the client and server to ensure the identity of both parties, clients do not require digital certificates to communicate securely. As the LDAP server listens for SSL connections on a special port, all the client needs to do is initiate the connection over that port.

To use SSL with LDAP you will need to have already installed SAS, PKIS, and NICI services. You will need to make sure that SSL is configured on the LDAP server. The Key Material object and the LDAP server must be in the same container.

NetWare
Operations

PART 2

LDAP vs. NDS Syntax

You will notice that LDAP and NDS use different syntaxes. The following are some important differences:

Commas   LDAP uses commas as delimiters rather than periods.

Typeful Names Only   LDAP uses only Typeful Names.

Escape Character   LDAP uses the backslash (\) in distinguished names as an escape character. If you use the plus (+) character or the comma (,) character, you can escape them with a single backslash character. Some examples include:

- CN=PRALINES\+CREAM,OU=FLAVORS,O=MFG (CN IS PRALINES+CREAM)
- CN=D. CARDINAL,O=LIONEL\,TURNER AND KAYE,C=US (O is LIONEL, TURNER AND KAYE)

Multiple Naming Attributes   You can define multiple object naming attributes in the schema. In both LDAP and NDS, the User object has two, CN and OU. The plus symbol (+) separates the naming attributes in the distinguished name. If the attributes are not explicitly labeled, the schema determines which string goes with which attribute (the first would be CN, the second is OU for NDS and LDAP). You can reorder them in a distinguished name if you manually label each portion.

For example, here are two relative distinguished names:

- SAMMY (CN is SAMMY)
- SAMMY+LISA (CN is SAMMY, the OU is LISA)

Both relative distinguished names (SAMMY and SAMMY+LISA) can exist in the same context because they must be referenced by two completely different relative distinguished names.

Optimizing Network Traffic

In this section, you'll learn how to optimize your network to achieve maximum speed and performance. You can use packet and buffer settings and the Packet Burst Protocol to streamline communication between the server and clients. NetWare 5 also supports Large Internet Packets, which can improve communication between multiple servers in an enterprise network. We'll discuss each of these optimization techniques in the following sections.

Optimize Network Architecture

The most important thing you can do to optimize network performance is to determine a baseline for the network. A *baseline* is a measure of performance speed over time. Establishing a baseline allows you to quickly determine if the network is running too slow. You can do this with the use of a network-monitoring tool such as ManageWise.

In addition to monitoring system performance, follow these tips:

- Use bridges and filters to keep data from being sent unnecessarily.
- Upgrade to Full Duplex 100BaseT NICs, 100BaseT switches, and Cat 5 twisted pair cabling. This gives you a total of 200Mb per port.
- For your LAN, use switches rather than standard hubs. This will allow you to take advantage of full duplex implementations, doubling your bandwidth instantly.
- If much routing is needed, consider using a dedicated router rather than your server.
- Try to use consistent protocols throughout as much of the network as possible.
- Limit the number of nodes to 200 per network.

These measures can improve your network performance, but you must use these only as a guide. Networks also include applications which can affect network performance.

Packets and Buffers

All communication between the server and clients is divided into *packets*, set amounts of bytes that are transmitted at the same time. Each packet includes a header that identifies the destination and source of the packet and the data itself. The size of the packets and the buffers used to transfer them can be changed to improve performance, as described in the following sections.

Changing Packet Size

The size of packets depends on the software and hardware used and on the topology of the network. Default packet sizes are 1,514 bytes for Ethernet and 4,202 bytes for ARCnet and Token Ring.

You can modify the packet size used with the Maximum Physical Receive Packet Size parameter, but not with the SET command at the server console. Instead, use Monitor, or change the STARTUP.NCF file manually. The change takes effect when the server is restarted.

You can use different packet sizes only if your network interface cards and drivers support them; consult their documentation for more information. If your network uses a router, you must consider the packet size that it supports; see the section called "Using Large Internet Packets (LIP)" later in this chapter for more details.

Packet Receive Buffers

NetWare reserves an area of memory for packet receive buffers. These buffers are used as an intermediate area to hold each packet as it is transferred between the server and other servers or clients. To ensure efficient communication, make sure that a sufficient number of packet receive buffers are available.

The main screen of the Monitor utility displays the current amount of available packet receive buffers. NetWare allocates additional packet receive buffers when needed. You can control the minimum and maximum amounts by using the SET commands for packet receive buffers:

SET Maximum Packet Receive Buffers Sets the maximum amount of buffers that can be allocated. This parameter defaults to 500. If the Monitor statistics show that the maximum number of buffers is being used, you should increase this number. A good range is 700 to 1,000.

SET Minimum Packet Receive Buffers Sets the minimum amount of buffers. NetWare allocates this amount when the server is started. This allows the server to run at optimal speeds immediately. The default setting is 128. If the server is slow after you start it, you can increase this number.

SET Maximum Service Processes Allows you to control the number of communications that can be processed at the same time. This may reduce the need for additional packet receive buffers.

SET New Packet Receive Buffer Wait Time Lets you set the amount of time that NetWare waits when additional buffers are needed without allocating them. This prevents the number of buffers from being increased by a brief period of high usage. This value ranges from .1 second to 20 seconds and defaults to the minimum .1 second setting.

Monitoring Network Interface Cards

You can use Monitor to display statistics for the Network Interface Cards (NICs) in the server. Access this information through the LAN/WAN Information option. The type of statistics you are provided depends on the NIC and driver software used on the server. The statistics include packets sent and received, errors, and other information.

For example, the Total Packet received and Total Packet sent statistics (provided for NE2000 cards) lists the amount of packets that the card transmitted and received since the server was loaded. If there is a big difference between these numbers (thousands of packets) this can indicate that the communication between the server and the network has a problem. You can resolve this, but you will need to analyze the network to determine the cause of the problem.

Using Packet Burst Protocol

Protocols are the languages that the server uses to communicate across the network. The IPX protocol sends data across the network, divided into packets. Packets are a specific size and contain a certain amount of information.

The packets are sent using a handshaking process. In this process, after each packet is sent successfully, the other machine sends back an acknowledgment. The sender waits until it receives this acknowledgment before sending the next packet. This requires two-way communication for each packet. Two-way communication can be particularly slow when a WAN link is involved, because each acknowledgment must be sent across the WAN before the next packet can be sent.

Using Packet Burst Protocol, multiple packets can be sent without individual acknowledgments. This protocol allows much faster transfers of large files. Up to 64KB can be sent in a single burst, or group of packets. Packet bursts can improve performance across the network between 10 and 300 percent, depending on the server and the way it is used.

How Packet Burst Works

The client (using the NetWare DOS Requester) and the server negotiate to determine the size of the packet bursts, also called the *window size*. The server may also use a delay, called the *burst gap time*, to ensure that packets are sent slowly enough for the client to keep up. These parameters are set automatically.

Once Packet Burst Protocol is enabled, the client sends a single request and receives an entire burst of packets. After the packets are received, it sends an acknowledgment. The acknowledgment specifies which packets were received correctly. If some packets were not received, they are sent again individually; there is no need to resend the entire packet burst.

Enabling and Optimizing Packet Burst Protocol

Packet Burst Protocol is automatically enabled on the NetWare 5 server. The NetWare DOS Requester provided with NetWare 5 also enables it automatically on the client. If clients are still using the NetWare shell, you must upgrade them in order to take advantage of Packet Burst Protocol, which requires the NetWare DOS Requester.

When a workstation establishes a connection with a server, the client and server negotiate to determine whether packet burst can be used. If a client is used that does not support packet bursts, the normal NetWare protocols are used instead. The DOS Requester also

NetWare
Operations

PART 2

supports servers that do not use packet burst; in fact, a client connected to two servers might use packet burst with one and not the other.

To disable Packet Burst Protocol for individual clients, set the PB BUFFERS parameter in the DOS Requester section of the NET.CFG file. This value can range from 0 to 10. Setting it to 0 disables packet burst entirely. Higher values can be used to increase the number of packets that can be sent from the workstation at one time.

Higher values for the PB BUFFERS parameter do not always increase performance. If this value is set too high, performance can actually decrease, because more memory is required. Low numbers such as 2 or 3 provide acceptable performance.

Using Large Internet Packets (LIP)

NetWare's Large Internet Packet feature provides another method of improving the speed of communication on the network. As explained earlier in this chapter, packet sizes can be changed to improve communication. The client and server negotiate to determine the packet size. Ethernet and Token Ring topologies allow larger packet sizes to be used.

When a NetWare server is used as a router, however, the packet size of routed packets is limited to 512 bytes. This causes all communication through the router to be limited to smaller packets. By using the Large Internet Packet feature, you can avoid this limitation and allow full-size packets to be routed.

LIP can be used in conjunction with Packet Burst Protocol for maximum performance. This allows several large packets to be sent across the network with a single acknowledgment. Using LIP with Packet Burst Protocol eliminates the bottlenecks associated with normal network communication and offers a streamlined alternative.

Large Internet Packets are enabled by default at the NetWare 5 server and the client using the NetWare DOS Requester. You must also ensure that the correct packet size is set for the router.

The SET Maximum Physical Receive Packet Size parameter can change the allowable packet size on each server that acts as a router. This parameter can range from 618 to 24,682. The default value of 4,202 is sufficient to allow LIP for Ethernet or Token Ring protocols.

9

Client Operations

Most of what we have discussed in this book has been about servers. While they are very important, they are useless without clients who access the services they provide. In fact, by some estimates, 90–95% of the total computing done on a typical network is done at the client. This makes sense if you think about it—your server provides data, and your client turns that data into information that your organization can use. That also implies that you need to think about the hardware that you give to your clients. The hardware they have will determine the performance of the users' computers, which is an important factor in their ability to get their jobs accomplished in a timely manner. Most analyses of network client performance show that Novell's clients are faster than the alternatives. In this chapter, we will begin with a very brief history of Novell's clients, followed by a review of the current clients for use with NetWare, including the DOS/Windows 3.1, Windows 9x, Windows NT, Macintosh, and OS/2 clients.

History of Novell's Clients

The purpose of this section is not to provide an in-depth analysis of Novell's clients, but rather a brief overview of each. This can help you see which particular client will work best and whether a client requires any special configuration. Table 9.1 shows the relationship between each client. The clients are presented in historical order, from the earliest to the current one.

Table 9.1 Novell Client Evolution

Layer	Linked IPX	ODI & NETX	ODI & VLMs	Client32 and the Novell Client
Redirector or Requester	NETX	NETX	VLM	Client32
Protocol(s)	IPX.COM	IPXODI.COM	IPXODI.COM	TCP/IP and/or IPX
LAN Driver (MLID)		LSL	LSL	NDIS Driver or Novell ODI driver
		MLID	MLID	

If you are familiar with the linked-IPX method, you may remember what a pain it was to use that client. When you went to a workstation, you would find a file called IPX.COM. That file was created by linking a LAN driver (often called an MLID, for Multiple Link Interface Driver) with the IPX protocol using a Novell utility called WSGEN. However, the resulting file wouldn't tell you what kind of network driver was installed. If you had multiple brands of NICs in your environment, you had no idea which driver was actually in the IPX.COM file. That would have been bad enough, but it got worse. All of the parameters for the NIC (I/O Port, base memory address, IRQ, and so on) were also hard-coded into that file; if you changed the settings on the card, you had to create a new IPX.COM file. If you missed those days, you didn't miss much (except large headaches).

With Novell's ODI (Open Data-Link Interface), you could run multiple frame types and protocols over the same NIC. In addition, the files were separated into the MLID (a .COM file), the Link Support Layer (LSL.COM), and the Protocol (usually IPXODI.COM). The first file was provided by the manufacturer of the NIC, while the other two were from Novell. They also placed the configuration information necessary for all of the components into a separate file, called NET.CFG.

You may notice that the first two client types used NETX.EXE. There are several versions in that family, as well as a NETX.EXE version that in later versions of the client replaced all the original NET commands. The important thing to know about NETX is that it is a redirector (sometimes also called a shell), not a requester. This means that it intercepts calls to drive letters or printer ports and sends them to NetWare without DOS knowing the call was ever made. Because DOS was not aware the call had been made, the most important configuration change that had to be made was to put LASTDRIVE=E (or another drive letter typically closer to A than to Z) in the CONFIG.SYS file. The letters at or below that letter were available for DOS use; anything higher was reserved for NetWare. There are still many client machines who are using this technology today. The big problem with it is that NDS connections are not supported, only bindery ones are. This means that many of the benefits of NDS can't be utilized until the client is upgraded. One of the biggest reasons this client is still in use is the low memory overhead compared to the other clients. Nevertheless, you should upgrade to one of the later clients to take advantage of NDS.

The next major client type was the NetWare DOS Requester also known as Virtual Loadable Modules (VLM). This technology had several advantages over NETX. First, it is a requester, meaning that it works with DOS instead of trying to intercept all DOS calls before DOS sees them. This means that you need a LASTDRIVE=Z statement in your CONFIG.SYS file. The primary configuration file used for this client is NET.CFG. Virtually all modern clients act in this manner, including Novell's newest client, the Novell Client. Second, it supports NDS, which is reason enough to upgrade. Third, it is modular, allowing you to load those features you need in your environment and saving memory with those you don't. This client needs to be used on 8088 and 286 computers (the latest client is not supported on these platforms) and on severely memory-limited client computers of all types. If you have the hardware described in the following sections, however, you will find that the 32-bit enhancements of Client32 are well worth the upgrade.

The current client type is generically called Client32 technology, which Novell has most recently called the Novell Client. This is the client that we will discuss in the next section in detail. In most circumstances, it is the client that should be used by all of your clients. Novell has ceased work, development, and most support of all older technologies.

> **NOTE** For the most up-to-date information on Novell's client offerings, refer to TID 2945422, available at support.novell.com. You can also find this information by going to www.novell.com/download and clicking on the link to that TID. This TID will also list the most recent Service Packs available for that client, if any. If you are using older versions of the Novell Client, refer to support.novell.com/misc/patlst.htm#client.

Windows-Based Clients

In this section, we will cover the features and requirements of Novell's Windows-based clients. We will then turn our attention to the optimizations that can be made to the clients. Finally, we will review the various installation methods for those clients, as well as when to use each. Specific directions on installation, optimizations, and so on will not be covered here; you can refer to the online documentation for all of the details.

NetWare Operations

PART 2

DOS and Windows 3.1

Many people today believe DOS is dead. It is not. A recent survey reported that approximately half of all computers in companies large and small still use DOS and Windows 3.1*x*. With various Y2K issues, that number is likely to shrink somewhat, but there are still many computers that run in this environment. Let's begin by reviewing the installation requirements, followed by the features and benefits of using this client. (The current, and Novell has announced final, version is 2.71.) Finally, we will look at optimizations that can be made.

Installation Requirements

The minimum hardware requirements to install this client are as follows:

- 386 or higher CPU
- 15MB free disk space (more for optional features, such as NDPS)
- 8MB RAM
- A Memory Manager (such as HIMEM.SYS)

As far as supported operating systems are concerned, you will need one of the following

- MS-DOS 5 or higher
- PC-DOS 5 or higher
- Novell DOS 7

You may also want Windows 3.1*x* or Windows for Workgroups.

Features and Benefits

Using this client offers many benefits. Some of the more important ones include:

- Supports connections to both IP- and IPX-based servers. Note, however, that IP-only servers are required to be running in Compatibility Mode (using SCMD.EXE) and a Migration Agent must be available on the network. More information on these topics is available in Chapter 5.
- Supports NDS, including accessing multiple trees simultaneously.
- Supports both 32 bit and 16 bit ODI drivers, although 32 bit drivers are recommended for the best performance whenever possible.
- Supports many Remote Access Service (RAS) features (see Chapter 8 for more information on RAS).

DOS/Windows 3.1*x*-Specific Client Optimizations

The optimizations that can be made to this client specifically are listed in Table 9.2. Optimization of the client involves editing NET.CFG, which is in the \NOVELL\CLIENT32 directory by default. Definitions of the parameters mentioned, along with the acceptable values for each, are available in the online documentation, as well as the help file that comes with the client, NWCFGDW.HLP, located in the \NLS\ENGLISH directory. After you have made all of the desired modifications, you will need to reboot for the changes to take effect.

Table 9.2   Parameters for the DOS/Windows 3.1*x* Client

Parameter	Recommended Value	Reason
Close Behind Ticks	> 18	This parameter keeps a file open for the specified number of ticks (1/18 of a second) before closing it, allowing a request within that interval to be served from cache and without the penalty of closing and then reopening the file. The range is 0–65,536 ticks (0–approximately 1 hour).
Max Cache Size	Varies, depending on amount of free RAM	The maximum amount of RAM used at the client for caching (0–9,999,999 bytes). When set to 0, the amount of cache is determined automatically based on available RAM (for example 1.5MB if you have 8MB RAM, up to 50% of free RAM if you have more than 24MB of free RAM). It will never be greater than 75% of free RAM, regardless of the setting.
PB Buffers	1–10	The value is irrelevant, as any number greater than 0 enables packet burst. The values are used for compatibility with the VLM client.
Frame Type(s) for IPX	Only those needed	Bandwidth is used connecting and maintaining connections over each frame type. Ideally, only one frame type should be in use on your network. Note that when using a 32-bit ODI driver, frame types are specified on the line that loads the driver in STARTNET.BAT, not in NET.CFG.

NetWare Operations

PART 2

Win95/Win98

This client is designed for Windows 95 and 98. Many of the features and benefits are the same as the Client 2.71 for DOS, so only new or different features will be mentioned. Version 3.1 is the current version of the client.

Installation Requirements

The minimum hardware requirements to install this client are as follows:

- 486 or higher CPU
- 16MB RAM
- 14MB free disk space for a typical installation; 28MB for a full installation

The following operating systems are supported:

- Windows 95A (If you have the original Windows 95, you can upgrade it to revision A by installing Service Pack 1 for Windows 95; the original version of Windows 95 is not supported.)
- Windows 95B
- Windows 98

You may also need Windows 9x CD-ROM or the .CAB files for your version of Windows. You will need to install support for long file names on the server if you want to take advantage of them (this is automatically installed on all volumes on NetWare 5 servers). Otherwise you will be limited to the DOS 8.3 naming convention.

The following software is *not* supported and will be removed if it is found when the client is installed:

- Microsoft Client for NetWare networks
- Microsoft File and Printer Sharing for NetWare networks
- Microsoft Services for Novell Directory Services
- NETX
- VLM
- IPXODI protocol (the 16-bit version that was used with NETX or VLM as described previously)

Features and Benefits

The Client for Windows 9x supports the following features:

- Support for IP- and IPX- based servers. (Unlike the client for DOS, there is no need for Compatibility Mode or Migration Agents, although they may be used.)
- Native NDIS drivers are used, not special proprietary ODI drivers, unless they are already installed.

- Synchronization of NetWare password with the local workstation's password.

- Supports multiple Directory trees.

- Contextless Login, allowing users to log in without knowing where their User objects are located in the tree. If multiple User objects exist in the tree with the same name, the user will be asked to select the appropriate user from a list of users with that name.

- Default capture settings can be set at each workstation, making capture settings much simpler in login scripts. These parameters include the number of copies desired, whether or not form feeds and banner pages are desired, and so on.

- Quick access via shortcut menus and the system tray to many popular NetWare features.

Windows 9x-Specific Client Optimizations

Some of the optimizations that can be made to this client specifically are listed in Table 9.3. Optimization of the client involves changing parameters in a GUI. This is accomplished by going to Control Panel ➢ Network ➢ Novell NetWare Client ➢ Properties and choosing the appropriate tab and parameter. Definitions of the parameters mentioned, along with the acceptable values for each, are available in the online documentation. Context-sensitive help is available by clicking on the "?" in the title bar and selecting the desired parameter. After you have made all of the desired modifications, you may need to reboot for the changes to take effect; fortunately many options don't require a reboot.

Table 9.3   Optimizations for the Windows 9x and NT Clients

Parameter	Value	Reason
Close Behind Ticks	Higher numbers are more efficient; 400 is the default	This parameter keeps a file open for the specified number of ticks (1/18 of a second) before closing it, allowing a request within that interval to be served from cache and without the penalty of closing and then reopening the file. The range is 0–65,536 ticks (0–approximately 1 hour).
Max Cache Size	Varies, depending on amount of free RAM	The maximum amount of RAM used at the client for caching (0–49,152K [48MB]). When set to 0, the amount of cache determined is automatically based on available RAM when the client loads, allocating 25% of free RAM. It will never be greater than 75% of free RAM, regardless of the setting.

Table 9.3   Optimizations for the Windows 9*x* and NT Clients *(continued)*

Parameter	Value	Reason
Packet Burst	On	Packet burst reduces network traffic and should normally be enabled. If your network card is slow and the network is slow, you might set this to Off to see if any changes are observed.
Frame Type(s) for IPX	Only those needed	Bandwidth is used for connecting and maintaining connections over each frame type. Ideally, only one frame type should be in use on your network. IPX-related settings are modified by selecting the IPX 32-bit Protocol for the Novell NetWare Client. By default, all detected frame types on your network are used.
Protocol Preferences: IP vs. IPX	The most used protocol on your servers	When selecting your protocol preferences, you should select whichever protocol is used most often on the servers in your environment. The preferred protocol will be tried first, and if it fails, the other will be attempted (assuming both are installed). Ideally, you will only have one protocol installed on the network. Changing the default setting affects the Name Resolution Order as well.
Protocol Preferences: Name Binding Order	The most used method in your environment should be at the top of the list	When configuring this parameter, you should place the most-used-name resolution method at the top of the list, arranging them in order from most used to least used. The default orders for IP are NWHost, SLP, DNS, DHCP, NDS, Bind, SAP. The default orders for IPX are NDS, Bind, SAP, NWHost, SLP, DNS, DHCP. NWHost is a standard Hosts file, and Bind stands for the server's bindery (not to be confused with a NetWare 3.*x* bindery) or table that contains known servers and their addresses.

Windows NT

This client is designed for Windows NT. Almost all of the features and benefits are the same as the Client 3.1 for Windows 9*x*, so this section will be very brief. Version 4.6 is the current version of the client for NT 4, but it is not compatible with NT 3.51. If you are using NT 3.51, you will need version 4.11b.

Installation Requirements

The minimum hardware requirements to install this client are simply the minimum requirements needed to install NT. There is nothing else required. The Novell Client for Windows NT can not coexist with Microsoft's CSNW (Client Services for NetWare) or GSNW (Gateway Services for NetWare). You will need to install support for long file names on the server if you want to take advantage of them (automatically installed on all volumes on NetWare 5 servers).

Features and Benefits

The Novell Client for Windows NT supports the same features as the Novell Client for Windows 9*x*. In fact, the two products are as close as Novell can make them, leaving the desired platform up to you, with no training cost involved (from the Novell Client perspective) with changing operating systems.

Windows NT-Specific Client Optimizations

The optimizations described for the Windows 9*x* client in Table 9.3 are the same ones you should consider for NT.

General Windows Client Optimizations

There are many ways that you can optimize your Windows and DOS-based clients. This section lists parameters that are common to all of the clients. Parameters that are specific to individual client types are already listed in their respective sections.

Clients are designed to perform well with moderate levels of data security and memory usage. You can choose to optimize the client to use less memory, maximize security, or maximize performance. Some of the parameters you can modify for each type of optimization are listed in Tables 9.4, 9.5, and 9.6, respectively. Complete details and other optimizations are listed in the online documentation.

Table 9.4   Parameter to Minimize Memory Usage

Parameter	Value	Reason
File Cache Level	0	Disables caching, freeing RAM

NetWare Operations

PART 2

Table 9.5 Parameters to Maximize Security

Parameter	Value	Reason
Checksum	2 or 3	Validates NCP packets to ensure they contain valid data. A value of 2 means it is desired and will be used as long as the server supports it, whereas a value of 3 means that it is always used and the server must support it to communicate with that server. (The server supports it by default; refer to server SET parameters in the online documentation for information on the server side.) This parameter is ignored when using the Ethernet 802.3 frame type as it does not support this feature.
Signature Level	3	Requires packet signature at the server or a connection can not be created with that server. It will force each packet to be signed to make it virtually impossible to forge a packet. (See Chapter 7 for more information on setting this at the server.)
True Commit	On	Requires the server to acknowledge each write, after it has been physically written to disk, before the client will remove the file from its RAM.

Table 9.6 Parameters to Maximize Performance

Parameter	Value	Reason
Cache Writes	On	This parameter saves changes to RAM first, then later to the network (in the background).
Delay Writes	On	Allows data to be written to the server after a file is closed. The delay is specified by the Close Behind Ticks parameter. With this parameter enabled, 8K of data are written per tick until the entire file has been sent to the server.

Table 9.6   Parameters to Maximize Performance *(continued)*

Parameter	Value	Reason
File Cache Level	2 or 3	Causes data to be read and written in 4KB blocks, as well as servicing requests for data from the client's cache when the file is open (levels 2 and 3) and even when closed (as long as no changes have been made to it; level 3 only). Level 3 is the preferred level, and the default in the 9x and NT clients.
Signature Level	0	Saves the overhead of signing packets, with a potential decrease in security. Any server with this value set to 3 will be inaccessible.
True Commit	Off	Speeds up saves as a save is considered complete as soon as it has been written to the server
Use Video BIOS	Off	Instead of writing to the video BIOS (more compatible), writes directly to the hardware for all character-based output. Only enable this if problems are experienced.

As you can see, there are many possible optimizations that can be made. The good news is that usually you don't have to make any; the client performs well in most circumstances.

Installation Options

Now that you have seen why you should install one of the Novell Clients instead of one that may ship with your operating system or an older version of one of Novell's own clients, we will turn our attention to how to do the actual installation.

There are several methods that can be used to install each client. Table 9.7 summarizes the options available on each platform and Table 9.8 covers the advantages and disadvantages of each. The right option for your environment will vary over time and as circumstances change, hence the multitude of offerings. Details on each option and specific implementation details can be found in the online documentation.

NetWare Operations

PART 2

Table 9.7 Installation Options by Platform

Platform	Installation Methods				
	CD or Network	ACU	ZENworks	Unattended Client	Client as Part of OS Installation
DOS and Windows 3.1x	Yes	Yes	Yes	No	No
Windows 9x	Yes	Yes	Yes	No	Yes
Windows NT	Yes	Yes	Yes	Yes	Yes

Table 9.8 Advantages and Disadvantages of Each Option

Method	Advantages	Disadvantages
CD or Network	Simple to set up for the administrator; useful in very small environments or in test labs with trained personnel; network connectivity is not required when using the CD.	User must know that a client needs to be installed and know how to do it; configurations will vary widely, as each user will make individual choices on configuration (can be automated with the DOS client); storage space on a server is required for the necessary files (network method); CD is required on each client (CD method).
ACU	No user intervention required; standard configuration of client is easily achieved; client can be pushed to each workstation.	Harder for administrator to set up (involves .INI files); storage space on a server is required for the necessary files; must have an existing network connection.
ZENworks	Same as ACU	Same as ACU plus the following: must have an existing client that supports ZENworks; requires application objects, which must be set up correctly.

Table 9.8   Advantages and Disadvantages of Each Option *(continued)*

Method	Advantages	Disadvantages
Unattended Client	Same as ACU plus the following: Does not require an existing Novell client; creating the configuration file is simpler with the Novell Client Install Manager.	Storage space is required on a server for the necessary files; must have an existing network connection; requires some administrator effort to set up, but easier than ACU or ZENworks.
Client as Part of OS Installation	Client is automatically installed as part of the OS installation so you don't have to go back and add it afterwards; standard configuration of client easily achieved; client can be pushed to each workstation; great when no OS exists or the OS is being upgraded to a different OS; can be burned to a CD and distributed to remote sites.	Storage space is required on a server for the necessary files (unless necessary information is burned to a CD); must have an existing network connection (unless a CD is being used); administrator effort; must follow strict rules required by Microsoft on the format of their automated installation files (using MSBATCH for Windows 9x or UNATTEND.TXT for NT).

NetWare
Operations

PART 2

MAC

If you have Macintosh computers on your network that need to access NetWare servers, you are probably already aware that Novell no longer has a Macintosh client as part of the operating system. Many of the related support files are included, such as the Macintosh name space (MAC.NAM) and the AppleTalk protocol (APPLETLK.NLM), but the client is now a separate product sold and updated by Prosoft Engineering, Inc. The latest version of the client is 5.12. Prosoft has a second option for integrating Macintosh computers into your network called NetWare 5 Services for Appleshare. We will review both in the following sections.

Macintosh Client

The requirements on the server side for Macintosh support are as follows:

- 4MB free RAM for 100 Macs (for the NLMs they require on the server).
- 3MB free space on the SYS: volume for the new files to be installed.
- Additional space will be required on traditional volumes if the Macintosh name space is added for the additional directory entries. (NSS volumes support Macintosh files automatically).

The client requirements are as follows:

- A 68030 or higher processor or any PowerMac
- System 7.6.1 or higher
- 5MB free RAM
- 7MB free hard drive space

The client is installed using standard Macintosh installation techniques. When installation has completed, the core functionality is installed, as well as several other files that may be useful, including:

- NetWare Remover to uninstall the client
- An installation log to document the changes
- The online documentation for the users in PDF format
- A Macintosh version of RCONSOLE (custom installations only)
- NetWare/IP client (not to be confused with native IP) custom install only

Once the client is installed, the user can use standard Macintosh mechanisms (such as the Chooser) to access NetWare resources. These mechanisms have been enhanced, however, to allow for encrypted access to NDS like PC clients in addition to the standard unencrypted methods that are native to the Macintosh. When using the enhanced features, even the dialog boxes look very similar to those on Windows systems, making it look more like part of the network than a distantly related cousin to the PC. Many of the features and optimizations described for the Windows clients are also supported with this client.

Prosoft is planning for native-IP support, as well as support for NDPS and some network and desktop management tools in future versions. Keep checking with Prosoft for the latest on these clients.

NetWare 5 Services for AppleShare

This product, while not technically a client, does allow for connectivity between NetWare servers and Macintosh clients. This solution doesn't require any special hardware on the servers, consuming only 25MB of hard drive space, and nothing special is required on the clients beyond System 6.0.5 or later with AppleShare 7.1 or later. This product requires SP3A or higher to be installed as well as an updated version of APPLETLK.NLM (5.11b or higher). Both are available from Novell's Web site and are described in the documentation that comes with this product.

This solution is simple to make operational because the product is simply installed on one or more NetWare 5 servers (the standard Novell-supplied connectivity mechanisms are used for older versions of NetWare). Once installed, both Macintosh and PC users can access files created on either platform with the tools native to that platform. To the Macintosh computers, the NetWare server simply appears like any other Macintosh, and can be accessed with the standard Macintosh methods such as the Chooser.

This tool includes AppleTalk routing support as well. It can be used to connect several Macintosh segments and route between them. It supports SNMP (including support for AppleTalk MIB I) and AppleTalk Phases I and II, and can automatically determine its zone. It supports both Ethernet and Token Ring as well.

Choosing a Macintosh Connectivity Solution

With all the simplicity offered by the NetWare 5 Services for AppleShare, why would anyone use the client? There are good reasons why both client solutions are offered. Table 9.9 summarizes the advantages and disadvantages of each, as well as when each solution may be appropriate.

Table 9.9   Macintosh Client 5.12 vs. NetWare 5 Services for AppleShare

	Macintosh Client 5.12	**NetWare 5 Services for AppleShare**
Advantages	Uses IPX (much faster than Apple-Talk). Allows access to all NetWare 3, 4, and 5 servers with IPX support. Supports NDS.	Simple installation on the server only (client software not necessary). AppleTalk Printers can be shared with Mac and PC-based computers.
Disadvantages	Must be installed on each computer.	Additional protocol to install and manage on the server. Additional protocol on the wire. AppleTalk is a "Chatty" protocol (similar to Microsoft's NetBEUI). NDS authentication is not supported without software on each client. Requires NetWare 5.
Recommended Use	Best choice in most situations as it provides the best performance and the ability to access more features of NetWare (including NDS).	Low-volume networks where there are many clients and few servers, such as a school computer lab.

> **NOTE** More information on Prosoft's Macintosh client and on NetWare 5 Services for AppleShare can be found on their Web site at: `www.prosofteng.com/netware.htm`.

OS/2

For those still using OS/2, your client options are the most limited. The good news is that Novell does have an OS/2 client and it is free. The bad news is that it hasn't been updated since January 1993, except for some patches made in December of 1998. The current version of the client is 2.12. This is the final release and will not be supported after 2000. It does support NDS, however and is a viable client if you still use OS/2. It does not support IP, NDPS, ZENworks, and many other modern innovations.

> **NOTE** The latest version of the client is discussed and available for download from Novell's Web site as part of TID 2938545. The address is `support.novell.com/cgi-bin/search/tidfinder.cgi?2938545`. The latest patches to the client (a file called OS2PT2.EXE) are available at: `support.novell.com/misc/patlst.htm#client`.

10

NDS Object Management

In this chapter, we will discuss the tools for doing basic administrative tasks and then discuss some basic objects. We will begin by briefly reviewing the tools that are at your disposal to administer the basic NDS objects. Following this, we will look at look at administering user and group objects and printing. We will then turn our attention to Catalog Services. Finally, we will conclude with a review of NDS security.

Tools for Administering NDS Objects

Today there are several tools at your disposal for administering the network. We will begin with a brief review of the most common and popular tool in use today, NWAdmin. Then we will turn our attention to the new rising star, ConsoleOne, and finally we will conclude this section with a review of a subset of ConsoleOne, ConsoleOne Web Edition. Before we begin, we want to make a quick note about the tools that will be discussed. All of the information, screen shots, and so on, comes from a NetWare 5 server with Support Pack 3 and NDS 8 installed. To get the most functionality with the fewest bugs, you should install these updates (or later) on your systems.

NWAdmin

This tool, which has been around since NetWare 4 days, was, and for many administrators still is, the primary administration tool. Through the use of snap-ins, this product can be extended to administer new types of objects and additional functionality, via links to other tools or wizards which can be added to the Tools menu.

All future development work, new tools, and so on will take place within the framework of ConsoleOne. There are still a few things that must be done in NWAdmin, but Novell expects to have all of the functionality available in ConsoleOne by the end of 1999 or early in 2000. See the section entitled "Comparison of NWAdmin and ConsoleOne" later in this chapter for more information on when to use each.

ConsoleOne

ConsoleOne is a Java-based administration tool. As such, it is cross-platform, allowing you to administer your server from any platform that supports Java, including the server itself. This (the cross-platform nature of the tool) is a goal more than reality at the moment due to the fluid nature of Java and the availability of updates on various platforms. Not all platforms support the latest version of Java, meaning that some versions of ConsoleOne will only run on certain platforms. For example, ConsoleOne 1.2b will only run on a Windows 9x or NT-based computer (or the server if SP3 or later has been installed) because the version of Java required to run it is only available on those platforms. Figure 10.1 shows what ConsoleOne 1.2b looks like.

Figure 10.1   The opening screen of ConsoleOne

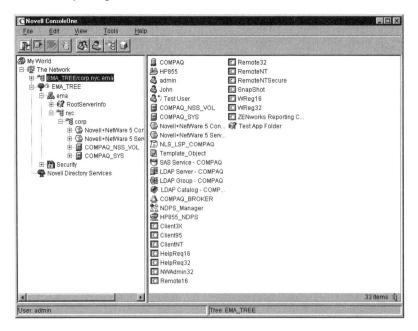

While you can create all types of objects with it, several of the more advanced objects are created with all of the properties on the Other tab. However, most of the object types are easily created and configured. In addition, you can view most of the properties of most objects with it. For common objects, such as User objects, the presentation is clean and easily accessible, as shown in Figure 10.2. Each tab with a downward pointing triangle has other options that display related screens of information. The other screens are accessible by clicking and holding on a tab, then selecting the desired screen from the list of choices that appears, also shown in Figure 10.2.

Figure 10.2   The properties available for a User object, along with other screens available on the General tab

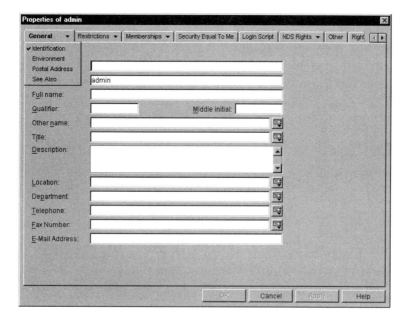

The properties that don't have a specific tab are displayed on an Other tab in a fairly user-unfriendly format as shown in Figure 10.3.

Figure 10.3 ConsoleOne Other tab for an Application object

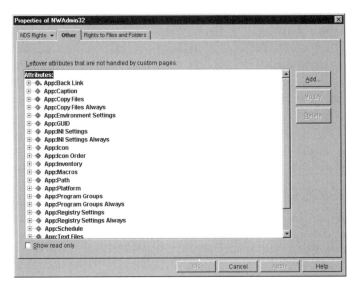

Figure 10.4 shows the dialog box in NWAdmin.

Figure 10.4 NWAdmin dialog box for an Application object

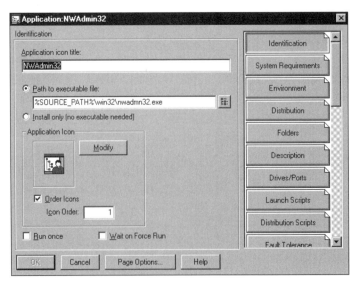

You can manage NDS security with this tool to the same extent possible as NWAdmin, including setting IRFs (Inherited Rights Filters) and trustees. The biggest difference is the interface; you choose to add a filter for desired object or property rights instead of picking them from a list box on screen. The other difference is minor: what NWAdmin calls Object rights are referred to as Entry rights in ConsoleOne.

ConsoleOne also allows you to move, rename, and delete any object. As with NWAdmin, you can copy, move, rename, and delete files and directories and set the attributes on them. Trustees for files and directories can also be set; IRFs can also be controlled through this interface.

There is also a version of ConsoleOne for use at the server. While you probably won't want to administer your network from the server, it is possible. The server-based version is useful when working at the server to view files, directories, and volumes, as well as configuration files for the server. You can even access a remote server from your server with RCONSOLEJ, allowing you to compare configuration files, for example.

The original server-based version of ConsoleOne is an older product that shipped with the original release of NetWare 5. Many objects show up with the "?" icon. All of the properties that have no associated property page are simply not displayed, leaving many objects only with NDS security options. While quite limited in nature, it does allow you to:

- View volumes, directories, files, and the contents of files (although, like the TYPE command in DOS, only text files are intelligible). A Java-based text editor automatically opens when you double-click a file, allowing you to modify text files.

- Cut, copy, and paste files between volumes and directories.

- Rename and delete files and directories.

- Create new folders.

- View and edit your primary configuration files from one place.

- View and manage some NDS objects (after logging into NDS as a user with the appropriate rights).

As you can see, it is not a full-featured tool, but it can allow you to do basic administrative tasks as you work on the server.

With ConsoleOne 1.2b and SP3, you have all of the features described above at the workstation. We recommend that you consider both versions of the tool in deciding which to use. With ConsoleOne 1.2b, you lose the ability to view your configuration files in one place, as well as the ability to view and edit text files. Those losses aside, we think it is generally still a better choice to use version 1.2b over the original version; those files can be edited with EDIT.NLM anyway.

PART 2

NetWare Operations

ConsoleOne Web Edition

The newest member of the ConsoleOne family of products is ConsoleOne Web Edition. This is also the least powerful tool because it is aimed at first-level help-desk administrators. It allows you to accomplish basic administration tasks through a standard Web browser.

It allows you to:

- Create and delete User objects
- Reset accounts that were locked due to Intruder Detection (though not for other reasons, such as an account expiration date)
- View and modify basic user information (all items on the Identification tab except Other Name and including the user's Internet E-Mail Address that is on the E-Mail Addresses tab)
- Set and change passwords
- Change a user's groups (though not create new groups)
- Disable a User account

> **WARNING** Once an account is disabled, it can not be re-enabled with this tool.

We find that this is a helpful tool to do basic management tasks from home (such as when a backup administrator forgets his or her password at 2 A.M.).

The requirements to install this product are quite modest and are available in the online documentation. Basically, all that is required is a NetWare 5 server with Support Pack 2 or higher and NDS 8 installed and either Netscape FastTrack or Enterprise server installed.

> **TIP** Installation may fail if you didn't install the Web server in the default directory, SYS:NOVONYX. If you installed it elsewhere, you should reinstall it in the default location before installing this tool.

> **WARNING** You should *strongly* consider the use of SSL on your server if you use this tool. Without SSL enabled, all passwords, user names, and so on are transmitted across your network (or even the Internet if you are doing remote administration) as clear text, totally unencrypted. SSL is covered in Chapter 8.

To use it, all that is required is Netscape Navigator 4 or higher or Internet Explorer 4 or higher. To get started, simply type the name or IP address of your server, followed by a colon and port number (if you are not using the default port), followed by **/ConsoleOne**. Figure 10.5 shows the opening screen.

Figure 10.5   The ConsoleOne Web Edition welcome screen

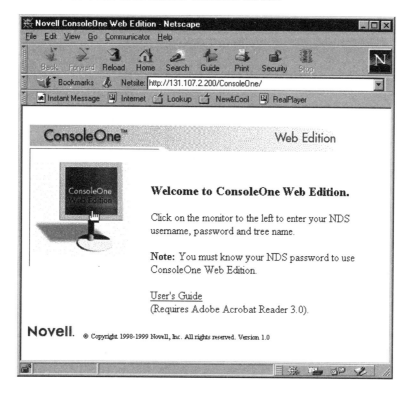

To log in and begin using the product, click the monitor and a login screen will be presented. You will need your user's distinguished name, password, and tree to successfully log in. Once you have done so, you will be presented with the screen shown in Figure 10.6.

For all tasks, you will be presented with a search area in the middle of the screen. When you find the user you want to modify, simply select it from the list and it will automatically fill in the appropriate box on the right. Figure 10.7 illustrates the screen that will appear when you choose to change a user's password.

Figure 10.6 ConsoleOne Web Edition home page

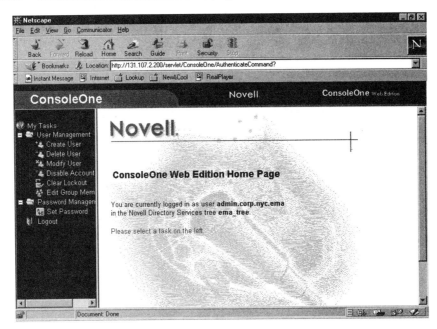

Figure 10.7 The Change Password screen

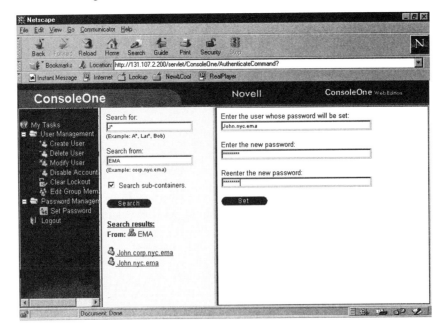

There are a few issues with this tool to be aware of, namely:

- The typical installation is tuned for 10 simultaneous users. If you expect a significantly higher number of users, you may need to increase the RequestThreads parameter, as described in the online documentation.

- To be able to do the administrative tasks previously listed, a user will need the appropriate rights, as described in the online documentation. This sounds simple, and it is, but read through them carefully if you intend to deploy this as a frontline support tool. Be sure that the correct NDS rights are in place and no unnecessary rights are given.

- If you don't use the tool for 10 minutes, you will be prompted to log in again.

- To further increase security, choose to log out and then exit your browser if you will be leaving your workstation. You may also consider disabling the cache on those browsers to be sure that NDS data will not be cached.

- You should not use the Back and Forward buttons in you browser; use the buttons in the frames only.

- New users will have blank passwords assigned; you should use the Set Password option to set an initial password for each user.

Comparison of NWAdmin and ConsoleOne

Obviously ConsoleOne Web edition has a very narrow target audience, but when should you use NWAdmin and when would ConsoleOne be more appropriate? In general, NWAdmin is better suited to small- and medium-sized trees, whereas ConsoleOne will perform best on very large trees.

There are some tasks that only certain tools can perform, as shown in the following list. For the remaining tasks, either tool will work. The online documentation offers more detailed descriptions of the issues surrounding the tools.

The tasks that require NWAdmin include the following:

- Creating the CA and Key Material objects necessary for SSL to function
- Setting up accounting
- Creating and managing NDPS-related objects
- Managing NetWare products that do not have ConsoleOne snap-ins yet

The only thing NWAdmin can't do is create an LDAP domain or domains in NDS; for that you will have to use ConsoleOne.

Some tasks can't be done with either tool. For example, currently DNS and DHCP must be managed with the DNS/DHCP Management Console, although there are plans to

NetWare
Operations

PART 2

eventually make this part of ConsoleOne. In addition, there are a few tasks that currently can only be performed in NDS Manager (although these functions are also slated for eventual control with ConsoleOne as well). They are:

- Managing partitions and replicas
- Removing NetWare servers from the tree

The remaining tasks can be performed in either tool, depending on your preference. That said, we recommend that you get used to ConsoleOne now; you will be forced to use it eventually as new objects and services come out that are only supported on ConsoleOne.

User and Group Management

The reasons that users and groups exist are obvious. In this section, we will briefly cover a few tips to make your life simpler. First we will look at the uses of Template objects, then we will turn to the Details on Multiple Users menu command.

Template Objects

Template objects have come a long way from when they were simply user accounts with the name *User_Template* in NetWare 4.10. With NetWare 5, you can even base templates on other templates, allowing you to have some standard information and/or rights for all users (with those in a location having information specific to those in that location, and so on). You can fill in values for all of your new users based on these Template objects.

Template objects let you specify almost all properties that are available for a user and a few that are unique to templates. Some of the more useful extensions to Template objects include the ability to do the following when creating a new user:

- Run a setup script (a script following login script syntax that runs only when the user is created). This could be used, for example, to copy some files to a user's home directory or to run a batch file that would create a user in a database or e-mail program.
- Be prompted to set an initial user password.
- Set a default list of trustees for the new user, such as assigning the manager of the department the ability to change passwords for everyone in his or her department.
- Assign default NDS rights (to take away a user's default right to modify his or her login script, for example).
- Assign default file system rights (to assign more limited rights to a home directory than are given by default, for example).
- Set default Volume Space restrictions.

- Assign Policy Packages to new users, such as a policy that disables roaming profiles for mobile users with laptops to make login faster. For more information on Policy Package objects, see Chapter 13.

- Assign Remote Operation settings for things like remote control and file transfer that may override settings in the policy package(s) the user is normally associated with. This may be useful to disallow remote control of administrative workstations without making a special policy just for administrators.

Another feature of Template objects is that if you select one and choose Details on Multiple Users instead of the normal Details choice, you can quickly modify any property on any of the pages of the Template objects for all users based on that template.

Details on Multiple Users

This is one of the most useful options in the menus. It allows you to select a group, template, container, or even multiple users and change any of the properties for all selected users or users associated with that object. Most of the options just discussed regarding Template objects also apply when making this choice. This choice can be useful if your company relocates—you can change the Location, Telephone, and Fax Number properties for all users at that location. You can get creative with this command in many cases, such as realigning departments, spinning off users to a new subsidiary, and so on.

Printing

Printing has got to be one of *the* biggest headaches of every administrator. Novell understands this and offers some great solutions to help make printing easier. The biggest advance is the creation of NDPS, which we will discuss in the beginning of this section. We will then look at Novell's latest extension to NDPS called NetWare Enterprise Print Services. Finally, we will review queue-based printing and how you can integrate it with NDPS.

Novell Distributed Print Services (NDPS)

NDPS was developed jointly by Novell, Hewlett Packard, and Xerox. It allows you to plug a printer into the network and print to it. It offers you a great deal of administrative control and the ability to check on the status of any printer on your network (to see if it is low on toner, jammed, out of paper, and so on). In this section, we will look at the components involved and the administrative issues and methods you can use to set up printing on your clients.

> ***TIP***   If you are not familiar with NDPS, want a general overview of it, or want to
> see how it can help you, you should view the multimedia overview of NDPS in the
> online documentation. It is available on the NetWare 5 Documentation CD in the
> following location: \NOVDOCS\NDPSVIEW and is named NDPS.EXE. That over-
> view covers only version 1; version 2 adds many new features.

Review of Components

There are several components that make NDPS work. This section is not designed to be
an in-depth discussion of the components, but rather a quick summary to be sure that you
understand the terminology that will be described in the sections that follow. The components are described in Table 10.1.

Table 10.1   NDPS Component Overview

Name	Associated Object	Purpose
Printer Agent (PA)	NDPS Printer	Represents one printer. Always a 1:1 relationship between PAs and Printers. Center of NDPS printing model. Acts as a combination printer, queue, and print server. Can be embedded in hardware or can be software handling a network, workstation, or server attached printer. Manages print jobs, answers queries about the status of the printer or print jobs, and produces events (such as out of paper). Can be public access (no associated NDPS printer object) or controlled access (with an associated printer object). Some NDPS features are not available with public access printers.
Manager	NDPS Manager	Supports software-based PAs. This object must be created before any PAs can be created. Can control an unlimited number of PAs. Used to create Public PAs.

Table 10.1 NDPS Component Overview *(continued)*

Name	Associated Object	Purpose
Gateways	N/A	Allow clients to print to printers that don't have NDPS built-in. Translates NDPS syntax to printer-specific syntax.
Third Party	N/A	NDPS ships with two third-party gateways—HP's and Xerox's. Offer more features as they integrate with specific printers. May allow PAs to be automatically created when plugged into the network.
Novell	N/A	Generic gateway allowing most printers to work with NDPS. Supports integration with workstation- and server-based printers, LPR-based printers, and queues.
PDS	N/A	A subcomponent of the Novell gateway. Stands for Print Device Subsystem. Loaded automatically when a PA is created using the Novell gateway. Gets printer-specific information and stores it for use by the gateway.
PH	N/A	A part of the Novell Gateway. Stands for Port Handler. Abstracts the PDS from the physical connection to the printer. Enables integration with all types of printers previously mentioned.
Broker	NDPS Broker	Provides support services to the rest of the NDPS system.
SRS	N/A	One of three subcomponents of the broker. Stands for Service Registry Service. Tracks public access printers and synchronizes this information with all other SRSs on the network. Keeps track of ENS and RNS services available.

NetWare
Operations

PART 2

Table 10.1   NDPS Component Overview *(continued)*

Name	Associated Object	Purpose
ENS	N/A	One of three subcomponents of the broker. Stands for Event Notification Service. Allows anyone to be notified when events (such as a paper jam or low toner) occur. Can notify those users by any of the following methods: pop-up message (always available when ENS is available); e-mail message sent via GroupWise or MHS; Log File (user must look in it); third party extensions (fully extensible by third parties for any mechanism, such as paging).
RMS	N/A	One of three subcomponents of the broker. Stands for Resource Management Service. Central location for storage of the following: Banners; Windows 3.*x*, Windows 9*x*, and Windows NT printer drivers; Novell Printer Definition (NPD) files (describe each printer's abilities specifically for use by NDPS). Allows for central storage of the preceding, reducing total disk space required and allowing automatic driver download for the clients.

Administrative Issues

The details on how NDPS is installed and set up are covered very well in the documentation, so only a few highlights will be covered here. Let's look at the objects and the NLMs on the server that are associated with those objects.

When you are installing NetWare 5, one of the options is to install NDPS. This extends the schema if necessary and installs a broker. A broker does not need to be installed on every server. It will be installed with the first server and may be created on subsequent servers. You will find a LOAD BROKER *name* statement in your AUTOEXEC.NCF file if a broker is installed on that machine.

The NDPS Manager object needs to be created before any software-based PAs can be created. You can have any number of these objects, but you are limited to a maximum of one per server. Any server that has a printer locally attached to it requires a manager. The manager will only be loadable on the server you designate. The database that it needs will be stored on the volume you specify and, by default, all printers will spool to this volume as well. The manager must be loaded on the specified server to be of use; to do so place a LOAD NDPSM *name* command in your AUTOEXEC.NCF file to be sure it is always available.

> **TIP** If possible, keep all NDPS files on a volume other than SYS: to ensure that it never fills up. You should at least store the spool files elsewhere. If this is not possible either, at the very minimum set space restrictions on the directory where data is spooled. This can be done directly on the directory or through the PA. This is very important to ensure that a large print job does not fill up SYS:.

The last object is the Printer Agent. To reiterate, there is only ever one PA per printer and one printer per PA. PAs will not exist as separate objects in the tree if they are public-access printers. Public-access printers are managed through NWAdmin by choosing Tools ➢ NDPS Public Access Printers. From this dialog box you can view all of your public-access printers and their settings. Controlled-access printers are represented by an object in NDS and as such can be viewed individually as with any other object.

NDPS can coexist with other systems, including queue-based printing if desired. NDPS can be configured to service queues or to send the data to a queue to be printed. Other migration and coexistence scenarios exist and are documented in the online documentation.

Client Setup

Setting up a printer for use with NDPS is a straightforward task and is documented in the online documentation. This section will briefly review the methods at your disposal to grant access to printers to your clients.

The first method, and one that involves no effort on the part of your users, is to use the Tools ➢ NDPS Remote Printer Management choice in NWAdmin. Note that you can also accomplish remote printer management by selecting a container or printer, choosing Details, and selecting NDPS Remote Printer Management. Figure 10.8 shows the dialog box that appears when you choose it from the Tools menu; other methods will produce slightly different output.

Figure 10.8 NDPS Remote Printer Management dialog box when selected from the Tools menu in NWAdmin

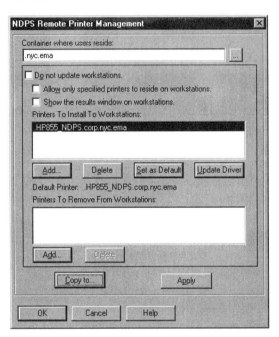

As you can see in the figure, you have a lot of control with this feature. You can restrict the printers that the user can use to those on the list, automatically add or remove printers, designate a default printer, and even update the driver if a new one becomes available. The printing updates take place automatically the next time the user logs in and requires no input from him or her.

A second method to automatically set up printing on users' workstations is through ZENworks. This is done by creating or modifying a workstation policy package for the appropriate platform. One of the advantages of this method is that printers can be installed based on queues or NDPS. This method also allows you to control the capture-related settings for queues, such as form feeds, banner pages, number of copies, and so on. If a queue is selected, any driver can be installed for the printer and it will be stored on the server so that it can be automatically installed. A default printer may also be specified.

The third approach is one that allows users to choose the printers that they want installed. This is done with Novell Print Manager (NWPMW32.EXE, located in SYS:PUBLIC\ WIN32 for Windows 9x and NT or NWPMW16.EXE, located in SYS:PUBLIC for Windows 3.x). This utility allows them to view all of the available printers, details about specific printers, including the protocol(s) it supports, and even filter the list based on criteria they specify. As Figure 10.9 shows, they can filter based on print mechanism (laser, ink jet, and so on), location, ability to duplex or print in color, minimum resolution and speed, and so on. It is a very powerful way for users to locate the printer(s) they need and automatically install the correct driver (assuming the user has sufficient rights to print to it).

Figure 10.9   Filtering the available printer listed based on user-defined criteria

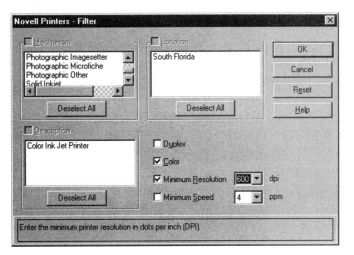

Fourth, the least automated and most generic approach is to browse the Network Neighborhood, either through the tree (which will show queues and NDPS PAs) or by looking on specific servers for printers (which will only show queues). When the desired printer is found, the user can right-click it to either capture the printer port (requiring the user to pick a port to be captured) or install the printer. If the user chooses to install the printer and a driver has been associated with it for that platform, the driver will automatically be installed; otherwise the user will have to select the make and model to be installed. In any case, the user will have the other standard questions to answer (print a test page, name of the printer, and so on).

Finally, there is the Add Printer wizard in the Printers folder on Windows 9x and Windows NT computers. If the user selects a Network Printer, he or she will be allowed to browse for it in the Network Neighborhood. This approach is very similar to the previous method.

NetWare Enterprise Print Services

Novell has announced an add-on (read: extra cost) option to NDPS 2 called NetWare Enterprise Print Services. This product allows UNIX clients (and any other operating system that supports it) to print to NDPS printers using LPR/LPD. In addition, it allows any user to send a print job to any printer on an intranet or the Internet by specifying a URL. This feature utilizes the IPP (Internet Printing Protocol). Additional gateways supporting printers from Lexmark, Epson, Tektronix, and Extended Systems are also supported.

NOTE   More information on this add-on can be found at Novell's online documentation site located at www.novell.com/documentation/lg/endps/docui/index.html.

Queue-Based Printing

Queue-based printing still exists and can be used just as it was in previous versions of NetWare. As mentioned in the previous section, it can also be used with NDPS. This offers the additional advantage of allowing any type of client to access NetWare's printers; most clients support NetWare's queues. If you want to use only queue-based printing, you can also use the quick setup feature in NWAdmin. To do so, simply choose Tools ➤ Print Services Quick Setup (non-NDPS). This is the same feature that was available in NetWare 4.11.

Catalog Services

This is an interesting feature. If you choose to install LDAP as part of your NetWare installation, you are asked if you want LDAP to use a catalog and if so, if you want to restrict searches to the catalog. You may also have heard of *Contextless Login*. But how do these things relate? What do they have in common?

Both of these applications use Catalog Services. What does this feature do? It scans NDS and keeps a user-defined subset of information in the catalog for quick access. Data in a catalog can span partitions, increasing the speed of searches through the directory as well. Catalog Services are enabled by loading DSCAT.NLM. This NLM will look in NDS for any catalogs hosted on that server and optionally update that catalog for you at specified intervals. You can choose what part of the tree will be searched, what attributes you want in the catalog, and which ones you would like indexed for faster access. You can also optionally configure slave catalogs, which are updated from master catalogs. This allows bandwidth and CPU time to be spent on only one computer, but the data can be replicated to any server or combination of servers on the network.

Now that you know what Catalog Services is, we want to turn to Contextless Login. This feature is often touted as a great reason to use NetWare 5, yet nowhere in the documentation are the steps listed on how to do so. There is some basic information in the Knowledgebase, but we want to discuss the procedure and walk you through the steps on how it is done. We found we had a few problems on our first attempt to get it working. After we show you how to set it up, we will show you what you need to configure on the client side and how this is used to simplify the login process.

Setting Up the Catalog Object

This is probably the most difficult part of enabling Contextless Login. It is probably also the most involved. We are assuming that Catalog Services was installed as part of your NetWare installation. If you didn't choose to install it, you can go back and add it. Once you have it installed, start the catalog dredger by typing **DSCAT** at a console prompt to load the NLM. To create the necessary object, follow these steps:

1. In NWAdmin, create a NDSCat:Master Catalog object wherever you wish. We prefer to place it near the top of the tree as we place all users in our tree in the catalog. Name it anything you wish. We prefer LoginCat. Check the Define Additional Properties dialog box (or go back and choose Details) and choose Create.

2. Specify the server that will be the host server, the one that will generate the data, the one with DSCAT.NLM loaded on it.

3. Enter the following values for the Primary and Secondary labels: **LGNCON** and **Users** respectively.

4. Select the Filter tab and in the Filter text box enter **"Object Class" = "User"** (including the quotation marks).

5. If you only want to search a portion of the tree (for example by region or division), select the starting context in the Context Limits and what you want to search (the entire subtree or just the immediate subordinates). To search the entire tree, leave the Context Limits blank and choose Search Subtree.

6. Select the Schedule tab and choose how often you would like the catalog updated. You will need to balance overhead (CPU utilization and bandwidth required to gather the data) vs. accuracy (how up-to-date you desire the catalog to be). We prefer an interval between one and six hours.

NetWare
Operations

PART 2

7. Select the Attributes/Indexes tab. As this is for Contextless Login, the only attribute required is Full Name, so choose Selected Attributes and then select Full Name. Choose that same field as the field you would like indexed.

8. Choose OK to save your changes.

9. Make the catalog a trustee of the [Root] object with Browse, Read, and Compare rights.

10. Make [Public] a trustee of the catalog object, assigning Browse, Read, and Compare rights.

11. Display the Details of the catalog object, select the Schedule tab, and choose Update Now.

12. This step is optional, but we believe it is more than worth it. Select the Summary tab and review the information for any errors. To test the catalog, choose Query Catalog, then click Query. All of your users should show up.

If you haven't made any mistakes, the catalog is now set up and you are ready to configure the client.

Setting Up the Client

Fortunately, configuring the client is simpler than configuring the Catalog object. To do so, follow these steps:

1. Display the properties of the Novell Client in Control Panel ➢ Network.

2. Select the Contextless Login tab and choose Enable.

3. Specify whether or not you want to allow wildcard searching (for example, to allow a user to enter user* and come up with User1, User2, and so on).

4. Enter the Tree Name (be careful—it is *case sensitive*) and the distinguished name of the catalog (including the leading period).

5. Reboot.

Using It at the Client

Using Contextless Login at the client is very simple. All that you need to do is enter a user name (or part of one if you enabled wildcard searches) and tree name and press TAB. If there are duplicate names, a dialog box will appear listing the matching user names. In either case, after you select the correct user and enter the appropriate password, you will be logged in. Only the tree name is needed in the advanced section of the dialog box. Figure 10.10 illustrates the dialog box that appears when there are multiple users with the same name in the tree.

Figure 10.10 The Matching User Names dialog box

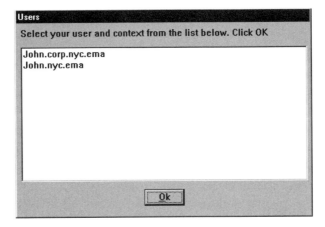

NDS Security

In the last section of this chapter, we will focus on NDS security. This topic has already been covered in Chapter 1, and many basic security guidelines are probably very familiar to you, so we will discuss only a few things in this section. First, we will review a few miscellaneous issues, then we will discuss the biggest change in NDS rights in NetWare 5, property-level inheritance and the Inheritable object and property rights.

The first general tip, and one of the most important in our view, is to make sure that you always have at least two users (or other objects) with Supervisor rights to [Root]. This also applies to any portion of the tree that may have an IRF that blocks the Supervisor object right. Object corruption, accidental deletion, and other problems make this a very prudent choice. While these problems are rare, they do happen.

Object Corruption and Supervisor Access to the Tree

NetWare 5 @Work

I was once working with a tree administrator for several days. One morning he walked in and received an error message indicating that his user account couldn't be found. After verifying that he had spelled it correctly, he logged in as another Admin-level user to investigate further. Upon starting NWAdmin, we found that his User object still existed with the same name, but that the type had been transformed to the Unknown type (the ? icon). Our first inclination was to run DSREPAIR, which we did. After it completed, we looked in NWAdmin again and found that his *user* account had been turned into an *Organizational Unit*! At this point we realized the value of having a backup administrator account. We simply deleted the user-turned-OU object, re-created a user with the same name, and reassigned rights to [Root].

In another instance, there wasn't a backup Admin object. Fortunately this was in a test lab, so NetWare was simply reinstalled and testing continued. If this were in a production environment, you would typically have to call Novell Technical Support or use one of the utilities (MakeSU or Recover) described in Chapter 6. Typically a backup would not even help, as you need administrative rights to the tree to restore the backup.

Second, anyone with the Write right to the *server's* ACL property (which includes everyone with the Supervisor right to the server's parent container) automatically has the Supervisor File System right to *all volumes on the server*. To reiterate, this is the only case where NDS rights grant file system rights, and it is on the *Server* object, not the *Volume* object.

Third, in terms of general review, rights granted explicitly at a lower level in the tree will override rights assignments made higher in the tree for the same object. Also, Selected Property rights override rights assigned to [All Properties].

> *TIP*   You can see any object's effective rights to another object by selecting the second object, choosing Trustees of This Object, clicking Effective Rights, and selecting the first object. That object's rights will be black, and the rest will be grayed out.

Finally, every object is Security Equivalent to its parent container and all of the Container objects listed in the object's distinguished name. This is implied and not seen through the

GUI in any way (except when viewing effective rights). This is also not configurable. These right are not affected even if there is an IRF on a container between where the assignment was made and the object. This is an often-overlooked source of rights problems.

Property-Level Inheritance

One of the most important advances in NDS security is the new Inheritable object and property rights, making possible property-level inheritance. This has been a feature that administrators have wanted since NetWare 4 shipped. This allows you to set rights for individual properties, such as Password Maintenance or City, at the Organization or Organizational Unit level, and then have that right or those rights flow down to all objects below it. This allows you to give help desk personnel the ability to change a user's password without being able to modify other attributes of the user. This also allows you to assign permissions to the HR personnel (typically through a group or OU) to maintain only address-related properties. The possibilities are endless. Take advantage of this new feature to really make your life simpler and at the same time help keep the Directory up to date.

11

NDS Partition and Replica Management

Managing partitions and replicas properly ensures the Directory's reliability and consistency. Users cannot access resources administrated by the Directory if it is corrupted or inaccessible. In order for you to have a Directory Service that performs and is redundant, you will need to follow guidelines when creating additional partitions and replicas, and know what to do to maintain their proper functioning.

Tips for Maintaining NDS

There is no way to avoid all NDS problems. In fact, if you deal with a NetWare 5 server for any length of time, you will undoubtedly need to handle several. However, most common NDS problems can be avoided with a bit of planning. Here are some tips to keep NDS running smoothly:

Placing Replicas Strategically   Always keep at least three replicas for each partition. It can't be stressed enough that you should have replicas of a partition strategically placed throughout your network, preferably close to the users, and at each end of the WAN links. This improves response times for logins as well as redundancy. If a replica is lost, even if it's the Master replica, it can be restored if another replica is available.

Regulating Partition Maintenance Rights   Use a single workstation to manage NDS partitions, such as when you are splitting partitions, merging partitions, or moving container objects. This will make it easy to keep track of the changes you have made and to avoid inconsistencies. Otherwise, conflicting messages can be received from different locations in the network, causing NDS corruption. You should also limit the number of users you allow to do maintenance functions on the tree.

Backing Up the Directory   Use your backup software to make frequent backups of the NDS database. The frequency depends on how often changes are made in your network, but it should be at least once a week. Many backup programs will back up NDS data automatically while other data is being backed up.

Planning Server Downtime   From time to time, you will need to take the server down for maintenance. This usually will not cause a problem with NDS. Once NDS notices that the server is down, other servers that need to send updates to a replica on that server will keep trying until the server comes back up. When you bring the server up, it may take several minutes to resynchronize the replicas.

Preventing the SYS: Volume from Running out of Space   Never let any server's SYS: volume run out of space. The NDS database is kept in a hidden directory on the SYS: volume. If the volume runs out of space, TTS is disabled, no changes can be made to NDS, and the server loses synchronization with other replicas. To be safe, keep at least 50MB free at all times, more if you use ZENworks with applications. If possible, keep space-consuming data, such as print queues, on a volume other than SYS:.

Maintain NDS Standard Version   In NetWare 5 you can also use the NDS Manager to update the NDS NLM (DS.NLM) remotely, thus allowing you to centrally maintain a standard version of DS.NLM. The process is available on a tree-by-tree basis and only with NetWare servers of the same version. You cannot maintain the same DS.NLM version across NetWare server versions. All the servers in the tree have to be updated with the same version in order for the new features in NDS to be made available.

NDS is a distributed database; each change you make to NDS begins at the replica where you make the change and is passed to each of the other servers that contain a replica. Depending on communication delays, network use, and the complexity of the change, it can take anywhere from ten seconds to an hour or two for all replicas to receive the change.

Fortunately, NDS was designed with this in mind. The NDS database is loosely consistent, which means that it remains functional even if replicas do not have exactly the same information. You may notice these inconsistencies, but they do not necessarily represent a problem with NDS.

Although some inconsistencies between NDS replicas are a normal occurrence, severe inconsistencies may be an indication of a corrupt NDS database or another problem. Here are the symptoms you should watch for:

- Changes made to an NDS object or its rights seem to disappear.

- An object or its properties change unexpectedly. For example, a user can no longer log in because their password is incorrect, but the user has not changed their password.

- Errors may be inconsistent. For example, a user may be able to log in successfully after several unsuccessful attempts.

- Unknown objects, shown with a question mark, appear in the Directory tree. It is normal for these objects to show up when a server has been removed or when a partitioning operation is in progress. However, if they appear without an apparent cause, there may be a problem.

If you notice any of these symptoms, or if any part of NDS seems to behave inconsistently, follow the instructions in the following sections to narrow down and correct the problem. If a corrupt Directory is left alone, it will probably become worse. Be sure to diagnose and correct the problem as soon as you notice any symptoms.

If the problems you are having with NDS are not severe, you should let the servers run for a few hours before attempting any repairs. NDS double-checks itself, and it may repair the problem automatically. Do not take any servers down; this would prevent NDS from synchronizing and correcting errors.

If the problem still occurs, you should check the synchronization of the server. You can use the NDS Manager, DSREPAIR and DSTRACE utilities to accomplish this, as described in the following sections.

In the following sections you will be exposed to NDS maintenance tools that can help you achieve these objectives, and a summary of NDS error codes that can be helpful in determining problems when they occur.

Tools for Maintaining NDS

The Directory is critical to your network and can grow to include a large amount of information. Fortunately, Novell provides you with various tools to monitor and maintain the Directory. They are DSREPAIR, DSTRACE, and NDS Manager.

NetWare
Operations

PART 2

It is best to concentrate your maintenance tasks on the Directory partitions and replicas. These are constantly being challenged and the probability for corruption is always a concern. By utilizing DSREPAIR, NDSTRACE and NDS Manager tools properly, you can effectively monitor and identify problems before they reach critical mass. You will also want to concentrate on time synchronization. Since all Directory Service transactions are time stamped, you should implement, monitor, and maintain a time provider plan that will support you network.

DSREPAIR

The DSREPAIR utility provides several options for checking and repairing NDS problems. These are listed on the utility's Available Options menu. The most useful of these is the first: Unattended Full Repair. When you select this option, NetWare scans the NDS database for errors. All errors found will be repaired if possible. The other options allow you to perform specific steps for troubleshooting, which may be useful if the Unattended Full Repair option fails or if you are troubleshooting a specific problem.

Checking Synchronization with DSREPAIR

The process that NDS uses to send information between replicas is called synchronization. Two replicas are synchronized if they contain exactly the same information. In a busy network, the synchronization process is happening constantly to update the latest changes. The process is different depending on the type of change.

Simple changes, such as adding a User object or changing a property, are synchronized quickly. All that is required is to send updates to each server that has a replica of the partition where the object is located. Creating a partition is also a relatively simple task.

Complex changes include joining partitions, moving partitions, and merging Directory trees. These changes require updates to multiple partitions, and each server with a replica of any one of the partitions must be contacted to send updates. These changes can take a long time.

If you suspect a problem in NDS, you should check the synchronization before performing a major operation, such as merging trees, splitting partitions, joining partitions, or moving a container object.

To check synchronization with DSREPAIR, follow these steps:

1. Start the DSREPAIR utility by typing **LOAD DSREPAIR** at the server console.

2. Go to Advanced Options ➤ Replica and Partition Operations.

3. The list of partition replicas on the server is displayed. Select the partition you want to check for synchronization.

4. A menu is displayed with a series of options; select Report Synchronization Status On All Servers.

5. DSREPAIR will check the synchronization status for all replicas and display a log file. Examine this log file. If no errors appear, the replicas on that server are fully synchronized.

Before you run DSREPAIR, make a backup copy of NDS using your backup software. If the NDS database becomes corrupted further, you may lose information on all replicas. Since there may be errors in the database, do not overwrite an older backup if you have one.

NDS Error Codes

Here is a short list of NDS error codes you will encounter while maintaining directory services:

- **601** Indicates unknown object
- **625** Indicates transport failure.
- **636** Server is unreachable.

There are many more error codes and they are all documented on the Novell Web site. That means you do not have to memorize them all. But it's good to be familiar with them.

Although DSREPAIR can repair most NDS corruption, you may lose some information. After DSREPAIR has finished its work, use NetWare Administrator to look at the Directory tree and make sure that all objects are intact. If there are still problems with NDS, you may need to force synchronization, as described in the following section.

> **TIP** You can also run most of the DSREPAIR procedures remotely, using the NDSMGR32 utility.

Forcing Synchronization   If DSREPAIR is unable to repair the problems you are having with NDS, you may want to try forcing synchronization. This option will send updates from the Master replica to all other replicas. Any changes waiting on those replicas will be ignored.

If you force synchronization, you may lose changes to NDS that were made at a replica other than the Master. Make a backup copy of NDS on each server before proceeding.

NetWare Operations

PART 2

After the forced synchronization process is completed, load DSREPAIR at the server and use the Unattended Full Repair option again. If there are still NDS errors that DSREPAIR cannot fix, you will need to restore a backup.

Removing NDS from a Server   There are some instances in which you are forced to remove NDS from a server. For example, you may have a corrupted replica on the server or you may have problems synchronizing with other servers in the replica ring. In any case, to remove NDS from the server you need to load the NWCONFIG utility on the server console and then select the appropriate Directory options. You can also force the removal of NDS without using the Admin account by entering **NWCONFIG –DSREMOVE** on the server console. Once NWCONFIG loads and displays its menu, select Directory Services ≻ Remove Directory Services. Using the –DSREMOVE option with NWCONFIG allows you to bypass the NDS authentication to the tree, permitting you to force the removal of the Directory Services from the server when you start the NWCONFIG utility.

Restoring an NDS Backup   As a last resort, you can restore NDS from a backup. Assuming the backup was performed before the NDS problems began, this should permit a full recovery. Note the date of the backup. If you have made changes to NDS (such as creating users or changing rights) since that date, you must reenter them after you restore the backup.

To restore NDS, first use the NDSMGR32.EXE utility to delete all replicas of the partition. Then restore the partition data using your backup software. This will create a new Master replica from which you can re-create the other replicas.

WARNING   Make sure that all users in the Directory tree are logged out of the network when you back up or restore NDS data. Do not bring down any servers during this operation; all servers that are members of a replica ring need to be available.

DSTRACE

DSTRACE was a special SET parameter with NetWare 4.*x*, but with NetWare 5 it is a server utility that can be used to monitor the activities of NDS. DSTRACE is primarily used to determine and track the health of NDS as it communicates with the other NetWare 5 servers in the network.

You can also use DSTRACE commands to monitor the status of NDS synchronization processes and view errors that occur during NDS synchronization. After you enable DSTRACE by typing **DSTRACE**, you can type **HELP DST**, which will display a list of options. Information is displayed each time NDS replicas are synchronized. This can be helpful when you are diagnosing an NDS problem.

In NetWare 5, the DSTRACE screen displays the important information in color. Different colors highlight key events that occur during the synchronization process for the server. The trace screen displays synchronization information for every replica stored on that server.

> **NOTE** Always check the DSTRACE screen to see that NDS is communicating before performing any partition operation. Never start a new partition operation if there is an error communicating to the other servers or replicas of the same partition. Look for the message "ALL PROCESSED = YES" for each partition on the server, especially the partition you are going to modify. This message indicates that all replicas in the partition are synchronized without error.

To enable DSTRACE for viewing and event logging, you can use the following commands:

DST ON Enables tracing the target device

DST OFF Disables tracing to target device

DST FILE Change command target to log file

DST SCREEN Change command target to trace screen

DST INLINE Display events inline

DST JOURNAL Display events on a background thread

DST FMAX={size} Specify maximum disk file size

DST FNAME={name} Specify disk file name

Once you have enabled DSTRACE, you can specify what you would like to view. You can select a whole array of information to view by specifying the DST command followed by a tag list.

To enable a tag, you simply type DST followed by the tag or item you want to view. Keep in mind that you have options of only viewing the file on the console, logging the item to a file, or doing both. A legend at the top of the screen tells you whether you are viewing, logging to a file, or both.

For example, you can type DST TIME to show event times. To disable this view, you would type **DST -TIME**, or to abbreviate, you can type **DST -TI**. The first two letters of each tag will work; however, you must always type all three characters of DST.

The quickest way to become familiar with the DSTRACE screen is to use it and learn what all the messages mean. Here is a standard set of DSTRACE commands that you can try:

DSTRACE   Load DSTRACE on the server

DST +   \<your preferred set of tags or flags\>

DST SCREEN ON   Enables viewing on the screen

DST FILE ON   Enables the events to be logged to a file

The following is the flag set:

ON, BACKLINK, ERRORS, EMU, FRAGGER, INIT, INSPECTOR, JANITOR, LIMBER, MISC, PART, RECMAN, REPAIR, SCHEMA, SKULKER, STREAMS, and VCLIENT.

When the DSTRACE screen is enabled, the information displayed is based on a default set of filters. If you want to view more or less than the default, you can manipulate the filters using the debugging message flags. The debugging messages help you determine the status of NDS and verify that everything is working well.

Each NDS process has its own set of debugging messages. To view the debugging messages on a particular process, use a plus sign (+) and the process name or option. To disable the display of a process, use a minus sign (-) and the process name or option. Here are some examples:

SET DSTRACE = +SYNC   Enables the synchronization messages

SET DSTRACE = -SYNC   Disables the synchronization messages

SET DSTRACE = +SCHEMA   Enables the schema messages

You can also combine the debugging message flags by using the Boolean operators "&" (which means AND) and "|" (which means OR). The syntax for controlling the debugging messages at the server console is as follows:

SET DSTRACE = +\<trace flag\> [\<trace flag\>]

SET DSTRACE = -\<trace flag\> [& \<trace flag\>]

TIP   The following DSTRACE setting is a favorite with Novell Technical support:
SET DSTRACE = A81164B91. This setting turns on (by setting the appropriate bits)
a predefined group of debugging messages.

In addition to the debugging messages, which help you check the status of NDS, there is a set of commands that forces the NDS background processes to run. To force the background process to run, you precede the command with an asterisk (*). An example would be: SET DSTRACE = *H.

TIP After completion of all DSTRACE checks enter the following DSTRACE commands: **Set DSTRACE=nodebug**; **Set DSTRACE=+min**; and **Set DSTRACE=off**. This will minimize filters and turn DSTRACE off.

Checking Synchronization with DSTRACE

To start tracing NDS synchronization data, type this command at the server console: **SET DSTRACE=ON**. To access the Directory Services Trace screen (DSTRACE or NDS TRACE) after you have started it, press ALT + ESC at the server console. You can leave DSTRACE running and check the screen periodically for problems. One of the most common problems will produce this message: "SYNC: End sync of partition name. All processed = NO."

If "NO" is displayed here, and the message keeps repeating after a few minutes, there is a serious problem with NDS. You should run the DSREPAIR utility, and repair the database.

When you no longer need the DSTRACE screen, type **SET DSTRACE = OFF** at the server console.

NOTE We could write a whole book on DSTRACE, but that is not the intent of this book. Novell's Web site has great documentation on this subject. These are just the tip of the iceberg.

NDS Manager

Once you have implemented your NDS partitioning and replication approach, we'll take a look at the actual process of creating, deleting, and managing partitions and replicas. NDS Manager (NDSMGR32.EXE) is the utility used for this.

You need to know some of the basic functions available for NDS Manager since you will be using this tool on a day-to-day basis. We have found this tool to be very helpful when it comes to monitoring the tree for signs of problems.

When you start NDS Manager, a split window is displayed. The main NDS Manager window is split into two sections. The left side displays the Directory tree. Only container objects and Server objects are shown. A container that is the root of a partition appears with an icon to the left of the container object's icon. The right side displays a list of replicas. If you have highlighted a partition's container, the replicas for that partition are listed. If you have highlighted a Server object, the replicas stored on the server are listed.

In the following sections you will review different activities you can accomplish with NDS Manager.

Creating (Splitting) a Partition

Creating a new partition is also called splitting a partition because the process involves splitting a child container object from its parent container's partition. Follow these procedures to create a partition:

1. Start NDS Manager and highlight the container object that will be the root of the new partition.

2. From the NDS Manager menu, select Object Create Partition.

3. The Create Partition dialog box will appear. Verify that you have chosen the correct object, and then click Yes to continue.

4. The new partition will now be created. Depending on the complexity of your network and the number of replicas to be made of the parent partition, this may take several minutes.

5. Create replicas of the new partition as needed. You will want to partition the tree to reduce the overall size of the Directory Services database which will help improve performance and redundancy, as described later in this chapter.

Deleting (Merging) a Partition

The process of deleting a partition is called merging partitions. When you merge a partition, it is combined with its parent partition. All of the objects that were contained in the partition become child objects of the parent partition. Follow these steps to merge a partition.

1. Start NDS Manager and highlight the container object at the root of the partition.

2. From the NDS Manager menu, select Object ➤ Partition ➤ Merge.

3. The Merge Partition dialog box will appear. Verify that you have chosen the correct child and parent partitions, and then click Yes to continue.

4. The partitions will now be merged. Depending on the complexity of the network and the number of replicas required, this may take several minutes.

Using this procedure can reduce the number of partitions and replicas. As your company evolves and your needs change, the tree can be reconfigured very easily.

Adding a Replica

NDS Manager allows you to manage the replicas for a partition easily. Follow these steps to add a new replica to a server.

1. Start NDS Manager and select the partition you want to add a replica to.

2. From the NDS Manager menu, choose Object ➢ Add Replica.

3. The Add Replica dialog box appears.

4. Choose a server to hold the new replica, and indicate whether the new replica will be Read/Write or Read only.

5. Click OK to add the new replica. This may take several minutes.

Adding replicas is an effective way to ensure redundancy on the Directory database. Placing the replicas in a strategic location improves network performance, as we discussed earlier in this chapter.

Removing a Replica

Removing a replica of a partition is also simple. To remove a replica, follow these steps:

1. From NDS Manager, highlight and expand the partition you want to remove a replica from.

2. Highlight the server that contains the replica to be removed.

3. In the right window, right-click the replica of the partition you want to remove from the server and select Delete.

4. Click Yes to confirm the deletion. Now that you've deleted this replica, be sure to create a new replica on a different server, if needed, to keep the partition safe.

As the need for replicas changes, you can reduce or increase their number. But you need to be very careful and plan properly so that you don't end up with too many replicas of a partition.

Moving a Container Object

You can't move a container object using the NetWare Administrator's Move Object option because it is considered a partitioning operation. But you can easily accomplish this using the NDS Manager utility.

To move a container object, follow these steps:

1. Split the container object you wish to move into its own partition.

2. From the NDS Manager menu, choose Object ➢ Partition ➢ Move.

3. Choose the new context for the container object.

4. Click Yes to begin the process of moving the container object. This may take several minutes.

NetWare Operations

PART 2

This procedure is another example of how configurable NDS is. You can easily reorganize a Directory at the Organizational Unit level, even in a large network.

These are general functions that are associated with NDS Manager. You can also perform DSREPAIR functions on partitions using this Utility.

Partitioning and Replication Rules

You should follow some basic rules when partitioning the tree:

- Before you perform any partition-related tasks, make sure all the replicas in the replica ring are accessible to each other.

- When you are adding a server to the tree, make sure the Master replica of the partition you are going to add the server to is available.

- Make it a habit to check the tree for any errors or synchronization problems.

- Use DSTRACE to verify that the tree is stable.

- Make sure that the tree is time synchronized.

- Create additional child partitions when you reach over 1,000 objects in a partition.

- Follow geographical boundaries at the upper layers of the tree.

- Avoid creating more than twelve child partitions.

- Do not create unnecessary child partitions.

- When deciding on partition boundaries, ensure that they do not span into the WAN.

- Keep users and resources local to each other when establishing partition boundaries.

- Keep the partition structure as simple as possible. Remember that less is more.

- Place at least three replicas of each partition on strategically placed servers on your network. Have at least one local server hold a Read/Write replica of the local partition. This establishes greater fault tolerance. By storing copies of partitions on multiple servers, you can help ensure that access to your Directory will remain intact, even if a disk crashes or servers go down. Also, you will give users greater freedom to log in without being dependent on one particular server's availability to provide authentication since any Read/Write replica can fulfill this role.

- Strategically placed replicas can improve network performance. If users need to use a WAN link to access Directory information, you can improve response time and network traffic by providing a replica that they can access locally. In addition, keeping an updated copy of a replica offsite is probably a good idea.

- Place all Master replicas in a central location (IS) where they can be administered locally.

- Do not place more than 15 replicas on a server; this will greatly reduce performance when the Directory is in maintenance mode or searching for resources.

- Each server used for Bindery Services must contain a Master or Read/Write replica of the partition that contains the User objects needing bindery access to the server.

- To minimize problems with subordinate references, create as few partitions as possible. Avoid too many replicas of the [Root] partition, because this partition tends to have many child partitions. Since a child partition or a subordinate reference must accompany its replica wherever it appears, the [Root] partition can create a lot of subordinate references, which can needlessly increase network traffic.

WARNING   You should avoid making too many replicas of the [Root] partition. But if you fail to replicate it at all, you are taking a dangerous risk. You need the [Root] partition to access the Directory tree.

Network Traffic Considerations

The NDS database remains consistent by transmitting any change made to an object in a partition to all replicas of that partition. Directory synchronization takes place across replica rings.

Each partition has at least one replica, the Master replica, with additional replicas (for example a Read/Write replica) for redundancy and load balancing. Because Directory synchronization requires that every replica be updated to reflect any changes to any object, a considerable amount of communication is required between NetWare 5 servers.

On LANs, this communication is not usually a major consideration because most LANs have plenty of bandwidth available. The extra bandwidth needed for this communication does become a concern on WAN links, where bottlenecks can occur.

Potential Problems with Subordinate References

When you want to change a partition that has a subordinate reference, make sure the subordinate reference is accessible before you make the change. If the subordinate reference is located on the other side of an unstable connection, you could be creating a potential problem because the data in the subordinate reference cannot be updated to match the Master.

NetWare
Operations

PART 2

Default Partitions and Replicas

When the first server is installed, NDS creates and stores a Master replica of the [Root] partition on that server's SYS: volume. The second and third servers receive a Read/Write replica of the [Root] partition. By default, any servers installed after that do not receive replicas. An admin can add additional replicas of a partition to any server in the tree at his or her discretion. We would recommend that you plan for this before you do it because unnecessary replicas will take up bandwidth on your network.

Replicas in Merged NDS Trees

When two or more Directory trees are merged, the source tree servers (servers of trees that are being merged into the [Root] of another tree) that hold replicas of their [Root] partition are given a Read/Write replica of the new [Root] partition. They also receive subordinate references to the child partitions of the new [Root] partition.

The servers of the *target* tree (the tree whose [Root] remains as the [Root]) are given subordinate references to the uppermost partitions in the source trees if the target tree servers currently hold replicas of the [Root] partition.

Server and Network Requirements for Replica support

We recently participated in a NetWare migration project. Company A needed to decide which servers were going to hold partition replicas. We put together a list of basic requirements for these servers with the goal of dedicating them for this function. In this project, we looked at the two basic weaknesses of major network installations: the servers and the LAN/WAN backbone.

We recommended that the servers be high-end systems and that bandwidth be increased to accommodate the anticipated network traffic.

We recommended the following specifics:

Server Configuration

The servers designated to support replicas, especially the Master replicas, should be high-end systems. All server vendors offer enterprise-level servers, which can easily accommodate the processing requirements of today's networks. We recommended the use of experienced vendors such as DELL, HP, Compaq, and IBM. The company chose HP Netservers for the bulk of the authentication and partition synchronization processes. We also took into consideration the bandwidth that's available and how close you can place the servers to the users.

We followed hardware recommendations and discussed these with each vendor. He or she will be more up-to-date with current Novell recommendations, and will make recommendations on their offerings.

LAN/WAN Configuration

We know CFOs hate the words *upgrade* or *replace*, but when you are going to support Directory Services over a WAN with multiple sites, 56K isn't going to do it. Here's what we recommend for the LAN/WAN topology:

- We recommend a single protocol, IP. We strongly suggest as open a protocol as possible; this means choosing TCP/IP. It will allow you more control over the network and will easily integrate with the Internet.

- Implement a Fast Ethernet–based LAN environment with backbone managed switches instead of active hubs.

- Use Fast Ethernet LAN cards on your servers and desktops.

- Use a fiber backbone when possible (ATM or FDDI) for your local backbone.

- Create multiple data paths to your servers by installing two or three network cards on them. This way you can balance the load between them.

- Install enterprise type routers and dedicate links to remote locations.

- Use high bandwidth WAN connections (T1 or above) for your main offices (250 users or more) and Frame Relay with dedicated services for the smaller offices. Make sure that the SLA is sufficient for peak times.

- Use a network management tool like ManageWise or OpenView, and monitor

24seven **CASE STUDY**

network performance. You want to catch problems before you get calls.

We incorporated these suggestions into the overall project, and installed a series of NetWare servers that support NDS functions and services. This infrastructure of servers maintains a high level of performance and availability for the users.

Part 3

ZENworks

Topics Covered:

- Designing and installing ZENworks
- Applying and administering ZENworks
- Registering workstations with NDS
- Distributing applications
- Managing desktops with ZENworks
- Remotely controlling and viewing a workstation
- Inventory your software and hardware
- Explaining benefits of ZENworks to end-users

12

ZENworks Design and Installation

This product, named ZENworks to remind us that it stands for Zero Effort Networks, is one of the most powerful tools in the Novell product lineup. In this part, we will focus primarily on version 2, which offers increased capabilities in many areas. Entire books have been written on this subject, so we have decided to concentrate on the capabilities of the various components and how they can be used to implement solutions to problems you may find in your network. We will also try and pass on a few tips and techniques along the way.

We will begin this chapter with an overview of the various versions of ZENworks and their capabilities. Next, we will turn to the objects related to ZENworks and the purpose of each. Once we have reviewed that, we can turn our attention to how the implementation of ZENworks will affect your tree design and give you some guidelines to maximize performance. We will then turn to a brief overview of the installation process. We will conclude this chapter with a review of additional resources to help you make the most of this very powerful product.

The next chapter will discuss the details of implementing software distribution. We will begin by covering workstation registration and some of the problems in registering them. This is a necessary prerequisite for some forms of application distribution and for most of the desktop management capabilities of ZENworks. Next, we'll cover how to create Application objects and then how to configure them to meet various needs, including just-in-time distribution, software metering, and the self-healing capabilities of applications distributed through ZENworks.

The last chapter in this part will cover each of the remaining components of ZENworks and how each can help you administrate the network more effectively. We will look at desktop management via policies, remote control (and several variations on it), help desk tools, and the anti-virus capabilities provided by McAfee and bundled with the product. We will conclude with some reasons that your end users may like it and how to "sell" ZENworks to them.

ZENworks will make your life better, even if you only implement a few of its capabilities. With a little brainstorming, you will probably find many, many ways that this tool can help you increase productivity, both for administrative personnel and users. We hope that you find this tool as useful as we do, and have provided several examples of how it has been implemented to solve common problems throughout the next three chapters.

Versions and Their Capabilities

Because there are several versions of this product around, we want to begin with a brief overview of each and how each fits into the big picture. You can also use this information to decide which product is right for you. Table 12.1 lists the different versions of ZENworks and the capabilities of each.

Table 12.1   ZENworks Versions and Their Capabilities

Capability	Starter Pack	ZENworks 1.1	ZENworks 2
Application distribution	Yes	Yes	Yes
Applications deliverable when no one is logged in	No	No	Yes
Criteria can be defined to ensure workstation is able to run an application, be updated by a patch, etc.	No	Limited	Yes
Macros can prompt user for preferences, information, etc.	No	No	Yes
Scripts can be run before and/or after application is distributed	No	No	Yes

Table 12.1   ZENworks Versions and Their Capabilities *(continued)*

Capability	Starter Pack	ZENworks 1.1	ZENworks 2
Reports available on application installation success or failure	No	No	Yes
Applications are self-healing	No	Yes	Yes
Software metering	No	Yes	Yes
Supports policies	Yes	Yes	Yes
Policies are extensible	No	No	Yes
Supports roaming profiles	Yes	Yes	Yes
Hardware inventory	No	Yes	Yes
Software inventory	No	No	Yes
Reports available on inventory information	No	Very Difficult	Yes
Supports DMI 2	No	No	Yes
Printers can be configured, managed, and assigned to specific users centrally	No	Yes	Yes
Remote control workstations	No	Yes	Yes
Remote workstation diagnostics	No	No	Yes
Remote file transfer without full remote control session	No	No	Yes
Remote execution of an application without full remote control session	No	No	Yes
Remotely view workstation without controlling it	No	No	Yes

ZENworks

PART 3

Table 12.1 ZENworks Versions and Their Capabilities *(continued)*

Capability	Starter Pack	ZENworks 1.1	ZENworks 2
Help desk utility for users to report problems	No	Yes	Yes
Ability to customize what information is sent with help request	No	No	Yes
Includes Y2K preparation tool (see note below)	No	Yes	Yes
Includes anti-virus software (see note below)	No	No	Yes

NOTE The Y2K tool, Check 2000, is included in a five-user version only. Additional licenses must be purchased separately. The anti-virus software, McAfee, is included, with one license included per license of ZENworks purchased. Software updates are included free for six months, after which additional updates can be purchased.

The starter pack is free and ships with NetWare 5. Updates are available for free from Novell's Web site. ZENworks 1.1 and 2 must be purchased on a per-seat basis. Upgrade pricing is available from 1 or 1.1 to 2.

ZENworks Objects

There are several NDS objects associated with ZENworks. This section is not designed to be an in-depth analysis of them, but rather a brief review of each before turning to how they impact NDS design. The objects are as follows: Application, Application Folder, Policy Package, Workstation, and Workstation Group.

Application Object The Application object is one of the best known (though not necessarily understood) objects associated with ZENworks. This object has been around since the old NAL days in NetWare 4.11. NAL (Novell Application Launcher) was a separate product for application distribution before the introduction of ZENworks. This is the primary object used in application distribution. There is a wizard to help you design or copy the object as well as a separate application, snAppShot, that helps you create the files and make the registry changes necessary for most applications.

Application Folder   The Application Folder is used to organize your applications. When you open your Start menu and choose Programs, you see applications and folders that contain either other folders or applications. This object lets you organize your applications in any order that makes sense to you. You can also use this feature to control the many folders that are typically in the Start menu, making it hard to use.

Policy Package Object   The Policy Package object is a type of object that you can choose when you choose to create an object; it actually starts a wizard that allows you to choose which type of policy package you desire. There are Workstation policy packages for Windows 3.1, 9x, and NT, User policy packages for users who use Windows 3.1, 9x, and/or NT workstations, and Search policy packages. Search policy packages control how NDS determines which policies will actually go into effect for a given user or computer by specifying where NDS will look for policies. User policies are set on a per operating system basis, so if you have users who use multiple operating systems, you will need to create a separate User policy package for each OS they use. Workstation policies are only in effect after the workstation has been registered in NDS.

Workstation Object   The Workstation object is used by NDS when Workstation polices are set. These objects are necessary for the inventory, remote control, and reporting capabilities of ZENworks, as well as for application distribution when a user isn't logged in.

> **WARNING**   ZENworks uses the *Workstation* object, not the *Computer* object. The Computer object is for documentation purposes only and is for your convenience.

Workstation Group Object   Finally there is the Workstation Group object. This object is designed to allow you to treat a group of Workstation objects like a single object, in the same way that groups are used to manage several users as a unit. File system rights, Workstation policies, and so on can be assigned either to each workstation individually or once to the Workstation Group, assuming each workstation in question belongs to the Workstation Group.

ZENworks and NDS Design

When designing your NDS tree to accommodate ZENworks, you have several factors to take into account: the number of objects per partition relative to your hardware, manageability questions, and so on. These issues vary depending on object type, so we will discuss each type separately.

Workstation and Workstation Group Objects

In most networks, each user has their own workstation. That means that there is one Workstation object per user, which basically doubles the number of objects per container. Depending on the number of objects in the partition, your hardware, and the version of NDS you are using, that number may exceed the recommended number of objects (see Chapter 1 for guidelines).

We and Novell recommend that you keep the workstation object in the same container as the user who uses it. This makes it fairly simple to maintain; the Workstation object stays with the user if it becomes necessary to partition or subdivide the container the user is in. Remember that users don't use this object, only administrators do.

Creating separate containers for each type of object (User, Group, Workstation, and so on) may result in the following issues:

- Reduction in user access performance. The server may need to go to other partitions, possibly on other servers, to get information it needs. This also raises NDS maintenance tasks.

- Reduction in the flexibility and scalability of the bottom of the tree. What will you do, for example, when the user's container approaches recommended capacity? Create a Users2 container? It probably makes more sense to divide by department, floor, or some other factor.

- Design is suited to administrators, not users. The design of your tree should take into account the needs of both administrators and users.

Nevertheless, there may be some circumstances when placing your workstations in a separate container makes sense. If you use a decentralized administrative approach, with some administrators dealing only with the workstations and the software on them, then using a separate container for Workstation objects may be best, as long as you plan on using the Workstation object primarily for inventory purposes. It allows you to easily control access to these objects without granting access to the rest of the tree or any objects therein.

TIP Maximum performance is achieved when the server containing the partition with the Workstation object is close to the actual workstation itself, not necessarily the associated User object.

Policy Package Objects

The guidelines for placing policy packages are quite simple:

- Place the Container Policy object as high in the tree as possible without placing it outside of your site container (without placing it on the other side of a WAN link).

- Place User and Workstation Policy objects in the same container as the users or workstations that will use them.

- Disable searching through groups if the policy package is on the other side of a WAN link. (If possible, you should avoid groups that span WAN links.)

- If you want to limit network traffic, search only to the *partition* root, not to the [Root].

Application and Application Folder Objects

This section is probably the most involved. Application and Application Folder objects are the focus of most user activity because users run applications provided by ZENworks. Application objects, along with the associated files on a volume, contain the applications that you would like distributed to your users. Application folders are for organizing those applications. (The purpose, creation, and configuration of these objects are discussed in greater detail in Chapter 13.)

In this section, we will focus on naming conventions for your Application objects, where they should be located in the tree, and some issues and tips in associating them with User, Group, Container, and Workstation objects.

Naming Conventions

If you have a single server that will provide applications to your clients, you can name your Application objects anything you wish. However, you should name them after the name of the application that they represent.

On the other hand, if you have multiple servers that have the same applications, you should create an Application object for each application *on each server*. The name should include both the application name and the server name. The format normally used is *ApplicationName_ServerName*. The simplest way to create an object for each application on each server is to create one object per application. Once all of your Application objects are created, you can use the wizard for creating objects from a copy of an existing object, or by using the same .AOT or .AXT file. Once you have done that, change the macro that contains the source server name to the new server's name, then change any mappings to point to the new server and modify any other properties necessary.

ZENworks

PART 3

WARNING Do *not* use any other method to copy an Application object, other than the one provided in the Create New Application Object wizard.

Location in the Tree

The Application objects should be created at the highest level in the tree that doesn't span the WAN—the container that represents the site level. If you have multiple sites, you should create an Application object representing each application in each site. If you only have a single site and you only have a single server, then a single Application object per application will suffice. If you have multiple partitions in a single site, you may want to place an Application object in each partition instead of at the site level. This is particularly true if the two partitions are on different servers.

Application Folder objects are for administrative use only, and so may be located wherever it is convenient for you. The configuration of the Application Folder is cached in the individual Application objects as well, causing less bandwidth to be used in the implementation of Application objects.

Associating with Groups, Containers, Workstations, and Workstation Groups

One of the new features in ZENworks 2 is that applications can be associated with Workstation and Workstation Group objects. This allows you to distribute software when no one is logged in (also called lights-out distribution). If you plan on utilizing this feature, you should place Workstation and Workstation Group objects near the Application objects.

Application objects are most often associated with User objects (and objects associated with them, including groups and containers), and allow users to run applications as needed. To simplify the management of applications, they are often associated with container objects, which allows all users in that container (and any subcontainers) access as well. As mentioned previously, you should create Application objects for each site and therefore shouldn't associate them with containers higher than the site level. You can control how far NDS searches up the tree for container associations with Application objects. You can specify how far NDS will look by setting the value of Set Application Inheritance Level on the container (Country, Organization, or Organizational Unit) or User object's Launcher Configuration tab for either the user or workstations in the container (depending on the tab selected), as shown in Figure 12.1. The values are as follows:

-1   Searches all parent containers to [Root] (should be used in LAN-only environments or substantial performance penalties may be incurred).

0   Does not search for any container associations (you will need to use user and group associations instead; this may cause more management overhead).

1 Searches the container the user is in only, not parent containers (recommended in many cases for maximum performance with minimal administrative overhead).

2 Searches the user's container object and that container's parent object only. (Use this setting as long as the user's container's parent container is in the same site—remember never to span the WAN.)

3-999 Same as 2, but more levels are searched.

Figure 12.1 Search behavior of NDS when looking for container associations with Application objects

Another very important performance consideration is the location and membership of Group objects. Ideally, Group objects will be placed near the Application objects, just as for User objects. Groups should only contain users from within the site, and preferably within the same partition. You should also consider limiting membership to approximately 1,000 users, minimizing the time it takes to search through the membership of the group. If this is not possible, you can turn off the searching of groups by setting Read Groups for Applications to No. This will increase performance, but may also increase management of Application objects.

Installation

The installation process is quite simple. Simply insert the ZENworks CD and choose to install the client or server portions. When installing the server components, you can choose the ZENworks components and/or Software Metering components. As shown in Figure 12.2, you can choose to install any combination of the following components when you choose to do a Custom installation:

Figure 12.2 ZENworks components

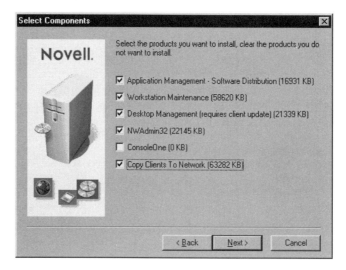

- Application Management and Software Distribution
- Workstation Maintenance, including both Hardware and Software Inventory components
- Desktop Management, including the following components:
  - Policies
  - Profiles
  - Remote Control in various forms
  - Help Desk Capabilities
- An update to NWAdmin to be able to manage the ZENworks-related objects
- An update to ConsoleOne to be able to manage more of the properties of the ZENworks-related objects (see Chapter 10 for more information on ConsoleOne and its capabilities)

- The ZENworks-enabled clients (including the installation of the Novell Workstation Manager option) to take advantage of the desktop management features (described below)

NOTE   The anti-virus and Y2K capabilities have separate installation programs. You should refer to the documentation of each for details and prerequisites for installation.

You can also choose to install portions of the listed components, including any or all of the following (the default installs all of them):

- The files actually used to implement the components
- Schema extensions needed to create the new object types
- A few default Application objects, showing how NWAdmin, the Help Requester, etc., are set up
- Workstation Registry rights settings, allowing workstations to register themselves in NDS

You may also choose which tree or trees to install ZENworks on. Note that you will need a user with Supervisor rights to [Root] to make the schema extensions, as well as the other NDS rights changes. The user will also need Write rights to the Public and System directories to write the files to the server. After the selections are made, a summary screen is given, which lets you know what will be done, and then the files are copied.

Server Requirements

To install ZENworks, you must meet the following minimum requirements:

- NetWare 4.11 with SP6 or higher, NetWare 5 with SP2 or higher recommended
- 64MB RAM (NetWare 4) or 128MB RAM (NetWare 5), with 7MB free RAM
- 160-185MB free disk space (the values will vary depending on options selected and may be more or less than this typical range)
- NDS rights as follows:
  - Supervisor right to the Server
  - Supervisor right to the container where the *server* is
  - Supervisor right to [Root] to extend the schema (if necessary)

These requirements are the minimum; increasing RAM and disk space will increase performance and provide room for growth.

If you will be storing inventory data on the server, the minimum requirements are higher:

- 128MB RAM minimum (see Chapter 14 for recommendations)

ZENworks

PART 3

- 220MB available disk space (additional room will be needed for the inventory data)
- 40MB free RAM

In addition, administration of those objects should be done with NWADMN32 for full functionality; ConsoleOne support is not fully functional but will be improved in the future.

Client Requirements

The requirements on the client side are rather modest. You will need to install the client that comes with ZENworks to take advantage of all of its features. The standard Novell client allows you to access some but not all of ZENwork's features. Specifically, you will need to install the desktop management and remote control features, as shown in Figure 12.3 (the Novell Remote Control Agent is off the bottom of the list).

Figure 12.3   Necessary features to install to take advantage of all ZENworks features

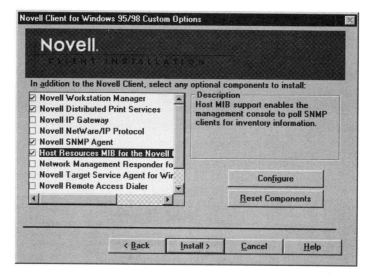

In particular, you need to choose the following components:

- Novell Workstation Manager
- Novell Distributed Print Services (NDPS), if you want to work with NDPS-based printers
- Novell SNMP Agent, if you want to use SNMP to report the results of software distribution

- Host Resources MIB for the Novell Client, if you want a management station to be able to query the client for inventory information (not necessary if you don't want to use SNMP for this, and will rely instead on the inventory feature of ZENworks)

- Novell Remote Control Agent, if you want the ability to remotely control the computer

The requirements on the client side vary with the version you choose to install. The minimum requirements for the DOS and Windows 3.1*x* client are as follows:

- 386 CPU (it will work better with a 486)

- 8MB RAM (more will be much better)

- 15MB free hard drive space (depending on options selected, the size requirements will vary)

- A memory manager, such as HIMEM.SYS or QEMM386.SYS

The minimum requirements for Windows 9*x* are as follows:

- 486 CPU (we recommend at least a Pentium)

- 16MB RAM (we recommend 32–64MB RAM)

- 28MB free hard drive space (depending on options installed, the size requirements will vary)

The requirements for Windows NT are simply the minimums required to run NT. We suggest that you at least double the minimums that Microsoft suggests. You will also need approximately 30MB of free hard drive space, depending on the options you choose.

The incompatibilities and optimizations listed in Chapter 9 also apply to the ZENworks client, which simply adds a few advanced capabilities to the standard client.

Additional Resources

There are many resources available as you begin your quest for ideas on how to maximize your use of ZENworks, as well as methods to implement your ideas. Besides the usual TIDs available at `support.novell.com`, there are many other resources. Finding them, however, can be difficult.

One of the best sites for finding information on ZENworks is the Cool Solutions Web site—part of Novell's Web site. Here you will find links to other sites on ZENworks, ideas on how you can use the various capabilities of ZENworks, and so on. The address is `www.novell.com/coolsolutions/zenworks`.

ZENworks

PART 3

TIP At the main Cool Solutions Web site you will also find sections devoted to NDS and GroupWise. Other products may be available in the future as well. The home page for Cool Solutions is `www.novell.com/coolsolutions`.

On this site, you will find many informative articles and tips on how to use it. There are several links that are particularly worth mentioning:

Vault   Provides a list sorted alphabetically by subject of all past articles, questions, tips, and so on. If you have a specific question in mind, check here first. They also have links to indexes of each type of article (tips, feature articles, Q&A, and so on). You can get there directly by going to `www.novell.com/coolsolutions/zenworks/subject_index.html`.

Feature Article   Takes you to the current feature article and an in-depth discussion of some facet of ZENworks.

Q&A   Provides a great place to ask your questions and find answers. Many forums are also dedicated to ZENworks. You can access them at `support.novell.com/forums`.

From the Trenches   Offers solutions using ZENworks that your fellow administrators have submitted. This is a great source for ideas on how to use the product to solve real-world problems.

Links   Contains links to other sites that are devoted in whole or part to ZENworks. There are many great sites where people have posted their own solutions and this is a great way to find them.

Downloadables   Contains useful tools to extend the power of ZENworks.

One other site worth mentioning (and available as a link from the Cool Solutions site) is `zenworksmaster.com/`. This site has lots of great information and is presented very succinctly. We have found that we often try this site first, as it gives us the answers to our questions without lots of background information and explanations as to why things should be done a certain way.

TIP We occasionally have trouble getting to the site when directly typing in this address. If this problem occurs, go to `www.novell.com/coolsolutions/zenworks/links.html` and click on the link `zenworksMASTER.com`. Once there, you may want to bookmark it; we have had no problems getting there from a bookmark. We don't know why this is, only that it consistently works.

For the most complete technical reference on how ZENworks works and all of the return and error codes associated with it, refer to Novell's LogicSource at `support.novell.com/logicsource/zenworks`.

13

ZENworks:
A Powerful Application
Distribution Tool

This chapter is a continuation of the previous chapter, with a focus on the features included in ZENworks along with some tips on how they can be used in your work environment. This chapter, like the last one, will focus primarily on version 2.

We will mainly review the capabilities of ZENworks in the following areas: workstation registration and application creation, configuration, and distribution.

Registering Workstations

To be able to use many of the ZENworks features, you must first register the Workstation object in NDS.

If you did not choose to grant the rights necessary for Workstations to automatically register themselves when users log in, you can either run SYS:PUBLIC\WIN32\WSRIGHTS.EXE or you can choose Tools ➢ Workstation Utilities ➢ Prepare Workstation Registration from NWAdmin. In either case, the container object will be granted Compare, Read, and Write property rights for the WM:Registered Workstation property for the container.

WARNING You must go through these steps whenever you create a new container. If you don't, that right will *not be assigned and no Workstation objects will be registered unless the user has the Write right to this property from another source.*

Once the appropriate rights have been granted, the workstation will need to register with NDS. This requires two things: the effective policy Workstation Import for the *User* object for the platform they are on, and the client software must register with NDS.

While policies in general will be discussed in detail in Chapter 14, we need to discuss the Workstation Import policy at this point because many ZENworks features depend on the workstation registering with NDS. To create the policy, select the desired parent container (see the section on search policy for a discussion of how NDS searches for effective policies) and choose Create ➢ Policy Package. In the wizard that appears, select the appropriate platform's (Win31, Win95-98, or WinNT) *user package*. The required setting for the workstation to register with NDS is Workstation Import Policy. This policy is normally scheduled to run at login, so it will automatically run each time the user logs in to keep the NDS data up to date. If you select the policy and choose Details, you will get a dialog box similar to the one seen in Figure 13.1.

Figure 13.1   Workstation Import Policy: Workstation Location tab

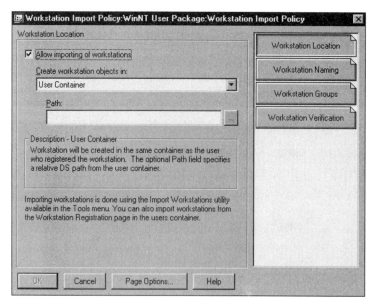

On the Workstation Location tab, you will need to check the Allow Importing of Workstations box and optionally the location you want those workstations created in. As mentioned in Chapter 12, this should normally be left at the default location of the user's container.

You must also specify how you would like the Workstation object named in NDS. The default is the name of the computer (its NetBIOS name) and network address (either IPX or TCP/IP) for Windows 9*x* and NT-based users. For Windows 3.1 users, it is the username and network address (again either TCP/IP or IPX). Adding the network address may be useful for those computers that have static addresses or ones that change very infrequently. If you have mobile users, however, the address portion of the name will quickly become out of date, and will therefore be misleading. The choices of components that you can place in a Workstation object's name include the following:

- CPU type
- Container the associated User object is in (especially useful if you place Workstation and User objects in different containers)
- DNS name (it is only the host name, not the FQDN [Fully Qualified Domain Name])
- Preferred server
- Operating system
- Any user-defined text you desire

If your naming standard allows for duplicate names, NDS will automatically assign a unique three-digit number to the end of the name to ensure that it is unique. As mentioned in preceding chapters, the importance of planning can't be overstated. Think carefully, then implement your standard.

Now that you've established the effective policy Workstation Import for the *User* object, you will need to register the client software with NDS. This will happen automatically if you have installed the desktop management portion of the ZENworks client. Alternatively, this can also be done manually by running SYS:PUBLIC\WSREG16.EXE for Windows 3.1 clients or SYS:PUBLIC\WSREG32.EXE for Windows 9*x* and NT clients. In either case, you can find the object registered with NDS by looking at the user's Parent Container object's details and viewing the Workstation Registration tab, as shown in Figure 13.2.

ZENworks

PART 3

Figure 13.2 The Workstation Registration tab of a container object

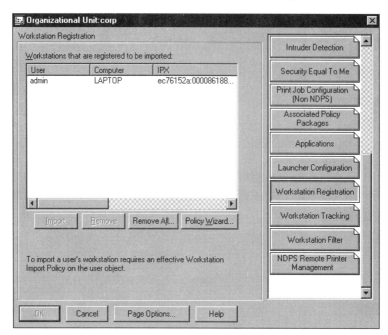

From the Workstation Registration tab you can verify that the object has been registered with NDS. Once registered, there is still one more task you must do to complete the process: create a Workstation object. This can be done by clicking on Import on the Workstation Registration tab or by selecting Tools ➤ Import Workstations in NWAdmin. This will create a Workstation object as shown in Figure 13.3.

Figure 13.3 A Workstation object

WARNING A workstation can only be registered once with NDS, and once registered, it will not reregister if the associated NDS object gets deleted, nor if the workstation is moved to another NDS tree. If you want the workstation to reregister with NDS, you will need to run SYS:PUBLIC\UNREG16.EXE for Windows 3.1–based clients or SYS:PUBLIC\UNREG32.EXE for Windows 9x and Windows NT–based clients. Refer to TID 2939246 for more information on troubleshooting the Workstation registration process.

Application Distribution

One of the most useful—and used—features of ZENworks is its ability to distribute applications to the appropriate users. This feature has been around for several years and was known by the name NAL (Network Application Launcher) before it was included (and upgraded) in the more powerful ZENworks. In the remainder of this chapter, we will review the process of creating an application, the details of an Application object, and several new features (including scheduling application delivery and application distribution when there is no one logged into the workstation). We will also cover the ability of a ZENworks-distributed application to repair itself if files are corrupted or deleted, as well as the software metering abilities of the product.

Overview of the Process of Creating an Application Object

In the realm of ZENworks, there are two kinds of applications, simple and complex. A simple application is one that doesn't modify any registry entries, .INI files, and so on. A complex application does modify one or more configuration files and/or the registry.

Creating a Simple Application Object

Simple applications don't require any updates to the target system; they simply make use of previously installed programs. Examples of simple applications are Windows Calculator and Notepad. Simple applications can also install new files, as long as no configuration files or registry entries are made or modified. They can have their own, product-specific .INI files, however, and still fall into this category. To create a simple application, follow these steps:

1. Select the container where you wish to create the application and choose Create ➤ Application.

2. Choose Create a Simple Application object (no .AOT/.AXT files) and click Next.

3. Fill in the object name and the path to the file then click Finish.

After creating the object, you will need to configure it by specifying the desired associations, operating system requirements, etc., as described in the "Overview of the Properties of an Application Object" section.

Creating a Complex Application Object with the Help of snAppShot

Complex applications are more difficult and time consuming to set up because they change Registry settings, modify .INI files, and otherwise modify various system configuration parameters. To help you create a complex application, Novell provides snAppShot. The process of using snAppShot is as follows (on a typical workstation on your network without the software installed):

1. Run snAppShot (SYS:PUBLIC\SNAPSHOT\SNAPSHOT.EXE)

2. Choose from the following list the method you would like to use when running the program:

   Standard   Use default settings, the simplest choice.

   Custom   Specify what you would like scanned or not scanned for changes: drives, folders, shortcuts, and the Registry. These choices may be saved for use by the Express option below.

   Express   Use custom settings saved earlier (useful when you install many applications and you would like to scan the same things each time).

The remaining steps in the process vary depending on the choice made in step two, but always include the following basic steps:

3. Enter the NDS object name and the icon title the user will see.

4. Enter the directory where you would like to store the files that your application creates or updates. The files will all have a .FIL extension. You will need one directory per Application object that you want to create; the directory should be located on a server.

TIP   Enter the path using UNC (Universal Naming Convention) syntax so that all users will be able to access the files, no matter how the drives are mapped on individual workstations. (A UNC path takes the format *SERVER\\VOL\\PATH;note that there is not a colon after the volume name.*)

---

5. Enter the name for the .AOT file that you will use when you create the Application object in NDS. This file should be in the same directory entered in step 4, and also entered using UNC syntax.

6. Confirm the settings snAppShot will use.

7. snAppShot will take the "before" image.

8. Install your application.

9. snAppShot will take the "after" image.

10. snAppShot will compare the two images, writing all file differences to .FIL files and generating an .AOT file for later use when creating the associated Application object.

Sage Advice

Whenever you install applications with snAppShot, start with a standard configuration that most, if not all, of your desktops use. Consider using Ghost, Drive Image, or another such product to take an image of your standard PC(s) and then always use that image when installing any application. Always install each application with the base image. For example, if you will be creating separate Application objects for each component of Microsoft Office (Word, Excel, and so on), do the complete process for each application, starting from that base image. While this will take a little more space on the server and a little more bandwidth when installing the program, it allows users to install any combination of applications in any order without problems.

When you have finished with snAppShot, you can use the .AOT file(s) to create the associated Application objects in NDS. The process of creating a complex application is as follows:

1. Select the container where you wish to create the application and choose Create ➢ Application.
2. Choose Create an Application object with an .AOT/.AXT file.
3. Enter the path to the .AOT or .AXT file.
4. Verify (and change if desired) the name of the Application object.
5. Verify and change if needed, the source and destination paths. Be very careful if you change either because the application may not function as desired. It is generally safer to change the source path (where the files will be copied from) than the destination path, which may impact registry locations, .INI file entries, and so on.
6. Click Finish.

As with creating a simple application, you will need to finish some settings to make the Application object functional. If you need to make copies of the object once you have created it, be sure to choose Duplicate an Existing Application object in the Create Application Object wizard dialog box. Never use the Object ➢ Copy command in NWAdmin to do so.

ZENworks

PART 3

Overview of the Properties of an Application Object

The Application object is one of the more complex objects in NDS and yet it is central to application distribution. It is also a very powerful object. In this section we will review the most important tabs of the Application object.

Identification

This is the standard tab for most objects, not just the application-related ones. On this tab, you can specify the name of the Application that the users will see, set the path to the application, choose the icon, and choose the order of the application relative to other applications (the default is alphabetical order). You can choose to run this program only once (per version ID, which you can set on the Distribution tab and change whenever you wish to update the application) and remove the icon after the application is installed so it doesn't confuse your users. One other choice is Force Run, which will automatically run the application when the user logs in. Force Run can be used in many circumstances—installing a service pack, for example. If multiple applications are specified as Force Run, they will be run in the same order as you see them on the screen and run at the same time.

System Requirements

This tab, shown in Figure 13.4, allows you to choose which conditions must be met for the application to be available to the applicable users.

Figure 13.4   System Requirements tab

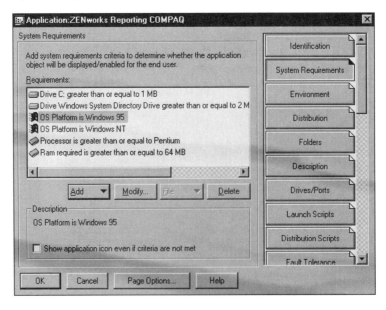

You can choose to set conditions on any of the following items:

- Operating System (Windows 3.*x*, 9*x*, or NT, as well as specific version numbers, such as to select Windows 95 OS/R 2 or higher only)
- CPU (386, 486, Pentium, Pentium Pro, Pentium II, or Pentium III)

NOTE Windows 3.*x* can't return values higher than 486, therefore setting it to anything higher than 486 is the same as setting it to 486.

- Memory (specified in MB)
- Disk Space available (in MB) on any of the following drives:
  - Windows System Directory drive
  - Windows Directory drive
  - Temp Directory drive
  - Any drive letter, A:–Z:

NOTE If you specify a drive more than once, for example 75MB on the Windows Directory drive and 50MB on C:, and the Windows Directory drive is C:, then there must be at least 125MB free on C:.

- Environmental Variable (any variable set to any value).
- Registry (any Registry Key does or does not exist; optionally you can look for specific values that are already in the Registry, not in the Registry, or are set to a specific value).
- Application object (present or not).
- Files (any of these options).
  - Existence (specified file is or is not present in a specified location).
  - Version (specified file in specified location is at least, at most, or equal to, a specified value).
  - Date (before, after, or equal to, a given date).

WARNING Although we have not found this documented anywhere, we have noticed that if you don't at least set the Operating System version, the icon will never appear for the user.

ZENworks

PART 3

Drives/Ports

This tab allows you to capture certain drive letters or printer ports as long as the application is running. While this is a very handy option, you must be careful not to interfere with local drives and ports, drives and ports mapped for other applications, and drives and ports needed by other Application objects. This is an area where planning and documentation are vital if the applications are all to be available in any combination at any time. Note that you can only capture non-NDPS queues and printers. You can also set Capture flags, and choose the behavior of the Map command (creating root drives or search drives). You will also specify for each mapped drive the action that should be taken if the drive letter is already mapped.

Launch Scripts and Distribution Scripts

Similar to the Drives/Ports options described above, these two tabs define scripts that will be executed every time an application is started and/or closed (in the case of the Launch Scripts tab) or before and/or after the application has been installed. These scripts follow login script syntax, and offer more versatility than the Drives/Ports option, in that it allows messages to be displayed, other programs to be executed, and so on.

Fault Tolerance

This tab allows you to set up two things: load balancing and fault tolerance. Load balancing allows you to have several Application objects that point to the same application on different servers and have NAL randomly select one when the application is executed. This spreads the load of starting an application across all of the servers that have the application on it. If that server is unavailable, another Application object is chosen at random and the process repeats until either the application starts or all objects have been tried. This should be done with local servers only; if you choose remote servers, it will take up considerable WAN bandwidth and time because of the random nature of this option.

Fault tolerance, on the other hand, allows you to specify other Application objects that may be chosen if the selected one is unavailable. They are selected in order, allowing you to put servers with greater available bandwidth to the selected object near the top of the list. Each object is tried in order until either the application is launched or all have been tried unsuccessfully.

Associations

This tab, shown in Figure 13.5, is probably the most important one. If you do not associate the application with any objects, it will never be available to any of your users. You can choose to associate an Application object with any of the following objects: User, Workstation, Group, Workstation Group, Organizational Unit, Organization, and Country.

Associating it with a container object allows all objects in the container (and any subcontainers below it) the ability to use the application. Associating it with a Workstation or Workstation Group object allows the computer (or all computers in the Workstation Group, if applicable) access to the application, without regard to who logs in at the workstation. This can be useful, because it is available even if no one is logged in at all (see the section below entitled Just-In-Time Distribution for more information on this feature).

Figure 13.5   The Associations tab

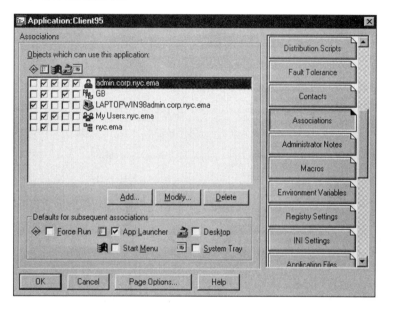

You can choose to have the application show up in any combination of the following locations: Application Launcher, Application Explorer, the Start menu, on the Desktop, and/or in the System Tray. To see the application in any location except Application Launcher, you must use Application Explorer, not Application Launcher. Also, the icon will disappear from all of those locations when you exit Application Explorer.

NOTE   Application Explorer only works on Windows 9x and NT.

Configuration Parameter Components

There are many similar configuration settings that can be updated. These appear on the following tabs.

Macros You can choose Macro settings to automate the installation of applications. An example of a macro is SOURCE_PATH, which contains the location of the source files. By making it a macro, you can easily copy the program's files to another server, duplicate the Application object, and change this parameter to point to the new server.

A great new feature in ZENworks 2 is the ability to do prompted macros. This allows the user to input information when the program needs specific input (such as for registered username, or installation drive). To do so, simply choose Add ➤ Prompted and choose either String or Drive. Name the macro anything you wish and then use that macro in a registry setting, .INI file, or whatever. Figure 13.6 illustrates several variables that are created when ZENworks Reporting is installed. (See Figure 13.7 below for how they are used.)

Figure 13.6 Macros related to the ZENworks Reporting Application object

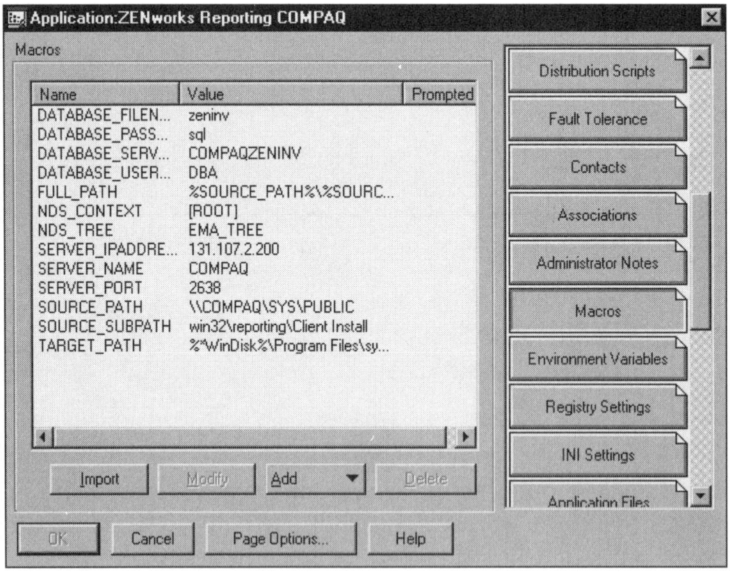

Environment Variables This tab allows you to see any environmental variables needed by the application and their values. You can also add your own variables here. You can also modify an existing environmental variable, such as when the path is modified. All that you need is the variable name, the value for it, and to decide whether you would like to append the data to the existing variable (if it exists). If you choose to add the data, you can specify the separator character (such as the semicolon in a path statement).

Registry Settings   Almost all 32-bit applications make use of the Registry in Windows 9x and NT. While a detailed discussion of the Registry is beyond the scope of this book, you can see that it is very valuable to be able to see the changes an application is making to the Registry.

There are several buttons that can help you make even greater use of this tab. When you click the File button, you can search for any text in the Registry, as well as import Registry changes from an .AOT file or export the changes the application makes in a standard .REG file. The Add button will allow you to add both keys and values. This can be a great way to track updates, installed components, or anything else you would like to track.

Figure 13.7   Registry settings related to the ZENworks Reporting Application object. Note the use of some of the macros (such as %NDS_TREE%) shown in Figure 13.6.

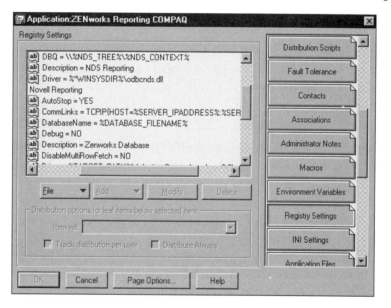

.INI Settings   Similar to the Registry settings described above, you can search for particular changes, use macros, import from an .AOT file, export to an .INI file, and so on. You can also add new .INI files, create a new section in an existing .INI file, or set a value. You can also choose to move the setting up or down in the .INI file. This can affect performance because they are read sequentially.

Text Files   This tab is similar in purpose to the INI tab, but it allows you to modify any text file, not just .INI files. This would allow you to modify CONFIG.SYS or AUTOEXEC .BAT, for example. You specify the file you want to change, then list all the text you want to add, delete, or modify. You can choose to place them at the beginning or the end of the file. You can also specify whether the changes you make require a reboot after distribution or not.

Application Files

This tab allows you to view the files and folders that will be affected, their location, and the source file name (usually a number with an .FIL extension). This tab is useful for the following three reasons:

- Allows you see what the .FIL files are really named when installed
- Gives you control over the file copying process and allows you to choose on a file-by-file basis any of these actions:
  - Always copy the file
  - Copy the file only if it already exists
  - Copy the file only if it isn't already in the directory
  - Copy the file only if it is newer (based on the dates and times of the two files) or if it is not installed
  - Copy the file only if it is newer (based on the dates and times of the two files) and is already installed
  - Copy the file if it is a newer version (based on version information that may be stored with the file when it is created; most useful for .EXE, .DLL, and .SYS files)
  - Request confirmation to overwrite files from the user
  - Delete files if they exist, unless they are marked as shared
- Permits you to add your own files, such as for forms or templates your company uses

The purpose of the Shared File setting is to mark as shared files that are used by other programs so they will not be deleted or otherwise modified accidentally by the program you are installing. Other programs use shared files, so making a change to one may affect many other programs that use the same file.

Sage Advice

One of our favorite uses of the Application Files tab is to install templates, forms, and other standard documents and files when the application is installed. This is a simple way to distribute macros, .DOT files for Word, .XLT files for Excel, and so on. You could even create other Force Run Application objects to maintain these files (when a new expense report template needs to be distributed, for example). You could also do this by properly setting the appropriate copy options and updating the template files on the servers. Note that if you want to update existing files on a distributed application, you will need to update the Version stamp on the Distribution tab.

Schedule

This tab lets you specify when the application should be available. By default, the application is always available (the Set schedule setting is none), but you can specify certain days or a range of days. For example, you may make the customer database only available to your salespeople during working hours Monday–Friday. You can optionally specify starting and ending dates of availability, as well as the times (in five-minute increments) it will be available. You can specify a Spread from start time value; the application will become available to any given user sometime between the specified Start time and Start + Spread time, randomly. This is very useful when you want to distribute a large application or service pack, for example, and don't want all of your users installing it when they arrive in the morning (consuming all available bandwidth, and significantly hampering the server's ability to service other needs). When the ending date and time arrive, the result specified on the Termination tab (described next) occurs. The Range of Days choice is shown in Figure 13.8.

WARNING We have often found that the application is available outside the *times* specified on this tab, but is not available outside the *dates* specified. We haven't found a reason for this behavior yet, though we have checked with Novell. This may be fixed in a future version; if you want this feature in your environment, ensure that it works as you expect.

ZENworks

PART 3

Figure 13.8   The Range of Days option selected on the Schedule tab for an application that is available only Monday–Friday from 8:00–5:00

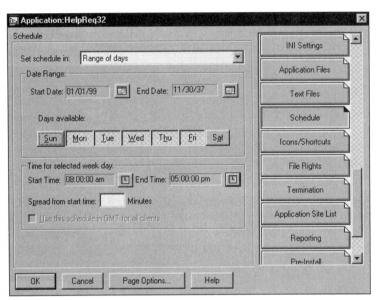

> **WARNING**   If the user still has the necessary file rights to the application, he or she can still run the application outside of these time limits.

Termination

This tab specifies what will happen when the application is no longer valid for that user. An application can become invalid for three reasons:

- The application is no longer associated with the user (or with a group or container associated with the user).
- The time the application is available to the user has expired (set on the Schedule tab).
- You have updated the system requirements to run the program (on the System Requirements tab) and the user's computer no longer meets them.

When this happens, you can choose to take any of the actions listed in Table 13.1.

As you can see, there are many actions you can choose depending on the application, who will be using it, and so forth.

Table 13.1 Termination Behaviors

Action	Description
None	The user may continue to use the application as long as desired, but the application will not open again until the cause for the termination has been taken care of.
Send message to close application	The user will be asked to exit the program at periodic intervals (from seconds to hours) with a message that you can specify.
Send message to close, then prompt to save data	With this choice, you ask the user to voluntarily exit the application a configurable number of times in a configurable amount of time (such as 5 times in 15 minutes) with a message of your choice, after which the Application Launcher (NAL) or Application Explorer will attempt to close it. If there is no data that needs saving, the application will be closed, otherwise the user will be prompted to save the data. The user may cancel out of the saving process and remain in the application. If this is done, a message will be sent to the user at the interval of your choice reminding them to save their data.
Send message to close, prompt to save, then force close	This choice is similar to the last choice, except that users will only be given a set amount of time to save their work and exit before the application is terminated, with or without the data being saved. In the latter case, a message may also be displayed explaining to the user why the application was ended.
Send message to close, then force close with explanation	This action is similar to the previous one, except the user will not be prompted to save the data. They will be told to exit a configurable number of times in a defined period then the application ends. You may specify a message to be displayed when this step is taken as well.

WARNING As with the Schedule tab, we have found that sometimes the Termination tab does not work properly. We have found in some circumstances that no matter what the cause of the termination and the action specified, that none of the specified actions have any effect. We recommend that you verify that the termination behavior you specify actually works before relying on it.

File Rights

This feature is probably one of the most anticipated features in application distribution using ZENworks. In previous versions, there was no way to make file system rights conditional on association with an application. This meant that you had to both associate an object with the Application object and also assign file system rights to the same objects. This also meant that when an association was removed, the user could still execute the program until file system rights were also removed. With ZENworks 2, file system rights can be granted in conjunction with the Application object. This is one of our favorite new features of ZENworks.

Application Site List

This tab allows you to configure other Application objects that can be used when a user is traveling. The idea is this: When a user travels from one site to another, they should, if possible, get the application from the closest server that has the application installed—not from one that is over a slow WAN link.

Here's how it works: ZENworks finds out the context of the server that responds the fastest and then checks with the application the user is configured to use to determine which other Application objects are listed in the Application Site List. NAL then compares the context of the server that responded first with the context of the Application objects in the Application Site List. It compares contexts until it finds those with the most similarities. For this to work properly, the upper layers of the tree must be based geographically, as we have pointed out throughout the book.

NetWare 5@Work: Application Site Lists and the Mobile User

Consider a company with three locations, one in Rochester, one in Boston, and one in Miami. The sales manager travels and uses a local computer in each location. Excel is used at each location to analyze sales, project future sales, and so on. With headquarters in Rochester, the sales manager's User object is located there and the Rochester OU is associated with the Application object .Excel.Rochester.Company. Without the Application Site List feature, the application would always be run from the server in Rochester, across the WAN when the sales manager is in Boston or Miami. Excel is already installed on the server at each of the other two locations, and is named .Excel.Boston.Company and .Excel.Miami.Company. On the Application Site List tab of each of the three objects, the other two objects are listed. When the Sales Manager travels to Miami, the .Server.Miami.Company server will respond first, the context .Miami.Company will match the context of .Excel.Miami.Company, and that Application object will be used when Excel is started.

NetWare 5@Work: Application Site Lists and the Mobile User *(continued)*

This also means that if there are multiple servers in Miami and the administrator has configured the load balancing or fault tolerance capabilities of the .Excel.Miami.Company object, these settings will be used in determining which server will actually provide the application, as described in the previous section, "Fault Tolerance."

Pre-Install

This is a new feature in ZENworks 2. It allows you to distribute applications to computers when no one is logged in. This is done by checking the box Pre-Install Application on the Pre-Install tab. The schedule for distribution is then determined as described in the section on the Schedule tab. The only thing you must be careful to do when using this feature is to associate the Application object with either Workstations or Workstation Groups, as users will most likely not be logged in.

Reporting

As shown in Figure 13.9, this feature is very easy to set up and can provide you a wealth of information on how and to whom applications are distributed, as well as used. You can choose to log information to a file (typically on a central server) or send SNMP traps (if SNMP is installed with the client). The figure also shows how you can monitor any of the following events:

- Successful launch of an application
- Failure to launch an application
- Successful distribution of an application
- Failure to distribute an application
- Icon visible in configured location(s)
- Icon hidden in configured location(s)

TIP   The SNMP abilities that come with the Novell Client work over TCP/IP and IPX/SPX.

To get reports based on this information, you will need to use the ZENworks reporting tool, described in the section "Reporting" in Chapter 14. There are many possible reports that can be generated, including application distribution successes and failures and application launch successes and failures, arranged by application, user, or workstation.

ZENworks

PART 3

Figure 13.9 Reporting configuration

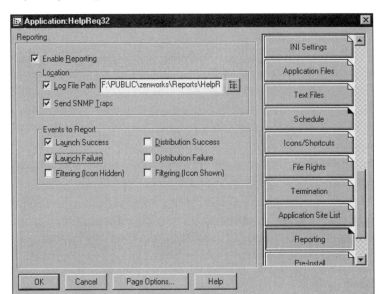

Software Metering

Software Metering is very important in your efforts to maintain proper licensing for all of your applications. While this feature will not help you with applications installed locally (use the inventory and reporting capabilities of ZENworks for these applications instead), you can use it to help you with any applications you run off of the server. To use it, you need to first set up NLS on one or more servers, then you will need to create License containers and License Certificate objects. Finally, all you need to do is associate the application with the appropriate License container. You can also choose whether the application will be available if NLS is not available.

The ability to do software metering gives you great capabilities when working with licensing because you assign the number of licenses you have to License Certificate objects. When all of the licenses are in use, no one else will be able to open the program, which keeps you legal. You can also run reports on licensing issues with Novell Licensing Services Manager (SYS:PUBLIC\WIN32\NLSMAN32.EXE). This can help you as you plan for the number of licenses you will need for various applications.

Just-In-Time Distribution

NAL offers great application distribution capabilities as described above. This also means that you can do "Just-In-Time" (JIT) distribution of applications so they can be installed only as they are needed. Of course, with the new ability to assign applications to workstations, you can also apply service packs, software upgrades, and so on in the middle of the night as well. Which is best? That depends on your situation.

If you have plenty of licenses for your applications but are more bandwidth challenged, you may want to distribute them when the demand for bandwidth is lower—often in the middle of the night. To do this, you will need to assign applications to workstations and then set the schedule of availability to the middle of the night. You will also want to set the applications as Force Run. You will also want to set the spread so that the applications will install starting at random intervals over the desired time period. You will not want to set a termination behavior; this way the application will finish installing even if the scheduled time runs out.

On the other hand, if you have plenty of bandwidth but few licenses, you may want to distribute them only as individual users need them. In such cases, assign applications to users and groups and allow the users to install them as needed. You will not want to make the applications Force Run.

You can also use a combination strategy. In this case, some things are done in the middle of the night, such as service packs, client upgrades, and so on. Other things, such as application software, are distributed on an as-needed basis. This is generally the strategy we prefer to employ.

Self-Healing Capabilities

Another major advantage to using ZENworks is that applications can be self-healing. This means that if an application gets damaged (a .DLL file gets corrupted, a template gets deleted, and so on), a user can right-click on it, choose Verify, and have NAL check each of the files and replace any missing or damaged ones.

The process is quite simple; it verifies all of the Registry settings, .INI and other text file changes, and files originally installed as part of the application, and restores all of them to the state they were in when the application was first installed. The user only needs to know that if the program doesn't work, they can simply right-click on the icon in Application Launcher or Application Explorer and choose Verify and it will be fixed. If the user does this and there is still a problem, then a call to the help desk would be warranted, as described in the next chapter.

ZENworks

PART 3

14

ZENworks: The Best Tool for Desktop Management

We will conclude this part with a review of how ZENworks can benefit both you and your end users.

ZENworks can help you manage your desktop with features such as support for policies, remote control, and both hardware and software inventory. We will also briefly review the included help desk tools and the anti-virus components that come with the product.

As for your end users, we will discuss some things you may want to point out at the impending rollout of ZENworks—specifically, how this product will benefit *them*.

Desktop Management with Policies

The desktop management features of ZENworks are a major reason to deploy it with NetWare. These features extend and enhance Microsoft's ZAW (Zero Administration for Windows) initiative. There are many ZENworks abilities that fall into this broad category, but we will concentrate on probably the most powerful and useful ability, the ability to manage each user's Registry with policies.

Policies are very, very powerful. You can control the settings associated with the Novell Client, Windows settings, and any other application that places settings in the Registry. In this section, we will discuss container policies, as well as user and computer policies for the Windows 9x and Windows NT platforms. Windows 3.1x has far fewer abilities to be managed than the other version of Windows, so we will focus on the Windows 9x and NT platforms in the following sections. Unless otherwise noted, all settings apply to both platforms.

Policies can be created by either selecting a container object and choosing Create ≻ Policy Package and then making choices presented by the Policy Package Wizard, or by selecting Tools ≻ ZENworks Policy Wizard. Note that the two wizards are similar but achieve the end result in slightly different manners.

Container Policies

Container policies, which can only be applied to containers, specify how the other policies will be applied. The container policies that can be set are the following:

Search Policy   This policy controls how far up the tree NDS searches for policies associated with users, groups, workstations, and so on, and the associated objects that will be searched.

You can choose to search a fixed number of containers above or below the choices specified here (the default is 0, to the selected choice only):

Object Container   The container the object resides in only.

Partition   To the root of the partition, regardless of how many or how few levels that is. This is our preferred choice as the partition level should be the site level in many cases, and this allows you to set policies at the site level.

Selected Container   Forces NDS to look in the specified container; use only if you have a dedicated container for policies. This is not recommended because it can cause a lot of WAN traffic as NDS searches for a replica that contains the necessary policy information.

[Root]   Searches to the [Root], which should only be done in LAN-only trees or other small networks where replicas of the entire hierarchy from the object to the [Root] are stored locally.

You can also specify the search order and which objects will be searched. They are (in default order):

Object   The User or Workstation object

Group   The group(s) the user or workstation belongs to

Container   Container(s) as specified by the search policy described above

> **TIP** Remove Groups from the policy if you are managing only users and you have groups that contain users across several containers, particularly if those containers are located in different sites.

SNMP Trap Target Policy   Allows you to specify how often SNMP Traps will occur and to whom they should be reported. This is often used with the reporting capabilities described in Chapter 13 on application distribution.

User Policies

User policies control the user's environment and (as the name implies) are applied on a per-user basis. They generally affect Registry settings stored in the HKEY_CURRENT_USER area of the Registry. In this section, we will concentrate on some of the more useful policies. We will ignore the remote control and help desk policies here, and discuss them in their respective sections below. The actual policies available vary depending on the operating system the user logs in on. User policies are operating-system specific, so if you have users who log on to multiple operating systems, you will need to set policies for the user on each operating system.

> **TIP** Always create a policy for administrators first and apply it to them before creating any others. Also, be sure to explicitly set the least restrictive settings so that if you inadvertently set a policy that is too restrictive, you can go back and fix it.

You will also want to take advantage of a new feature in ZENworks 2 for both user and workstation policies that allows you to add new policies as needed by using .ADM template files. This allows you to control various settings your application programs (such as Office 2000 and Outlook 2000) make in the Registry. We will discuss this in the user extensible policies section later.

> **TIP** When setting policies, be sure to test them on an isolated network or only apply them to a test user to be sure that your users can still accomplish the work they need to. After you have verified that all of the settings are acceptable, apply them to the bulk of your users.

Desktop Preferences

Desktop preferences control the appearance and behavior of the user's desktop. The settings you can control with this policy are:

Accessibility Options   These options configure Windows to help those with visual and tactile disabilities. If you choose to enable some of these policies for some of your users, we recommend that you create an explicit policy that disables them for the rest of your users, or they may become quite frustrated with these settings.

Display   These settings allow you to control the wallpaper, screen saver, and color scheme choices, among other things. You can also choose where the screen saver and wallpaper files are located (on a server for example) and enable the power management features for the monitor if the user's computer supports them. We like the ability to control colors for those users who like to change colors (for example, black text on a black background), and then complain that the monitor doesn't work or that there is no text on the screen.

Keyboard   Allows you to set the keyboard delay before repeating characters when a key is held down and set the rate at which they will repeat. The blink rate of the cursor can also be set here.

Mouse   Allows you to set the mouse for left- or right-handed operation, set the double-click speed, the speed of the mouse, and the mouse pointers displayed. We recommend that you are very careful when changing these settings, particularly for left- or right-handed operation, or you may find that you have a very large management headache on your hands. This occurs as you create separate policies for left- and right-handed users and keep track of which users are left- or right-handed.

Sounds   Allows you to set your sound scheme for those users with sound cards installed.

You can also control roaming profiles, as described in the next section.

Roaming Profiles   Your desktop settings, such as colors, wallpaper, Start menu contents, and so on, follow you from computer to computer. Roaming alleviates the need to spend fifteen minutes configuring colors, wallpaper, and so on that some people feel when sitting down at a new computer.

For roaming profiles to work well, you need to have standards that define what applications will be installed where. To implement them, you need to modify a Windows 95-98 or Windows NT User policy, enable 95 (or NT, depending on the platform) desktop preferences, and then click the Roaming Profiles tab. From here, you can check the box to enable Roaming Profiles, as well as set the location to store them. You can choose from the following two options:

Store User Profile in User's Home Directory   Allows the user to have an individual profile, which he or she can modify at will and which will follow him or her from machine to machine.

Find Mandatory Profile in a NetWare File System   Lets you specify a profile that can't be updated by the users (a mandatory profile). When you make this choice, you must also specify the path to the mandatory profile.

For more information on roaming profiles, as well as personal vs. mandatory profiles, refer to Microsoft's documentation.

User-System Policies

User-system policies are settings you can choose that control how the system behaves. While there are a few overlapping settings (such as for wallpaper), this category of policies primarily controls what the user can do with the system. The list of policies you can set is quite extensive and very similar to Microsoft's policies (which are created with System Policy Editor). Rather than list all of them, we will highlight a few of the more useful policies and leave you to study Microsoft's documentation on all of the standard policies they offer.

A few of the more useful policies that you can set include:

Control Panel   Allows you to restrict or allow access to the icons (or tabs within them) listed below. These settings, when judiciously applied, can prevent many common help desk calls, as users can no longer disable DHCP, delete the default printer, and so on. We highly recommend that you review the restrictions you can place on the following areas of Control Panel:

- Display
- Network (*9x* only)
- Passwords (*9x* only)
- Printers (*9x* only)
- System (*9x* only)

Network (*9x* only)   Allows you to enable or disable file and printer sharing

Shell   Allows you to lock down your system through various restrictions, such as removing (and therefore disabling) any of the following:

- Start ➤ Run
- Start ➤ Find
- Drives in My Computer
- Network Neighborhood or Entire Network in Network Neighborhood (to prevent browsing for other resources on the network)

System   Allows you to place restrictions that enable or disable the following:

- Registry editing tools
- MS-DOS prompt and MS-DOS Mode applications (Windows *9x* only)

ZENworks

PART 3

Applications   You can choose which programs a user can run (listing them by filename); all other Windows applications can't be run. Although this is a very powerful choice, we generally prefer to let other restrictions and NAL do this instead. This allows new applications and upgraded applications with different filenames to be run without updating policies.

Windows NT System (NT Only)   Among other things, the policies included here allow you to enable or disable Task Manager, which can be used to terminate applications such as NAL, and to show or hide the Welcome Tips. There are many great NT tips that you may or may not want your users to know. Since the welcome tips are stored in the Registry, some companies replace the default text (by other custom policies or by duplicating a hard drive with the default text already modified) with company policies, announcements, and so on.

ZAK Policies ➤ Windows 95 (or Windows NT, depending on the platform) ➤ Internet Explorer Security   With most companies allowing Internet access from user's desktops and with the growing threat of malicious ActiveX and Java-based applets, the security of user's computers becomes a bigger issue. In addition to the McAfee anti-virus capabilities described later, you can also set the level of security you desire on ActiveX and Java applets here.

Most attributes are set with check boxes that can be set to any of three values:

Checked   Enable this setting, regardless of the previous value.

Unchecked   Disable this setting, regardless of the previous value.

Gray-colored   Don't change the existing value in the Registry; if enabled, leave it enabled and if disabled, leave it disabled.

Sage Advice

Associate a policy with all of your users. In most cases, containers should do this, with exceptions handled with groups or individual users (depending on the number of users needing exceptions). Without a policy in place, the settings for the previous user will prevail in many cases, which may be more or less restrictive than you desire. As noted above, always be sure to create a policy for administrators that has no restrictions so that you can make any and all needed changes.

Dynamic Local User (NT Only)

The dynamic local user policy specifies how the NetWare client handles authentication to the local workstation. There are several possibilities that can be configured and you can choose which is best suited to your environment. The options are as follows:

Use an existing account   Use this choice if accounts are already set up on your NT workstation or if it belongs to a domain where the account is defined. If the account can't be found, however, the user can't be logged in.

Use a dynamic local user   With this option selected, a user will automatically be created by NetWare when the user logs in, thus allowing the user to log in to the workstation as well. When you choose to create this type of user, you have two additional choices that deal with how long the user will remain in the local SAM (Security Accounts Manager) database. They are as follows:

Volatile   When this is chosen, the account will automatically be removed after a specified number of days (see the section on "Configuring the Volatile-User-Account Caching Interval"). This accomplishes two things: it reduces the number of objects in the SAM database and it keeps users from logging into the workstation without also logging into NDS (after the cache time expires). You can also specify that the user will belong to any of the standard NT groups that you desire (the default is that they belong to the Users group). You can even assign them to non-standard groups as described in the section on Custom Groups, below. You may also specify a full name and description if desired when creating the user. Note that accounts that belong to the Guest group in NT are never cached, but are automatically removed when the user logs out. One other important note that should not affect most implementations of NDS is that the NDS name must be 48 characters or less.

Nonvolatile   The user account is created, if it doesn't already exist, in the local SAM and is not automatically removed. It is a standard account and can be used at any point in the future to log in, without necessarily logging into NDS first.

Custom Groups   Custom Groups allow you to create additional groups (beyond the standard NT groups) for the dynamic users you create and then assign the dynamic users to them. The primary purpose of creating these groups is to assign system rights (such as the ability to do backups, log on locally, add workstations to the domain, and so on) to the users you are creating. To create them, simply click on Custom ➤ New then enter the new group name and an optional description. Next, assign the privileges you would like to assign to the group and click OK twice. This capability is convenient when you need to assign system rights to specific users.

Configuring the Volatile-User-Account Caching Interval By default, volatile user accounts are deleted when the user logs out. If you desire to keep the user in the SAM database for a few extra days, you will want to enable this feature. This is useful in situations such as for a laptop user who may not be connected to the network for a few days but still needs the ability to log into the NT workstation. To do so, go to Control Panel ➤ Network ➤ Services ➤ Workstation Manager ➤ Properties. In this dialog box, check the box to enable caching and then specify the interval (in days) that you would like the user account to remain available. Note that if you wish to set this to a long period of time, you may want to consider using a non-volatile account instead.

Sage Advice

We prefer using volatile accounts because nonvolatile accounts pose a potential security threat. Users can log in at any point in the future with an old NDS name and password. In addition, users can still log in to the workstation, even if the account was deleted in NDS. Think carefully before implementing nonvolatile accounts.

We also recommend that when creating volatile accounts you use the Description property to note that NetWare created the account. This allows you to see where the user came from and maintain or delete the account as needed in the future.

User-Extensible Policies

This new feature allows you to extend the policies that come with ZENworks 2 with any policy or policies you wish by specifying .ADM files. Many new 32-bit applications come with predefined .ADM files for that very purpose. You can also create your own, but be aware that this is not for the faint of heart. It can take many, many hours to write your own .ADM file (it is just a text file, but it has very specific syntax) and get it debugged. This does offer you enormous flexibility, however, and may be desirable in some cases.

To implement user-extensible policies, you will need access to the .ADM files. These files can be stored on the server or on any workstation, as they are only needed once to import the policy into NDS. After that, they are not needed again unless you want to remove the entries that the .ADM file creates. To allow you to remove those policies, you should keep the .ADM files somewhere. Novell recommends that you keep them in SYS:PUBLIC\ WIN32\ADMFILES. This keeps them easily accessible on the server. They are small files, so disk space should not be an issue, even on the SYS: volume.

Standard Microsoft policy (.POL) files can still be used in addition to setting policies through NDS. These policies are created and maintained through the standard Microsoft tool, System Policy Editor (POLEDIT.EXE). This tool is only installed by default on NT Server–based computers. It can be installed on Windows 9*x* and NT machines if desired. If you choose to set policies through both NDS (via ZENworks) and policy files, you need to be aware of the order that policies are processed in. The order is as follows:

1. ZENworks User policy.

2. ZENworks Computer policy.

3. Microsoft policy file (for Windows 9*x* it will automatically look for the file SYS:PUBLIC\CONFIG.POL or, for Windows NT, SYS:PUBLIC\NTCONFIG .POL). If you place it elsewhere or rename it, you will need to configure a policy that tells the workstation where to find it.

TIP In ZENworks 1.*x*, all of the policies were hard coded. In ZENworks 2, policies are extensible, but the old hard-coded policies still exist. This means that it is possible to set the same policy twice: once through the hard-coded policy and once through the .ADM file that the hard-coded policies are based on. This is *not* recommended, as the order of the two policies is not guaranteed. Novell recommends that you use extensible policies when possible because they are more easily debugged.

Workstation Policies

As the name implies, these policies are computer-specific, not user-specific. They generally affect settings stored in the HKEY_LOCAL_MACHINE portion of the Registry. These settings are also operating system–specific, so you will need to create multiple computer specific policies, one per platform if you have multiple operating systems in use. In this section, we will focus on the following policies: general computer, Novell client configuration, login restrictions, and, as with user policies, the new ability to install your own policies via .ADM files.

Computer System Policies

Computer System policies affect the operation of the system itself, more than the interface to the system that the user sees. Some of the more useful parameters that can be controlled include (note that the location of specific policies may differ between Windows 9*x* and NT):

Logon Banner   When enabled, this policy will display a dialog box before login with whatever text you desire. The purpose is to inform users that only authorized users are allowed to log in and that all others will be prosecuted for trespassing. This is in response to a court case where it was found that a company didn't warn a hacker that data was confidential and that access was forbidden except to authorized users, so the hacker was acquitted. You should always have this enabled with a security policy in place to protect your company and its data.

Require Validation by Network for Windows Access (Windows 9x only) If enabled, it will force the user to be authenticated by NDS before getting their desktop. This effectively disables the Cancel button at login. (It will still be there, but a dialog box will inform the user that they must log in first.) We recommend that you enable this policy if data is stored on your client computers to protect them from unauthorized access. If the Cancel button is disabled and the user clicks Cancel, network access will be disabled anyway so there is not the same security threat.

Disable Password Caching (Windows 9x only) Passwords are stored in .PWL files that are easily hacked by many virus and Trojan horse applications, such as Back Orifice. This policy, when enabled, will disable these files and make your network more secure, but it requires users to enter passwords whenever they need access to various shares, Web sites, and so on. Users may write their passwords down (and often keep them near their computer) which potentially opens other security holes in your network. You need to decide which is the bigger threat to your network.

Disable file sharing and Disable print sharing (Windows 9x only) These two policies can enable or disable file and printer sharing. We recommend that you disable file sharing in general, forcing your users to store their data on the server instead, particularly when they need to share it with other users. You have a lot more security on the server than on your clients.

Disable Peer-to-Peer Server (Windows NT only) Similar to Disable file sharing, this policy will disable the Server and Browser services. This also overrides the Create Hidden Drive Shares policies.

Create Hidden Drive Shares (workstation) and Create Hidden Drive Shares (server) (Windows NT only) These two policies control whether or not the administrative hidden drive shares are created on workstations and servers, respectively. They are for administrative use only, but they allow complete access to the root of each hard drive if enabled, and are named C$, D$, and so on, one for each drive letter. The directory that Windows NT is installed in (\WINNT by default) is also shared as ADMIN$ by default, unless disabled by this policy. Many viruses, Trojan horses, and so on, as well as hackers, target these shares. We generally recommend that these shares be disabled to increase security. If you need them for remote administrative access, consider disabling them with this policy and then sharing them with different names (still as hidden shares) to increase security.

SNMP   This category of policies lets you configure SNMP, including the communities the workstation belongs to, managers to report traps to and receive requests from, and so on.

Run   This policy lets you run an application (or multiple applications) when the user logs in. This can be helpful in setting up a user's environment instead of using the Start menu.

Enable User Profiles (Windows 9*x* only)   This policy allows you to enable a separate profile for each user who logs into the computer, allowing each user to have his or her own desktop settings.

Network Path for Windows Setup (Windows 9*x* only)   This policy lets you specify where the Windows source files are stored, so the user is not prompted whenever a new component requiring the original Windows CD is installed. This happens a lot, even when applications such as the Novell client are installed.

Novell Client Configuration

You can control many of the configuration options of the Novell client with this category of policies. The policies may differ between NT and 9*x*. We highly recommend that you browse these policies to see how they can help you deploy and maintain client-configuration settings. Some of the more useful policies include:

- Enable Workstation Manger (Windows NT only): Allows you to enable or disable workstation manger remotely, as well as specify the number of days that dynamic local users are cached.

- The ability to set any parameter in the Novell Client configuration dialog box, including protocols, first network drive, contextless login, and so on.

- NetWare/IP configuration.

- IP Gateway: Allows you to enable or disable the Novell IPX/IP gateway, which allows you to run IPX on all of your workstations, yet still offer your users the ability to surf the Web. This happens because the IPX packets used internally are converted to IP packets at the IPX/IP gateway computer. This will decrease performance, but will also act as a firewall between your computers and the Internet. IPX-based computers are considered to be virtually unhackable from IP.

Computer Extensible Policies

Very similar to the extensible user policies described above, these policies are also implemented via custom .ADM files. For a discussion on extensible policies, refer to the User Extensible Policies section.

ZENworks

PART 3

Restrict Login

In addition to the login restrictions you can set on individual users, you can also set them on individual workstations and workstation groups, thereby restricting who can use individual workstations. You can restrict access to workstations to individual users, groups, or containers. You simply configure those you deem appropriate to use the workstation. The advantage of setting login restrictions this way is that you can take entire groups of computers and restrict them to certain users. For example, accounting computers can only be used by accounting personnel. This can be done without regard to the subnets they are on, portions of IPX or IP addresses they do or don't have, and so on. We personally prefer to set login restrictions this way.

Remote Control

Remote control is a broad category in ZENworks 2. In previous versions, the only option was to take complete control over a user's workstation. While this is useful at times, other times you just need to send a file, such as a missing .DLL or .SYS file or need to ask the user a few questions.

We will begin by reviewing the setup procedure to enable the various forms of remote management. We will then discuss the ability to completely control the workstation as well as the ability to send files, run remote diagnostics, chat with the user of the computer, and the ability to view, but not take control of, other workstations. You can perform any of these tasks by selecting the desired task from the Tools ➤ ZENworks Workstation Remote Operations menu in NWAdmin.

Remote Control Setup

Setup of the remote control portion of ZENworks is quite simple. You will need to install the ZENworks version of the client to get the remote management agent installed on the client, and you will need to decide who will be able to remotely manage your clients and then assign them the appropriate NDS rights. You will also need to create the appropriate remote control policies.

Before we begin, let's overview the process of actually remotely managing a workstation. To actually use the remote management capabilities of ZENworks, you must meet four criteria, namely:

- The workstation must be imported into NDS.
- The remote management policies must be set and associated with any of the standard objects for policy associations.

- The appropriate NDS rights must be set for those who will have the ability to remotely control various workstations.

- The correct remote control agent must be installed.

Remote Management Policies

You can set policies for remote management with workstation or user policy packages or both. If you set conflicting policies for remote control (user and workstation), the user policies will supersede the workstation policies. You may also set remote control policies for individual users that will override the settings for either of the remote control policies that may be set for groups of users or computers.

The remote control policies that can be set and the tab each can be found on are listed in Table 14.1. With the exception of "Display Remote Operation Agent icon to users" and the default protocol choice, all of the settings are available for each object associated with remote management described previously.

Table 14.1   Remote Management Options, Locations, and Notes

Feature	Tab(s)	Notes
Display Remote Operations Agent icon to users	General	Displays the icon (in the system tray for Windows 9x and NT, as a minimized application on 3.x) for remote control; users can select and view information on who is controlling them, permissions assigned, and they can also terminate the agent. We recommend that you disable this for most of your users and consider doing it for your power users as well. We also recommend that you enable it for administrators.
Default protocol (for Remote Control and Remote View)	General	IP or IPX (note: ZENworks 1.0 supports only IPX).
Enable Chat	General	Chat is described later in this chapter.
Enable Diagnostics	General	Diagnostic abilities are described later in this chapter.
Enable Remote Control	Control	Remote Control is described later in this chapter.

ZENworks

PART 3

Table 14.1 Remote Management Options, Locations, and Notes *(continued)*

Feature	Tab(s)	Notes
Enable Remote View	View	Remote View is described later in this chapter.
Enable File Transfer	File Transfer	File Transfer is described later in this chapter.
Prompt user for permission	Control, View, File Transfer	Asks the user whether to allow or disallow the particular remote management action; many administrators disable this. We recommend doing so for normal users; consider doing so for power users and not doing so for administrators.
Audible and/or visible signal when being remotely controlled or viewed and the interval for the signal	Control, View	Allows the user to be notified visually and/or audibly when being remotely managed and the interval of that notification. Our recommendations are the same as for the "prompt for permissions" option.

NDS Rights

To be able to remotely manage a workstation, the user will need the effective Read right to the WM:Network Address property. In addition, the user will need the Write right to the properties listed here to perform the associated form of management:

DM: Remote Control   To take full control of the workstation

DM: ZEN Remote Execute   To run applications on the remote workstation

DM: ZEN Remote View   To view, but not control, the remote machine

DM: ZEN File Transfer   To send or receive files to/from the remote computer

You can assign the necessary rights in any of these ways:

- Select the Workstation object(s) desired and select the Remote Operators tab. You will be able to see and modify those who have rights as well as what they can do (Remote Control, Remote View, or File Transfer).

- Manually assign the rights described to the selected properties of the Workstation object.

- Assign the rights to a container object, and if you have NetWare 5 (but not NetWare 4.1x), assign the selected property rights and also make each right

Inheritable as well. This will allow the desired rights to be valid for all Workstation objects in that container and any subcontainer.

- From the Tools ➤ ZENworks Workstation Remote Operations menu, select Manage Remote Operators and follow the prompts the wizard provides. You will be prompted for the Workstation objects or containers to manage, the rights to grant, and the objects to grant the rights to.

Unfortunately, you can't assign these rights to a Workstation Group object. But with the ability to assign rights to the container object, however, it is not a big limitation.

Remote Management Agent

The remote management agent is the program that allows you to remotely control a workstation. The actual program that is executed depends on the client operating system. The program names and operating systems are listed in Table 14.2 (all are located in SYS:PUBLIC\ZENWORKS and are installed locally when the client is installed).

Table 14.2   Remote Management Agent Information

Operating System	Application Object Name in NWAdmin	Application Object Title in NAL	File Name
Windows 3.x	Remote16	ZENworks Remote Control 16-bit	WUSER.EXE
Windows 9x	Remote32	ZENworks Remote Control for Windows 95-98	ZENRC32.EXE (or WUSER98.EXE)
Windows NT	RemoteNT	ZENworks Remote Control	NTSTACFG.EXE to install and configure WUSER32.EXE

The remote management agents are installed as executables for Windows 3.x and 9x. They must be run from a login script, the Start menu, or as force run applications in Application Launcher before you will have any remote management capabilities. This is a key point, so let us reiterate it again: If the remote management agent is not loaded, you will have no remote management capabilities until it is loaded. For Windows NT, however, it is installed as a service.

Normally, you will use the 32-bit remote management agent when your clients are running Windows 9*x*. You can, however, choose to use the 16-bit version instead. Using the 16-bit version has advantages and disadvantages, as listed here:

Advantages	Disadvantages
Faster	Only works with IPX
Works with full-screen DOS screens	Unstable with IP installed
	Does not support many common video cards (including some by ATI, S3, and other major video chip manufacturers), LAN cards, and computer systems (including some made by Dell and Compaq)

WARNING   No matter which remote control agent you choose, you may only use *one*. You may load it any way you wish, *but you may only choose one*   .

You also have the ability to ping the agent, as well as unload and reload it. Obviously, you will have no ability to remotely control a workstation if the agent is unloaded, and you will lose any open remote access sessions when the agent is unloaded as well.

WARNING   You will lose your remote control session if the display settings are modified. You should consider a policy that removes that ability from users to prevent them from disconnecting you.

Remotely Controlling a Workstation

This capability has been available since the beginning of ZENworks. It allows you to take control of a remote workstation and do anything as if you were actually sitting at the remote machine. In fact, you can even do a remote control of a machine from a machine that you dial into. This capability is a great troubleshooting tool and can help you diagnose and fix problems at the workstation.

When you take remote control of a workstation, only the keyboard and mouse inputs get sent to the remote machine, where they are processed, along with any running applications, and the screen I/O is returned to you. This keeps traffic on the wire to a minimum.

Once you take control, you can do anything just as if you were at the workstation, including change settings, run applications, and reboot the computer.

TIP Remember that your abilities on the remote workstation will be those that the user who is logged into the computer has.

There are several optimizations that you can make to tweak the performance of the session by selecting the control icon at the top-left corner of the remote control window and choosing Configure. However, the only choice that will generally be considered is the Force 16 Color Viewing option, which displays the remote machine in 16 colors instead of whatever the remote machine is configured for. This causes less traffic on the wire and faster screen updates, but the screen may not match what the remote user sees.

There are also buttons on the top of your remote control window that allow you to send various special keystrokes to the remote machine. The keystrokes you can send and the purpose of each (on the remote system) are as follows:

- CTRL + ESC: Opens the Start menu
- ALT + TAB: Switches between open applications
- CTRL + ALT + DEL: Causes different actions, depending on the remote computer's operating system, as follows:
  - Windows 9*x*: Reboots the machine
  - Windows NT: Opens the Windows NT Security dialog box where you can change passwords, lock the workstation, log off, reboot, or open Task Manager

There is also a button called the Navigate button that allows you to see and scroll to other parts of the remote workstation's desktop area that don't fit into the window on your workstation.

On the remotely controlled machine, right-clicking on the agent will allow you to view the status of the agent. The three tabs and the purpose of each are described in Table 14.3.

Table 14.3   Information Available from the Remote Management Agent

Tab	Available Information
General	The object that is currently controlling you, along with the date and time that control was taken, as well as the default protocol
History	Displays information on the last 10 remote management sessions, including type of management (remote control, remote view, or file transfer), name of object that took control, and the date and time control was taken

ZENworks

PART 3

Table 14.3   Information Available from the Remote Management Agent *(continued)*

Tab	Available Information
Security	Allows the user to view, but not modify, the remote control settings set in the remote control policy, as described in the Remote Management Policies section

Sage Advice

We like to use remote control with the remote diagnostics to gather information on problems before going to the user's location. By doing so, we can bring the appropriate disks, CDs, and other necessary tools to fix the problem the first time if it can't be fixed remotely. The only time we have to go to the user's desk without this information is when the problem is network related.

One administrator who had once used Microsoft's SMS (and paid the big price they charge) was very happy when the change was made to ZENworks. He has more free time for other projects and fewer headaches because managing SMS is no longer a full-time task.

Remotely Viewing a Workstation

The purpose behind Remote View is that you can look but you can't touch. It is designed for help desk personnel and others who need to be able to see problems occurring on remote workstations, but don't necessarily need to control them and get data off of them. This can be helpful in larger networks where front-line help-desk personnel are granted this capability. When they can't solve the problem, it can be escalated to second-level support where the ability to initiate a full remote control session is given. For smaller networks, generally only the full remote control option will be used.

File Transfers to and from Other Workstations

The ability to transfer files to and from a remotely controlled machine is a new feature in ZENworks 2. This allows you to send updates to the remote computer, copy data files that need to be worked on to your computer, and much more.

For this feature to work, SRVFTP32.EXE must be in the search path of the machine you want to work with. This feature does not work on Windows 3.*x*–based machines, only

Windows 9*x* and NT systems. It is installed with the ZENworks client in the \NOVELL\ ZENRC directory and is also available in SYS:PUBLIC\ZENWORKS. If the application is not in the path, you will need to copy it to a directory on the path or update the path to include its location.

> **NOTE** This feature only works with fixed (hard) drives. You can't access floppy disks, CDs, ZIP disks, and so on with this tool.

For those who have used LapLink, the interface will seem familiar. You will be able to see files and directories on both your own system and the remote system. You can do basically any file or directory management task with this tool, including the following:

- Create new folders.
- Copy and move files.
- Rename files.
- Delete files and folders (the folder must be empty to be deletable).
- Open a file on your machine with Notepad, Wordpad, or any application you specify. This can be very useful for application and macro developers who are trying to diagnose problems with their applications.
- View the properties of a file or folder, just as when you right-click on one in Explorer.

> **NOTE** When copying and moving files, the following terminology is used: Upload is *to the remote*   machine and Download is *to your* machine.

Remote Diagnostics of Client Workstations

The ability to get information about a remote machine is a great feature in ZENworks. If you are using NT workstations, you have many remote administration tools already available to you, such as Event Viewer, Windows NT Diagnostics, Server Manager, and NT's Registry Editor. Remote Diagnostics will probably be most used in NT environments in conjunction with NT Diagnostics. If you are using Windows 9*x*, however, remote administration capabilities are limited at best. Therefore, the remote diagnostic capabilities included with ZENworks may become your primary tool for viewing information on remote stations running Windows 9*x*.

ZENworks

PART 3

WARNING The remote diagnostic application is Java-based and functions only over IP. You will not be able to use this tool if either the target computer or your computer runs only IPX. The remote diagnostics capability of ZENworks only works on Windows 9x and NT machines, not 3.x-based computers.

Table 14.4 highlights a few of the seventy different pieces of information you can display with Diagnostic. While most of the categories of information are available on both platforms, there are a few categories of information not available on one platform or the other. The missing categories are listed in Table 14.5.

Table 14.4 Useful Information from Diagnostics

Category	Field	Notes/Purpose
Windows Memory	Memory Load (%)	% of memory in use; formula is 100–([Free Physical Memory / Total Physical Memory] * 100).
	Total Physical Memory (MB)	Size of RAM in MB. Useful in troubleshooting slow workstations due to insufficient RAM; compare with Free Physical RAM (MB).
	Free Physical Memory (MB)	Free RAM in MB. If this number is smaller than expected, determine what else is running. In particular, on Windows 9x machines, verify the typical role of this computer in Control Panel ➢ System ➢ Performance ➢ File System. If it is set to Network Server, most of the available RAM will be set aside for caching until another application needs it, thus this number will be artificially low.
	Total Paging File Size (MB)	On Windows 9x machines where the virtual memory settings are set to let Windows manage it, the value may be up to the free space on the drive that Windows is installed on. On NT machines, it will be the maximum size of the page file on all drives.

Table 14.4   Useful Information from Diagnostics *(continued)*

Category	Field	Notes/Purpose
Environment	Variable and Value	All of the environmental variables are listed here. Especially useful are the Path, Temp, and Windir variables.
Device Driver Information	Name and State	Names and states (running or stopped) of all device drivers.
Service Information	Name and State	Names and states (running or stopped) of all services; useful in debugging.
NDS and NetWare Connections	Server Name	List of servers that the remote user is currently connected to.
	User Name	Name that the remote user is logged into server as; useful in troubleshooting rights problems.
	Authentication State	Bindery or NDS; useful when troubleshooting resource access problems.
	Transport Type	Protocol (IP or IPX) used by the server and workstation for that connection.
Novell Client Information	Preferred Server and Preferred Tree	The preferred server and tree can be used in login scripts and is useful when login is not functioning as expected.
	Name Context	Current context of the logged-in user; useful in troubleshooting resource access problems.
	First Network Drive	Useful in troubleshooting when local resources are unavailable due to mapped drives overwriting them and when login scripts have conflicts with local resources.
	Client Version	Version of the Novell Client in use; useful in determining if an updated client is available for the workstation.

ZENworks

PART 3

Table 14.4 Useful Information from Diagnostics *(continued)*

Category	Field	Notes/Purpose
Network Drives	Path	Server and volume that each drive letter is mapped to.
	Name Space	Name spaces supported on mapped drive; long name space may show up as OS/2.
	Effective Rights	Displays all standard rights (RWCEMF), with Erase displayed as D (for delete) and O (for Ownership). S and A rights are not displayed.
	Free Clusters	Free space on the drive (as seen by the currently logged-in user) in Clusters. Can be calculated in Bytes using this formula: Free Clusters * Sectors per Cluster * Bytes per Sector.
Printers	Printer Device Name	Name of ports (LPT1, and so on). Number listed is the number that can be captured.
	Port State	Captured or not. If printing directly to a queue- or NDPS-based printer or NT-based printer, it will not display as captured.
	Captured Queues	Name of the captured queue if captured, otherwise blank.
Network Protocols	Protocol Name	Lists installed protocols (TCP, UDP, IP, IPX, and/or SPX). One line per protocol; much more information also available, but this is typically paramount for troubleshooting.
Network Services	Service Provider	Lists names of all registered (with WinSock 2 APIs) services; typically includes NDS, SAP, SLP, and DNS.

Table 14.5   Diagnostic Categories Not Supported on Listed Platforms

Windows 9x	Windows NT
Event Log	WIN32 Processes
Device Drivers	WIN32 Modules
Services	

Chatting with Remote Users

This new capability is another great troubleshooting tool. Often, you will speak to the user experiencing problems directly, but you can also communicate to the user in writing using chat. This may be useful for those with hearing impairments and who have trouble communicating via the phone. Some users simply prefer this mode of communication. It also allows you to keep a written transcript of the conversation.

For chat to work, you must have a 4.3 BSD OTALK–compatible daemon installed on both machines. Novell has implemented this through WTALK32.EXE, located in SYS:PUBLIC\ZENWORKS.

This tool offers little configuration. Only administrators can initiate a chat session, and the target user must accept the incoming request. The interface is very simple, with one party's communication on the top half of the dialog box and the other user's on the bottom half. Either user may close the chat session.

Help Desk Tools

ZENworks makes it easier for users to request help from you. You can see how their workstations are configured which makes diagnosing problems easier, especially when combined with the remote control abilities described in the previous section. In this section, we will explore the primary tool to help your front-line help-desk personnel, and maybe even you, the help requester application.

To enable users to report their problems with this application, you must enable the Help Desk Policy User Policy. When you do so, you can fill in the name, phone number, and e-mail address of the person or group the user should contact for help. You can also choose to allow users to run the Help Requester program (which we recommend in most cases and which you can accomplish with NAL) and send trouble tickets to you. You can choose to have those tickets delivered via either GroupWise or any standard MAPI-compliant e-mail

ZENworks

PART 3

package (such as Outlook or Outlook Express). You may also specify the subject lines the user has to choose from: hardware problem, application problem, and so on. This can assist you in routing the request to the appropriate help personnel. Finally, you can choose what information you would like to include in the e-mail, including information about both the user (name, context, phone, and location) and the user's computer (ID [the distinguished name of the Workstation object], Primary Tree, and Inventory).

The user can access the application by choosing ZENworks Help Request for Win32 for 9x and NT systems or ZENworks Help Request for Win3x in NAL or by running SYS: PUBLIC\HLPREQ32.EXE or SYS:PUBLIC\HLPREQ16.EXE, respectively. The user can either e-mail the problem ticket or can get contact information and phone the ticket in.

If the user wants to e-mail the ticket, he or she must choose from the predefined subjects created in the policy, and can enter a message describing the problem and e-mail it. The user and computer-related information that the administrator configured to be sent with the message can also be viewed.

If the user chooses to phone in the ticket, he or she can view the contact's name and phone number and can call with the same user and workstation information available with the e-mail option.

The user can also view the tickets that they have submitted which allows him or her the ability to track the resolution to the problems that have been sent.

To reiterate, this is a very basic system that can greatly simplify problem tracking, resolution, and the reporting process. This is especially true if you use e-mail to submit the issues to the technical support personnel.

Software and Hardware Inventory

While the ability to do hardware inventory has been part of ZENworks since its inception, the ability to also obtain a software inventory is new in version 2. It uses a new program on the client to obtain this information, as well as some new capabilities on the server. In this section we will look at the client software as well as the server-based portion and how to install and configure both. We will also look at how to optimize the server portion, do a quick overview of the information that can be gathered, and learn how to get reports on that information. Finally, we will review some troubleshooting ideas.

Inventory Components

The client portion is composed of a scanner program that gathers the information that will be stored in a database. The scanner engine is platform-specific and is located in SYS:PUBLIC\ZENWORKS. The files and platforms are as follows:

- Windows 9*x*: WINSCAN.EXE
- Windows NT: NTSCAN32.EXE

NOTE The inventory capabilities only work on Windows 9*x* and NT-based computers, not Windows 3.*x* systems.

The server uses the following components:

Inventory Gatherer   Collects the information from the scan programs and saves them as .STR temporary files (by default in SYS:SYSTEM\STRFILES)

Inventory Storer   Moves the information from the .STR files to the actual inventory database

Inventory Database   A SQL database (in Sybase format) that stores all of the hardware and software data gathered

The relationships between the components described here are illustrated in Figure 14.1.

Figure 14.1   Relationships between inventory components

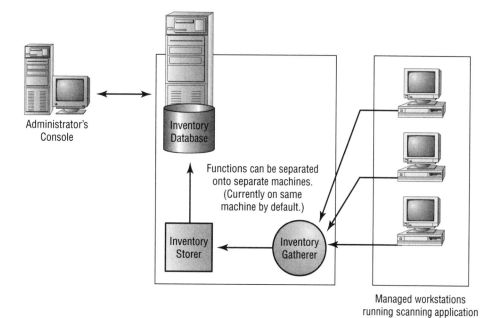

Administrator's Console

Inventory Database

Functions can be separated onto separate machines. (Currently on same machine by default.)

Inventory Storer

Inventory Gatherer

Managed workstations running scanning application

ZENworks

PART 3

Setup and Configuration

To take advantage of the inventory-related capabilities of ZENworks, do the following:

1. Install ZENworks (covered in Chapter 12).

2. Load the software on the designated server(s).

3. Set up the appropriate inventory-related policies and schedule them to collect the information.

Loading the Server-Based Components

When you configure ZENworks, you specify if you want the inventory portion of the product loaded, and if so where. We will discuss the simplest scenario here, one where all server-based components are loaded on the same server. For those with larger networks or multiple sites, refer to the optimization of the server components section for more information.

If components are loaded and specified incorrectly, you will encounter problems with inventory functions on your server. To aid in troubleshooting these problems, we will list the contents of AUTOEXEC.NCF as it relates to inventory functions and provide a few notes on some of the lines. The lines in AUTOEXEC.NCF are as follows:

```
SEARCH ADD SYS:\PUBLIC\ZENWORKS\DATABASE

SEARCH ADD SYS:\PUBLIC\ZENWORKS\JAVA

LOAD JAVA.NLM

SYS:\SYSTEM\JVORBCFG.NCF

LOAD ORBCMD.NLM

LOAD OSAGENT.NLM

SYS:\PUBLIC\ZENWORKS\DATABASE\SYBASE.NCF

SYS:\PUBLIC\ZENWORKS\JAVA\ALARMMGR.NCF

SYS:\SYSTEM\GATHERER.NCF

SYS:\PUBLIC\ZENWORKS\JAVA\MASTER.NCF

SYS:\PUBLIC\ZENWORKS\JAVA\STORER.NCF
```

The first six lines simply prepare the environment and load Java, if it isn't already loaded. SYBASE.NCF simply starts the Sybase server with the environment that it needs and opens the inventory database. GATHERER.NCF loads the inventory gatherer component (ZENINV.NLM) to receive the information from the client scanning programs. It exists as a .NCF file simply to facilitate adding a parameter to specify the temporary directory where the .STR files will be placed, if SYS:SYSTEM\STRFILES is not desired. If you change that path, you must also specify that path in STORER.NCF. MASTER.NCF and STORER.NCF together and start the inventory storer component that will take the data in the temporary .STR files and move them into their permanent home in the Sybase database.

Configuring the Inventory-Related Policies

Once everything is installed and configured, you must create the policies that will cause the inventory information to be gathered on the clients. To do so, enable the Workstation Inventory policy in a Workstation Policy object. After the policy is enabled, you need to choose when it will run. Scanning can take several minutes, so you may wish to schedule it for the middle of the night or another time when usage is likely to be light, both on the inventory-related server(s) and the clients being scanned. If your systems are in use around the clock, consider scanning them at a shift change or at login, but be aware that it may take a few minutes to complete; longer on older, slower equipment.

In addition to scheduling the policy, you need to configure it. You need to specify the distinguished name (or IP address) of the inventory server. If you split up the storer/gatherer functions from the actual database server, this will be the name or IP address of the storer/gatherer server. After selecting the server, you will also need to select the name and location of the scanner application for the client to run at the scheduled intervals. Be sure to use the correct name and location as described, or inventory will fail. Finally, you can choose whether or not to scan for software as well as hardware. Doing so can be a great aid in troubleshooting, but it will take longer to gather the data and more disk space to store the gathered data. If you choose to enable it, you can choose individual applications you would like to scan for, or select them all.

Optimization of the Server Components

The server can be optimized for several different scenarios. In this section, we will look at how the inventory collection process can be optimized at the server. We will begin by looking at various sizes of LANs and then we will turn our attention to WAN environments. We will use the general recommendations from Novell, based on their internal testing, when listing network sizes. From there, we will look at how to configure multiple inventory servers with only a single database server and how to configure the size of the cache for Sybase to maximize the performance of the database server.

LAN Scenarios

Novell has broken the network down into three basic sizes for the purposes of inventory collection and storage. Table 14.6 reviews the size of each, the recommended hardware and configuration for acceptable performance, and the notes associated with that size of network.

> **WARNING** The recommendations listed here are intended as starting points only and will need to be tested to determine actual configurations in your working environment. Inventory collection and storage can cause quite a load on a server; consider dedicating one or more servers exclusively to inventory functions as your network grows. These recommendations assume that you are using dedicated servers for inventory purposes. Adding other demands to the server will necessitate more powerful equipment than that listed here.

Table 14.6 LAN Configurations and Notes for Inventory Collection and Storage

Size	Hardware	Optimizations	Recommendations and Notes
Small (less than 3,000 managed workstations)	64MB RAM for the low end of the range to 256MB RAM at the high end	Increase the cache for Sybase as RAM increases, up to 64MB for a server with 256MB RAM	Stagger the collection of inventory data to reduce the load on the server. This can be achieved by scheduling collection to take place at different times in different policies or using an event that will happen at a random time, such as a screen saver becoming active. If you choose to use the screen saver, be sure to set a long timeout so scanning doesn't take place frequently, overloading the network and the servers involved.

Table 14.6   LAN Configurations and Notes for Inventory Collection and Storage *(continued)*

Size	Hardware	Optimizations	Recommendations and Notes
Medium (3,000–10,000 managed workstations)	256MB RAM for the low end to 512MB at the high end	Database cache should be at least 64MB, up to 128MB for a server with 512MB RAM	In addition to the notes for a small network, this size of network will most likely require several servers to be involved in the collection and storage of inventory data. You can most likely still use a single database server, but you will probably need three to four servers to collect and send the data to the database server. You will need to create several policies and divide your workstations roughly equally across the inventory servers. The process of sending the inventory data to the inventory servers will probably take several hours a day; plan for appropriate bandwidth, CPU time, hard drive space, and so on with this in mind.

ZENworks

PART 3

Table 14.6 LAN Configurations and Notes for Inventory Collection and Storage *(continued)*

Size	Hardware	Optimizations	Recommendations and Notes
Large (greater than 10,000 managed workstations)	See Notes column	See Notes column	With a network this size, the volume of data will almost certainly overwhelm a single database server. You will need to divide the network into smaller pieces and then implement multiple database servers. When dividing the network, use the recommendation for small- and medium-sized networks as a guideline for needed equipment and configuration. Consider dividing the network by department or some other logical manner, keeping in mind that the reports you will get back will be based on the divisions chosen. If a composite view is desired, data can be exported from the reports, and the exported data can be consolidated into a comprehensive view.

WAN Scenarios

Novell has broken the WAN scenarios down into four basic sizes for the purposes of inventory collection and storage. Table 14.7 reviews the size of each, and the recommendations and notes associated with that size of network. The same warnings listed in the LAN scenarios section apply here as well, with even more importance. WAN bandwidth varies widely, as does available WAN bandwidth, which necessitates thorough testing to ensure adequate performance.

Optimization Configurations

There are two main issues involved in configuration options. The first is how to configure multiple inventory servers with one database server and the second is how to optimize the inventory database cache size.

Table 14.7 WAN Configurations and Notes for Inventory Collection and Storage

Size	Recommendations and Notes
Single user	There is a two-minute timeout for the inventory gatherer; if it does timeout, no data will be received.
Small office (5–100 managed workstations)	Install a local inventory server that reports to a central inventory database over the WAN. WAN bandwidth is likely to be the limiting factor, with the storer often needing one minute or more to transfer each .STR file into a record in the database. When DMI scans are also enabled, 100KB of data can be collected per workstation. Be aware that there may be a lengthy lag between the collection of the data and its availability in the database for reporting purposes. As for NDS issues, a Read/Write replica of the partition that contains all of the workstation objects and all relevant Workstation Policy objects should be available locally.
Medium office (101–3,000 managed workstations)	This size network should be implemented as described in a small LAN environment above. This means that there will be multiple database servers (one per site). You will need to export the reports generated at each site for centralized correlation, if needed.
Large sites (> 3,000 managed workstations)	The same issues mentioned in the medium network apply here as well, with the difference being that you should use the medium-sized LAN guidelines described above.

To configure multiple inventory servers to send data to a single inventory server, you can take either of two approaches. The first is to choose to install the inventory portion and then point it to the inventory database server during the installation of ZENworks. The second is to manually edit SYS:PUBLIC\ZENWORKS\JAVA\STORER.NCF file and modify the –dbloc switch with the IP address of the database server.

As for the second issue, when deciding what the optimal cache size is, use the recommendations from the tables above, keeping in mind that the general recommendation is to set the size of the cache to 25% of the database size, but not more than 50% of total memory. You should set this value very carefully if other demands are being placed on the server above and beyond the inventory server, as all memory dedicated to the inventory server is unavailable for any other use. Using average information listed yields the general information provided. To actually change the size of the cache, edit SYS: PUBLIC\ZENWORKS\DATABASE\SYBASE.NCF and modify the –c parameter. The

ZENworks

PART 3

value of the –c parameter is the desired size of the cache followed by the letter *m* (for example, 64m). Next, stop the server and then restart it (using the SYBASE.NCF file) to cause the new parameter to take effect.

Inventory

The inventory information that can be collected is extensive. You can view a list of the software installed, including size, date, and version information, and hardware installed. While a great deal of data is collected, and more can be collected with hardware-specific DMI drivers (refer to the online documentation for more information on this capability), only a few summary items are stored in NDS. Most are stored in a separate inventory database, as we have previously described.

The data stored in NDS are:

- Computer type and model
- Model number
- Serial number
- Asset tag
- OS type (for example Windows 95 or Windows 98)
- OS version (for example, Windows 98 is reported as version 4.10 Build 1998)
- Novell client (version number)
- Processor (Pentium II processors are reported as Pentium Pro and speed is not reported)
- Video type
- NIC type (Brand and model of NIC)
- Memory size (extended memory only reported)
- Disk info (hard drive letter(s) and size(s) [note: we have had incorrect sizes reported in some cases])
- MAC address (this could be useful in finding the computers that have conflicting IP addresses when their MAC addresses are reported in the error message)
- IP address and subnet mask
- IPX address

Sage Advice

While all of the information stored in NDS is useful, one of the most useful things is the MAC address. If you are like us, you have seen many error messages letting you know that you have a conflicting IP address and then listing the MAC address of the machine you have a conflict with. Knowing the MAC address has been useless, however, because who knows where the machine is located? Even with other automated packages that collect it, there is still no link to who uses the machine and where it is in the network. With ZENworks and a good naming convention, however, you can tell who uses the machine, and from that, a quick phone call will let you know where it is physically located.

This is just one more case where ZENworks can save a lot of time by putting needed information at your fingertips.

Many things are collected beyond those few things that are stored in the NDS database. You can view them through the reporting methods described in the next section, as well as by clicking on the More Workstation Information button on the ZEN Workstation Inventory tab of the Workstation object. A few of the more useful things collected include:

- Last scan date (in the title bar of the Workstation Inventory dialog box, as well as under Scanner Information) ensures that you are looking at up-to-date data
- Mouse and keyboard information, including number of mouse buttons and number of function keys
- Display resolution, number of colors, and chipset
- BIOS release date and type
- Processor family (486, Pentium, and so on) and speed
- Statistics (including drive letter, size—both total and free—file system, and so on depending on the particular type of drive selected) for all of the following drive types:
  - Floppy
  - Hard
  - CD-ROM / DVD-ROM
  - Mapped network
- NT Services installed and their status

While looking at this information for a single workstation can be valuable, particularly when troubleshooting and when combined with the remote diagnostic capability described previously, it becomes even more valuable when analyzed with the reporting tools described next.

Reporting

Reporting abilities are greatly improved in ZENworks 2. There is a Java-based utility that lets you view the inventory data for any given workstation and generate various reports on what was found. Most of the reports can also have filters applied, allowing you to search for workstations meeting criteria that you specify.

Installation

To install Reporting, choose the ZENworks Reporting application object in NAL. It will install the necessary files to your local drive, consuming approximately 2.5MB of space. Once you have installed it, you will be able to choose Tools ➤ ZENworks Reporting in NWAdmin (otherwise it will be grayed out).

WARNING There will be a separate application icon for each inventory *database* server on the network. If you have multiple database servers, be sure to install and use the desired one. *Only one database server can be configured data time* . To use a different server, exit the reporting tool and run the desired application that points to the desired server in NAL. That server will then be the server used until the process is repeated.

Available Reports

Reports are divided into two general categories, which are then subdivided further into various subcategories. The two primary categories are Inventory and NAL. They correspond to information generated by the inventory components and information on application distribution, respectively.

Some of the more useful inventory-related reports and suggestions for when and how to use them are listed in Table 14.8.

Table 14.8 Some Useful Inventory-Related Reports and Suggestions for Their Use

Name	Description	Possible Uses and Notes
Workstation Operating System	Name and version of the OS on each computer	Useful when deploying new applications to determine that the necessary OS is in place, in determining budget for OS upgrades, and in conjunction with the workstation memory reports and the hardware report.
Workstation Memory More Than and Workstation Memory Less Than	Useful in determining a list of workstations that have more or less memory than a value you specify (in KB)	Useful when deploying applications that have minimum and recommended amounts of RAM when considering OS upgrades and the RAM required for it. Great budgeting tool, as RAM is often the component that will yield the greatest return if upgraded.
Workstation Network Adapter	Type of NIC in each computer	Useful in migrations to new technologies to see where the older technology is still being used for capacity planning and budgeting, as well as determining brands in use for hardware compatibility testing when upgrading OSs.
Workstation Software	Software installed on each computer, sorted by software name	Useful in determining which applications are installed throughout the network for licensing compliance and for budgeting for new licenses. Useful in ridding the network of software applications that aren't approved, such as games or illegal software.
Software Product by Workstation	Software installed on each computer, sorted by computer	Useful in monitoring a few problem workstations for unapproved software and for creating policies for those machines limiting the ability of those users to install and use those applications.

ZENworks

PART 3

Table 14.8   Some Useful Inventory-Related Reports and Suggestions for Their Use *(continued)*

Name	Description	Possible Uses and Notes
Software Product Summary	Name and version of each application and the number of workstations it is installed on (individual workstation names are not listed)	This report is often used to find out what is in use on the network overall and is often followed by the workstation software report to see what is where. This is a great tool to manage licensing issues; the workstation software report can help you make sure that packages are only installed where they are needed.
Asset Management	Model number, asset number, name, and so on for security personnel	A great report for security personnel to track what is supposed to be installed where and for spot-checking to make sure machines are where they should be.
Hardware	Most hardware related information for each workstation	A great tool for monitoring workstation configurations, for changes and for application and OS upgrades. Also a great tool to help determine the value of the computer assets for insurance purposes and for making claims when property is stolen or damaged.
Networking Information	NIC, MAC, IP and IPX address information and so on	Useful in setting firewall restrictions. A great report to summarize the networking configuration of your network for documentation purposes.

A portion of a sample hardware report is shown in Figure 14.2.

Figure 14.2 A sample ZENworks report

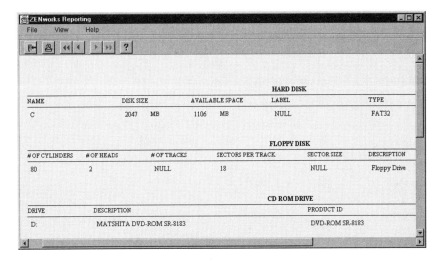

In Chapter 13, we reviewed the NAL-related reports, and so we won't discuss them here.

Exporting Report Data

Once you have generated a report, you need to do something with it. Often this involves printing it and possibly storing the report for later use. Sometimes, however, this data needs to be used in another format, in conjunction with another application, or even aggregated from multiple inventory database servers. Once you have generated the report, you can choose to export it in any of the following formats:

HTML One file per page of the report; useful to put on Web pages for internal use, to highlight problem workstations (for illegal software, for example) or for project status as a migration is taking place.

PDF Adobe Acrobat format; useful as a cross platform, small (in terms of disk space) format for e-mail distribution, for example.

ASCII text The most versatile option, it lets you import the data into any other tool for further analysis. An example is to take the data into Excel or Access to generate a graph or to do statistical analysis on the data. This is the method we like to use most often.

Troubleshooting

In terms of troubleshooting, the two biggest areas of ZENworks are application distribution and inventory management. We presented ideas and tips in the application-related portion of the book to guide you in your troubleshooting efforts. In this section, we will focus on problems that may occur with the inventory portions of the product.

If you have trouble with the inventory functions in ZENworks 2, there are quite a few things you can do to troubleshoot the problem. To simplify the process, we have broken them down into three categories: client and server configuration problems, problems collecting the data, and problems accessing or viewing the reports.

Client and Server Configuration Problems

The issues and suggested solutions in this category are:

- The ZENworks client needs to be installed, including the workstation management component. In particular, be sure that WM95INV.DLL (for Windows 9x) or WMINV.DLL (for Windows NT) is located in the Windows directory structure.

- If you get errors when generating reports, go back and check the shortcut or NAL icon that you started NWAdmin from. The working directory must be set to SYS:PUBLIC\WIN32 (via either a mapped drive or UNC path) or you will likely see this kind of error. This is especially true if you upgraded from ZENworks 1.1 to 2, as the NWAdmin icon that was created with version 1.1 did *not* set a working directory, whereas the ZENworks 2 shortcut does.

- If loading the Sybase database abends the server, there are two likely causes. The cause and solution for each is as follows:

  - Multiple CPUs on the server: The database server needs to be on a single processor machine, though you can certainly upgrade RAM, NICs, and so on to increase performance.

  - The database (ZENINV.DB) needs to be on a standard NetWare volume for the server to use direct I/O when accessing the database. When using a mapped file, such as with the NFS Gateway, direct I/O is not possible. The solution is to either place the database on a standard NetWare volume or modify the SYBASE.NCF file, adding the –d switch to the line that loads the database engine.

Problems Collecting the Data

This is probably the biggest category and the most difficult to troubleshoot. To prevent as many problems as possible and keep your troubleshooting time to a minimum, refer to the following techniques and suggestions:

- The workstation must be registered in NDS before any inventory functions will work. Verify that the workstation is properly registered first.

- Verify that the correct type of workstation policy is associated with the Workstation object based on the machine's operating system.

- Make sure there is an effective policy enabling Workstation Inventory on the Workstation object in order for scanning to take place. You can view the effective policies on a workstation by selecting the workstation object, viewing the details, selecting the Effective Policies tab and clicking on the Effective Policies button. This will show you the policies that NDS sees when policies are applied to the object.

- Verify that you have specified the schedule for the policy and the necessary inventory settings (at least Inventory Server and Inventory Scanner, as well as the Scan List option if you want to do software scanning). You can open the Novell Desktop Management icon and you should see an entry for workstation inventory. If it is there, select it and choose Run Now to gather the data immediately. If the Novell Desktop Management icon is not visible, make sure it is installed and start it for the Novell-generated events to occur.

- If you have made changes to the inventory scanning policies and the changes aren't taking effect, try logging off and then back on again or rebooting to update the scheduler.

- Review the contents of the files listed (all are located in either \WINDOWS\TEMP on Windows 9*x* machines or in \TEMP on NT machines) to see if there are any clues as to the problem.

  ZENERRORS.LOG   This is best source of troubleshooting information; it includes the error that caused the scan to fail.

  DMISTAT.INI   This file contains the configuration the scanner used.

  DMISCAN.TXT   The results of the DMI portion of the scan (if DMI is enabled, otherwise it is any empty file).

  MINFO.INI   The data that will end up in the NDS object.

  SCAN.TXT   Results of the hardware and software portion of the scan.

Problems Accessing and Viewing Reports

This category includes the following problems and solutions:

- If you have access problems when attempting to view the database information, try to log in with a supervisor account to the database. You can log in to the inventory database when prompted as user DBA with a password of *sql*.

- The reporting programs rely on Java on IP. If IP is not correctly configured, you will not be able to connect to the database. In addition, if you specify an IP address or the DNS name of the server, scanning will take place only over IP; any IPX-only workstations will not scan. If you specify the NDS distinguished name, it should work correctly over either protocol, although we have experienced trouble occasionally when not using IP. Name resolution problems are often the cause of scanning problems. Therefore, if possible, we recommend using the IP address of the server for both the Inventory server and the Inventory Database server.

- Verify that the minimal information that is stored in the NDS object is there; if not, scanning most likely hasn't happened. If it is there, it may be due to a problem with the Storer process getting the data to the inventory database server. This is probably due to slow WAN links or incorrect configuration in STORER.NCF.

Remember, Novell has some excellent online resources to help you track down solutions to problems. Two in particular are worth mentioning: support.novell.com, the general support site for all Novell products, and support.novell.com/forums/, the online forums for asking questions of your peers and Novell's support engineers.

Bundled Capabilities

In addition to all of the built-in capabilities of ZENworks, there are two other applications that come with the product. The first is a program called Check2000 that gathers information on Y2K readiness, and the second is McAfee anti-virus by Network Associates (NAI), which can protect both your servers and your clients. As most Y2K problems have probably already been dealt with by now, we will only discuss McAfee anti-virus. A six-month license for the same number of users you purchased with ZENworks is included. Before that introductory period is over, NAI will send you information on how to keep your subscription up to date and the cost to do so.

Anti-Virus Capability

McAfee is a very respected name in the anti-virus business. By teaming up with Novell and by automating the entire process with ZENworks, you can be sure you have virtually complete virus protection, while avoiding the administrative overhead of keeping all of your clients up-to-date. This section is intended to be just a brief overview of the product and its integration with ZENworks. Complete information can be found in the online help files and in the online documentation.

McAfee offers many capabilities to protect you network from viruses, including from all of the following sources:

- Media (Floppy disks, CD-ROMs, ZIP disks, and so on)
- Downloads from the Internet
- E-mail attachments

- Malicious ActiveX controls
- Malicious Java Applets
- Files in compressed files

When a virus is found, you may choose any of the following actions to occur (among others):

- Clean the virus, if possible
- Move it to another location for later analysis
- Delete it

WARNING   The version of McAfee included with ZENworks is specifically designed to be used with ZENworks. This means that to work properly, ZENworks must be installed first. There are two separate installations, one for ZENworks, the other for McAfee. Once installed, you will need to register the McAfee portion separately, as described in the online documentation.

NOTE   The actual client files are installed in SYS:PUBLIC\ZENWORKS\NAI on each server you choose during installation for distribution by the application objects (described in the next section).

In the next section, we will review the application objects that are created and some of the modifications you may wish to make to those objects, and how upgraded products and virus signatures are obtained.

Anti-Virus-Related Application Objects

There are seven application objects that are created when McAfee is installed. They fall into three categories: the VirusScan application, the scheduler application for obtaining virus signature and program updates, and the administrator's component.

The VirusScan application-related objects are as follows:

- VScan31
- VScan9x
- VScanNT

These objects install the client application on each workstation. The objects should not be modified, except to possibly Force Run them on all of your client machines to ensure that all of the clients are properly protected.

ZENworks

PART 3

The second set of objects, the scheduler-related objects, can be modified. Just as with the application-related objects, there is one for each operating system. The objects are as follows:

- VSched31
- VSched9x
- VSchedNT

The modifications that can be made to these objects consist of changes to either .INI files or Registry entries. The purpose of the changes is to determine when the scheduler will check for upgrades to the client software or the virus definition (.DAT) files. Rather than list all of the changes that can be made and where to make them (which are described in the online documentation), we will instead list some of the values you may want to modify. The things you may wish to modify include how often the scheduler should look for updates: once, hourly, daily, weekly, or monthly. Depending on how often you choose to look for updates, you can specify the minute (within the hour or randomly within the hour), hour of the day, day of the week, or day of the month.

Sage Advice

We recommend that you schedule the anti-virus updates daily. With the proliferation of viruses and the pace at which anti-virus manufacturers update their products, this seems to be the best balance between timeliness and the load on the clients, servers, and network bandwidth to process the updates. We recommend that you instruct your users to leave their computers on when they leave for the day and then schedule the updates to take place in the middle of the night or at a shift change when few users are likely to be using their computers and when server utilization is expected to be low.

The third component is for you, the administrator. This component is called BackWeb, and it helps you keep the system up-to-date. The process of doing so is described in the next section.

Obtaining Updates to the Anti-Virus Capabilities

The key to a good anti-virus defense is keeping the virus signature files and the scanning applications as up-to-date as possible. This is done, from the client perspective, using the scheduling capabilities of McAfee. However, the scheduling program simply looks for updates in a predefined location. How do those updates get there? You put them there. How do you get the updates? BackWeb.

Unlike the other application objects that should be associated with large groups, such as containers, to ensure that all users get the application, BackWeb is designed for administrator use only. You should associate this object only with your user account, or the organizational role object that contains your administrative staff.

Once this product is installed and you have registered the product, you have a link to NAI by which they will push you updates to both the client software and the virus definition files. This is done through what NAI calls an InfoPak. An InfoPak simply contains the latest updates in a compressed format. InfoPaks are automatically sent to BackWeb's InBox. From there, you can open them and copy them to SYS:PUBLIC\ZENWORKS\ NAI\DATFILES, where the clients are configured to check for updates.

End-User Benefits of ZENworks

Once you have been sold on how useful ZENworks is, you need to sell your boss and the network users. Showing the possible productivity gains and cost savings to your boss is often enough for management. Your users, on the other hand may be somewhat distrustful of this new technology. They may wonder why there is a new interface or how this new technology will help them be more productive. The following reasons may be presented to them:

- ZENworks offers easy access to applications, regardless of which computer they use.

- Troubleshooting can be done remotely. This means that their computer and the applications they need can be repaired quickly, allowing them to get back to work. This can also be a great way to get help when they don't know how to perform a given task instead of trying to walk a user through a complicated series of tasks over the phone.

- If an application gets damaged, a hard drive crashes, a critical file or directory gets deleted (or almost any other problem the user may run into), it can often be fixed quickly. Applications can be delivered quickly and as they are needed. Applications damaged by a missing or corrupt file can automatically repair themselves. The user does not need to wait for long periods for a technician to come to the desk and manually solve the problem.

- Printing can be automatically set up and new drivers can automatically be distributed. Errors, including out of paper or low toner, can be sent to the user whose print job is currently being processed as well as to printer technicians to solve the problem quickly. Information on these capabilities can be found in the NDPS section of Chapter 10.

Before implementing ZENworks, you may wish to send out a memo or an e-mail describing the additional capabilities and how they will benefit users individually. Feel free to borrow heavily on these reasons in that e-mail. We have found that by simply informing users in advance of the rollout of ZENworks, the changes to be expected, and how they will benefit from the change, that most users react very positively and welcome the change.

Managing the Desktop

Figuring that the more expensive packages had to be better (otherwise, who would buy them?), we had tried many distribution applications in the past at Company A, but none had worked very well. Finally, one administrator suggested that we try ZENworks. With nothing to lose, we decided to try it to distribute our upgrade to Microsoft Office.

We set up workstation import policies and imported workstations. We created the Office Application objects using snAppShot and tested them thoroughly in the lab. Finally, we believed it was time to see how well the product would perform on our production network.

8:30 A.M.: Users from Company A start strolling down the hallways, headed for their computers to start their day. At the same time a prayer meeting is held in the IT department's conference room. IT managers and support personnel hold hands, reassuring each other that everything will be okay. A team of counselors review how they are going to deal with the deluge of calls from IT to help them deal with the stress.

Yes, it's Monday morning, the day after Office was upgraded on the desktops (using the lights-out application distribution capabilities of ZENworks), and the unknown was about to occur. We were worried that the application might not have been distributed correctly, may have been distributed to only some of the desktops, or may have been only partially distributed, making both the old and new versions of the applications unusable. As users sat at their workstations and proceeded to log on to their systems, you could feel the tension in the air. The help-desk personnel held on to their chairs for dear life, waiting for that complaint call. Fear, no, panic, streaked through everyone's veins, puncturing any trace of confidence left in one's mind.

It was 9:00 A.M. now, and total silence filled the IT department. A cool, soft breeze swirled through the room, almost giving a feeling of relief to all. Not a phone rang, not an e-mail was transmitted. Could this be possible? A successful software upgrade to the desktops? No users complaining? Could it be?

10:00 A.M. now and all is calm, just the usual call of missing icons, and those defective coffee cup holders that users keep calling about. You could see a few smiles starting to pop up, but caution still reigned heavily.

12:00 P.M.: It's lunchtime now but no one moves from their desks, still disbelieving that all is well. Suddenly the phone rings. All heads turn in the direction of the phone. Anticipation is replaced with an utter sensation of loss. With all attention focused on the call a smile is seen. It was the front desk informing that the pizza was waiting to be picked up. Wow, what a relief.

6:00 P.M. All is quiet and the hallways are empty. Workstations are silent, and users are home. In the IT department, laughter and happiness spreads all over the room. Hugging, dancing, you name it. We were all happy, the worst was over. The upgrade was a success.

CASE STUDY

24seven

Thank you ZENworks!

As a postscript to this experience, Company A has now standardized on ZENworks as its application distribution mechanism. Other deployments are planned that will distribute only selected components of Office to some users, while others will get the whole suite. Some users will be able to choose to upgrade (such as the IT department when new software is being evaluated) and others will have the software automatically distributed to them.

Part 4

Maintenance and Troubleshooting

Topics Covered:

- Maintaining time synchronization
- Maintaining SYS: and NSS volumes
- Creating a disaster recovery plan
- Monitoring the network
- Monitoring servers and desktops
- Setting up and protecting your file system
- Designing an effective file system
- Backing up servers and workstations
- Using tested troubleshooting methodologies
- Recovering from disaster

15

Maintenance

This chapter covers advanced maintenance issues, including maintenance tools and maintenance strategies, that will help you ensure a smooth operation. Specifically, we will cover NDS error codes, time synchronization, volume maintenance, and managing server downtime. We will conclude this chapter with some thoughts on creating a disaster recovery plan. Once created, this plan should be tested periodically to make sure that it is up-to-date and accurate for your current situation.

Users cannot access resources administrated by the Directory if it is corrupted or inaccessible. NDS cannot function if your server's SYS: volumes are corrupt or out of space. You want to maintain the SYS: volumes on your servers, since all NDS data is kept on them. You can never run out of space on this volume because it holds the Directory database files. Another reason to avoid running out of space on the SYS: volume is that the Directory counts on TTS for ensuring that the right data is posted to the database. If the SYS: volume runs out of space, the TTS is disabled, which allows corrupted data to be posted.

The essence of our job is to monitor services and prevent our servers from crashing. This involves the implementation of maintenance standards for the company that must be adhered to.

NDS Error Codes

Here is some useful information you can use to manage your servers when NDS error conditions exist. NDS error codes are usually displayed in decimal numbers. Sometimes an application displays these codes using hexadecimal values.

Error code numbers can be categorized as follows:

NDS Operating System Error Codes   Certain NDS background processes or operations require the use or functionality provided by the operating system on which NDS is running. These functions, such as communication and transaction services, can return operating system-specific error codes to NDS. These error codes are then passed on to the NDS background process or operation that initiated a request. In NetWare 4.*x*, versions of NDS can also generate operating system error codes. Generally, all operating system error codes that are generated by NDS have a negative numerical representation. while all other operating system error codes have a positive numerical representation. The numerical range for operating system error codes generated by NDS is -1 through -256, while the numerical range for operating system error codes is 1 through 255. To provide backward compatibility with older applications, NDS will return the positive numerical error code rather than the negative error code normally used by NDS. Therefore, any occurrence of an error code within the range of 1 to 255 or -1 to -255 should be treated as the same error.

NDS Client Error Codes   Certain NDS background processes or operations require the use or functionality provided by other NDS servers. Use of these functions, such as bindery services, requires that an NDS server act as an NDS client to the server providing the functionality. Consequently, these functions can result in client-specific error codes being returned to the NDS background processes and operations. The NDS client that is built into NDS (DS.NLM) generates these error codes. The NDS client error codes fall in the range of codes numbered -301 through -399 (or FED3 through FDA6).

Other NDS Error Codes   Certain NDS background processes or operations require the use or functionality provided by other NLM programs, such as TIMESYNC.NLM or UNICODE.NLM. If any of these modules encounter an error, it can be passed on to the DS.NLM. Unicode and other errors in this category range from -400 to -599.

NDS Agent Error Codes   Error codes numbered -601 through -799 (or FDA7 through F9FE) represent errors that originated in the NDS Agent software in the server that are returned through NDS. Because the NDS database is designed as a loosely consistent database, temporary errors are normal. You should not be alarmed if NDS error conditions exist temporarily. However, some errors might persist until the error condition is resolved.

NOTE The most complete reference source of NDS codes (as well as ZENworks codes, ManageWise codes, and GroupWise codes) is LogicSource. You can find it at `support.novell.com/logicsource`. You must purchase it, but at approximately $200, it is a bargain. We highly recommend it.

Maintaining Time Synchronization

This service is used to coordinate time in an IP or mixed IP/IPX environment. The IPX-based servers can only be secondary time servers in a mixed IP and IP/IPX environment. IP-based servers can be one of two modes; they can be server mode (analogous to Reference Time server) or peer mode (analogous to a primary time server).

You should be using TIMESYNC.NLM v5.09 or later on the Single Reference or Reference servers to support NTP services. NTP relies on multiple redundant sources of time; therefore, you should coordinate what external time sources you should use. The protocol recommends that you use at least three external reference sources.

You need to identify the primary NTP time sources on the NTP network; these are the time sources that obtain time from a source external to NTP and then distribute it to the rest of the NTP network.

If you configured time to flow from Timesync to NTP, then any atomic clock or an authentic Internet source of time should be applied only to the Timesync network and not to the NTP network. You will find that NTP is a very sensitive protocol—if it detects large differences of time between reference time sources, it will likely reject one or more of them. When configuring NTP, you only need to worry about the primary or reference servers, since these are the ones synchronizing with NTP time sources.

You need to also be aware of the fact that NTP uses UDP port 123; your routers and firewalls need to be aware of this. You will need to configure them to allow this traffic so that time can be synchronized.

NOTE We strongly recommend that you check the Novell support site for the latest TID on the subject. They constantly update this information.

Maintenance and Troubleshooting

PART 4

NetWare 5@Work: The Importance of Synchronization

We had just been adding several servers to Company A's network and proceeded to install replicas on them. Server 1 received a replica of the [Root] partition and the other servers obtained replicas of other partitions. We had been working for quite a while when all of the sudden DSTRACE displays started showing incomplete synchronization processes on the [Root] partition, which in turn had a domino effect on other partions.

Soon we were unable to add servers to the tree and had several severs left to install.

We started troubleshooting and checking for corrupted replicas and other possibilities when we noticed that time wasn't synchronizing.

After going around in circles trying to determine the cause (by now synthetic time messages were all over the place), we stumbled on the TimeSych.CFG files. We noticed that Server 1 was configured as a primary time server, and we also noticed that its internal clock was several days behind the current time and date.

That just goes to show you that you need to make sure your servers are set properly and that time is synchronized, or you won't be able to perform complicated NDS tasks like adding servers or working on partitions.

Maintaining SYS: and NSS Volumes

Maintaining the NetWare file system is a critical area for the Directory services. This involves managing its usage and anticipating the impact users and applications will have on the available space. It would be great if all your data could be saved on a separate volume other than the SYS:, but even the Directory services and the operating system generate their own data which is saved on the SYS: volume. A well-designed file system will minimize the use of the SYS: volume, as well as provide ease of management and security.

NetWare is also introducing a new file system, NSS (NetWare Storage Services), and we will cover some considerations on this file system. You will also need to manage its usage to prevent any issues with it.

Occasionally, DET and FAT table mirrors get corrupted, which will lead to the volume not mounting. You have two tools available for the purpose of correcting most problems with the file system: VRepair and Rebuild. VRepair solves traditional NetWare file system problems and Rebuild addresses NSS volume issues. But these tools can't fix everything, especially hardware problems. That's where your backups save the day.

VRepair

You will want to use VRepair when one of the following occurs:

- A hardware failure either prevented a volume from mounting or caused a disk-read error. After you have rebooted the system, VRepair will automatically run. If you had a disk-read error you will want to check the Hot Fix areas for redirected blocks. You might have to replace the drive.

- A power failure corrupted a volume. This might take several VRepair runs. (Hope that the tape backup ran; damage by power failure is pretty destructive.)

- The server displays memory errors and can't mount a volume after a name space (such as Macintosh) is added to the volume. For this type of problem, you need to add more memory to the server or use VRepair to remove the newly added name space.

- The volume has bad blocks. VRepair will usually fix this. The following kinds of errors in FAT or Directory tables signal bad blocks: read errors, data mirror mismatch errors, fatal DIR errors, and Write errors.

Make sure you have the latest version of VRepair, which you can get with the service packs. Service Pack 3 for NetWare 5 is out and provides many updates for server utilities. Using Version 4.33 of VRepair dated 09/04/98 and version 4.33 of V_LONG.NLM dated 09/04/98 and later, solves problems generated by the initial shipping version of VRepair that was delivered with NetWare 5. Version 4.33 of VRepair and V_LONG.NLM can be downloaded from the support.novell.com Web site. The name of the file to download is VRPNW5A.EXE.

Rebuild

You will use the Rebuild utility to recover corrupted Novell Storage Services (NSS) volumes. The Rebuild utility salvages the data it finds on your corrupted NSS volume and recovers it.

Rebuild verifies and uses the existing leaves of an object tree to rebuild all the other trees in the system. The NSS volumes that are verified and rebuilt are placed in maintenance mode. This means the NSS volumes are unusable until this process is finished, and the volume is remounted.

After running Rebuild, you must run the Verify utility. Verify accounts for all blocks in the system. If errors are found, they are reported to the screen, and the NSS volume is left in maintenance mode. Run Rebuild again until no errors are found. If errors are not found, the volume is placed back in the active state. You may have to mount the volume.

WARNING   NSS volumes could be spread over multiple drives; if one of the drives fails, the entire volume needs to be recreated.

Managing Server Downtime

At one time or another, your file server will go down. You might take it down to perform maintenance or reset the server, or it may go down unexpectedly due to a hardware or software problem.

Because NDS is constantly doing self-maintenance, you should be careful when you are planning to bring down a server for maintenance. In these situations, you should make sure that your tree is stable, and that the server being brought down is not a member of a replica ring during the maintenance period.

NDS is always checking on servers that hold replicas of partitions. If a server goes down, NDS will hold information intended for the server that is down. If the server is down for maintenance or for a short period of time (less than two days), then it's okay—NDS can handle short periods of downtime. But if the server is down due to a crash and you are replacing it with another server, you need to remove the crashed server from the tree. The following sections discuss how to deal with unplanned downtime, as well as how to remove a server from the tree permanently.

Unplanned Downtime

A hardware or software problem can cause a server to go down unexpectedly. If this happens, diagnose the problem. If you can bring the server up within an hour or two and the hard disk containing the SYS: volume is undamaged, NDS will resynchronize, and there shouldn't be any NDS problems.

If you are going to take down the server that contains the Master replica for a partition, you may need to set up another Master replica. If the downtime will be brief, another Master should not be required. If the server will be down for an extended period (several hours to a day or more), you should change another replica to Master status. This will allow you to make changes to NDS objects in the partition without the use of the server that is down.

If you are bringing a server down for an extended period, you should remove any replicas that are on the server first. This will prevent the large amount of traffic resulting from other servers trying to contact the downed server. After you bring the server back up, you can recreate the replicas. If you have lost the SYS: volume on the server, you will need to reinstall NetWare 5 on the server.

Sage Advice

The Master Replica of a partition is used for only a couple of things:

- Partitioning operations

- Janitor process, which involves cleaning up deleted, renamed, or moved objects

- Limber process, which handles server address and name checking

- Other NDS background processes

This means that when you are doing restores or replica removals, you do not want to perform more than one partition operation at a time.

Removing a Server Permanently

You may wish to remove a server permanently if it is no longer needed. When you remove a server, be aware that you are also removing replicas of the NDS database. Be sure you recreate the replicas on other servers to maintain fault tolerance.

If, on the other hand, the server crashed, you will need to use NDS Manager or DSRepair. Either way, you must make sure that the partition the server belonged to has a live Master replica, or you won't be able to remove it. After you have removed the server, you must delete the volumes using NWAdmin.

Running DSREPAIR in a Mixed NetWare Environment

NetWare 5 introduces many new features in NDS. Although it is backward compatible with NetWare 4.11, NetWare 4.11 servers need to be upgraded to DS.NLM version 5.99 or later (whatever is the newest version) to take full advantage of the new features in NetWare 5. In addition to the upgrade, you may need to run DSREPAIR v4.56 or higher.

Changes in DSREPAIR v4.56 include the following:

Added Reset Schema Option   This function will reset the schema on non-Master [Root] servers. It requires DS v5.99 and higher of DS.NLM to work. This change was added to clean up any schema objects that were not deleted from servers without replicas.

Incorrectly Reporting on NetWare 5 Servers   When previous versions of DSREPAIR are run, they incorrectly report that NetWare 5 servers "are not NDS servers." DSREPAIR v4.56 reports the correct information.

The features included also allow for more thorough understanding and troubleshooting of obituaries. Clicking Advanced Options ➢ Check External References, will give information regarding obituaries as they exist on the server in which DSREPAIR is run.

Creating a Disaster Recovery Plan

A disaster recovery plan is vital for organizations of all sizes. In it, you plan for what your response will be to any and all disasters that may come your way. They may vary from region to region and business to business, but every business needs to have one. A large retail chain has a disaster plan for non-technical issues that addresses all of the following issues (and more):

- Lost children
- Civil disturbances
- Fires
- Hurricanes
- Tornadoes
- Flood
- Hostage situations
- Armed standoffs
- Power loss

While many of these situations may not apply to us technically, many do, and there are probably many others that you can think of. We will break this section down into three sections: issues and topics that should be included, testing your plan, and additional resources for help in creating your own plan.

Issues and Topics to Address in Your Disaster Recovery Plan

In this section, we will review many of the things that should be in your plan. This is not meant to be a comprehensive list of all possible issues and considerations, but we hope it will get you thinking.

Risk Assessment

What kinds of threats does your particular company face? It varies widely from region to region, country to country, business to business, but can generically be broken down into the following categories:

Natural Examples of disasters in this category include the following: floods, fires, earthquakes, tornadoes, hurricanes, snow and ice storms, volcanoes, and disease epidemics that may cause many of your staff to not report to work.

Technical   Examples of disasters in this category include the following: hardware and software failures, viruses, corrupted data, and telecommunication failures (voice or data).

Human   Examples of disasters in this category include the following: theft, embezzlement, extortion, terrorism (including kidnappings), sabotage, war, chemical, biological, or nuclear contamination, and vehicles crashing into your building (including cars, trucks, and airplanes).

Other   Examples of disasters in this category include the following: electrical failures, nuclear accidents, asbestos and other environmental hazards, and gas leaks.

While we often think of big events in our plans (such as fires and earthquakes), we hope that the foregoing list has inspired you to think of many other things that can also be considered disasters.

Risk assessment and disaster recover are very broad topics, not only in terms of determining the source of the threat, but also in addressing the following issues:

- How often would the type of threat effect you?
- Can the threat be predicted in advance? If so, how accurate will the prediction be? How much advance warning will you have?
- Does the threat happen all at once or will the effects increase gradually?
- How long will the disaster last?
- What will be the short and medium term consequences?
- Will redundancy be required? If so, how much and in what areas?
- What will the economic impact be? Remember to consider all of the following in estimating this value and for determining the proper amount of insurance needed to cover the loss:
  - Salaries of workers
  - Goods/services not provided
  - Cost of raw materials lost
  - Legal actions that may be taken against your company
  - Negative press
  - Cost of redundant materials

While this sounds like a lot, and it is, there are many good articles, newsletters, books, and other resources to help you with this. Many companies also specialize in this field.

Maintenance and Troubleshooting

PART 4

Computer Hardware Issues

This is a well discussed topic and one that is probably familiar to many of you. Let us briefly cover some of the things to consider in this category:

- Backups, including the following:
  - Type of backup hardware
  - Type of backups done and the frequency of each
  - Where and how often backups are stored off site
  - Where and how often backups are stored on site
  - Tape rotation and number of tapes needed
- UPSes, including on all connectivity devices (hubs, routers and so on) and servers
- Generators for the UPS systems for longer term power outagages
- RAID 1 (mirroring/duplexing) or 5 (stripe set with parity striped) implementations

Data Accessibility Issues

When considering the various types of disasters that may occur, keep in mind that the goal of disaster recovery is to recover from the effects of the disaster. That sounds logical, right? The biggest thing that we want to recover, as IS professionals, is our company's data. Some of the things that should be addressed in the plan in this regard are:

- E-mail availability. Can it be rerouted elsewhere, for example?
- Web site accessibility. (If your Web server is down, do you have a replica elsewhere or at your ISP to provide for continual access?)
- Phone numbers for your telecommunications people.
- Phone numbers for your ISP.
- Is your data replicated elsewhere so that network operations can continue from another location? Can the data be at least accessed by users who were unaffected by the disaster in other locations?

Keep in mind that you need to plan and prepare for these things now so that they will be in place when disaster strikes.

Non-Computer-Related Hardware Issues

Not only do you need to plan for computer problems and failures, but there are also other things you need to consider in your plan. Some of the more important issues include:

- HVAC (Heating, Ventilation, and Air Conditioning) issues, especially for computer rooms that have lots of equipment that may make the room hot and lead to premature failure of various systems

- Water cooling for large computers that require them (such as some mainframes)
- Fire suppression systems (portable, sprinklers [not unless absolutely necessary unless you want the equipment to be destroyed], halon systems, and so on)

Plan carefully in this category to minimize any problems, as well as to figure out any necessary contingency plans.

Legal Issues

Considering the propensity of so many to sue whenever they feel they have been injured, the legal issues surrounding this kind of plan are important. While we aren't qualified to dispense extensive legal advice, we do strongly recommend that you review your legal liability with a qualified attorney to make sure that you have properly protected your company. You should review the following areas with him or her:

- Statutory requirements
- Contract requirements
- Common law issues (including suits against the company for not having a disaster recovery plan in place)
- Business insurance recommendations

Disaster Recovery Teams

Consider the use of teams that are specialized into specific areas to recover from a disaster. This can also make the training for these teams easier, and make it easier to test your preparedness. Each team should have a leader and an alternate should something happen to the leader. These leaders should report to top-level management.

The specific teams you will need vary based on the size and type of your business, among other things. Consider all aspects of the business in this plan, not just those that are computer related. As businesses vary widely, however, we will focus on the computer-related teams, which may include:

- Computer recovery or replacement
- Computer backup (and probably at this point, restore)
- Off-site storage and/or operations
- User support (including most of the help desk personnel)
- Application support (especially to get business-critical functions up, including payroll)

Many others may be needed and these may be subdivided depending on the size and complexity of your organization.

Writing Your Disaster Recovery Plan

When writing the plan, keep in mind that you are writing for a group of people who have just undergone a catastrophe. They may have gone without sleep for an extended period of time (especially as the recovery process proceeds) and stress levels may be high. Therefore, keep the following guidelines in mind as you write:

- Be very specific and detailed. Remember that the normal administrative people may have been affected by the disaster and may be unavailable. You don't know in advance who will be performing these tasks.

- Use short and simple sentences that can be easily understood. Avoid jargon and technical words that may not be familiar to the people who will need to follow the instructions.

- Keep paragraphs short and simple. Keep the topic focused and stay on it.

- Don't assume anything.

- Use active verbs in the present tense. Don't write as if you are looking back on the event or looking forward to it. When the instructions are being used, it will be in the present.

- Refer to titles, not individuals; persons named may have been affected by the disaster and so may be unavailable.

- List the events that can be done concurrently and those that must follow a predetermined sequence, and label them clearly. List them at the beginning of the document and relist the pertinent ones at the beginning of each section on the manual.

- Use descriptive words that tell the reader specifically what to do. The corollary to that is to avoid non-descriptive terms, such as *make*, *get*, and so on. Examples of descriptive terms include *count*, *declare*, *contact*, *deliver*, *print*, and *report*.

While this list is certainly not comprehensive, it does provide some good general guidelines to keep in mind. You may also wish to refer to the additional resources section of this chapter for some links to Web sites that have detailed information and some existing plans.

Testing Your Disaster Recovery Plan

All of the planning in the world is of no value if you don't test your plan and make sure it works in your specific situation. I know of many companies that thought they had a working plan in place until a disaster struck (such as a hurricane) and no one knew where the plan was, who was to do what, and so on.

Many companies mandate that their plan be tested periodically, at least annually and often more frequently than that. We whole-heartedly concur with that idea. Simulate various disasters and see how well your IS team deals with them. Keep in mind, however, that you will need spare equipment to do the tests and you may also require time off for portions of your staff to run the plan.

Another issue that must be addressed in the plan and on an ongoing basis is the required level of training for all those involved so that they will know how to respond when disaster strikes.

Additional Resources

There are many sites and companies that deal with creating your own disaster recovery plan, providing an off-site location to work from after a disaster, and so on. A few of those that we have found most useful include the following:

Federal Emergency Management Agency (FEMA)   A US federal government agency, it has ideas and tips to protect many of your business's assets. Their home page is at `www.fema.gov`. They have a section devoted to business issues at `www.fema.gov/mit/how2bus.htm`.

Binomial International   An international company that offers seminars, consulting, and other resources to aid you in disaster planning. They also have a free newsletter on the subject that will bring you ideas and tips on the subject monthly. In addition, they have links to about 800 other sites on the issue. They can be found on the Web at `www.binomial.com`.

The Disaster Recovery Journal   An Internet-based resource that offers many ideas for creating your own disaster recovery plan. They can be reached at `www.drj.com`. They offer two especially important resources on their site: a free newsletter on the subject, and a how-to section for people new to creating a disaster recovery plan. Both of these resources are available at `www.drj.com/new2dr/newbies.htm`. If you are new to this, you may also want to check out some sample plans. They have some links to some great plans at `www.drj.com/new2dr/samples.htm`.

The SANS Institute   They have an excellent publication on security-related information and how to secure your computer resources. This is something we have discussed throughout the book, but we want to point out that this should be an important part of your plan. They can be found on the web at `www.sans.org/newlook/publications/roadmap.htm`.

The Journal of Business Continuity   A free newsletter that is published every other week on the subject of Business Continuity and how to plan for and handle disasters. All of the previous newsletters are available on line and you can also subscribe to receive the newsletter as it is published. They are available at `www.business-continuity.com/journal.html`.

The previous list presents just a few of the literally thousands of Web sites on the Internet and companies that deal with this subject. Be sure to check them out and design and test your plan to make sure it works for your organization—your job may depend on it.

Maintenance and Troubleshooting

PART 4

Hurricane Andrew

About six months before Hurricane Andrew hit southeast Florida, we started an ambitious project to develop a disaster recovery plan.

This project was divided into three phases that covered everything from the scope of the recovery plan to annual updates and reviews.

Phase 1: Project Scope

The Institution we were consulting for first decided at the board level that a disaster recovery plan was needed to deal with any eventuality. It was very important to have the full support of the board of trustees, since this project would take considerable resources in both human and capital terms. The project determined the scope and procedures to execute when a natural disaster occurred. Since most departments had basic recovery procedures, it was determined early in the project that this disaster recovery plan would focus on major disasters only. Because a computer shutdown would not disable the institution by itself, extreme effort was taken to come up with very difficult scenarios, such as complete devastation of the campus.

This phase included the selection of the disaster recovery team at the executive level and representatives of all departments. The overall unifying departments were determined to be HR, MIS, and Physical Plant. These departments were responsible for

key tasks to ensure the success of the recovery:

- HR would have to devise a plan to make people available before, during, and after a disaster.

- MIS was responsible for systems and telecommunications availability.

- Physical Plant was responsible for infrastructure access and transportation.

- The reasoning was that if a major disaster ever occurred, you need to have people, systems, and communications available in order to recover.

Phase 2: Tasks and Procedures

The second phase involved a series of meetings involving all the departments. Tasks were assigned to prepare a department for before, after, and during a disaster. This phase focused on the individual departments and what they needed to do to recover from a devastating disaster. Special attention was given to the possibility that replacements might be needed; therefore, the procedures would have to be detailed enough for a non-department member to follow. This phase took the longest and involved considerable resources. One of the key dictums of the board of trustees was to establish a recovery priority schedule. This meant that a recovery order would have to be established by importance. Also, the recovery would by phased by 24hr, 48hr, 72hr time tables.

Phase 3: Review and Updates

The final phase of the project was determined to be an ongoing process. Once the Board approved the plan, then a series of yearly reviews would follow, and a review counsel was established by the institution to enforce this. If a disaster did occur, the counsel would review its effectiveness and assess the results. Care was taken to give this counsel broad authority to enforce the recovery plan.

As you can see, a disaster recovery plan doesn't include just the MIS department; it's a company-wide process.

As a footnote, Hurricane Andrew hit the Institution six months after it started the project and just after its completion. The Institution and the surrounding area, including the homes of the employees, suffered great damage ($20 billion). The institution had its core services up and running within 72 hours, and proceeded to help its more devastated employees. Had it not planned for this disaster, the institution would not have survived.

24seven **CASE STUDY**

16

Tools for Monitoring the Network

Aside from monitoring your network, you also need to monitor, manage, and support your applications, servers, and desktops—all from a central location. Monitoring your network will help you identify potential problems, but the monitoring data can also help you analyze and forecast future performance. To accomplish these tasks there are many products available (called asset management applications). In the following sections you will get an overview of these products and their use.

Tools for Monitoring the Network

Network monitoring and management can be accomplished with the use of products developed for this task. You will find that most of these products cover a variety of levels in your network topology. These products identify network trouble spots, help you establish a baseline, and forecast future needs. They also help you inventory and track hardware and software assets.

Here are some tools you will want to consider:

- HP OpenView, from Hewlett Packard, is a well-established, high-performance network monitoring and management tool. We have used it extensively and in many companies it's the de facto tool. This is an SNMP-based product that provides graphics and reporting capabilities. There are many products that take advantage of OpenView as their platform, such as Peregrim.

- Vendor specific tools are provided by the vendor as a benefit to using their product. Microsoft includes with SMS a full version of Network Monitor, and Novell offers one with ManageWise.

- OEM vendors such as Compaq and 3Com offer SNMP-compliant monitoring tools also. These come as part of the network and server products. We especially like 3Com's Web-based tools that allow you to view all of their products and centrally manage them from a browser client.

- On the WAN side you have COMNET Predictor 2 from CACI Products. This product is a network-performance planning tool that models infrastructure and traffic changes for ATM and frame relay networks before they occur.

- Network*IT* Pro from Computer Associates has graphical, reporting, and protocol analyzing features that compete with OpenView from HP.

- Network Inspector from Fluke is a compact, full-featured network-monitoring suite that can support an entire enterprise. Fluke is famous for developing hardware stand-alone sniffers for network troubleshooting, but is now entering the full-featured network-management field.

- Sniffer Pro 99 v2 from Network Associates. This product can monitor LAN and WAN traffic and is NA's entry into the Windows world. Previous versions were DOS based.

NOTE You need to use promiscuous-mode compatible network cards in order to use network-monitoring products. Check with your vendor for the proper NIC and driver for this task. This is especially important if you plan to take your show on the road; most models of PCMCIA network cards do not support promiscuous mode.

Cable Management

We have always known that an unstable network causes a lot of problems, but we haven't really spent a lot of time monitoring the cable infrastructure, which in many cases causes the instability. A well-planned and installed cable infrastructure is the first step in providing a stable environment. Cable management is the process that delivers that stability.

As the requirements for increasingly fast, complex, and bandwidth-hungry networks increase, you may find yourself confronting a number of infrastructure-related questions:

- Should you stick with copper, or do you need to move to fiber?

- If you opt for copper, should you look at a higher-category product?
- Should you invest in Structured Cabling System (SCS)?
- What additional hardware and software do you need to accommodate the upgrades?
- Are your installation and testing procedures sufficient?
- How can you ensure compliance with current standards and accommodate changes that may occur in the future?

Planning to implement higher-speed technologies such as Fast Ethernet, Gigabit Ethernet, and ATM bring concerns related to your cabling structure. The performance of these technologies is related to issues such as the integrity of the cabling infrastructure, cable length, the quality of connecting hardware, the number of connectors within a segment, and the number of wire pairs used during transmission.

A great source of information on cabling standards is the Telecommunications Industry/ Electronic Industries Association organization (TIA/EIA). This is a standards group that oversees cabling management, among other telecommunications issues.

A must-have document for the network administrator and the network engineer is the TIA/EIA 568A, "Commercial Building Telecommunications Cabling Standard," which governs many cabling infrastructure issues. As with many other standards, the TIA/EIA standards are under constant revision. Many of the proposed revisions are necessary to meet the increasingly stringent requirements of today's networks, such as running higher-speed technologies like Gigabit Ethernet over copper cabling.

Sage Advice: Providing High-Speed Services over Copper

There's been extensive debate over copper cabling's capacity to support higher-speed technologies. Perhaps the biggest image boost for copper came from the ATM Forum, which approved using 155Mb/sec ATM over copper cabling.

However, if you plan to run higher-speed technologies over copper, you should be aware of several issues. One is that as frequency increases, so does the vulnerability to problems such as attenuation and Near-End Crosstalk (NEXT).

Failure to give the installation process the attention it deserves can lead to disruptive network behavior.

Fortunately, good installation tips can help you prevent future growing pains in high-performance configurations. As a baseline, it's crucial to follow the TIA/EIA 568A guidelines related to factors such as degree of twist, bend radius, and termination.

Sage Advice: Providing High-Speed Services over Copper *(continued)*

If you're using cable ties to join a bundle of cables, avoid cinching the ties too tightly. Overcinching the ties can have the same effect as an insufficient bend radius, particularly with the cables on the outside of the bundle. When installing cabling to patch panels, make sure to provide adequate strain relief. Reinforcing support becomes increasingly important as you add more cables to a patch panel over time.

The first 50 feet or so of a cable run are particularly susceptible to NEXT, a fact that should be kept in mind during the cable planning, installation, and management phases. Also, according to TIA/EIA 568A, the limits for attenuation and crosstalk for Category 5 cabling at 100MHz are 24 decibels (dB) and 27.1dB, respectively. Proper testing techniques are necessary to ensure that cabling complies with these specifications.

Fast Ethernet transmissions use only two twisted pairs within four-pair Category 5 UTP copper cable, whereas Gigabit Ethernet uses all four pairs. Thus, it's critical to comply with Category 5 requirements across all four pairs if you're going to run Gigabit Ethernet over the network. Among other things, this requires highly accurate test equipment.

The 802.3ab draft standard for Gigabit Ethernet over twisted pair cable (1000BaseT) incorporates recommendations for enhanced performance. These include converting to high-performance patch cables, reducing the number of connectors along a run, and refitting existing connectors. The draft standard also includes three additional test parameters: return loss, delay skew, and Equal-Level Far-End Crosstalk (ELFEXT).

Finally, keep in mind that with high-speed technologies, a cabling infrastructure must maintain consistent performance levels throughout the entire system—including the cabling itself, as well as patch panels, cross-connects, connectors and connector interfaces, and WAOs. For example, if substandard materials are used in the construction of certain cabling, delay skew may exceed the limits established in TIA/EIA 568A.

Using Copper

The TIA and the ISO are working on a Category 6 standard, which specifies performance levels for cabling at a minimum of 200MHz. The standard is expected to include an eight-pin modular connector jack and plug.

The Category 7 standard is expected to include a specification of up to 600MHz and a requirement for a new connector interface. Category 7 cabling may not be backward compatible with existing equipment with eight-pin modular connectors.

While a few vendors have cabling that they claim meets the requirements of some of these proposed standards, Category 6 and Category 7 products in particular will probably take quite some time to become popular. However, the future management implications for this type of cabling shouldn't be ignored. It's likely that higher-category cabling will be prone to some of the same problems.

Gigabit Ethernet over copper is vulnerable to Far-End Crosstalk (FEXT), not to mention a number of other hardware-interconnect issues. This means that you will have to take a serious look at your cabling. If your organization is considering moving to enhanced cabling, the time to break out the drawing board is now.

Using Fiber

Fiber cabling presents its own set of management issues. According to the TIA/EIA 568A specifications for fiber backbone cabling, the maximum distance between the main cross-connect and the horizontal cross-connect for multimode cabling is 2,000 meters. For single-mode cabling, the limit is 3,000 meters.

Recent developments on the standards front include IEEE 802.3z, which defines requirements for Gigabit Ethernet over multimode and single-mode fiber. The 1000BaseSX standard includes specifications for using multimode fiber for short-haul applications. 1000BaseLX defines the parameters for using multimode or single-mode fiber for long-haul applications.

Structured Cabling System (SCS)

Structured Cabling System (SCS) is a technique for designing, installing, and maintaining cabling structures, that has been around for a while and will likely become more significant. The TIA/EIA 568A standard specifies the contents of an SCS, which are founded on a star-based topology. Other standards that contain useful guidelines pertaining to structured cabling systems include TIA/EIA 569, "Commercial Building Standard for Telecommunications Pathways and Spaceways"; TIA/EIA 606, "Administration Standard for the Telecommunications Infrastructure of Commercial Buildings"; and TIA/EIA 607, "Commercial Building Grounding and Bonding Requirements for Telecommunications."

According to TIA/EIA 568A, each wall jack must be linked to a cross-connect in a wiring closet, and each wiring closet must be linked to the building's main equipment facility. In a campus environment, each building is linked to a centralized administration point. The standard also stipulates that horizontal cable running from the wiring closet to the wall jack can be no longer than 90 meters. (This applies to any type of transmission media.)

Maintenance and Troubleshooting

PART 4

An additional 10 meters is allotted for patch cords in the wiring closet and the work area. A maximum of four interconnections between the wall jack and the wiring closet are allowed.

For backbone cabling, the distance requirements vary. As mentioned earlier, for multi-mode fiber on the backbone, TIA/EIA 568A stipulates a maximum distance of 2,000 meters. The maximum distance for single-mode fiber on the backbone is 3,000 meters. Deviation from these requirements can result in significant performance problems.

Although they can require a substantial up-front investment, SCSs can yield substantial long-term advantages. Many manufacturers guarantee system performance for a certain number of years, providing a degree of future proofing. SCSs can also take a lot of the guesswork out of the cabling system design process.

One example of an SCS is Lucent Technologies' well-established Systimax Structured Cabling System. Systimax is based on a scheme called zone wiring, where a permanent section of horizontal cabling runs from the wiring closet to a second section of cabling divided among multiple work areas, or zones. Available for both copper and fiber, Systimax can be configured to incorporate other Lucent products, such as its GigaSPEED® copper cabling and OptiSPEED™ LC fiber connectors.

As the complexity of cabling increases, so will the importance of devices such as cross-connect switches. These types of systems typically reside in the wiring closet. Connections to user equipment are on one side of the switch matrix, and links to networking equipment such as hubs and switches are on the other. The cross-connect switching system connects ports on one side of the matrix to ports on the opposite side.

Network Analysis

So, what do you do with all this information going through your head right now? Well, there is a lot you can do, starting with surveying your current network infrastructure. You will want to identify your trouble spots (areas that are not up to standards, potential bottlenecks) and then decide on a plan to correct these issues. A good network analysis tool will take you a long way to reaching your goals.

A good combination of tools will include the following:

- A handheld Microtest Omniscanner Advanced Cable Certification Tool. This is a really neat piece of equipment. It will certify up to category 7.

- ManageWise Lanalyzer or a similar network analyzer, first to establish baselines and bottlenecks and then to collect data.

- Visio or similar technical drawing application.

- Excel or similar spreadsheet for archiving and reporting.

- SNMP compliant systems.

TIP   It may be hard to convince your managers to buy a $5,000 handheld cable tester with certifying capability, but it's even more cost-prohibitive not to have one. A badly installed network is hard to diagnose without one of these tools.

NetWare 5@Work: Our Cabling Nightmare

Day one, 3:00 P.M.: The entire network freezes at Company A. After initial trouble-shooting, no signs of a problem surfaced, and it was determined that the freeze was a fluke of nature.

Day two, 3:15 P.M.: Another freeze. You could feel the panic streaking through the corridors of the IS department. There was a migration in progress and the possible causes were unimaginable.

Day three, 3:25 P.M.: Another freeze. We were getting ready to leave the country. Corporate was breathing down our necks, and still no suspect in sight.

After two weeks of watching CRC errors on sniffers building up to the point of freezing the network at approximately the same time every day, we had no clue what was causing this.

We thought we had installed the best infrastructure in the world. It was all Category 5 100 Mbs, with state-of-the-art HP-100 Mb switches, and a T3 redundant WAN backbone. NDS managed the users, and TCP/IP and IPX were the standard protocols. There were no indications in the analysis as to which system or network segment was causing the CRC storms.

Then a team member, going on a hunch (based on the fact that we had just installed new fast Ethernet NIC's and switches) took a look at the configuration and noticed that the NICs had a half duplex setting and the hubs were set at full duplex.

Well, what can we tell you? The settings on the switches were reconfigured and there were no more problems.

The moral of the story is never give up.

Maintenance and Troubleshooting

PART 4

Monitoring Servers and Desktops

Providing our users with a stable user platform, secure links to their servers and applications, and high performance have been our objectives as system administrators throughout our careers. But incompatibilities, downtime, bottlenecks, and system crashes always hamper us.

To address these issues we rely on network management products that maintain and monitor servers and desktops. These products, in conjunction with network monitoring tools, provide us with a platform to completely manage network resources and user desktops. We also test future implementations before they go online, and we train users in their use. In essence we try to be as proactive as possible.

Management Products

If we were to identify a single priority in system delivery it would be availability. This sums up all our tasks into one objective; that is, to ensure that users have access to their resources at all times, with minimal downtime. To accomplish this, you need to perform a series of maintenance procedures throughout the life of the network. You would need a very large staff to implement these procedures unless you use applications that are dedicated to these processes.

The following are solutions available to you from various vendors, including Novell:

- High-Availability Software for NetWare 5

  - **Standby*Server* for NetWare 5** by Vinca (Vinca, 1201 N. 800 E., Orem, UT 84097, (801) 223-3100, www.vinca.com.) is the newest high-availability software product. Standby*Server* for NetWare clusters two servers with a high-speed link and employs NetWare 5's real-time mirroring function for automatic failover and full redundancy with no single point of failure. The product lets the standby machine access data and applications stored on a disk subsystem such as a RAID device, and users can continue working without having to log in to the system again.

  - **Novell Cluster Services for NetWare 5**, is a Novell clustering system that provides high-server availability without losing performance capabilities. In the cluster, two or more servers share a storage subsystem and all are available to users, but if one server fails, the other servers on the cluster take over the functions assigned to the failed server. Novell's *AppNotes* issue of May 1999 has a great article on this product.

More software solutions can be found in the following list:

Desktop management software products	Company contact information
Attachmate: NetWizard Plus	www.attachmate.com
Bendata: Heat Workgroup Asset Manager	www.bendata.com

Desktop management software products	Company contact information
BindView Development: EMS/ NETinventory	www.bindview.com
ClickNet: ClickNet Professional	www.clicknet.com
Comdisco: ComPlete Buyer ComPlete Asset Manager	www.comdisco.com
Compaq: Insight Manager	www.compaq.com
Computer Associates: AimIT ShipIT Unicenter TNG	www.cai.com
Hewlett-Packard: AssetView OpenView Desktop Administrator	www.hp.com
Intel: LANDesk Management Suite	www.intel.com
Janus Technologies: Argis	www.janus-tech.com
MainControl: MC/Empower 3	www.maincontrol.com
Microsoft: Systems Management Server (SMS) 2	www.microsoft.com
NetBalance: IT Ledger	www.netbalance.com
Network Associates: Zero Administration Client Suite	www.nai.com
Novell: ZENworks and ManageWise	www.novell.com
Peregrine: AssetCenter	www.peregrine.com
Platinum Technology: AutoAnswer AutoConfigure AutoXfer	www.platinum.com
Seagate Software: Desktop Management Suite Wininstall and Winland	www.seagatesoftware.com
Tally Systems: Cenergy	www.tallysystems.com
Tangram: Asset Insight 3	www.tangram.com
Tivoli: Inventory Module	www.tivoli.com
WRQ: Express	www.wrq.com

Maintenance and Troubleshooting

PART 4

This wide variety of products can seem overwhelming. But we recommend that a good implementation of ZENworks coupled with NDS resources can provide a formidable desktop management platform.

NetWare 5@Work: Company A's Desktop Management Implementation

Company A, as part of its overall design, wanted to establish a network management platform that not only supported the network, but also its desktop and laptop systems.

To accomplish this they evaluated various products and services with the intention of centralizing the management and distribution of applications to the desktop. They also wanted to provide centralized help desk functionality and remote control to the desktop. This would in turn reduce the number of out calls to the sites for support. Considering that this was a statewide enterprise with over 30,000 users, implementation was not considered lightly.

After all the evaluation processes, they decided to take a combined approach to monitor and manage their network. The following is a summary of their approach:

1. For network monitoring tasks, the company decided to use OpenView from HP. This product has an excellent reputation and is known for its stability. OpenView was deployed throughout the company network, and it now resides on Sun workstations. The help desk has a wall screen for the view of the help desk personnel.

2. Peregrine's AssetCenter product and other SNMP utilities were installed on top of OpenView to provide additional features such as server monitoring and intruder-detection services.

3. NetWare 5 servers dedicated to NDS, and ZENworks support, were deployed throughout the company network to assure user and software management services. The help desk also added two additional large wall screens to view the tree. Having servers dedicated to these tasks provides a stable and redundant infrastructure for the management system.

These solutions added up to a very reliable, high-performance, centralized management system for Company A.

Asset Management

Nobody wants to spend money unless it makes money. The same goes with systems management. Is your current system helping increase revenues or reducing them? How can you approach your corporate managers with an answer if you don't have the data to back you up? That's why it's so important to monitor and maintain your network, servers and workstations. Without the tools we discussed earlier, you cannot collect the data needed to come up with your estimates or projections on utilization and need.

Total Cost of Ownership (TCO)

A network system is a collection of assets and people that function in harmony, which over time accumulate a total cost for the year. This total cost divided into the number of user desktops equals the TCO. This value is what it costs you to buy and support each desktop in the company and is a consideration for the actual cost of doing business when the company tries to determine if their systems were an asset or a detriment to the company's profit goals.

The TCO includes hardware that is rarely standardized in even the most diligent of companies. It also includes software that presents an even more complex situations because of the variety of OSs, applications installed (and their version), hard drive partitions, you name it.

Of these assets, many have short life cycles and need constant support or service. The installed software may or may not match the licenses a company has paid for. And most users, given that they have a similar desktop computer at home, feel willing and able to meddle with their system configurations (not to mention those pesky downloads from the Internet users always seem to insist on).

Employee turnover causes extra problems, too. Users always seem to add their touch to the system they use, and then a new employee takes their place, adding their two cents to the fray.

What can we say? Desktops are not easy to manage or maintain. Asset Management software can cut, according to some estimates, the TCO tab by as much as $2,500 per annum per PC. By learning what you have out there and making better use of it, you can save substantial amounts of money.

Asset Management Software

Asset management software automates the task of tracking IT hardware and software throughout their life cycles. What you track might just be simple information like model number, serial number, or manufacturer name. It might include information about

Maintenance and Troubleshooting

PART 4

financial issues and help with procurement; it can track and manage software licenses. It can also be tied into help desk software.

There is a distinction between asset-management products that are passive and just do inventory and those that are active, which distribute software and meter it.

Inventory tools often have a financial orientation, and this certainly is the case with the HEAT Workgroup Asset Manager from Bendata (www.bendata.com). BindView Development (www.bindview.com) recently released version 6 of its BindView EMS/NET-inventory software, targeted at NetWare 3.*x*, 4.*x*, and Windows NT. This software, aimed at tracking both hardware and software, employs multiple servers, including a master server that holds configuration information for an entire enterprise. Separate audit and login servers may be distributed for the least-expensive routing of audit information, yet the ability to perform enterprise-wide reports is not sacrificed.

Novell offers two asset-management products: ManageWise and ZENworks (discussed in Part 3 of this book). ManageWise, the older and more traditional of the two, performs a wide variety of functions: autodiscovery/network mapping, software and hardware inventorying, software distribution, and even server monitoring. The NDS-centric ZENworks, aimed at workstation and application management, had previously confined itself to hardware inventorying, collecting only such asset data as could be reasonably stored in the directory. Whether or not this limitation was a real problem, it provided the grist for several Microsoft white papers. Therefore, Novell's new ZENworks 2 performs software inventories as well, storing data in an ODBC-compliant SQL database. Other new features include desktop virus protection and reporting capabilities.

A year from now, when Y2K concerns have faded, the need for effective desktop asset management will remain. New products and services will be available, helping us keep the cost of ownership at a reasonable level.

Sage Advice: Tracking Assets on Systems That Are Not Turned On

How do you use a program to inventory the hardware and software on a desktop computer when it isn't turned on? This is the problem that Intel and IBM addressed in 1997 when they introduced Wake on LAN, which allows a NIC, when prompted remotely, to power up a host computer.

> ### Sage Advice: Tracking Assets on Systems That Are Not Turned On *(continued)*
>
> Wake-on-LAN-compatible computers always draw a trickle charge of power. Last year, Intel and IBM capitalized on this fact by devising Alert on LAN. With this refinement, a PC will send regular status packets to a management server whether or not it is "turned on." Therefore, alerts can be generated if a PC is unplugged from its power source, disconnected from the network, or suffers an unauthorized processor blue screen of death.
>
> Alert on LAN 2, announced in February 1999, builds on this by allowing a management console to work directly with a PC. For example, when the desktop sends an alert, the console can send back an acknowledgment. In the event of a software freeze or apparent hardware failure, an administrator can reboot any client into a diagnostic mode.
>
> These advancements have extended the reach of a centralized administrator to the entire company reducing even further the costs associated with sending tech personnel on site.

Software Distribution

As part of your asset management, you will also want to manage software distribution to the desktop and take control of it remotely, which would really increase the value of your services to your users and reduce the cost of hands on support.

It's human nature to be frustrated if you have just discovered that you have two copies of Word 6 for DOS, three copies of Winword 2, twelve copies of Winword 6, two hundred forty-six of Word 97, and twenty-five betas of Office 2000—and you can't do anything about it. By adding software distribution to your network, you can solve problems associated with maintaining the latest versions of user software and also resolve problems that occur with corrupted desktop configurations as soon as they are discovered.

Most Software Distribution products that push software to the desktop also perform metering (the recording of program launches). This may operate regardless of whether the programs are launched from a server or from a local hard drive. Metering allows a warning message or prohibition to be sent to the user when running a program that would violate licensing parameters. However, since concurrent-use licensing—which allowed a single software license to be shared consecutively by multiple users—has fallen out of fashion, metering is not as significant as it used to be.

Maintenance and Troubleshooting

PART 4

If you decide you want metering, Computer Associates' Unicenter TNG is the quintessential framework. As of the recent version 2.2, it includes agents for over 40 operating systems, including Windows 95, Windows NT, NetWare, AS/400, Tandem NSK, and a wide range of Unix OSs. Data repositories can reside on either Windows NT or Unix. As you would expect, Unicenter TNG includes solutions for inventory, software distribution, and metering. The news here is that in 1998, Computer Associates knuckled under, breaking Unicenter into pieces for those who don't want—or can't afford—the whole thing. The asset and inventory management component is sold as AimIT, while the software distribution component is sold as ShipIT.

17

Setting Up and Protecting Your File System

Your job as a network administrator is to make sure users have full access to their applications and data. Designing a standard file system structure for your servers is a critical component of these duties.

The file system involves system-created and administrator-defined volumes and directories on your NetWare servers. It doesn't matter if you have one or more servers. In every case you are going to design your file system structure for performance, administration, and security. A well designed file system, and one that is implemented as the standard for the servers, will make it easier to manage, back up, and secure.

NetWare is also introducing a new file system, NSS (NetWare Storage Services), which will allow you to address the issue of large databases, and also data warehousing. You should consider using NSS in very limited circumstances, since at the time of this writing NSS cannot replace the SYS: volume.

You should also consider Novell Replication Services when you are managing a large number of servers that contain the same directory structure and files. Using Novell Replication Services, discussed in Chapter 1, involves some planning, but it is very effective in managing redundant and large environments.

For successful backups, you must establish an effective plan, and when it comes to the disaster recovery plan, the entire company should be involved. When hurricane Andrew hit Miami, Florida whole communities were leveled to the ground. Just having a backup plan wouldn't have recovered a business to its state before the hurricane. Only a disaster recovery plan that included physical relocation contingencies would have enabled a company to survive.

This chapter will focus on designing a file system with ease of access and management in mind. We will go over some design fundamentals and also cover backup strategies. For details on disaster recovery and available solutions, see Chapter 18.

An Effective File System Design

One of the most important aspects of configuring the network is the assignment of directories for data and program files on your servers. Before you install a NetWare 5 server, you will want to design a file system with one or more volumes, and a directory structure that places files at least one level of directories from the root of the volume. If you are upgrading from a previous version of NetWare, you might not have to worry about this unless you want to redesign the file system.

File System Design Considerations

When you install applications on the network or provide a location for data files, keep the directory structure simple so that the users can easily find files. You also want to position the directories so that it will be easy to make security assignments for them. Take advantage of the fact that child directories inherit rights from parent directories. For example, you can create a single directory for spreadsheet data and then subdivide the directory for particular projects. Giving a user access to the data directory allows him or her access to all of the projects.

Here are some file system design basics:

- Think of volumes as you would a file cabinet; they are meant to store information in a logical manner so that the data can be retrieved easily.

- Separate program and data volumes to make it easy to perform backups. Then the files you need to back up—the data files—are always in the same place. Also decide at installation if you are going to use the SYS: volume for all data storage or if you are going to create multiple volumes, including the SYS: volume, to separate the user data from system data.

- Look at directories as the drawers in the file cabinet. To further subdivide a directory, you can use subdirectories as you would folders in a cabinet. Directories and subdirectories allow you to organize data in greater detail. Keep in mind that the more complicated your directory structure, the harder it will be to find files.

- Be careful when creating a large number of directories off the root of the volume; the root of a "non-NSS" volume is limited to 512 entries.

- Store files in directories. Files are the most basic storage units of a file system. They contain critical information and are what you ultimately want to protect. Avoid saving files on the root of a volume. Create directory names that reflect the type of files to be held in each directory.

You should always take into consideration the server's function and whom it serves. Your structure should reflect that. In a file server you will have home-user directories, whereas an application server should only have directories storing the applications run from a server.

Figure 17.1 shows a sample of a file system meant for a file server.

Figure 17.1   A sample NetWare file structure

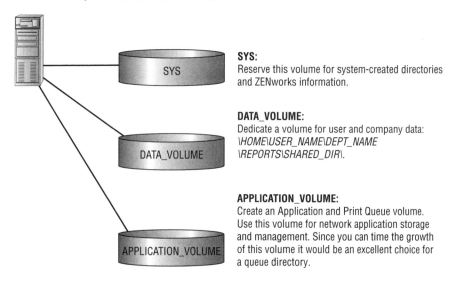

SYS:
Reserve this volume for system-created directories and ZENworks information.

DATA_VOLUME:
Dedicate a volume for user and company data:
\HOME\USER_NAME\DEPT_NAME
\REPORTS\SHARED_DIR\.

APPLICATION_VOLUME:
Create an Application and Print Queue volume. Use this volume for network application storage and management. Since you can time the growth of this volume it would be an excellent choice for a queue directory.

By properly designing your file system, you will ensure that your users have access to data and applications on the file server, and at the same time provide security and protection for valuable resources.

The following sections cover system-created volumes and directories, and you will be given suggestions on how to design or create a file system that fits your users' needs. You will also learn how to provide security for directories and files.

Maintenance and Troubleshooting

PART 4

System-Created Directories

When you install a NetWare file server, a SYS: volume is created with system-created directories. System-created directories allow for the successful operation of the server. You will find that each directory supports different functions, some at the server and others for administrative tasks.

Here are the system-created directories and their functions:

CDROM$$.ROM   When you mount a CD-ROM volume, the index of the information on the CD-ROM is stored in this directory. You should make sure you have enough free space to store this information.

DELETED.SAV   All volumes contain this hidden directory. When directories are deleted, the files they contained are stored in this directory.

ETC   Contains TCP/IP configuration and related files.

JAVA   Stores Java support files.

JAVASAVE   Contains other Java-related files.

License   Contains server license files.

Login   Stores files that allow users to log in. This is the only directory available to users before they log in.

Mail   This directory is used for backward compatibility to bindery services.

NDPS   Contains files supporting Novell Distributed Printing Services (NDPS).

NETBASIC   Stores NETBASIC support files.

NI   Contains NetWare installation files.

Perl   Holds Perl-related files.

Public   Stores the NetWare client files, utilities, and commands that are available to users and administrators.

Readme   Contains documents relating to NetWare topics.

SYSTEM   Stores NetWare operating system files, NLMs, server console utilities, and commands.

You should not delete any of these directories because loss of any system directory could cause the server to crash. It is highly recommended that you dedicate the SYS: volume to only the system-created directories. In doing so, you ensure protection for the system directories by allowing access only to administrators. By keeping user data and applications in a separate volume, you can restrict access to the SYS: volume, avoiding harmful mistakes by users.

Suggested Directory Structures

When creating your file system structure, strive for ease of administrator and user access. There is no single right way to design a file system, but you should follow these guidelines before you plan and implement your file system:

- Use the SYS: volume for server system directories and files only.

- Create additional volumes for user data and applications.

- Create a separate volume to hold print queues if the printing levels require it.

- Consider adding name space modules to volumes to support the various desktop platforms your users will be using.

- Decide on naming conventions for volumes and directories that reflect their purpose.

NOTE Additional information on planning and creating NetWare volumes is provided in the CNE course called "Service and Support." You can also access the Novell Web site for additional information on this subject at www.novell.com.

Sage Advice

ZENworks offers desktop management tools to administrate your workstations from a centralized location. But in order to support these, you not only have to prepare your servers but you must take into consideration the workstations; they will be the running agents.

- At the server level, take care to structure a file system that makes it easy to manage and locate information provided by ZENworks.

- By providing a common file system structure, you can take advantage of NRS to replicate information like application files and snapshots (images) of workstations throughout your servers.

- In some circumstances, it's a good idea to dedicate servers for ZENworks functionality.

- Follow the guidelines given by Novell and its partners.

- There is a lot of support available to plan your server file system to best suit your needs.

The NSS File System

NetWare 5 offers an optional storage access system, Novell Storage Services (NSS). NSS is a new technology developed by Novell to provide quick and unlimited access to storage devices. NSS is independent of the operating system, yet it is compatible with NetWare 5 and the NetWare file system. NSS is not limited by the FAT file system constraints as in previous versions of NetWare.

NetWare 5@Work: NSS File System Advantages and Disadvantages

There are advantages and disadvantages to consider before implementing an NSS file system. Among the considerations are its advantages over previous NetWare file systems:

Advantages

- Files created in an NSS volume can have a much greater capacity, up to 8TB instead of the 2GB file size limit NetWare volumes previously had.

- You can access and store an unlimited number of files on an NSS volume.

- NSS volumes load very quickly and require much less server memory and fewer resources.

- NSS volumes can be repaired in the same amount of time it would normally take to mount them without errors.

- NSS also provides improved support for CD-ROM files, detecting and then mounting them as read-only volumes.

- Before implementing NSS, you should also consider its disadvantages:

Disadvantages

- NSS can't create a SYS: volume because NSS doesn't support TTS.

- This system does not support many fault tolerance features of traditional Net-Ware partitions.

- NSS doesn't support disk suballocation, file compression, or file migration.

NSS may support these features in the future.

You need to balance the advantages with the disadvantages to decide if NSS is appropriate for your needs. If you are managing large databases, NSS is probably the best file system for you.

> **NOTE** You can find more information on the support for CD-ROMs at the Novell Web site (www.novell.com). Go to the section on utilities within the reference area of the site.

Securing the File System

To design a secure file structure, you need to consider whether you are going to go beyond the physical and login security already active on NetWare servers and NDS. You also need to consider file system security on the servers as well. This requires planning on your part, and also establishing a set of standards that can be documented.

You should start by establishing a team consisting of users and supervisors from the departments involved. They will be your best source of information to determine who needs access to what. After detailing and gathering the information you may want to document this with a form (an example is shown in Table 17.1), that captures specific data. Believe us, you will want a similar form for future reference when you are trying to troubleshoot a problem with a user.

Table 17.1   An Example of a File System Security Form

Resource | User\Group	SYS:	SYS:PUBLIC	SYS:HOME\ UserA	SYS:\ACCT\ Data	SYS:\Apps\ DB
Container Object	N\A	Default	N\A	N\A	N\A
UserA	N\A	N\A	ALL	N\A	N\A
Accounting	N\A	N\A	N\A	RWFEC	RF

This is really the hardest part of setting up secure access to the file system. Determining the right combination of rights is a cooperative effort with other department heads. There is no one way to do this. In addition to file system rights you should also consider physical security of the servers.

Maintenance and Troubleshooting

PART 4

Backing Up Servers and Workstations

The main focus of a network administrator is to guarantee users fast and secure access to their data and applications. To do this, you need to ensure the reliability and performance of the systems you manage. But no system is foolproof. You will want to establish a backup strategy to protect you from simple data loss to complete system loss. You will also want to implement a restore plan and test it just to make sure your backup strategy will work.

As part of Novell's complete backup solutions strategy, NetWare Storage Management Services (SMS) can back up files, systems, NDS directories, and workstations. There are also a number of third-party solutions that support NetWare backups with more features than NetWare's SMS. We will also discuss backup strategies for ongoing backups.

Storage Management Services (SMS)

Along with disk storage, your network should include a backup device—typically a tape drive. We'll start this section with a technical explanation of how NetWare 5 supports backups. We'll then explore the different types of backups and their advantages.

NOTE   NetWare 5 also lets you back up NetWare 3.1x servers, client workstations, and the NDS database.

Understanding Enhanced SMS

NetWare 5 includes built-in support for backup utilities, as did previous versions of NetWare. This system is called Enhanced SMS, or Storage Management Services. The Enhanced part of the name refers to new components incorporated into the NetWare 5 version of SMS which includes a really neat client-backup tool called NWBACKUP32 .EXE for Windows 95/98. SMS is a system that allows backup software to work with the operating system to allow it to back up and restore data. SMS includes NetWare Backup/Restore and Target Service Agents, described below. NetWare Backup/Restore is a group of NLMs and executables that provide the backup engine and the user interfaces. Here are some of its components and their functions:

SBCON.NLM   Loads the Enhanced SBACKUP (Backup/Restore) on the host server.

QMAN.NLM   Manages the job queue.

SBSC.NLM   Holds the SBACKUP Communication Module, which is auto-loaded with QMAN.

SMSDI.NLM   Holds the Storage Management Services Device Interface, which is also auto-loaded with QMAN.

SMDR.NLM   Contains the Storage Management Data Requestor, which is responsible for requesting data from the target and sending it to the tape storage device on the host server.

NWBACK32.EXE   Runs at the workstation. You can choose the type of backup or restore job you want done and submit it to the host server that has NetWare Backup/Restore running on it.

Target Service Agents (TSAs) are components that allow a particular device—or target—to be backed up. Several TSAs are available for a wide variety of systems:

TSA500.NLM   Supports backups of NetWare 5 server volumes and NSS volumes.

TSA410.NLM   Supports backups of NetWare 4 server volumes.

TSA312.NLM   Supports NetWare 3.12 server volume backups.

TSA311.NLM   Supports NetWare 3.11 server volume backups.

TSANDS.NLM   Supports backup and restore of the NDS database.

TSADOS.NLM   Runs on the server and supports backup of DOS workstations. You must also load the TSA executable file on the workstation.

TSAPROXY.NLM   Runs on the server and supports backup of OS/2, Unix, Windows 95, Windows NT, and Macintosh workstations. Again, you must also load a workstation version of the TSA.

TIP   When you install client software for DOS, OS/2, Windows 95, Windows NT, or Macintosh, you have the option of installing the workstation TSA component. You can also install it at any time by running the client-software installation program, NetWare Backup/Restore.

Implementing SMS

Although many of you will implement different backup software products, it is important to know that NetWare includes its own backup and restore utilities. NetWare Backup/Restore runs on the server. To use it, you'll need a tape drive or other backup device attached to the server. If your tape device is attached to a workstation, you will need to use third-party backup software. NetWare Backup/Restore doesn't support tape devices attached to a workstation.

You can run NetWare Backup/Restore from the server or from a workstation, but the tape device must be connected to the server. The server utility is called SBCON.NLM, and the workstation utility is called NWBACK32.EXE.

TIP NetWare Backup/Restore must run at the host server. You can configure and submit backup or restore jobs from SBCON.NLM at the server console or from NWBACK32 on a Windows 95 workstation.

NOTE You can find more information on NetWare Backup/Restore on the Novell Web site at `www.novell.com`.

Choosing a Backup Strategy

Unlike many utilities, a backup program isn't very useful if you only run it occasionally. Instead, you should have a backup strategy. This strategy determines when you make backups, which type of backups you make, and the tapes you use for backups. In the following sections, we will look at the types of backups and tape rotation you can include in your strategy.

Full Backup

A full backup is the simplest and safest type of backup. It includes all the data on a volume or workstation. For servers with relatively small amounts of data storage, a regular full backup is the best solution. There are several advantages to this strategy:

- All files are available on each backup tape if you need to restore them.
- A minimum configuration is required to run the backup.

There are disadvantages, however:

- The backup and restore process can be very slow with large amounts of data.
- If you have a large amount of data, a single backup tape may not be enough to hold a full backup.

Incremental Backup

An incremental backup strategy begins with a full backup at regular intervals—perhaps once a week. Backups that take place between the full backup store only the files that have changed since the previous backup. For example, if you make a full backup on Monday, Tuesday's backup includes only the files changed since Monday, Wednesday's backup includes only the files changed since Tuesday, and so on. This system has a few advantages:

- Incremental backups are the quickest strategy to execute (but restore times will be longer, as we'll explain below).
- The latest changes are always available on the most recent tape.

However, there are some significant disadvantages to this strategy:

- Restoring a group of files can be time-consuming because they may be located on several different tapes.

- If you must restore all files, you will need all of the incremental tapes, along with the last full backup tape; if any tape is damaged or missing you will not have an up-to-date backup of some files.

Differential Backup

The differential backup strategy is popular because it offers the best of both worlds; it is something of a compromise between the full and incremental strategies. In this system, again, you make a full backup regularly. Between full backups, you make differential backups, which include the information changed since the *full* backup.

For example, if you make a full backup on Monday, Tuesday's backup includes all files changed since Monday. Wednesday's backup also includes all files changed since Monday, and so on. The advantages of this strategy are clear:

- Backups are reasonably fast because a large amount of data usually remains unchanged.

- To restore a file, or even all files, you need a maximum of two tapes (or sets of tapes, if your backup spans several tapes): the last full backup and the last incremental backup.

As you might have guessed, each successive differential backup will be larger and more time-consuming than the one before. For a successful differential backup strategy, you should schedule full backups frequently enough so that the differential backups don't become inconvenient. This will depend on your users and how often data is changed on your volumes.

Tape Rotation

With any backup method, you need a number of tapes—a minimum of one for the regular full backup and one for each day for incremental backups or one for differential backups. However, you should add additional tapes to provide a regularly archived backup.

In deciding on a tape-rotation scheme, realize that backups have two purposes for most companies. While they are obviously useful in case of data loss or system problems, they can also be handy for accounting and auditing purposes.

For example, a company may need to run a report on the data from the end of the previous month or year. The company might have five tapes, labeled MON through FRI. FRI is used for a full backup and MON through THU for differential backups. To keep an archive, the company might have four FRI tapes and use FRI1 one week, FRI2 the next week, and so on. This ensures that backups are available for the previous four weeks, along with the current backup. Many companies take this one step further and make a month-ending tape that is rotated once a year.

The last and one of the most important principles related to backups, is to keep at least one copy of the data off-site, such as in a safe deposit box. Some companies use the week-ending or month-ending tape for this purpose. No matter which strategy you choose, be sure to keep copies off-site. All of the backups in the world are of no value if they are destroyed in an earthquake, flood, hurricane, fire, or other disaster—along with your network.

There are many products you can use that provide additional features than the ones supported by the NetWare Backup/Restore utility. For example, DELL has a package based on a fiber-channel backbone that can connect to several servers. Compaq servers come with a backup and restore package from ArcServ with an automated system recovery tool. You need to evaluate these products and select the one that best supports your environment.

NDS Backup

If you don't have more than one replica of a partition, or if your tree is completely corrupted, you can restore NDS from a backup. Assuming the backup was performed before the NDS problems began, this should permit a full recovery. Note the date of the backup. If you have made changes to NDS (such as creating users or changing rights) since that date, you must re-enter them after you restore the backup.

To restore NDS, first use the NDSMGR32.EXE utility to delete all replicas of the partition. Then restore the partition data using your backup software. This will create a new Master replica from which you can re-create the other replicas.

WARNING Be sure all users in the Directory tree are logged out of the network when you back up or restore NDS data. Do not bring down any servers, however.

18

Troubleshooting

Out of the blue, your network crashes. Sound familiar? Well it happens to the best of us.

There are many things that you can do to prepare for and anticipate all the possible scenarios that could occur. To plan for these situations, start with a viable disaster recovery plan and maintain a backup strategy you can test on a continuous basis. At best, you can minimize the occurrences of problems and downtime.

If you've had training similar to ours, you may have learned that there are some basic troubleshooting rules you can follow. We didn't make any of these up, and we wouldn't dare take credit for any of them, but we have used them and they work. You can apply these to any situation you come up with, and believe us when we tell you that it is very time consuming to troubleshoot a problem alone.

Part of the methodology is to use resources made available by the manufacturers and the software developers. These resources are typically referred to as Knowledgebase (Microsoft) and TIDs (Novell). They are an invaluable resource when you are trying to troubleshoot a problem.

In this chapter, you will be exposed to a methodology that Novell and most other companies like to follow, and we will cover some specific issues with servers and NDS. We will also cover some disaster recovery techniques and solutions that some third parties have to offer. Finally, we will conclude with a table that lists the troubleshooting information available elsewhere in this book. We hope that this helps you when confronting system crashes.

NOTE Of all the things you do to prevent or repair crashes, backing up your system is the most important. See Chapter 17 for help with backing up your system.

Troubleshooting Methodology

There you are, in front of a server that has just crashed a few seconds ago. What do you do now? Well, if you are like most of us who have been in the business for a while, you curse and then start isolating the problem. Unfortunately, because our users are breathing down our necks, we take shortcuts when we try to troubleshoot a problem and minimize downtime. This might seem like a good way to save time, but in reality you hurt yourself. Following the methodology essentially forces you to eliminate some possibilities or check for previous occurrences of the problem. This actually saves you time and headaches. You also can take a more proactive approach to potential problems. A server that is performing poorly, for example, would display high utilization on its memory and processor. In this situation you might want to approach management to add an additional server or upgrade the current one before you experience any downtime.

Troubleshooting Methodology Basics

Methodology is a structured approach to a process; therefore, a troubleshooting methodology implies using a structured process to isolate and solve a problem.

Let's review the methodology:

- Always check the problem logs, TIDs, Knowledgebase, hardware inconsistencies, or user procedures prior to starting the troubleshooting process.
- If this doesn't solve your problem, develop a list of symptoms and their characteristics (how many users, which applications, and so forth).
- Establish a plan to isolate the problem, one assumption at a time.
- Implement the plan.
- When the problem is isolated and resolved, you should document it and develop a problem database for future use.

You also want to be familiar with Novell's Web site (www.novell.com). You will find that most of the tips and suggestions come from the site and from personal experience. We also recommend the CNENet secure site for valuable information. There are also tools such as the Support Connection CD by Novell and the TechNet CD from Microsoft.

User groups are also a great source of information. In this respect, you will learn something new every day.

Sage Advice: Service Packs As the First Step in Troubleshooting

All major software developers are constantly improving their software and repairing bugs associated with them. It's impossible for any company to anticipate when, how, and what will cause a problem, and it's impractical to continuously release new versions of an application. Hence the advent of the service pack—a very convenient way for developers to update their software without having to deliver a completely new release.

From a troubleshooting standpoint, you are almost obligated to ensure that a service pack for an application hasn't been released before you call technical support. Most first-level help-desk support will ask if you have installed the latest service pack.

Novell is no exception to the rule. The latest service pack for NetWare 5 as of this writing is Service Pack 3. It contains the following items:

- Directory Services v7.30
- All of the fixes from NW5SP1
- Added compatibility with eDirectory
- Added ability to install NetWare 5 and Support Pack simultaneously
- Added support for languages: Chinese Simplified, Chinese Traditional, and Russian
- Web server updates
- Updated SLP and SCMD components
- Updated NLS licensing files
- Updated Timesync
- Updated Winsock

As you can see, service packs resolve a multitude of problems, but we would like to add a word of caution: You do not want to be the first to use the newest service pack. Just as they can resolve problems, they can also create them. We would strongly suggest setting up a test lab and trying out the service packs on a test server before you deploy on the production servers. It's not unusual to see service packs released and then followed by a new one right away.

Maintenance and Troubleshooting

PART 4

Troubleshooting the Network

It is not unusual for the network itself to be the cause of many problems. An unstable network, be it by cabling or protocol configurations, can directly or indirectly be the source of many problems. Whether these problems are related to user access to resources, or client server applications being able to complete processes, you must take a proactive approach to preventing problems. If problems do occur, your main objective is to minimize downtime as much as possible. You are not there to show off your troubleshooting skills.

A proactive approach, of course, is the best approach to take in this arena, but if the damage is done, it can be a very laborious process to straighten things out. In this section, we will take a dual approach to solving and preventing problems caused by the network. We also like to follow the OSI model as our map to resolving problems. Take heart; we have made a lot of the same mistakes and assumptions you might.

Preventing Network Problems

To prevent network problems, you must manage your network from the ground up in a proactive mode. What we mean by this is that you must follow some basic rules and religiously document your activities. Think of the situation that could occur if you weren't there. Can the people left behind find their way around the network with the documentation at hand? You must start with that paradigm to ensure that the system can be recovered if all is lost.

Here are some proactive measures that we recommend you incorporate to your network management tasks:

- Start from the physical topology. Follow the data flow and make sure that the network parallels this flow. Sending data through a route that doesn't make sense could delay delivery. Also, having multiple routes to a destination can help with preventing downtime and provide load balancing. Chapter 16 covers cable management issues useful in the implementation of proactive measures.

- At the Datalink layer, minimize the number of frames and broadcasts. Reducing the number of live protocols and the use of DNS services for name resolution can do this. You should also implement DAs to resolve directory requests in a complicated network configuration. Standardizing on a single topology on your LANs will also help.

- At the network and transport layers, standardize on a single protocol and preferably use TCP/IP as your core protocol. This will simplify network management and troubleshooting. Ensure that your routes are not able to loop back and cause a major broadcast storm. Use DHCP and DDNS; they are very effective in preventing duplicate addresses, which is a common situation on TCP/IP networks.

Use SNMP compliant network management tools like ManageWise to monitor network activity. A firewall is also highly recommended if you are connected to the Internet.

- At the session, presentation, and application layers make sure that you impose basic security measures. These measures should include logon and file system security. If providing Internet access, enable VPN or SSL security measures. And by all means do not forget about virus protection. Chapter 5 covers a good amount of network stability issues and so does Chapter 16.

- User training is also a proactive measure to implement. A smart user doesn't try to fix their own problems. Instead, they call IT and describe the symptoms of their problem.

As you can see, you don't have to reinvent the wheel to develop some proactive measures for your network. We covered a lot of issues in the preceding chapters that will help you.

Resolving Network Problems

You incorporated proactive measures into your network, but it still went down. Now you have to resolve it and minimize the downtime so that your users can get back to work. Following is advice on what you can do to bring your network back up quickly rather than to troubleshoot it. Remember that your users don't care how good you are at troubleshooting; they want to have their connections restored. The following are some measures you can take to quickly recover from a network shutdown:

- At the physical and datalink layers, you will want to have hot swappable capable systems; this should include your LAN cards and drive adapters for your SCCI drives. Implement RAID 5 on your servers, and have additional drives included with the system. We have encountered problems with drive replacements on RAID 5 systems when the replacement drive was purchased at a later date.

- With network and transport layer functions, you should document your configurations. Many times, we have encountered networks that took much longer to troubleshoot because they were badly documented.

- When troubleshooting session, presentation, and application layer problems, check for any recent changes made to the applications or permissions. Having a log recording changes can be very helpful in these situations. Also have a standard server and client image that you can refer to restore servers and workstations in a more timely manner.

- As you can see, these are but a few measures that you can take. It would be impossible to cover all possibilities since there are so many different network configurations, so we encourage you to expand from these.

Maintenance and Troubleshooting

PART 4

Troubleshooting NDS

NDS is the most important feature of NetWare 5. It is also the most common source of problems. In this section, you will learn how to correct NDS problems when they happen.

You should use NDS Manager or DSREPAIR (described in Chapter 11) to check synchronization before performing any complicated NDS operations. You will also use these tools to perform repairs on the tree database. This same methodology can be applied to just about any situation when you are facing a problem with your network.

Each change you make to NDS starts a series of events that can carry over to your entire network. Beginning at the replica where you made the change, the change is passed to each of the other servers that contain a replica. Depending on communication delays, network use, and the complexity of the change, it can take anywhere from ten seconds to an hour or two for all replicas to receive the change. (eDirectory has just been released and the verdict is still out.)

Fortunately, NDS was designed to handle large time delays due to WAN or LAN traffic bottlenecks and downed servers. The NDS database is loosely consistent, which means that it remains functional even if replicas do not have exactly the same information. You may notice these inconsistencies, but they do not necessarily represent a problem with NDS.

The process that NDS uses to send information between replicas is called synchronization. Two replicas are synchronized if they contain exactly the same information. In a busy network, the synchronization process is happening constantly to update the latest changes. The process is different depending on the type of change.

Simple changes, such as adding a User object or changing a property, are synchronized quickly. All that is required is to send updates to each server that has a replica of the partition where the object is located. Creating a partition is also a relatively simple task.

Complex changes include joining partitions, moving partitions, and merging Directory trees. These changes require updates to multiple partitions, and each server with a replica of any one of the partitions must be contacted to send updates. These changes can take a long time, and some of the repairs involve locking the NDS database.

Symptoms of NDS Problems

Although some inconsistencies between NDS replicas are a normal occurrence, severe inconsistencies may be an indication of a corrupt NDS database or another problem.

Here are the symptoms you should watch for:

- A change made to an NDS object or its rights seems to disappear.

- An object or its properties changes unexpectedly. For example, a user can no longer log in because the password is incorrect, but the user has not changed the password.

- Errors may be inconsistent. For example, a user may be able to log in successfully after several unsuccessful attempts.

- Unknown objects, shown with a question mark, appear in the Directory tree. It is normal for these objects to show up when a server has been removed or when a partitioning operation is in progress. However, if they appear without an apparent cause, there may be a problem.

If you notice any of these symptoms, or if any part of NDS seems to behave inconsistently, follow the instructions in the following sections to narrow down and correct the problem. If a corrupt Directory is left alone, it will probably become worse. Be sure to diagnose and correct the problem as soon as you notice any symptoms.

Checking NDS Synchronization

If the problems you are having with NDS are not severe, you should let the servers run for a few hours before attempting any repairs. NDS double-checks itself, and it may repair the problem automatically. Do not take any servers down, because this would prevent NDS from synchronizing and correcting errors.

If the problem still occurs, you should check the synchronization of the server. You can use the DSREPAIR and DSTRACE utilities to accomplish this, as described in Chapters 11.

NetWare 5@Work: Understanding NDS

Not long ago a friend of ours who ran a fairly large NetWare 4 network ran into a problem with an NDS replica on a particular server. Replicas on severs in other locations where doing fine, so it was determined that the replica was corrupted. When he tried to repair the replica, it would show that it was locked, or in other words, inaccessible. We also found that the way he made a backup of the tree was to put a replica on a server and take the server offline. This was a large problem because the replica ring could never reach a state of synchronization.

The first thing we did was remove from the replica ring the server that was offline. This would allow the tree to finalize synchronization. Then we forced the removal of NDS from the server with the corrupted replica. After the server object was removed from the tree, we reinstalled NDS on the server and reinstalled the replicas of the partitions that were in the original server. Problem solved. This shows you that NDS is a very easy service to maintain and support. With that in mind, we still strongly encourage you to take some hands-on classes to better understand NDS.

Server Abends

At one time or another, your file server will go down. Worst of all, your server might abend, and you know that could be a nightmare. Although most of the time abends are due to an abnormality, such as a bad application or loss of resources, you still need to understand their impact on your system.

First, what is a server abend? Abends happen when the server detects a critical error condition, which then invokes the server's fault handler. The fault handler idles the server and displays the abend message on the server console. An error that is detected by the server CPU is called a *Processor Exception*, and if NetWare detects the error it is called a *Software Exception*.

The primary function of an abend is to protect system data from being corrupted. In a sense, you should be thankful when one occurs because the server detected a fault, such as incorrect cache pointers, and stopped the system from corrupting itself.

Troubleshooting Abends

When you encounter a server abend, or any other server error for that matter, you should consider these preliminary steps:

- Apply the most recent patches and drivers on your server. This means that you should install the latest patches or service packs on the operating system (currently Service Pack 3 for NetWare 5) and also the latest LAN and SCSI drivers.
- Note that you have a hardware problem if the abend message displayed says "Non-Maskable Interrupt."
- Look for NLMs that are outdated and replace them.
- Check for viruses on the DOS partition.
- Re-seat cards and cables, check that fans are working properly.

Once you have covered the preliminary steps, you can proceed with troubleshooting the abend.

- The first step is to collect data. In other words, collect symptoms and console messages, and record them. Go beyond the immediate symptoms; check for *any* abnormal events like new applications, patches, or NLMs that have been installed recently.
- Watch for trends over a period of time. This helps to isolate the cause of the problem.
- Look at the system error log for clues that haven't surfaced anywhere else, such as an error on a certain node just before the abend, an error on a certain file, a print queue, volume dismounts, etc.

- Check which resources (like printing, file, tape, com port, memory access, etc.) were being used at the time of the abend.
- Check for a pattern in the time of day that the abend occurs.
- Break into the debugger and record basic information such as the EIP (instruction pointer), running NLM, and running process. (Learn to use the debugger if you don't already know how.)
- Watch the DSTRACE screen for errors, or for an "All processed = NO" message. Be sure to give any DS errors time to go away before you worry too much. Fifteen minutes to several hours is usually adequate.
- MONITOR.NLM and NWCONFIG.NLM are valuable NetWare utilities to check your server's health. Use them to find information.
- Use CONFIG.NLM (included in TABND2.EXE) to collect server configuration information. This tool can help you troubleshoot abends by displaying server information. You may notice something here that raises a red flag that you hadn't noticed before. Use it to document your configuration before you make any changes to the server. If you place a call to tech support, you will often be asked for this information, anyway.

NOTE The most important thing you can do to protect your server from abends is to establish what is normal for your environment so that you can accurately determine when you have a real problem and when you have simply hit against the limitations of your hardware and/or software.

If going through the steps doesn't solve the problem, you will need to troubleshoot the abend. To troubleshoot a problem, you will want to isolate it or duplicate it. Here are some ways to do that:

- Use **SERVER -NS** or **SERVER -NA** to bring the server up without executing the STARTUP.NCF or the AUTOEXEC.NCF, respectively. Loading **SERVER -NS** will allow you to bring up the server without the volume mounting automatically. These parameters also work for SFT3.
- Check the abend message itself to see if it suggests anything. Messages may indicate problems with LAN channel, disk channel, memory corruption, system board, a certain NLM, printing, a certain piece of hardware, a certain LAN segment, a workstation, a router, an environmental condition, etc. NetWare will create a file called ABEND.LOG in the SYS: SYSTEM directory that will contain the current and previous abend messages, as well as a list of modules loaded at the time of the abend.

- Use **SERVER -NA** to prevent the AUTOEXEC.NCF from running. Then load NLMs manually, one at a time. This follows the basic principles. Start your server with just the kernel, and work your way up, one process at a time, until you run into the corrupted process.

- Use SERVER -NDB to prevent the DS database from loading and thereby eliminating directory services. Note that you won't be able to log in without the database loaded.

- Check for weather conditions the day before. A severe storm could have damaged the surge protectors and even the UPS, causing damage to the server.

- The abend message is very generic, but it can still be used to point you in a direction. Most abends indicate memory corruption. Some will be disk related, others LAN related. Often an abend will include a function name.

- When an abend message mentions the word "interrupted," take a look at the LAN because the LAN does more interrupting than anything else in the server does. As is always the case, this becomes more intuitive from experience.

If all else fails, go back to basics. Use an NE2000 NIC, and eliminate any unnecessary hardware on the server. Replace the SERVER.EXE file, and work your way up. As you gain in experience, you learn to document as much as you can on your network, not just your servers. We have learned that there are no rules when it comes to problems; the only thing going for you is your documentation and your backups.

NetWare 5@Work: Keeping NDS Healthy

Company A's administrators follow a fairly strict regimen when it comes to maintaining its directory services. Here are some steps that they follow:

- They check that the tree is synchronized before anything else is done. If there are any communication or synching errors in the tree, steps are taken to stabilize the tree.

- On the Master of [Root] in DSREPAIR, run Report Synchronization Status. Look for errors. If there are errors, they must be addressed. For example, a -625 error means a communication error with a specific server. Search the Web for specific problem references or talk with Novell Technical Support about fixing them.

- Time synch, or report synch status, is run at different points in the tree to guarantee that there are no problems.

NetWare 5@Work: Keeping NDS Healthy *(continued)*

Company A takes a very proactive approach to its directory services health. When difficult problems are encountered, logs provided by these procedures are used to quickly determine the cause of the problems. Also, Novell technical support uses these logs to help in the troubleshooting of problems.

Disaster Recovery

If a tornado hit your office, what would you need to make the offices operational again? That is a question you need to ask yourself when considering a disaster recovery plan. Notice we said *plan*; that's because you need to develop a set of procedures that ensures the recovery of the business.

All good plans start with a process. Detailing a disaster recovery plan involves a process that spans several steps. We strongly recommend that you follow a methodical approach when deciding on a disaster recovery plan.

The following is the methodology used in many disaster recovery plans:

1. Establish priorities. The company as a group must decide the order in which systems and departments must be recovered. This way you maximize the resources available on a few areas at a time.

2. Designate members for the disaster team. You will need to select individuals from each department to participate in the disaster recovery plan. These individuals should have a high level of understanding of their business and its priorities.

3. Establish a timetable. As a team you will need to establish a timetable for the complete recovery of all systems and business units. Some departments need to be up within the first twenty-four hours after a disaster, while others can be brought up much later.

4. Allocate the necessary resources. Most of the resources needed for the recovery should be standby elements. This means that you have spare components ready to replace the damaged ones. You will also need to anticipate relocation of essential company staff and services to an alternate site. There are companies that specialize in this service.

5. Schedule practice runs. You want to test your plans. This can be done on a large or small scale. It is very important to make sure that your assumptions are correct, especially when it comes to an alternate site. This may include running the company from this site at least once a year.

Maintenance and Troubleshooting

PART 4

6. Anticipate employee needs. The company will have to make disaster services available for employees and their families in order to facilitate their availability to the company.

7. Train disaster recovery team members. Last but not least, you will want to make sure your team members are trained in the tasks assigned to them.

Trust us—using a methodology will make your planning process more efficient and enjoyable. Also, the more participation you get from the company, the better plan you will develop.

Avoiding Downtime

A fair amount of effort and resources are dedicated to keeping your servers up and running at all times. But you can't guarantee that all servers will be running 100% of the time. You must also consider times when you need to do maintenance or just need to replace systems and applications. These always incur downtime.

There are now many solutions, once available only to large systems, which are available to NetWare to ensure minimal downtime. These solutions include SFTIII (System Fault Tolerance Level Three), Clustering, and Standby services. Their purpose is to avoid lengthy downtime and enable quick recovery.

SFT III

SFT III, System Fault Tolerance Level Three, has been around for a while and it basically involves the use of two identical servers. These servers are a mirror image of each other and are interconnected with fiber. You will usually purchase this as a package because it's a very complicated setup.

The resulting product is a constantly updated backup server so that when the primary server fails, the image server picks up the services. The drawback to this solution is that you lose the use of an entire server. This solution is available to v3.*x* or earlier versions of NetWare.

Standby Server

This solution is very similar to SFT III; you designate a server as a standby server so that when the primary server crashes, the standby takes its place. The difference is that the two servers do not have to be next to each other (NDS controls this environment) and you can still use the standby server for other services. The advantage over SFT III is that you don't waste a server.

Novell has made this solution available with NetWare 4.11 and will release the NetWare 5 version in the near future.

Cluster Server

This solution provides the highest reliability and uptime possible while optimizing performance. This solution involves a group of servers acting as one large system and sharing the same storage system, which in itself is redundant. Performance is shared among all servers, but when one crashes, the other servers pick up the slack.

This solution is available with NetWare 4.11 and NetWare 5, and its current configuration will support two or more servers. Novell is currently on Beta v1.0 for Novell Cluster Services.

Solutions from Novell OEM Partners

Just as we have seen in Chapter 4 that there are Novell OEM (Original Manufacturer Equipment) partners that specialize in supporting NetWare products, you will also notice OEM companies that develop disaster recovery applications tested and approved by Novell.

The following is a list of partners and their products that are recommended by Novell, and some by us, the authors, that can help you protect your data.

Advanced storage systems are available from:

- Fujitsu Computers Limited
- Hewlett-Packard
- IBM
- Maxtor
- Quantum
- DELL Corporation

Advanced backup systems are available from:

- Seagate (not officially approved for NetWare 5, but is for NetWare 4.*x*)
- Legato Systems (approved for previous versions of NetWare)
- ArcServ (although not on the list of Novell's approved software, it has been a name stay in the industry and we certainly recommend it)

Failsafe server platforms are available from:

- Plain Tree Systems
- SysKonnect

NOTE Even Novell's failsafe products, such as Clusters and Standby Servers, have just been released.

Troubleshooting Information Elsewhere in This Book

While we have provided some troubleshooting information in this chapter and given you a good methodology, there is also a great deal of troubleshooting information throughout the book. We decided that it probably makes more sense to have troubleshooting information in its relevant chapter, instead of only in one place. Table 18.1 summarizes the troubleshooting information found elsewhere in this book, by chapter and section.

Table 18.1 Troubleshooting Tips Locator

Problem	Chapter	Section
Adaptec AHA 1540 and 1542 HBAs will only install if they are revision C or higher.	2	"Other Issues to Consider Before Installation"
Video card must support VESA 1.2 or 2.0 to work with the SVGA video setting.	2	"Other Issues to Consider Before Installation"
Older 3C5x9 cards in Legacy mode aren't auto detected.	2	"Other Issues to Consider Before Installation"
AHA2940 PCI SCSI card on a Pentium II 200MHz (or faster) computer with four or more processors.	2	"Other Issues to Consider Before Installation"
Adapter cards set to use the memory at 0A0000h.	2	"Other Issues to Consider Before Installation"
Secondary time servers don't find time providers.	2	"Time Synchronization Issues"

Table 18.1   Troubleshooting Tips Locator *(continued)*

Problem	Chapter	Section
Multiple IP servers installed together point to each other for time.	2	"Time Synchronization Issues"
Mouse issues.	2	"Hardware Issues (Mouse and NIC)"
Server-to-server installs with the NetWare 5 CD mounted as a volume on a NetWare 5 server.	2	"CD-ROM Issues"
Accessing CDs on a NetWare 4.11 server.	2	"CD-ROM Issues"
Installing an IP-only server into an IPX-only tree.	2	"Protocol Issues"
IPX-only and IP-only servers in the same tree.	2	"Protocol Issues"
Required versions of DS.NLM and DSREPAIR.NLM for interoperability of NetWare 4.1*x*, 4.2, and 5 servers in the same tree.	2	"Installing a NetWare 5 Server into a NetWare 4.1*x* or 4.2Tree"
Error 0xC0001003 and Policy Manager Error 5.00-89.	2	"Licensing Issues"
License ownership issues.	2	"Licensing Issues"
License installation and RCONSOLE.	2	"Licensing Issues"
Installation takes a long time or appears to hang when installing licensing.	2	"Licensing Issues"
Message "Error Installing DS, Error Code 1 when installing NDS".	2	"Directory Services Installation Error"

Maintenance and Troubleshooting

PART 4

Table 18.1 Troubleshooting Tips Locator *(continued)*

Problem	Chapter	Section
NetWare won't install if the year is greater than 2039.	2	"Date and Time Issues"
INSTALL.BAT switches.	2	"General Troubleshooting Techniques for Installation Problems"
General installation trouble-shooting information in C:\NWINST.TMP directory.	2	"General Troubleshooting Techniques for Installation Problems"
Dealing with corrupted STARTUP.NCF file.	2	"When STARTUP.NCF is Corrupted, What Next?"
FPNW on NT Servers: Interoperability with Client32.	3	"FPNW"
Changes made with Exchange Administrator not replicated back to NDS.	3	"Exchange Interoperability Issues"
Mailbox Manager doesn't support custom recipients.	3	"Exchange Interoperability Issues"
Replication issues, unknown objects, time synchronization issues and other issues to be addressed before migrating NetWare 4 to 5.	4	"Make Sure Your Tree Is Healthy"
ROLLCALL.NLM must be version 4.10 or higher before migrating NetWare 4.11 servers to 5 servers.	4	"Preparing for the Migration"
NLS must be operational when using NetWare 5.	4	"Preparing for the Migration"
Run BINDFIX.EXE before upgrading a NetWare 3 server.	4	"Preparing for the Migration"

Table 18.1   Troubleshooting Tips Locator *(continued)*

Problem	Chapter	Section
NetWare 2 can't be upgraded to NetWare 5 directly.	4	"Preparing for the Migration: Migrating from NetWare 2.*x* and 3.*x*"
Troubleshooting NLS issues.	4	"Licensing Services Administration Tools"
Licenses with a nine-digit serial number cannot be installed while upgrading an existing server to NetWare 5.	4	"Licensing Services Administration Tools"
Users can't connect to FTP server.	5	"Troubleshoot FTP Services"
Connection refused by FTP server.	5	"Troubleshoot FTP Services"
Users cannot download a file.	5	"Troubleshoot FTP Services"
Config and Config Reader: Tools to aid in troubleshooting.	6	"Config and Config Reader: A Simple Method of Viewing and Documenting Server Configuration"
Troubleshooting NDS rights problems.	6	"DSRights: A Utility to See What Rights One Object Has to Another Object and/or Effective Rights and Where They Come From"
Creating a new Admin account when the old one is lost or damaged or the password is forgotten.	6	"MakeSU and Recover: Powerful Backdoors and a Hacker's Delight"
Tracking the size of the NDS database components.	6	"NDSDir: A Tool to View the Hidden Components of NDS and Keep Track of Their Sizes"
Managing and updating your NetWare servers.	6	"OnSite Admin Pro: The NetWare Equivalent of the Swiss Army Knife"

Maintenance and Troubleshooting

PART 4

Table 18.1   Troubleshooting Tips Locator *(continued)*

Problem	Chapter	Section
Schema issues.	6	"Schema Compare: A Tool to View the Schema and Optionally Compare it with Another Server"
Debugging NDS problems with DSTRACE.NLM.	8	"DSTRACE"
ConsoleOne Web Edition installation may fail if the Web server isn't in the default directory.	10	"ConsoleOne Web Edition"
Replica issues when merging trees.	11	"Replicas in Merged NDS Trees"
Symptoms of problems with NDS	11	"Symptoms of NDS Problems"
Fixing NDS errors.	11	"Checking Synchronization with DSREPAIR;" "Forcing Synchronization;" "Removing NDS from a Server;" "Restoring an NDS Backup"
NDS Error Codes.	11 & 15	"NDS Error Codes"
Workstations aren't registered in NDS.	13	"Registering Workstations"
Applications don't appear in NAL or NAL Explorer.	13	"System Requirements"
Applications are available outside the scheduled times.	13	"Schedule"
Remote control session ends when display settings are changed.	14	"Remote Management Agent"
Remote diagnostics works only over IP.	14	"Remote Diagnostics of Client Workstations"

Table 18.1   Troubleshooting Tips Locator *(continued)*

Problem	Chapter	Section
Inventory doesn't work properly.	14	"Loading the Server-Based Components;" "Client and Server Configuration Problems;" "Problems Collecting the Data;" "Problems Accessing and Viewing Reports"
Inventory reporting doesn't show all workstations.	14	"Installation;" "Problems Accessing and Viewing Reports"
Corrupted traditional volumes.	15	"VSrepair"
Corrupted NSS volumes.	15	"Rebuild"
Network problems (tools to help you solve).	16	"Monitoring the Network"

Maintenance and Troubleshooting

PART 4

Design and Implementation from Start to Finish

Company C needed to migrate its existing single office NetWare 3 network with three servers to NetWare 5 with the following objectives:

- Maintain the current naming convention.

- Maintain current users and groups with their existing permissions to file systems and applications.

- Add NDS for NT and integrate NT administration with Novell Directory Services. Company C wants to include an NT 4 Exchange 5.5 server.

- Migrate to TCP/IP as the only protocol, and provide Internet access.

- Ensure that all applications will work on the new platform.

This project was divided into four phases. We considered it a simple network project since it involved less than 15 servers and a single office location. This was important because it illuminated the need to deal with more complicated tasks such as time synchronization and partitioning.

Phase 1

The first phase involved selecting a point of contact with the company and establishing the project's scope. Data was collected on the current data flow and applications, and the network topology was analyzed for additional components needed to connect the company to the Internet. User needs were analyzed and documented. Any network configuration not documented was recorded, and backup solutions were tested and verified.

Phase 2

In this phase, we designed the Directory services tree outline:

- We decided on a single organization container and we also used default time and partition configurations. This was more than sufficient to support the administration capabilities of the company.

- Only a subcontainer (OU) was added to support the NT 4 Exchange server.

- A diagram of the extended network structure was also drawn to show the additional components needed to gain access to the Internet.

- A list of additional applications was recorded to include a firewall (BorderManager), NDS for NT, and ManageWise so that the project objectives could be met.

- A test lab was installed to ensure that current applications and user needs could be met when the new platform was installed. The migration also needed to be tested.

- Since the current servers met the hardware requirements for NetWare 5, it was also determined that new servers would not be needed.

- Because the DOS and SYS partitions weren't large enough, we used Server Magic from Power Quest to increase the DOS partition and the SYS: volume so that we could do in-place upgrades.

- All applications were tested and client images were retooled for the latest Novell client.

- We made sure the network was stable and that all topology related equipment was installed and operational.

- A tentative rollout schedule was determined.

Phase 3

The implementation phase started with the pilot location to fine tune the rollout schedule and execute the backups. Once the pilot location was done, the rest of the office was completed. The only surprise we encountered was the discovery of a large amount of unlicensed applications being used by users. This was attributed to poor discovery techniques on our part.

Phase 4

By phase 4, we had a working network, but a few of the objectives were not yet implemented. These were migrating to TCP/IP, integrating with NT 4, and installing the firewall.

- Once the network was operational and all components are installed, we selected one of the servers to be an IP/IPX gateway server to maintain connectivity. Then we proceeded to convert the other two servers to IP-only. By selecting an IP/IPX gateway server and taking advantage of compatibility mode, we were able to migrate to IP-only without a hitch.

- DNS and DHCP were installed and clients configured as DHCP clients.

- NDS for NT was installed and configured.

- Once the network was all IP, we proceeded to install BorderManager and set up the firewall between the LAN and access to the Internet.

Final Note

After completing the project, we decided that greater emphasis on the discovery process in the first phase was recommended. This should include the visit to a larger number of user desktops. This is especially true on networks without a full time administrator.

24seven **CASE STUDY**

Netware 6.5 includes Virtual Office allows multiple users to access Same web-files with Chat Capabilities

e GUIDE - Software integrated to consolidate all directory info into the Virtual Office Browser.

SnapShot Backup tool: Automated Backups

Open Source technology

Appendix

DNS/DHCP Services

This appendix will briefly review the DNS and DHCP services that NetWare 5 offers. We will build on the information contained in Chapter 5, where the creation and configuration of the objects associated with these services were discussed. This appendix offers a more detailed explanation of the DNS and DHCP capabilities of NetWare 5 as well as providing some troubleshooting tips that you may find useful if you run into trouble with either service. We will also briefly review how to initially install these services.

Installation

The files necessary to use DNS and DHCP are copied as part of the installation process. Note that we said copied, not installed. You can choose at installation to have them installed as well, or you can choose to do that later. Doing it later involves running DNIPINST.NLM to extend the schema to support the new objects.

You will also need to install the client portion so that you can manage these services. The administrative tool is called the DNS/DHCP Management Console. To install it, run SYS: PUBLIC\DNSDHCP\SETUP.EXE. It is a Java-based GUI that will allow you to manage both services. Note that you can't administer either DNS or DHCP through NWADMIN or ConsoleOne, although ConsoleOne support is expected in mid-2000. The files will be installed to your local hard drive in C:\PROGRAM FILES\NOVELL\DNSDHCP. The name of the actual program is DNSDHCP.EXE. Installation takes approximately 13.5MB of hard drive space on the client. The client does allow you to manage all DNS and DHCP servers in the entire network, however, so you don't need to install this tool on many workstations unless you desire distributed management of these services.

> ***TIP*** Novell recommends that you install the management console on an NT-based machine (with at least NT's SP 3 installed) for better performance.

In the next few sections, we will review the NDS rights that are required to view and manage DNS and DHCP and offer some troubleshooting tips and tricks.

NDS Rights Required

The rights required to manage DNS and DHCP vary depending on what you wish the administrators to be able to do. Table A.1 lists the required NDS rights to create new configuration objects (such as DNS Server and DHCP Server objects, Zones, DHCP Subnets, and so on) and modify existing objects. Table A.2 lists the requirements for administrators who manage individual zones or subnets. For those who need to be able to view, but not manage, DNS and DHCP, all that is required is the Browse object right and the Read property right to all properties to the following objects:

- DNS/DHCP Locator
- DNS/DHCP Group
- Existing DNS and/or DHCP objects

Table A.1   NDS Requirements for Managing the Configuration of DNS and DHCP Services

Object	Object Rights Required	Property Rights (for All Properties) Required
DNS/DHCP Locator	Browse	Supervisor
DNS/DHCP Group	Browse	Supervisor
Existing objects	Supervisor	Supervisor
Parent container when creating new objects	Create	N/A

Table A.2   NDS Requirements for Managing the Individual Subnets or Zones

Object	Object Rights Required	Property Rights (for All Properties) Required
DNS/DHCP Locator	Browse	Read
DNS/DHCP Group	Browse	Read
Existing objects	Browse, Create, and Delete	Supervisor

General Troubleshooting

There are quite a few tips and tricks that can help you as you attempt to manage DNS and DHCP. In this section, we will list some of the more popular problems and solutions as well as some helpful tricks.

DNS/DHCP Management Console Requires TCP/IP on the Client

While the management console can be run on a client that has only IPX installed, functionality will be lost. Specifically, the following buttons will be disabled:

- Start and Stop Service
- View Audit Trail Log
- View Events/Alerts

In addition, the server objects will show as inactive, regardless of their actual state. We recommend that you install TCP/IP on at least the workstations where administration will be done.

Minimizing the Time Necessary to Start the Management Console

When you start the console, it must first locate the DNS/DHCP Locator object. This can cause WAN traffic and delays as it searches for it. To eliminate the search, add the –C switch and the context of the object to the shortcut you use to start the management console. For example, if this object was located in DNSAndDHCPConfig.Organization, the command line you would enter in the Target line of the shortcut would be as follows:

```
"C:\PROGRAM FILES\NOVELL\DNSDHCP\DNSDHCP.EXE" -C
DNSAndDHCPConfig.Organization
```

CAPS LOCK and the Management Console

If CAPS LOCK is on, you may see strange characters in the management console as you type. There is a bug in the Java code that causes this. Capital letters entered with the

Appendix

SHIFT key do not cause any problems. This problem is corrected in Support Pack 3 as the underlying Java files are updated.

> **TIP**   After installing Support Pack 2 and NDS 8, we no longer saw this problem in the GUI.

Management Console Won't Load

There are several possible reasons why the management console won't load, including the following:

- Client is not logged in.
- Client can't access DNS/DHCP Locator object (due to NDS rights, WAN links down without a local replica, and so on).
- Schema hasn't been extended yet (you can extend it with DNIPINST.NLM).
- Corrupted DNS and/or DHCP objects. Try to repair with DSREPAIR.NLM, or delete and recreate them.
- Client 3.0 or higher isn't loaded.
- Video configuration issues (we haven't run into them, but others have reported problems). The minimum recommended configuration is:
  - 800 x 600 resolution
  - 256 Colors

Inability to Create DNS or DHCP Objects

There are a few reasons why you may not be able to create these objects (besides the obvious NDS rights issues). They can be solved by installing Support Pack 1 or higher (we always recommend that you use the latest). Possible reasons include:

- NDS is unavailable (WAN link issues without a local replica, for example).
- Management console is having trouble with a replica that is damaged or not fully synchronized. To force the console to use the Master replica of the partition, start it with the –mr switch.

DNS

DNS (Domain Name System), as described in Chapter 5, allows you to resolve Host names to IP addresses. It also allows you to resolve FQDNs (Fully Qualified Domain Names, for example www.sybex.com) to an IP address. In this section we will review the features of Novell's implementation of DNS, how it can be used as a primary or secondary server, its support of DDNS, and some troubleshooting advice.

> **NOTE** A full explanation of DNS is beyond the scope of this book. *The* authoritative reference on the subject is *DNS and BIND* by Paul Albitz and Cricket Liu (O'Reilly, 1998). Currently in its third edition, it now covers DDNS in addition to standard DNS. We highly recommend this book for all DNS administrators.

DNS Features

Novell has created a full-featured, RFC-compliant DNS server for use with NetWare 5. Some of the key features it offers include:

- Supports multiple zones per server (several hundred have been demonstrated on a single server).
- All NetWare DNS servers are peer DNS servers, not the standard master/slave relationships that normally exist between DNS servers. This is because all DNS data are stored in NDS (not in Btrieve, like in previous versions).
- Can import and export standard BIND-formatted files.
- BIND 4.96 and 8.1.1 compliant, providing interoperability with virtually all DNS servers, including most UNIX DNS servers and NT's DNS implementation.
- Supports the following RFCs: 819, 920, 974, 1032, 1033, 1034, 1035, 1036, 1101, 1122, 1123, 1183, 1535, 1536, 1537, 1591, 1597, 1627, 1713, 1884, 1886, 1912, 2010, 2052.
- All DNS data is cached for faster performance.
- Changes made in the management console are dynamically applied (no need to unload and reload the server).

> **NOTE** BIND is the Berkeley Internet Name Daemon, the de facto DNS server that all others are compared to.

Operation as a Primary or Secondary Server

NetWare's DNS server stores all of the data in NDS, as mentioned previously. This means that a change to DNS data can be made from anywhere, not just at primary name servers. Changes will be replicated in the same manner as any other NDS data, allowing redundancy in DNS data across any number of servers. The replication mechanism is better than standard DNS replication, which takes place with a zone transfer. A zone transfer is simply the process of copying the DNS data from one server to another. There is no concept of changed records in zone transfers, so all DNS data goes in every zone transfer. As you can see, Novell's implementation is more efficient in terms of bandwidth, and provides better fault tolerance due to data being replicated frequently.

Figures A.1 and A.2 show how NetWare DNS servers can be configured as either primary or secondary DNS servers. Notice that in A.1 changes can be made on any NetWare server and they will automatically be replicated to the rest. However, one server is configured as the "primary" DNS server for the foreign DNS server. Figure A.2 shows the opposite configuration, where the foreign DNS server is the primary DNS server and it replicates with one secondary NetWare DNS server. That secondary server then replicates changes it receives to all other DNS servers that service that zone. Remember that in this case, all changes must be made at the foreign primary server only.

Figure A.1   NetWare servers configured as primary DNS servers with another type of server as a secondary server

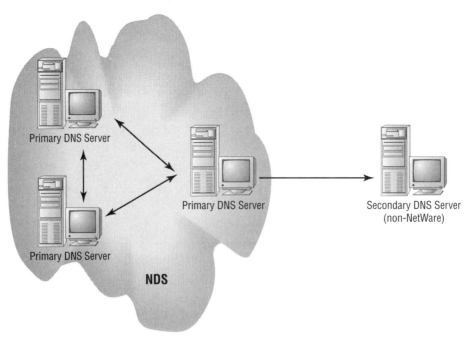

Figure A.2   NetWare servers configured as secondary DNS servers with another type of server as the primary server

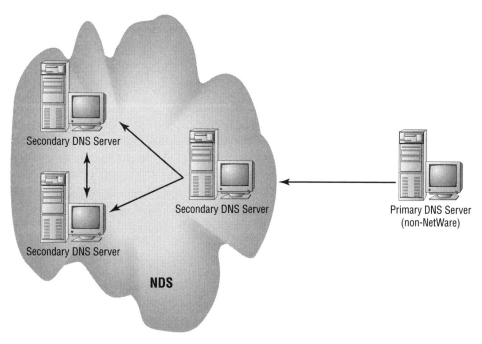

Dynamic DNS (DDNS)

Dynamic DNS is the latest concept in DNS. This concept makes administration simpler and reduces errors due to outdated data. This feature can be used in conjunction with DHCP, as illustrated in Figure A.3.

Figure A.3   How DHCP and DDNS are used in the process of a client getting an IP address

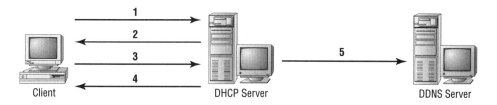

1. Client broadcasts for DHCP Server(s).
2. DHCP Server(s) respond with an IP address.
3. Client accepts one IP address.
4. Server acknowledges the client's acceptance.
   Client now has an IP address.
5. DHCP Server registers client's FQDN and IP address
   with the DDNS server (they may be on the same machine).

As you can see in Figure A.3, when a client requests an IP address from a DHCP server, the DHCP server gets the client's host name and returns an IP address to the client. It then forwards the FQDN (made from the client's host name and the domain name you specify for the subnet), along with the IP address it assigned to the designated DDNS zone. A DDNS server will then create the appropriate A and PTR records and replicate that information with the other servers in the zone. When the lease expires or is otherwise dropped, the DHCP server will notify the DDNS server, which will flag the appropriate records as inactive. The DHCP server sends the information as a background thread, meaning it is a low-priority thread, thus allowing more important tasks (if there are any at that moment) to receive more CPU time.

One question that may come to mind is "But what happens if the DDNS server is down?" No problem. The DHCP server will create a file (SYS:ETC\DHCPDNS.LOG) in which it will store the information until the DDNS server is back online. At that point, the records will be sent to the DDNS server and the file will be removed.

Troubleshooting DNS

Novell has built in the capability to create both an event log and an audit log for DNS. Both are controlled through the DNS Server object. These two files are very useful in troubleshooting. The event log tracks all of the DNS related errors that occur, as well as entries that track when the DNS server is brought up or taken down. The audit log tracks all DNS activity and can be used to see what is happening on the server.

You can also load NAMED.NLM with the –V switch and it will display additional debugging information. You will see all the steps taken to initialize and shut down the server, as well as other information on the status of DNS as it is processing requests.

DHCP

DHCP (Dynamic Host Configuration Protocol), as discussed in Chapter 5, was created to simplify the administration associated with distributing IP addresses and related parameters (such as default gateways, subnet masks, and so on). This is a very popular protocol and one that will make your life substantially easier. Without DHCP, you have the overhead of touching each machine to set up this information; there is the administrative overhead of tracking which IP addresses are in use, and the probability that you will make mistakes as you enter all of these parameters. In addition, if a machine is moved from one subnet to another, all of the IP information must be re-entered, and the system will have no network connectivity over TCP/IP until this is done. With DHCP, however, most of the configuration problems are solved as long as the DHCP server is properly configured. We think you will find this a compelling solution to your IP addressing needs.

In this section, we will discuss the features of Novell's implementation of DHCP; the files that are created and used by DHCP; the process of failing over to another DHCP server when your usual DHCP server goes down; and some troubleshooting hints and tricks.

DHCP Features

Novell has upgraded its DHCP server with NetWare 5 and added many improvements, including the following:

- Performance is much better than in previous versions (the database has been moved out of Btrieve and all of the data is cached).

- The configuration options have been greatly expanded. In addition to the standard options that most DHCP servers can give, Novell's implementation of DHCP can give out all of the following pieces of information:

  - SLP (Service Location Protocol) Directory Agent and SLP service scope

  - CMD (Compatibility Mode) network number and the IP address(es) of any migration agent(s)

  - SMTP and POP3 servers

  - IP address(es) of NetWare server(s)

  - NDS tree name

  - Default NDS context

- One NLM (DHCPSRVR.NLM) is now used for both local (LAN-based) and remote (remote access, including dial-in) workstations, instead of the two that were used in previous versions.

- Supports DDNS (as described previously).

- Addresses can be pinged before being assigned to greatly reduce duplicate IP address errors. The address is pinged before it is needed so that when a client needs it, it has already been verified. As soon as an IP address is given out, the next address in the range is pinged to make sure the server is ready when the next request arrives.

- DHCP data is stored in NDS, allowing it to be replicated like any other NDS data.

- Supports the following DHCP-related RFCs: 2131, 2132, 2241, 2242.

- Supports the following BOOTP-related RFCs: 1497, 1534, 1542.

- Has been tested handling tens of thousands of IP addresses on a single server.

Appendix

DHCP Files

DHCP uses several files to help keep it accurate and up-to-date, as well as for diagnostic purposes. The files are all located in SYS:ETC\DHCP. The files and the purpose of each are described in Table A.3.

Table A.3   DHCP-Related Files and Their Purpose

Filename	Contents/Purpose
DHCPSYNC.LOG	Provides information on when and which IP addresses were given out by this DHCP server; used when the DHCP server is restarted to be sure cache is up-to-date relative to data stored in NDS.
DHCPLOC.TAB	Contains global options and MAC addresses that have been excluded from using DHCP. This information comes from the DNS/DHCP Locator object and is updated each time the service is started. It is kept in this file as a backup in case the Locator object is unavailable when the service starts.
DHCPLOG.LOG	This is used as an overflow file when the service can't write data to NDS until that ability is restored. The loss of the ability could be due to loss of access to a replica where the data is stored (for example while doing a DSREPAIR or attempting to access a remote replica while the WAN link is down). The server may also be too busy for the service to get access to NDS. When the ability is restored, the transactions will be written to NDS. When that process is completed, the file will be deleted.
DHCPDNS.LOG	Similar in purpose to DHCPLOG.LOG, this file is created when access to a DDNS server is not possible. When the ability to access it returns, the data will be flushed and the file deleted.
DHCPCACHE.LOG	This file is created when the service is shut down and is similar in purpose to DHCPSYNC.LOG; it contains all of the DHCP information that was cached when the server went down. You can force this file to be created at any time by typing **SET DHCP DUMP = 2** at the server's console prompt.

Failover

DHCP failover is not an automatic process in NetWare 5. The process is not difficult but does involve administrative intervention. There are also a few issues that need to be discussed in conjunction with this process. The process is as follows:

1. Configure a subnet with a default DHCP server (ServerA). Every subnet needs a default server.

2. When ServerA goes down, simply reconfigure the subnet to use another DHCP server (ServerB) instead.

3. Load DHCPSRVR.NLM on ServerB. Because the data is in NDS, it knows about the existing IP assignments that have been made.

4. When ServerA is back online, update the configuration for the subnet to point the default server back to ServerA.

5. Reload the DHCP server NLM to use the new configuration.

This is a simple process that works well in most situations. Remember from our discussion of files in the previous section, however, that DHCP keeps various log files to track data that hasn't made it to NDS yet. Even though the data hasn't been put in NDS yet, the assignments have been made. This means that ServerB may hand out addresses that it thinks are unassigned, which have, in fact, already been assigned by ServerA. There are three solutions to this problem, namely:

- If ServerA is going down for planned maintenance and ServerB is not normally a DHCP server, copy the log files already mentioned to ServerB before bringing the server up. Of course, it is not always possible to meet all of these conditions.

- Configure ServerB to ping ahead to verify that the next address it is going to hand out is unused first. If it is already in use, it will choose the next address and repeat the process until it either finds an unused IP address or it has checked all of the addresses it is configured for and none of them are available.

- Assign *two* DHCP servers with different scopes of addresses for each subnet. In this case, if either fails, the other can still give out IP addresses and there won't be any duplication.

Appendix

Troubleshooting DHCP

There are a lot of diagnostic abilities that are built into DHCP and configured through the DHCP Server object. Things that you can configure that relate to troubleshooting fall into the following categories:

- Trouble Reporting

    Audit Logs   Track IP assignments and releases.

    Event Logs   Track events, such as the server starting or stopping, as well as problems with the synchronization log and addresses that are declined on renewal (for example, due to the moving of a machine from one physical subnet to another).

- Problem Prevention

    - Configure SNMP to report problems to a SNMP Management Station.

    - PING ahead to greatly reduce or eliminate duplicate IP address errors.

You can also load the DHCP server in debug mode, much like with the DNS server. The syntax is DHCPSRVR and one of the following switches:

D1   Shows all of the packets that are sent and received

D2   D1 and additional debugging information (for example on the startup and shutdown of the service)

D3   D2, with the output going to a file (SYS:ETC\DHCP\DHCPSRVR.LOG) instead of to the screen

Index

Note to the Reader: Throughout this index **boldfaced** page numbers indicate primary discussions of a topic. *Italicized* page numbers indicate illustrations.

Index

for licensing, 104–105, 444
for removing NDS from servers, **290**
for STARTUP.NCF file, 53
for support packs, 56
NWLink protocol, 60
NWPA (NetWare Peripheral Architecture), 39
NWPMW16.EXE tool, 276–277
NWPMW32.EXE tool, 276–277

O

Object container, search policy for, 340
Object Create Partition command, 294
Object menu
Add Replica command, 295
Partition menu
Merge command, 294
Move command, 295
ODI (Open Data-Link Interface), 246
OEM disaster recovery support, **441–442**
off-site data storage, 428
1.NDS FILE, 161
100BaseTX topology, 23
Online processors parameter, 205
Open Data-Link Interface (ODI), 246
Open files parameter, 206
operating systems
for Application objects, 325
for ConsoleOne, 171–173
error codes for, **388**
for MAC clients, 258
in migration, 84
for NDS for NT, 68
for Windows-based clients, 248, 250
for ZENworks, 313
optimization, **183**
guidelines for, **210–212**
Monitor for, **203–210**, *204*, *207–209*
of server traffic, **240–244**
SET parameters for. *See* SET parameters
Windows-based clients, **253–255**
Options menu in RCONSOLE, 215

OptiSPEED cabling, 408
Oracle 8, 29
Organization objects
associating Application objects with, 326
in tree structure design, 6
Organizational Role objects, **11–12**
Organizational Unit objects
associating Application objects with, 326
in domains, AD, and NDS, 75
in tree structure design, 6
Original Cache Buffers parameter, 205
OS/2 clients, **260**
Other tab, 263, *264*
Owners tab, 102
ownership of licenses, **45**, **102**

P

PA (Printer Agent) component, 272
Packet Burst parameter, 252
Packet Burst Protocol, **243–244**
packet-filtering routers, **129**
Packet Forwarding option, 180
Packet Receive Buffers (PRBs), **185–186**
Packet Receive Buffers parameter, 206
packets
in performance, **241–242**
receive buffers for, 206, **242**
size of, **241–242**, **244**
PAP (Password Authentication Protocol), **228**
PARTIO.DNS file, 159, *162*
partitions
creating, **294**
default, 298
and licensing issues, 44
maintenance rights to, 286
merging, **294**
in migration, 88, 92
MLAs for, 46
for NDS for NT, **68–69**
rules for, **296–297**
search policy for, 340

Index

Index

Build Your Own Networking Reference Library

with Sybex Network Press™ books

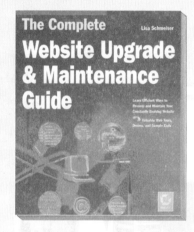
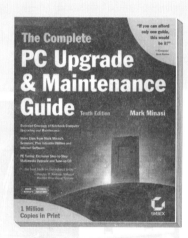

NETWARE® 5 CNE®
STUDY GUIDES FROM
NETWORK PRESS®

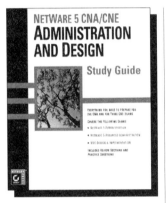

NetWare® 5 CNA℠/CNE®: Administration and Design Study Guide

ISBN: 0-7821-2387-2
864 pp.; 7½" X 9"
$44.99, Hardcover

Covers:

NetWare® 5 Administration
(the CNA test)

NetWare® 5 Advanced
Administration

NDS Design & Implementation

NetWare® 5 CNE®: Core Technologies Study Guide

ISBN: 0-7821-2389-9
512 pp.; 7½" X 9"
$44.99, Hardcover

Covers:

Networking Technologies

Service & Support

NetWare® 5 CNE®: Integrating Windows® NT® Study Guide

ISBN: 0-7821-2388-0
448 pp.; 7½" X 9"
$39.99, Hardcover

Covers:

Integrating Windows® NT®

NetWare® 5 CNE®: Update to NetWare® 5 Study Guide

ISBN: 0-7821-2390-2
432 pp.; 7½" X 9"
$39.99, Hardcover

Covers:

NetWare® 4.11 to
NetWare® 5 Update

www.sybex.com

CISCO® STUDY GUIDES
FROM NETWORK PRESS®

- · **Prepare for Cisco certification with the experts**
- · **Full coverage of each exam objective**
- · **Hands-on labs and hundreds of sample questions**

ISBN 0-7821-2381-3
768 pp; 7½" × 9"; $49.99
Hardcover

ISBN 0-7821-2403-8
832 pp; 7½" × 9"; $49.99
Hardcover

ISBN 0-7821-2571-9
704 pp; 7½" × 9"; $49.99
Hardcover
Available Summer 1999

CCDA™: Cisco® Certified Design Associate Study Guide
ISBN: 0-7821-2534-4; 800 pp; 7½" × 9"
$49.99; Hardcover; CD
Available Fall 1999

CCNP™: Cisco® Internetwork Troubleshooting Study Guide
ISBN 0-7821-2536-0; 704 pp; 7½ × 9
$49.99; Hardcover; CD
Available Summer 1999

CCNP™: Configuring, Monitoring, and Troubleshooting Dial-Up Services Study Guide
ISBN 0-7821-2544-1; 704 pp; 7½" × 9"
$49.99; Hardcover; CD
Available Summer 1999

SYBEX
www.sybex.com

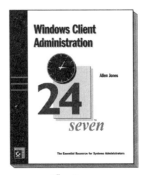
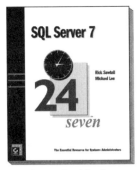

TAKE YOUR CAREER TO THE NEXT LEVEL

with 24seven books from Network Press

- This new series offers the advanced information you need to keep your systems and networks running 24 hours a day, seven days a week.
- On-the-job case studies provide solutions to real-world problems.
- Maximize your system's uptime—and go home at 5!
- $34.99; 7½" x 9"; 544–704 pages; softcover

Paul Robichaux
0-7821-2531-X

Craig Hunt
0-7821-2506-9

Gary Govanus
0-7821-2509-3

Matthew Strebe
0-7821-2529-8

John Hales, Nestor Reyes
0-7821-2593-X

THE ESSENTIAL RESOURCE FOR SYSTEMS ADMINISTRATORS

Visit the 24seven Web site at www.24sevenbooks.com for more information and sample chapters.

How to: